BROADENING JEWISH HISTORY

T0366904

THE LITTMAN LIBRARY OF
JEWISH CIVILIZATION

Dedicated to the memory of
LOUIS THOMAS SIDNEY LITTMAN
*who founded the Littman Library for the love of God
and as an act of charity in memory of his father*
JOSEPH AARON LITTMAN
and to the memory of
ROBERT JOSEPH LITTMAN
who continued what his father Louis had begun

יהא זכרם ברוך

*'Get wisdom, get understanding:
Forsake her not and she shall preserve thee'*

PROV. 4: 5

*The Littman Library of Jewish Civilization is a registered UK charity
Registered charity no. 1000784*

BROADENING
JEWISH HISTORY

◆

Towards a Social History of
Ordinary Jews

TODD M. ENDELMAN

London
The Littman Library of Jewish Civilization
in association with Liverpool University Press

The Littman Library of Jewish Civilization
Registered office: 4th floor, 7–10 Chandos Street, London WIG 9DQ

in association with Liverpool University Press
4 Cambridge Street, Liverpool L69 7ZU, UK
www.liverpooluniversitypress.co.uk/littman

Managing Editor: Connie Webber

Distributed in North America by
Oxford University Press Inc., 198 Madison Avenue,
New York, NY 10016, USA

First published in hardback 2011
First published in paperback 2014

Catalogue records for this book are available from the
British Library and the Library of Congress

ISBN 978–1–904113–02–7

Publishing co-ordinator: Janet Moth
Copy-editing: Mark Newby
Index: Todd M. Endelman
Designed and typeset by Pete Russell, Faringdon, Oxon.

Printed and bound in Great Britain by
CPI Group (UK) Ltd., Croydon, CR0 4YY

To the memory of my parents

◆

ALBERT LEWIS ENDELMAN

1915–1983

◆

MARCELLE NADINE TODRESIC ENDELMAN

1917–1961

◆

*Publication of this volume was facilitated by
a generous donation in memory of*

LEON DRUCKER

1932–1998

and

GRAHAM DRUCKER

1936–2008

◆

Acknowledgements

MANY FRIENDS and colleagues read and commented on the essays in this book prior to their initial publication. I am particularly grateful to those who repeatedly took time from their own work to offer criticism and advice: Miriam Bodian, Deborah Dash Moore, David Feldman, Zvi Gitelman, Deborah Hertz, Brian Porter, Jack Rakove, Meri-Jane Rochelson, and Sheldon Rothblatt. The Frankel Center for Judaic Studies at the University of Michigan has been one of my academic homes for more than twenty-five years. Its generous support allowed me to travel to archives and libraries in New York, London, Cambridge, Oxford, and elsewhere. I also want to acknowledge, as well, the vision and commitment of Jean and Samuel Frankel (may his memory be for a blessing), without whom Judaic studies would not have flourished in Ann Arbor, and the steadfast support of Stanley and Judy Frankel, who have carried on the family tradition.

The essays in this volume were originally published as follows.

INTRODUCTION: 'In Defense of Jewish Social History', *Jewish Social Studies*, NS 7/3 (2001), 52–67.

CHAPTER 1: 'Jewish Self-Identification and West European Categories of Belonging: From the Enlightenment to World War II', in Zvi Gitelman (ed.), *Religion or Ethnicity? Jewish Identities in Evolution* (New Brunswick: Rutgers University Press, 2009), 104–30.

CHAPTER 2: 'The Legitimization of the Diaspora Experience in Recent Jewish Historiography', *Modern Judaism*, 11 (1991), 195–209.

CHAPTER 3: 'The Englishness of Jewish Modernity in England', in Jacob Katz (ed.), *Toward Modernity: The European Jewish Model* (New Brunswick: Transaction Books, 1986), 225–46.

CHAPTER 4: 'Welcoming Ex-Jews into the Jewish Historiographical Fold', in Marc L. Raphael (ed.), *The Margins of Jewish History* (Williamsburg, Va.: Department of Religion, College of William and Mary, 2000), 14–22.

CHAPTER 5: 'The Social and Political Context of Conversion in Germany and England, 1870–1914', in Todd M. Endelman (ed.), *Jewish Apostasy in the Modern World* (New York: Holmes & Meier, 1987), 83–107.

CHAPTER 6: 'Jewish Self-Hatred in Britain and Germany', in Michael Brenner et al. (eds.), *Two Nations: British and German Jews in Comparative Perspective* (Tübingen: J. C. B. Mohr, 1999), 331–63.

CHAPTER 7: 'German-Jewish Settlement in Victorian England', in Werner E. Mosse (ed.), *Second Chance: Two Centuries of German-Speaking Jews in the United Kingdom* (Tübingen: J. C. B. Mohr, 1991), 37–56.

CHAPTER 8: 'The Checkered Career of "Jew" King: A Study in Anglo-Jewish Social History', *AJS Review*, 7–8 (1982–3), 69–100. Copyright © 1982 Association for Jewish Studies. Reprinted with the permission of Cambridge University Press.

CHAPTER 9: '"A Hebrew to the End": The Emergence of Disraeli's Jewishness', in Charles Richmond and Paul Smith (eds.), *The Self-Fashioning of Disraeli, 1818–1851* (Cambridge: Cambridge University Press, 1999), 106–30. Copyright © 1998 Cambridge University Press. Reprinted with permission.

CHAPTER 10: 'Benjamin Disraeli and the Myth of Sephardi Superiority', *Jewish History*, 10/2 (Fall 1996), 21–35.

CHAPTER 11: 'L'Impact de la expérience conversa sur l'identité Sépharade en Angleterre', in Ester Benbassa (ed.), *Mémoires juives d'Espagne et du Portugal* (Paris: Publisud, 1996), 79–90.

CHAPTER 12: 'The Frankaus of London: A Study in Radical Assimilation, 1837–1967', *Jewish History*, 8/1–2 (Winter 1994), 117–54.

CHAPTER 13: 'Jewish Converts in Nineteenth-Century Warsaw: A Quantitative Analysis', *Jewish Social Studies*, NS 4/1 (Fall 1997), 28–59.

CHAPTER 14: 'Memories of Jewishness: Jewish Converts and their Jewish Pasts', in Elisheva Carlebach, John M. Efron, and David N. Myers (eds.), *Jewish History and Jewish Memory: Essays Honoring Yosef Hayim Yerushalmi* (Hanover, NH: University Press of New England, 1998), 311–29.

Contents

Note on Transliteration

THE transliteration of Hebrew in this book reflects consideration of the type of book it is, in terms of its content, purpose, and readership. The system adopted therefore reflects a broad approach to transcription, rather than the narrower approaches found in the *Encyclopaedia Judaica* or other systems developed for text-based or linguistic studies. The aim has been to reflect the pronunciation prescribed for modern Hebrew, rather than the spelling or Hebrew word structure, and to do so using conventions that are generally familiar to the English-speaking reader.

In accordance with this approach, no attempt is made to indicate the distinctions between *alef* and *ayin*, *tet* and *taf*, *kaf* and *kuf*, *sin* and *samekh*, since these are not relevant to pronunciation; likewise, the *dagesh* is not indicated except where it affects pronunciation. Following the principle of using conventions familiar to the majority of readers, however, transcriptions that are well established have been retained even when they are not fully consistent with the transliteration system adopted. On similar grounds, the *tsadi* is rendered by 'tz' in such familiar words as bar mitzvah. Likewise, the distinction between *ḥet* and *khaf* has been retained, using *ḥ* for the former and *kh* for the latter; the associated forms are generally familiar to readers, even if the distinction is not actually borne out in pronunciation, and for the same reason the final *heh* is indicated too. As in Hebrew, no capital letters are used, except that an initial capital has been retained in transliterating titles of published works (for example, *Shulḥan arukh*).

Since no distinction is made between *alef* and *ayin*, they are indicated by an apostrophe only in intervocalic positions where a failure to do so could lead an English-speaking reader to pronounce the vowel-cluster as a diphthong—as, for example, in *ha'ir*—or otherwise mispronounce the word.

The *sheva na* is indicated by an *e*—*perikat ol, reshut*—except, again, when established convention dictates otherwise.

The *yod* is represented by *i* when it occurs as a vowel (*bereshit*), by *y* when it occurs as a consonant (*yesodot*), and by *yi* when it occurs as both (*yisra'el*).

Names have generally been left in their familiar forms, even when this is inconsistent with the overall system.

Introduction

IN SURVEYING WORK on modern Jewish history at a conference in 1987 marking the centenary of the Jewish Theological Seminary, Paula Hyman captured the transformations that swept the field from the 1960s to the 1980s when she spoke of its 'normalization'.[1] By this she meant that the rules of writing and analysis in the field had become similar to those in other fields of historical research. Jewish historians of the late twentieth century, she observed, were no longer concerned, at least in their published work, with overarching questions of Jewish existence and destiny. They did not feel obliged to create a politically viable historical memory to serve extra-scholarly communal ends. Specifically Jewish ideological commitments—to nationalism, integrationism, socialism, or traditional belief and practice—that drove earlier scholarly work had no place in theirs. The transcendent master-narratives (the 'big story' into which historians fit their own 'small stories' and with which they make sense of their own research) that structured the telling of Jewish history in earlier generations had lost their power, a development that the later ascent of postmodernist currents in the academy at large reinforced. As Eli Lederhendler wrote in 1994, 'history on a grand scale is a model we no longer *choose*', because it means selecting 'a red thread of continuity' or 'an "essence" of the Jewish experience', 'imposing a superstructure based on that essence', and then 'choosing a defining characteristic of each successive "stage" of development'.[2]

The essays in this volume are a product of this 'normalization' process and of one current in it in particular—the rise of social history in the academy. Although they range widely in time and place, they share in common a commitment to writing the history of 'ordinary' or 'everyday' Jews rather than highly articulate, widely admired, and thus exceptional Jews. In one way or another, they seek to expand the arena of modern Jewish history, introducing less well known actors and examining emotional states and mundane behaviours. By shifting and expanding the focus of the historian, they seek to redefine the very content of modern Jewish history. To

---

[1] P. E. Hyman, 'Ideological Transformation'.

[2] Lederhendler, *Jewish Responses to Modernity*, 193–4. See also Rosman, *How Jewish Is Jewish History?*, 47–55.

understand whence this new emphasis arose and how it came to influence
my work and that of others in my cohort of Jewish historians, we need to
return to the mid-twentieth century.

In the United States the 'normalization' of Jewish historiography was
linked to the decline of antisemitism that began in the 1960s and in turn to
the integration of Jewish studies into American universities and colleges
that this decline enabled. Until the 1970s the writing and teaching of Jewish
history was largely a parochial enterprise. The few who wrote and taught the
subject in the United States were more likely to hold appointments in seminaries and Hebrew teachers colleges (or in departments of Near Eastern
studies) than in departments of history in research universities and liberal
arts colleges. (Some earned their living as pulpit rabbis.) The pre-eminent
publisher of scholarly Judaica in the United States was the Jewish Publication Society, not a university press. Leading historical journals, such as the
Journal of Modern History and *Past & Present*, rarely published the work of
Jewish historians. In short the field was very much on the institutional
margins of academic historiography in the United States, if not outside it
altogether.[3]

This began to change in the 1970s. Programmes, professors, and graduate aid in Jewish studies began to proliferate. Graduate students intending to teach and write Jewish history enrolled in doctoral programmes in
departments of history at distinguished research universities—in particular Harvard, Columbia, and the University of California campuses at Los
Angeles and Berkeley. As chance would have it, their graduate training
coincided with a revolution in the orientation of historical scholarship in
the United States and other Western countries. The traditional subjects
of academic historiography—intellectual, diplomatic, and political history
—were losing their precedence, yielding ground to a relative newcomer—
social history—with its myriad subdivisions, offshoots, and spin-offs, including the histories of labour, immigration, urbanization, poverty, demography,
crime, women, peasants, family life, and sexuality. Graduate students
were attracted to social history for several reasons. First, it was both novel
and critical. It questioned the assumptions of 'establishment' historiography, positioning itself as progressive and even revolutionary, and thus it
complemented the outlook of 'baby-boomer' historians, who had embraced
sex, drugs, rock 'n' roll, and generational revolt a decade earlier in the turbulent sixties. Second, the cohort of budding historians who entered graduate
school in the late 1960s and 1970s was more ethnically diverse than earlier

[3] On the evolution of Jewish studies as an academic field in American higher education,
see Ritterband and Wechsler, *Jewish Learning in American Universities*.

cohorts. 'Graduate students with strange, unpronounceable surnames, with Brooklyn accents and different skin colors, appeared in the venerable ivy-covered buildings that epitomized elite schooling.'[4] Many were the children and grandchildren of immigrants; some were women. The conventional ways of doing history that they encountered focused on the activities and ideas of the powerful and well born, along with innovators and intellectuals, few of whom were female. Social history, in contrast, was history from the bottom up, history that made room for those who were politically, intellectually, and economically unremarkable, like the parents and grandparents of the new social historians. Between 1958 and 1978 the percentage of Ph.D. dissertations in social history quadrupled and social history overtook political history as the most popular area of research.[5]

The enthronement of social history was more than a switch from writing about statesmen and intellectuals to writing about washerwomen and criminals. There was a strong ideological dimension to this shift. For many, doing social history meant a commitment to championing the dispossessed, the downtrodden, and the inarticulate and rescuing them and other 'casualties of history' from obscurity and what E. P. Thompson famously called 'the enormous condescension of posterity'.[6] Even those historians who practised social history without embracing radical politics endorsed—intentionally or implicitly—a radical understanding of the history of cultures and societies. Social history turned the world upside down. What had been marginal at best became central. By focusing on the textures, structures, and challenges of 'ordinary life'—that is, life as most men and women lived it—social history democratized the historical landscape and subverted conventional notions of what constitutes significance and worth. By refusing to privilege the activities of the rich and the famous (which is not the same as denying their importance), it affirmed a radical egalitarianism, a faith in the value of understanding how a broad and diverse range of people experienced and even influenced historical change. In the case of modern Jewish history, it started from the assumption that all Jews—rich and poor, articulate and inarticulate, male and female—experienced the disruptions of modernity, that few if any were immune to or exempt from the large-scale changes that transformed Europe in the two centuries before the Second World War. Thus it became possible to claim that the life of London's notorious 'Jew' King (1753?–1824), the subject of Chapter 8, was as important as that of Berlin's revered Moses Mendelssohn (1729–86), for each in his own way pioneered

[4] Appleby, Hunt, and Jacob, *Telling the Truth about History*, 147.
[5] Darnton, 'Intellectual and Cultural History', 334.
[6] Thompson, *The Making of the English Working Class*, 12–13.

Jewish integration into state and society at the start of the modern era. More-over, since there were more Jewish scoundrels and bounders than Jewish philosophers in eighteenth- and nineteenth-century Europe, it could be said that it was Mendelssohn who was atypical and marginal, not 'Jew' King. In addition, Mendelssohn's reconciliation of reason and revelation in Judaism, as opposed to the symbolic value that Jews attributed to his career, was idio-syncratic. His disciples were disciples in name only and did not follow his intellectual lead. The creators of Reform Judaism, for example, owed more to Hegel than to Mendelssohn.

The social-history perspective challenged the dominant ways of writing modern Jewish history. Historians who were trained before the 1970s focused on the activities of articulate elites—ideologues, pamphleteers, re-formers, and *shtadlanim* (intercessors and spokesmen), the makers and shakers of communal life, those who voiced their hopes, fears, and dreams in the public sphere. They showed little interest in the history of 'ordinary Jews', who in effect they treated as passive bystanders, waiting patiently for change to trickle down from above. They assumed that new visions, ideas, and outlooks drove change and that these were embedded in self-reflective, ideologically structured thinking. They considered changes in behaviour historically significant and worthy of attention only when they were self-con-sciously willed, the outcome of deliberation and reflection. They showed lit-tle interest in the emotional havoc that emancipation and acculturation wreaked in the lives of either famous or obscure Jews. The *locus classicus* of this perspective is Jacob Katz's much-cited and influential *Out of the Ghetto*, which was written in the 1960s but published only in 1973. It tells the story of Jewish modernization—how Jews 'made their first steps towards integrat-ing into the mainstream of European life'[7]—by recounting the attitudes and activities of a sliver of the German Jewish community (probably less than 1 per cent of the total population): the maskilim (proponents of the Haskalah, the Jewish Enlightenment) and their wealthy patrons. It tells the story, more-over, while ignoring the two largest Jewish communities in Europe at the time—those in Amsterdam and London—where integration and accultura-tion were more advanced, but intellectual activity less brilliant. This was a bit like writing a history of American Jewry without reference to New York and Los Angeles.

Social historians questioned in particular the centrality of Moses Mendelssohn and the maskilim in narratives of Jewish transformation in the West. As is well known, nineteenth-century historians canonized him, giving him the central role in the emergence of the Jews from medieval dark-

---

[7] Katz, *Out of the Ghetto*, p. v.

ness to modern enlightenment. For Heinrich Graetz (1817–91), he was the instigator of Jewish rebirth, the reviver of 'the slumbering genius of the Jewish race', the prophet who summoned 'the captive daughter of Zion' to shake off the dust and loosen the bonds around her neck,[8] whereas for Isaak Markus Jost (1793–1860), he was the third divinely chosen Moses, after the biblical Moses and Maimonides, sent 'to raise those who were bowed down and to free the fettered'.[9] Hagiographical treatments like these were no longer in vogue when social history began its ascent in the academy, but Mendelssohn still loomed large in the Jewish historical imagination. Alexander Altmann's magisterial biography appeared in 1973, the same year as Katz's *Out of the Ghetto*. In the decades that followed, despite the fading star of the Berlin Haskalah as an agent of transformation, Mendelssohn continued to invite the scrutiny of Jewish historians. In the 1990s Allen Arkush, Edward Breuer, and David Sorkin published well-received studies of Mendelssohn, while in the next decade Dominique Bourel, following Altmann's example, weighed in with a hefty biography (640 pages in French; 800 in German), whose subtitle—*La Naissance du Judaïsme moderne*—made clear the interpretative tradition to which it belonged.[10]

The social history perspective did not challenge—nor address, for that matter—the substance of Mendelssohn's thinking or its place in the history of Jewish thought. It claimed, rather, that what many Jews did was more central than what a few Jews thought, thus refocusing the historian's gaze. It also claimed that all Jews, whatever their rank and gender, experienced the disruptions of modernity. The same large-scale transformative currents that demanded a response in elite circles also influenced behaviour outside them. Poor Jews, Jews of middling intelligence and culture (or not much culture at all), undistinguished and unintelligent Jews, as well as Jewish women in general, were not immune from the changes and pressures reshaping the lives of bankers and brokers, publicists, and philosophers. They too had 'eyes . . . hands, organs, dimensions, senses, affections, passions' and bled if pricked, laughed if tickled, died if poisoned, and took revenge if wronged.[11] In short, they were as fully human as those Jews who monopolized the attention of historians heretofore, and thus if for no other reason were worthy of notice.

From this perspective Mendelssohn was irrelevant. Of course, if it were the case that his outlook and example sparked transformations in European

---

[8] Graetz, *History of the Jews*, v. 292–3.   [9] Jost, *Die Geschichte des Judenthums*, iii. 296.
[10] Altmann, *Moses Mendelssohn*; Arkush, *Moses Mendelssohn*; Breuer, *The Limits of Enlightenment*; Sorkin, *Moses Mendelssohn*; Bourel, *Moses Mendelssohn*.
[11] Shakespeare, *The Merchant of Venice*, III. i.

Jewry more broadly, then he would merit a more central place. But, as I argue in Chapter 3, the conventional view that German Jewish currents, not just Mendelssohn alone, contributed to the weakening of traditional beliefs and customs elsewhere in Europe exaggerates the appeal and influence of these currents in other settings. On the other hand, for those who privileged the history of ideas, measuring significance by shifts in self-definition and self-consciousness, the behaviour of inarticulate Jews or Jews whose thoughts went unrecorded was irrelevant. For these historians, the life of the mind trumped other dimensions of human experience. In the end, it is difficult to know how to judge one approach as more valuable or authentic than the other, since ultimately each reflects irreducible core values. As Max Weber recognized a century ago, scholars examine only those segments of reality which are significant to them in light of their relevance. Recognizing the existence of a historical issue 'coincides, personally, with the possession of specifically oriented motives and values'. The question of knowing what is worth knowing among 'an infinite multiplicity of successively and coexistently emerging and disappearing events, both "within" and "outside" ourselves', is linked to values—that is, deeply held ideological, cultural, social, and emotional commitments.[12] In other words, both approaches produced histories that were 'true'. What was open to debate, however, was the often unarticulated claim of conventional historiography that it was the only story to be told, that the history of a few Jews encompassed and represented the history of all Jews.

The influence of social history on the writing of modern Jewish history was profound. It legitimized new avenues of research, enlarging its content and expanding its boundaries. To an unprecedented extent, 'ordinary' men and women, people distant from influence, power, and ideological foment, those who everywhere and at all times constituted the majority of the Jewish people, attracted the attention of historians, especially younger historians. Village Jews in Alsace and Germany; east European immigrants in London, Paris, and New York; impoverished Ashkenazim in Amsterdam; yeshiva students in Lithuania and religiously indifferent civil servants in France; homemakers and their daughters in imperial Germany; housewives and consumers on the Lower East Side; converts, renegades, criminals, and no-goodniks everywhere—all took their place alongside maskilim, Reform ideologues, Zionist functionaries, communal magnates, and philanthropists. In particular, the boom in social history, which coincided with second-wave feminism, paved the way for the study of Jewish women, the family, and gender more broadly. At the same time the shift from the history of ideas

[12] Weber, '"Objectivity" in Social Science and Social Policy', 61, 72, 84.

to the history of society broke the link between rabbinical training and the writing of Jewish history. It allowed students—women and non-Jews in particular—whose education did not include years of studying rabbinic texts to enter a field that at the time was dominated by graduates of yeshivas and seminaries.[13]

Critics at the time charged social historians with being preoccupied with the outré and the transgressive and said that their work lacked gravitas. A now deceased notable of the Jewish Historical Society of England, for example, once claimed (not in my presence) that I was preoccupied with Jewish vagabonds and criminals. For these critics, the activities of Jews who behaved badly—quacks, criminals, converts, and the like—were in a category of their own, unconnected to and distinct from the activities of admirable Jews. Social historians, however, argued that Jewish 'misbehaviour' was not aberrational, at least in historiographical terms, and that its study revealed stresses and strains to which all Jews were subject. Structurally, this claim was similar to the psychoanalytic claim that neurotic thinking and behaviour exist on a continuum. When extreme, neuroses are crippling; when mild, they are merely anxiety-provoking. In their aetiology, structure, and operation, however, they are similar, so that studying the extreme illuminates the moderate as well. The study of Jews who left the Jewish fold—through conversion and other modes of radical assimilation—is a case in point, one that I discuss at length in Chapters 4, 5, 13, and 14. Jews who shed their Jewishness (or at least tried to) might seem, at first, peripheral to writing modern Jewish history. These were Jews, after all, who did not want to be Jews and who took steps to free themselves from the constraints of Jewishness and the burdens of Jewish history. If so, why include them? One answer is that their flight from Jewishness was an extreme manifestation of behaviour that was common in most Westernized Jewish circles. Everywhere acculturated Jews who identified with the societies in which they lived were subject to assimilatory pressures. Only a minority, those whose attachment to Judaism was as weak as their ambition was strong, chose radical assimilation. A greater number considered taking this step but in the end held back for various reasons. Even more experienced the hurt and distress that the few who left the fold found unbearable. Because Jewish responses to exclusion and stigmatization constituted a continuum of behaviours rather than a series of discrete, disconnected behaviours, studying those at one end of the spectrum brings the whole phenomenon into focus. The same is true of Jewish self-hatred, which I discuss in Chapter 6. Few Jews internalized the antisemitic critique of Jewishness to the extent that they became virulent

---

[13] I owe this point to Deborah Moore.

antisemites themselves, compelled emotionally to declaim the shortcomings of the Jews in public. But many Jews incorporated what antisemites said about them into their own thinking and tailored their behaviour accordingly.

The integration of 'ordinary' Jews into the historiographical fold represented—and was made possible by—the abandonment of special pleading. Most Jewish historical writing in the nineteenth and early twentieth centuries was animated by ideological and apologetic aims, largely because the Jewish Question was still alive. In tune with their own commitments, Jewish historians highlighted the spiritual worth of Judaism and its contributions to Western civilization, *or* the centrality of the Land of Israel and national consciousness in the diaspora, *or* the primacy of class relationships in communal life, *or* the pioneering presence of Jews in one country or another in its formative years. They preferred well-behaved, respectable Jews, or at least ideologically driven Jews, to run-of-the-mill or disreputable ones, who could not be pressed into service as role models, precursors, or heroes. When Jewish history entered the American academy, the tendency to make it a vehicle of Jewish politics weakened (though, as I explain in Chapter 2, it did not disappear). This was, in part, a result of exposure to the values and methods of the academy, which at the time celebrated objectivity and value-neutrality in scholarship, but it was also a result of the normalization of Jewish status that made this integration possible in the first place. In the last three decades of the twentieth century Jews in the United States came to feel more 'at home' and secure than in earlier periods, whether in Europe or America. More acculturated and integrated than earlier generations, they were less likely to encounter antisemitic obstacles to their happiness and advancement. (The best evidence of this is the sharp increase in the intermarriage rate towards the end of the twentieth century.) As the lives of American Jews became more 'normal', their historians became less inclined to use their work to advance this or that solution to the no longer pressing Jewish Question.

However, though integration into the American academy weakened special pleading in Jewish historiography, it also exposed it to intellectual and political currents that were animating and dividing the academy as a whole. Thus, at the same time that social history broadened the stage of modern Jewish history, it also infused it with concerns that owed more to contemporary American stresses and strains than to Jewish politics. Because social history was a left-wing rather than right-wing project, its practitioners often undertook to do more than recover ignored voices. In restoring the poor and the humble to their place in the historical landscape, social historians with an eye to contemporary politics often embellished their portrait, transforming them into heroic figures, the bearers of virtues and viewpoints that were close to their own heart. Some were tempted, for example, to portray east European immigrant workers in New York, London, and Paris as class-conscious proletarians, dreaming collectivist dreams while rejecting liberal individualism, capitalism, and the claims of Jewish solidarity. Others were tempted to represent Jewish criminals and toughs as primitive political radicals, flaunting and resisting the constraints of bourgeois respectability. Still others were tempted to depict Jewish women as heroes in the struggle to preserve Jewish traditions and loyalties in the face of career-minded male indifference and even hostility. Once maligned in historical literature as the vanguard of radical assimilation, Jewish women were now represented as the first line of defence in the struggle for ethnic continuity. Reassessments like these flowed from the integration of Jewish historical writing into the American academy. They reflected the concerns of American radicalism and feminism rather than those of the old warhorses of internal Jewish politics—socialism, nationalism, assimilationism, and orthodoxy.

From the mid-1980s Jewish historical writing was exposed to a new set of influences, those connected to the rise of postmodernism, cultural studies, and literary theory in the humanities and the 'softer' social sciences (history and cultural anthropology). Postmodernism, by which I mean the French-born, anti-Enlightenment, intellectual project that questioned modernist assumptions about the nature and reliability of knowledge and the ability of this knowledge to capture reality external to it, arrived in the American academy in the mid- to late 1970s, when literary critics and philosophers discovered French theorists like Jacques Derrida and Michel Foucault. At first its influence was limited to departments of literature and philosophy, but within a decade or so it spread to departments of history as well. There it intersected with—and further fuelled—growing dissatisfaction with social history, which was in part a disenchantment with its economic reductionism (at least in its Marxist varieties), its reliance on no longer compelling teleological master-narratives, and its neglect of sentiment and emotion. Social history, critics claimed, ignored what people felt and believed and the meanings they assigned to their experiences; it failed to confront the realm of culture—structures, processes, states of mind. Even its champions were compelled to concede that it could lapse into a mechanistic materialism that accorded little agency to subjective feelings. The cultural turn in historiography focused on 'the mind as a repository of society's prescriptions, as the site where identity is formed and reality linguistically negotiated' and as the residence of culture, 'society's repertoire of interpretive mechanisms and value systems'.[14] Armed with the insights of literary theory and cultural

[14] Appleby, Hunt, and Jacob, *Telling the Truth about History*, 218.

anthropology, the new cultural historians worked beneath the surface of societies and their formal social institutions and cultural productions to excavate the conscious and unconscious understandings that animated them. Not only did the new way of doing history take root in the 1980s and 1990s, it became hegemonic, struggling with and then supplanting the old social history at the 'cutting edge'. Incoming graduate students took to cultural history as enthusiastically as their predecessors had to social history in the 1970s. Their embrace of the new approach, however, was not an act of rebellion, for their teachers were also retooling their methodological outlook.[15]

The ascendancy of cultural history at the turn of the century grew from a confluence of trends and events. First, a new set of political passions, rooted in gender and racial issues, rose to the fore. Identity movements—feminism especially—called into question understandings of history that privileged class and economic relations as analytical categories. Second, the demise of the Soviet Union dimmed the flame of Marxist thought in the academy and fuelled scepticism about totalizing utopias and the theoretical schemes that predicted their emergence. The effort to identify 'big structures' yielded to micro-histories, local perspectives, questions of identity, and histories of subjectivity. Third, to summarize William Sewell's insight, the post-war economic boom, which buttressed the confidence of baby-boomer historians in their ability to understand macro-historical social structures, faded in the 1970s and gave way to cycles of financial and industrial crisis, which undermined that confidence. The seeming inability of established analytical categories and methods to make sense of the present, Sewell writes, encouraged historians to turn 'from the pursuit of big structures to micro-history, from socioeconomic determinism to studies of culture, from master processes to the sources of subjective identity'.[16]

The rise of cultural studies in the academy provoked angry, at times vituperative, criticism, often from those with antiradical and neoconservative credentials, but also from those on the left who remained committed to materialism and determinism and felt betrayed. Critics charged that cultural studies, with its roots in postmodernist thinking, was morally relativistic; that it was not critical enquiry, let alone *Wissenschaft*, but a system of beliefs about transforming society; not scholarship but identity politics with a veneer of scholarship. Even some who were sympathetic to its tendentiousness were troubled by its indifference to verbal clarity. Cultural studies-inflected history writing was (and largely remains) dense, convoluted, inelegant, self-referential, pretentious, and often impenetrable. Littered with

---

[15] See e.g. Eley, *A Crooked Line*.   [16] Sewell, 'AHA Forum on *A Crooked Line*', 401.

clumsy neologisms and awkward wordplays, it was often like a kabbalistic text—opaque, except to those already familiar with its concerns, vocabulary, and world-view. In these complaints, there was an element of truth. Still, critics usually failed to see the positive side of the cultural turn—how it brought scepticism and caution to the reading of texts whose meanings were once considered self-evident, how it addressed layers of human experience that social history had ignored, and how it problematized the master-narratives that had become conventional and all too familiar. They also failed to see that both ways of writing history shared at least one object in common—inclusivity. Social history worked to expand the stage of history by making room for, or in some cases foregrounding, those who had previously been excluded. Cultural history worked to expand the range of human experiences deemed worthy of historical investigation.

The postmodernist element in the rise of cultural studies (that is, the anti-Enlightenment critique of commonsense empiricism and the representation of reality) had little if any impact on the writing of modern Jewish history. No one in Jewish studies argued that the very effort to represent the past was so fundamentally flawed from the start—due to the subjectivity of historians and the evidence they use—that it was not worth the effort. The reason, I suspect, is that Jewish historians are too emotionally invested in the past that is the focus of their research to treat it as an arbitrary construction, perpetually in flux, without fixed reality. Indeed, for them, modern Jewish history is too 'real'—too serious a matter to be treated as an intellectual play-thing, tossed about here and there. In other ways, however, postmodernism did oblige Jewish historians, at least the methodologically self-conscious among them, to examine a number of assumptions about the nature of Judaism and Jewish history that had hitherto been axiomatic—including the belief in a coherent, unified, transnational Jewish experience. As Moshe Rosman wrote in his collection of essays *How Jewish Is Jewish History?*, postmodernism problematizes the existence of the collective entity 'the Jewish people' and the very word 'Jewish'. In his words:

If the word 'Jewish' signifies no essential features continuous over time and place, if it can be—or if it has been—constructed in an infinite number of ways, if it is always and everywhere contingent, then, as a practical matter, how do we go about defining the subject which we seek to research and write about? . . . If Jewish can be everything, is it anything?[17]

Perhaps then Jewishness is in the eye of the beholder, the Jews are 'an imagined community' (*pace* Benedict Anderson), and the very notion of Jewish

---

[17] Rosman, *How Jewish Is Jewish History?*, 4.

history is constructed for this or that end. At a minimum, it can be said that postmodernism encouraged Jewish historians to pause before pronouncing what was authentically Jewish and what was not.

The impact of the cultural turn on the writing of Jewish history was stronger at a more concrete, less abstract level. Whether philosophically hostile to empiricism or not, cultural studies-inflected history privileged subjective states—how people understood and voiced their experiences and what cultural resources were available to them in doing so. Discourses, representations, and states of feeling, what men and women wrote or what others wrote about them, took centre stage. What they experienced subjectively—how they felt and thought—trumped what they actually did. It was this dimension of the new cultural history that was most appealing towards the end of the century and this dimension that threatened to reverse earlier gains.

The great achievement of social history was its expansion and democratization of the historical landscape. It foregrounded the doings of 'average' flesh-and-blood men and women, those who were typical by virtue of their numbers, and undermined the identification of Jewish history with the history of Jewish thought, ideology, and philosophy. While the champions of the new cultural history did not intend to narrow the stage of history, they did so nonetheless because they focused on perceptions, attitudes, sensibilities, and feelings; how and why they shifted; and how these shifts expanded or limited the possibilities for agency. They downplayed or marginalized behaviour, the plenitude of acts, large and small, that constitute the stuff of everyday life, and privileged thinking and feeling. In doing so, they constricted rather than expanded the historical stage, for the average Jew of the past, like the average Christian, was inarticulate (at least before the rise of opinion polls) and left little evidence to allow historians to intuit how he or she made sense of the world.

In retrospect, the choice between social history and cultural history was a false one. It seemed to be an either/or proposition because of the close identification of social history with Marxist materialism, which in the view of critics was incapable of evaluating inner states of experience on their own terms. In Great Britain and the United States in particular, social history and the history of the poor, the downtrodden, and the dispossessed were often viewed as one and the same project. While it is understandable why the two were identified with each other, the link between them was contingent, the result of the circumstances surrounding the birth of social history, rather than logically necessary. When detached from the radical politics that nourished its growth, social history held the potential to be more inclusive in its sweep and supple in its approach, capable of examining both behaviours and states of mind, not just among workers but among all those whom historical scholarship previously marginalized. In the debate between social and cultural historians, it was easy to forget that one impulse of the social history revolution was the desire to broaden the stage of history in general, to foreground diverse kinds of people. When the overriding aim of social history is defined as inclusion, rather than the construction of a past with political relevance, the question of method—how one studies those whom one wants to include—loses its urgency. The way in which the historian addresses his or her material will depend, then, on what he or she wants to know and what, given the evidence that survives, it is possible to know.

At a time when cultural history is in the ascendant, the essays in this volume restate the case for social history. Their aim is twofold: to people the stage of Jewish history with an expanded cast of characters *and* to show how this move reconfigures views of Jewish history whose correctness is assumed rather than explored. In short, my claim is that the social history of the Jews is not a diverting sideshow—even though it features at times diverting characters. Rather, I argue, it speaks to key, mainstream issues in Jewish history. I also hope to show that social history, when conceived broadly, that is, when detached from the materialist assumptions that nurtured it in the 1960s and 1970s, can address the subjectivities that its critics believed it ignored. The essays that follow return repeatedly to the question of how otherwise successful Jews coped with stigmatization and exclusion, whether the topic is the much-studied Benjamin Disraeli (Chapters 9 and 10) or the now forgotten cigar merchant and novelist Gilbert Frankau (Chapter 12). While Disraeli was not in any sense an 'ordinary' Jew, and while his strategy for coping with anti-Jewish taunts and barbs was unusual (if not bizarre), his need to respond in one way or another to exclusion and hostility was a common experience. I have included the essays about Disraeli, along with essays about how less flamboyant Jews responded to the absence of acceptance, to illustrate both the ubiquity and gravity of the problem and the range of responses that emerged. Similarly, in asking why the project to make Jews modern 'went wrong' (that is, failed to turn out as its promoters wished), the first chapter foregrounds feelings and sentiments, expectations and hopes, among broad swathes of the Jewish population and explores how these both drove and reflected behaviour.

A secondary aim of this volume is to tout comparative history.[18] From its inception in the nineteenth century, critical Jewish historical scholarship

---

[18] For a fuller discussion see my introduction to Endelman (ed.), *Comparing Jewish Societies*, 1–21.

was transnational in its focus, which is not surprising given the diasporic character of the Jewish people. In fact, at times it was so avowedly transnational, because of its faith in the cohesion and uniqueness of the Jewish experience, that it ignored the impact of local, regional, and national circumstances. However, history writing that thinks outside the framework of the nation-state is not the same as comparative history. The latter assumes that the societies and states in which Jews lived shaped (but did not necessarily determine) their actions and attitudes, asking how, why, and to what extent, but it also assumes that their Jewishness, what they shared regardless of where they lived by virtue of common historical memories and traditions, was also a critical ingredient. The comparative method alone establishes what is unique and what is shared in each national Jewish experience. Ironically, it alone, in distinguishing the similar from the dissimilar, reveals the Germanness of German Jewish history or the Englishness of English Jewish history. For example, comparing the origins of Jewish modernity in Germany and England, as I do in Chapter 3, reveals the peculiarity of the German case, not its universality or representativeness, thus undermining the claim of an earlier generation that Jewish modernity went forth from Germany, like the Torah from Zion. It alone allows us to assess the relative strength of currents of hostility and tolerance in various settings and in various periods, a matter of some historiographical dispute, especially in regard to Europe's long nineteenth century. Some historians, for example, claim that antisemitism in imperial Germany was no stronger than in late Victorian England or *fin-de-siècle* France. Chapters 5 and 6 speak to this question by asking how Jews in different national contexts (England and Germany) perceived and responded to antisemitism. By shifting the focus from what antisemites said to how Jews experienced what was said, it becomes possible to avoid the chief stumbling block to measuring the strength of antisemitism from country to country: the ubiquity of antisemitic discourse. Even in the most tolerant societies and in the most tolerant times, Jew-baiters were active. The question, of course, is not their presence, but the ways in which their ideas were mobilized in concrete social and political situations. Exploring conversion and self-hatred, two extreme responses to antisemitism, in Germany and England taps the methodological strengths of both social and comparative history.

As detailed above (pp. vii–viii), the essays in this volume initially appeared in Israeli, British, German, French, and American journals and collections over the past three decades. In every case, I have updated and revised the essays, taking note of recent work and, more importantly, correcting statements of fact and interpretation in light of this work and changes in my own thinking. Many of the essays are substantially different from their original versions. By bringing them together in one volume I hope to make a case for the rehabilitation of social history, demonstrating its compatibility with newer ways of describing the past, and to encourage transnational comparisons in the writing of Jewish history more generally.

PART I

METHODS AND PERSPECTIVES

CHAPTER ONE

Making Jews Modern

Jewish Self-Identification and West European Categories of Belonging

I

IT IS AN ARTICLE OF FAITH in much of the academy that 'identity'—everywhere and at all times—is fluid, fragmented, and contingent. This assumption, whatever its value in illuminating Jewish behaviour in recent centuries, is not very useful in understanding the experience of Jews in earlier periods. In medieval and early modern Europe, Jews constituted a well-defined collective unit for whom questions of self-identification—who are we and what is our place here?—rarely arose. Pre-modern European Jews differed from their neighbours by virtue of their religion, nationality/ethnicity, legal status, and in most cases language, costume, employment, and social and cultural habits. Most lived in quasi-autonomous, self-regulating corporations (*kehilot*), chartered bodies with well-defined privileges and obligations. With the frequent exception of late medieval Italian and Spanish Jews and those in small, isolated communities elsewhere, their contacts with Christians were largely instrumental. Religious traditions (Jewish and Christian alike), social structures, and legal categories defined the borders of the Jewish world, which remained more or less stable throughout the medieval and early modern periods. 'Jewishness' was not endlessly constructed and renegotiated. The line between Christian and Jew was clear and stable, not fuzzy or indeterminate, for over one thousand years. Within the Jewish world the nature of correct belief and practice (what Judaism required) was much disputed of course. The rabbis clashed over how best to know and serve God and how best to interpret the Law. These were not, however, debates about the boundary between Jews and non-Jews or about the fundamentals of Jewish self-definition such as origins, chosenness, exile, redemption, and the like.

The one exception to this generalization—the case of former New Christians or Conversos—is the proverbial exception that proves the proverbial rule. The descendants of Iberian Jews who had converted to Catholicism in the fourteenth and fifteenth centuries under duress, Conversos lived as nominal Christians before resettling in tolerated Jewish communities in the Netherlands, Britain, south-western France, northern Germany, and the New World. Regardless of the extent to which they harboured a sense of Jewish descent or maintained remnants of Jewish observance, they were educated and socialized as Christians. In Yosef Yerushalmi's now classic formulation, they were 'the first considerable group of European Jews to have had their most extensive and direct personal experiences completely outside the organic Jewish community and the spiritual universe of normative Jewish tradition'. Before leaving the Iberian peninsula, and especially afterwards, they experienced the tensions that later became characteristic of Jews whose identities were multiple and fragmented as the result of living simultaneously in two or more overlapping worlds. Ex-Converso communities confronted the task of collective self-definition, requiring them to balance, reconcile, or negotiate two clusters of traditions—one associated with the normative, rabbinic Judaism of professing Jewish communities; the other with the values, norms, and behavioural traits of Spain and Portugal.[1]

Former Conversos, however, were unrepresentative of the European Jewish population with its roots in northern and central Europe (Ashkenaz). The Jewishness of the Ashkenazim (by which I mean their subjective self-understanding and their objective behavioural and situational distinctiveness, rather than any essential spiritual or biological quality) remained undisturbed until the eighteenth and nineteenth centuries. It became problematic for them, a matter of reflection and debate, only when the structure of state and society that had supported it weakened and then dissolved. When the *ancien régime* gave way, when states ceased to be constituted as clusters of legally structured corporate ranks and orders, and Jews, like others whose civil status previously derived from the collective unit to which they belonged, were incorporated into the emerging liberal order as individuals, only then did Jews turn to forging new self-definitions.

2

The transformation of the Jews, their movement 'out of the ghetto' (to use the title of Jacob Katz's well-known account), did not follow a unitary, linear trajectory. It was a complex, multidimensional, messy process, with at least four distinct components—emancipation, acculturation, secularization, and

---

[1] Yerushalmi, *From Spanish Court to Italian Ghetto*, 44. Nuanced treatments of this negotiation are Bodian, *Hebrews of the Portuguese Nation*, and Graizbord, *Souls in Dispute*.

integration—which, while interdependent, were also distinct from each other both conceptually and in practice. In western and central Europe the transformation of the Jews entailed the acquisition of citizenship and the rights it bestowed (emancipation); the adoption of new social and cultural values and new modes of deportment, dress, and speech (acculturation); the rejection or neglect of time-honoured religious beliefs and practices, including both those sanctioned by custom and those required by law (secularization); and the struggle for social acceptance in non-Jewish circles (integration).[2] Their transformation also included far-reaching changes in self-perception, for as Jews moved from exclusion to inclusion, from periphery to mainstream, they found themselves reconsidering and redefining how they saw themselves—and how they wanted others to see them. Formerly, they had viewed themselves—and were viewed by others—as a discrete people, different in kind from other peoples. In the words of the Aleinu prayer, the closing prayer of the Jewish liturgy, God had made them different from the other nations of the world and assigned to them a distinct fate. Moreover, they were a people whose national and religious identities were indissolubly linked and whose ties to the Christians among whom they lived were more instrumental than affective. Religion and ethnicity were omnipresent and inseparable, filling the whole of their existence. The integration of Jews into states increasingly built around individual rights rather than collective privileges made the survival of this undifferentiated sense of self-identification difficult if not impossible.[3]

[2] On the transformation of the Jews in the eighteenth and nineteenth centuries, see Katz, *Out of the Ghetto*; Endelman, *The Jews of Georgian England*; P. E. Hyman, *The Emancipation of the Jews of Alsace*; Lowenstein, *The Berlin Jewish Community*; the essays in Katz (ed.), *Toward Modernity*; Birnbaum and Katznelson (eds.), *Paths of Emancipation*; and Frankel and Zipperstein (eds.), *Assimilation and Community*.

[3] Some social scientists employ the term 'assimilation' to describe the combined process of changing one's culture (what I am calling 'acculturation') and changing one's subjective identity. For several reasons, I prefer to avoid the term. First, historically, the term was partisan and prescriptive, used to describe a political programme for Jewish social and cultural transformation. The political uses to which it was put in the past still hinder its employment as a value-free, descriptive concept. Second, when used in historical scholarship, it is often deployed without precision or rigour. Historians who write about Jewish modernization frequently fail to distinguish between 'assimilation' as a complex of processes and 'assimilation' as a cultural and political programme. They often also fail to distinguish between 'acculturation' and 'integration'. Third, 'assimilation', when used to describe subjective identity transformation (becoming Jewish *and* something else), refers to a state of mind rather than concrete practices. While social scientists, armed with the tools of quantitative survey research, can sample the thinking of entire populations, historians must make do with the ideologically driven programmatic statements of elites. The *behaviour* of 'average' Jews in the nineteenth and twentieth centuries (their acculturation, integration, and secularization) is more accessible than their sense of self-identification.

The states that took shape in the West in the eighteenth and nineteenth centuries eliminated or weakened the estates, corporations, chapters, guilds, chartered bodies, and other intermediate units that previously determined the legal status of their members. In particular, they eroded the unity between ecclesiastical community and national identity, replacing it with categories of universal citizenship and individual rights. Religion, in theory, ceased to be a criterion for membership in the nation and became little more than 'one feature among others in the diversity of a people, neither more nor less than having different jobs or coming from this or that region'. It was reduced to 'no more than one of the numerous variables that distinguished between subjects or citizens'.[4] This process of civil levelling and homogenizing was aimed at imposing order, coherence, rationality, and uniformity. Even if Jews had wanted to remain a people apart, with their own distinctive legal niche, the states in which they lived would have been unwilling to tolerate such separatism. There was no room for the anomaly of a legally privileged Jewish corporation exercising authority over its members. As Salo Baron recognized decades ago, 'emancipation was an even greater necessity for the modern state than it was for the Jew'. Once corporate distinctions were abolished, it would have been 'an outright anachronism' to allow the Jews to remain a separate body, with privileges and obligations that were different from those of other citizens.[5]

Both Jewish and Christian supporters of the entry of the Jews into the modern nation-state acknowledged that an undifferentiated sense of Jewishness was an anachronism, a vestige of intolerant epochs when Jews were legally and socially marginalized. In the words of an 1889 editorial in a liberal Hungarian publication, if Jews 'want to be regarded as completely equal, they must not differ in any detail from the other inhabitants of the nation'. They had to alter 'their external appearance, their clothing, their way of life, their occupations'.[6] The Jewish component in their identity was to shrink and become compartmentalized as their civil status improved. They reasoned that if Jews continued to consider themselves a separate nation, with their own distinct allegiances and hopes, they could not be incorporated into nation-states that no longer recognized corporate or collective membership. (Further to the east, in the multi-national Romanov empire, the survival of a dynastic regime into the early twentieth century allowed an undifferentiated, non-compartmentalized Jewish identity to endure longer.) Jewish people-

---

[4] Rémond, *Religion and Society in Modern Europe*, 119.

[5] S. W. Baron, 'The Modern Age', 317. Baron first advanced this view in the interwar period (see 'Ghetto and Emancipation' and *Social and Religious History of the Jews*, vol. ii, ch. 11).

[6] 'Újabb tanács', *Egyenlöség*, 10 Feb. 1889, quoted in Gluck, 'The Budapest Flâneur', 7.

hood was to be abandoned, Jewish particularism to be muted. Judaism was to be transformed into a religion, like other religions, adherence to which was to be one among several strands in the identity of emancipated, modern Jews. Inclusion in state and society could occur on no other basis. In the oft-cited declaration of the count of Clermont-Tonnerre in the debate on Jewish emancipation in France in December 1789: 'Il faut refuser tout aux Juifs comme nation et accorder tout aux Juifs comme individus . . . il faut qu'ils ne fassent dans l'Etat ni un corps politique, ni un Ordre; il faut qu'ils soient individuellement citoyens.'[7] Jews who refused emancipation on these terms, Clermont-Tonnerre continued, were to be expelled.

While Jewish notables and pamphleteers did not dwell on the consequences of failing to accept the terms of emancipation, they were as adamant as their Christian counterparts that emancipation called for a fundamental shift in Jewish self-identification. Following the emancipation of the Jews of Alsace and Lorraine in September 1791, Berr Isaac Berr, a wealthy maskil from Nancy, wrote an open letter to his newly emancipated 'co-religionists' reminding them 'how absolutely necessary it is for us to divest ourselves entirely of that narrow spirit, of *Corporation* and *Congregation*, in all civil and political matters, not immediately connected with our spiritual laws; in these things we must absolutely appear simply as individuals, as Frenchmen' rather than as 'a distinct body of people and a separate community'.[8] In the German states, where public debate about the transformation of the Jews was more protracted and charged, maskilim and reformers were just as adamant.

From the perspective of the early twenty-first-century academy, with its validation of ethnic diversity and cultural pluralism, the link between emancipation and transformation, the demand that Jews refashion their self-definition and behaviour, seems harsh, even unreasonable. However, in the context of the period, it represented an advance, a sharp break with the pre-modern past, when the source of the Jew's defect was a matter of faith and baptism the sole remedy, the only avenue to integration and acceptance. Moreover, while those Christians who championed emancipation also believed that Jewish morals and customs were in a sorry state and in need of reform, they did not trace this to the basic teachings of Judaism or to any essential trait, spiritual or corporeal, of the Jews. Disciples of the

---

[7] 'One must refuse everything to the Jews as a nation but bestow everything on them as individuals . . . They can remain neither a political body nor a nation; they must become individual citizens' (*Opinion de M. le comte Stanislas de Clermont-Tonnerre, député de Paris, le 23 décembre 1789*, quoted in Girard, *Les Juifs de France*, 51).

[8] Berr Isaac Berr, *Lettre d'un citoyen . . . à ses confrères*, in Tama (ed.), *Transactions of the Parisian Sanhedrim*, 15–17.

Enlightenment, they rejected the traditional Christian claims of God's eternal damnation and punishment of the Jews and of their ineradicable malevolence. In their view there was no unchanging Jewish essence. As the English deist John Toland wrote in 1707 (in what may be the earliest statement of this position), whatever 'genius' or 'bent of mind' reigned among the Jews, it proceeded 'from accident and not from nature'. 'The different methods of government and education are the true springs and causes of such different inclinations all over the world.'[9] If Jews were unsocial, unproductive, devious, and immoral (which was the common Enlightenment view), the reason was that circumstances—bad measures and bad treatment—had made them that way. The Whig historian and essayist Thomas Babington Macaulay was explicit about this in calling for the removal of Jewish legal disabilities in Britain. If English Jews lacked 'patriotic feeling' and viewed Dutch Jews rather than English Christians as their compatriots, it was because an oppressive state had failed to protect them. 'If the Jews have not felt towards England like children', he wrote in the *Edinburgh Review* in 1831, 'it is because she has treated them like a step-mother.' Once treated as equals, they would 'know that they owe all their comforts and pleasures to the bond which united them in one community' and would be overcome with feelings of patriotism. In short, the Jews of his day were 'precisely what our government has made them'.[10]

This belief in the power of environmental influence was central to all Enlightenment and liberal proposals to ameliorate the condition of the Jews. In France the three prizewinners in the Metz essay contest of 1785–87 (on the question: 'Are there means of making the Jews happy and more useful in France?') accepted the premise that persecution was the major cause of Jewish degeneration. In this they followed the lead of the Prussian civil servant Christian Wilhelm von Dohm, whose *Über die bürgerliche Verbesserung der Juden* (1781–3) was the classic Enlightenment statement of this position. Dohm, for example, traced the concentration of Jews in low-status trades (money-lending, peddling and hawking, trading in second-hand goods) to government measures to regulate their economic activity. To the unfortunate Jew, he wrote, 'whose activity is restricted on all sides, whose talents have no scope for free utterance, in whose virtue nobody believes, for whom honor is almost non-existent, to him no other way but commerce is open to acquire means for improving his lot for earning a living'.[11] Central to the argument of Dohm and other reformers was the conviction that human

[9] Toland, *Reasons for Naturalizing the Jews in Great Britain and Ireland*, 18.
[10] Macaulay, *Critical and Historical Essays*, i. 142–4.
[11] Dohm, *Concerning the Amelioration of the Civil Status of the Jews*, 3.

character was universal and plastic, and thus subject to environmental influence. Enlightenment and liberal supporters of emancipation were buoyant optimists, firm believers in the oneness of human nature and the perfectibility of human character, confident that toleration would make the Jews more productive and honest and less tribal and superstitious. 'A life of normal civil happiness in a well ordered state', wrote Dohm, would do away with their 'clannish religious opinions'. 'How would it be possible for [the Jew] not to love a state where he could freely acquire property and freely enjoy it, where his taxes would be no heavier than those of other citizens, where he could reach positions of honor and enjoy general esteem?'[12]

3

While Jewish reformers and their Christian friends agreed that emancipation and integration required the overhaul of Jewish behaviour and identity, they did not agree—or even discuss—the scope of this transformation. In retrospect the vagueness of the discussion—its fuzziness, lack of rigour, reliance on catchwords—is striking. What, after all, did those who urged the transformation of the Jews mean when they called for their *régénération, assimilation, rapprochement,* or *fusion sociale*; their *bürgerliche Verbesserung, Veredelung,* or *Reformezirung*; their 'complete fusion . . . with their fellow subjects of every other denomination'?[13] At a minimum, they meant that Jews should speak and dress like other citizens, that they should embrace secular education and culture, and that they should identify with their country of residence, becoming law-abiding, patriotic, productive citizens. About these there was little confusion or disagreement. But more than this was expected. Jewish reformers and Christian critics also targeted the 'clannishness' of the Jews (that is, their preference for mixing and marrying among themselves), their concentration in commerce and finance, and their attachment to 'backward' or 'superstitious' religious customs, including dietary laws that hindered social intercourse. However, while reformers and critics saw these matters as ripe for reform, they failed to specify what constituted sufficient change or to establish criteria to measure it. For example, did the progression of Jews from peddling to shop-keeping meet their expectations? Were Jews expected only to abandon low-status street trades or were they expected to forsake trade altogether, becoming farm and factory workers, hewers of wood and drawers of water, so that their occupational profile resembled that of the non-Jewish population? They also failed to indicate what they considered a reasonable time for this and other changes to occur. Was the transfor-

---

[12] Ibid. 14.   [13] *The Voice of Jacob*, 31 Jan. 1845.

mation of the Jews a long-term project, stretching over many generations, or was it a change that would occur swiftly in the immediate wake of their emancipation from the restraints of the past?

Expectations about Jewish acculturation and integration—how much and how far—were as fuzzy as those regarding Jewish productivization. Jews and non-Jews alike assumed that Jewish particularism and marginality would diminish following emancipation. Jews would be found in universities, lodges, fraternities, literary and philosophical societies, concert halls, casinos, and clubs. They would drink, carouse, whore, and gamble in pubs, cafés, beer halls, and wine cellars in non-Jewish company. This vision of integration, even if never articulated in these terms, would not have met with opposition from either Jewish or Christian emancipationists. But the problem was more complex than this. Little was said about whether Jews were also expected to stop choosing their closest friends and marriage partners from among their own community. If the ideal was 'a random pattern of interaction, where Jews [were] no more likely to interact with each other than with non-Jews',[14] and the expectation that in time they would seek husbands and wives outside the tribal pond, then the eventual outcome of their integration would be their demographic decline if not disappearance as an identifiable or cohesive social unit. Similarly, while even Orthodox Jews in Western countries endorsed the idea of acculturation, there was a point at which the process threatened to erase the most distinctive marks of Jewishness. To what extent were Jews to identify with the dominant culture? Were they to be inconspicuous and even unrecognizable as Jews outside their homes and synagogues? Were they to pursue acculturation to the extent that they embraced the religion of the dominant culture as well and disappeared from the scene by the path of total fusion?

Although those who wanted to reform the Jews were vague about their expectations, some, it is clear, hoped that emancipation and integration would end in the full absorption of the Jews and their disappearance as a collective unit. In Britain Christian defenders of the Jew Bill of 1753 argued that allowing foreign-born Jews to become naturalized citizens would encourage their conformity to English customs and accelerate their integration into English society, in time preparing the way for their conversion to the Anglican faith. For example, in a sermon to a fashionable London congregation, the Reverend Thomas Winstanley predicted that naturalization would incline the Jews 'to cultivate a friendship and familiarity with us; which, of course, must bring them in due season, to a conformity of manners, and an imitation of our ways and customs'. Social contact would

---

[14] Goldscheider and Zuckerman, *The Transformation of the Jews*, 7.

engender more favourable feelings regarding Christians, and 'these more favourable sentiments concerning us may be improved, e'er long, into a more favourable opinion of our religion'.[15] In France the Abbé Grégoire, one of the three co-winners of the Metz essay contest, urged improvements in the socio-economic status of the Ashkenazim of Alsace and Lorraine for the same reason. The state, he believed, should scatter Jews throughout rural France, thus undermining the influence of their rabbis, while compelling their children to attend state schools, thus exposing them to French culture. This would lead to more interaction between Jews and Christians, and in time bring the former to Christianity.[16]

There were Jews as well (not many, of course) who envisioned a future in which Jews qua Jews would disappear and be absorbed into some larger unit of humankind. Baptized Jews presumably held such views—to the extent that they thought about the collective fate of the Jews at all, as distinct from their own personal fortunes. More unusual were those Jewish secularists and deists who dreamed of a future that was neither Jewish nor Christian, who envisioned a world in which divisions among religions, nations, and in some cases ranks and classes as well were effaced.[17] David Friedländer's well-known 'dry baptism' letter on behalf of Berlin Jews to Provost Wilhelm Teller in 1799, in which he proposed that Jews who had given up their ancestral rituals be admitted to Protestantism without having to accept its dogmas and mysteries, rested on the premise that there was one rational, natural religion that was the essence of both enlightened Christianity and enlightened Judaism.[18]

A generation later Jewish Saint-Simonians—Gustave d'Eichthal, Léon Halévy, the Rodrigues and Pereire brothers—spun dreams of a new universal order of one religion, one dogma, one cult, in which Judaism and Jews were to be absorbed. In their vision of the future, which belonged to a larger movement of utopian system-building in the wake of the social upheaval and intellectual confusion engendered by the French Revolution, nations disappeared, religion and politics merged, and universal harmony reigned.[19] In his *Lettres sur la religion et la politique* (1829), for example, the young Eugène Rodrigues, son of a Paris stockbroker, confidently asserted that humanity was advancing towards an immense unity—*la société universelle*—in which

[15] Winstanley, *Sermon*, 12–14.
[16] Necheles, *The Abbé Grégoire*.   [17] Endelman, *Leaving the Jewish Fold*, ch. 7.
[18] Littmann, 'David Friedländers Sendschreiben'. Also helpful is Richard Cohen, Introduction to David Friedländer, *Sendschreiben*.
[19] On the Jewish Saint-Simonians, see Ratcliffe, 'Some Jewish Problems in the Early Careers of Emile and Isaac Pereire'; Graetz, *The Periphery Became the Centre* (Heb.), ch. 4; Simon-Nahum, *La Cité investie*, 25–39.

nations would disappear, the spiritual and temporal realms of life merge, and the new religion include both Christians and Jews within its temples. Church and state would become identical, for religion would absorb all of society within its bosom. The reign of Caesar would cease, the reign of God commence. Although not a Saint-Simonian, their contemporary Joseph Salvador worked out a similar scheme of religious development, culminating in an imminent messianic era in which Mosaism (in effect, ethical monotheism), preserved by the Jews for centuries, provided a foundation for universal organization.[20]

In central Europe Karl Marx and his Jewish disciples also looked forward to a future in which the categories 'Jew' and 'Christian' would disappear.[21] The Austrian social democrat Otto Bauer, for example, taught that the Jews were fated to disappear from among the nations of Europe because they no longer performed a historical task. Before the rise of capitalism they pioneered trade and commerce, but with its advent and the 'Judaization' of Christianity they lost their historical role and were condemned to blend in socially and economically. In imperial Germany most Jewish advocates of Jewish dissolution saw the future in terms of absorption into the German nation rather than a universalistic utopia transcending particularistic identities. Writing in Maximilian Harden's journal *Die Zukunft* in 1904, the semiticist Jakob Fromer advised Germany's Jews,

Dive under, disappear! Disappear with your oriental physiognomy, with your ways that contrast with your surroundings, with your 'mission' and, above all, with your exclusively ethical worldview. Take the customs, the values, and the religion of your host people, seek to mix in with them and see to it that you are consumed in them without a trace.[22]

The notary and jurist Adolf Weissler, writing in the arch-conservative *Preussische Jahrbücher* in 1900, urged the dissolution of German Jewry through child baptism. Although he believed that Judaism was morally stagnant and inferior to Christianity, he knew that even Jews who agreed with him were unable to believe in the divinity of Jesus and accept baptism. Because he also regarded conversions of convenience as unprincipled, but nonetheless wished to see German Jewry disappear, he urged Jewish parents

[20] Graetz, *The Periphery Became the Centre* (Heb.), ch. 6; P. E. Hyman, 'Joseph Salvador'.

[21] The literature on this topic is enormous. See in particular Silberner, *Sozialisten zur Judenfrage*; Wistrich, *Socialism and the Jews*; Berlin, 'Benjamin Disraeli, Karl Marx and the Search for Identity'.

[22] Quoted in Levenson, 'Jewish Reactions to Intermarriage', 136. See his discussions of advocates of Jewish dissolution (ibid., ch. 4, and 'The Conversionary Impulse in Fin-de-Siècle Germany').

to baptize their children, who, not having been raised as Jews, could not be accused of insincerity and opportunism.[23]

4

Views such as these were exceptional by virtue of their radicalism. In addition, they were exceptional—along with all prescriptive statements about the Jewish future, whatever their tone—by virtue of their very existence. Few Jews bothered to tell the world what being Jewish meant and what the future of the Jews would or should be. Those who did were public figures (notables, publicists, rabbis) seeking to influence the outcome of Jewish modernization. Their views did not necessarily reflect the sentiments of 'ordinary' Jews (traders, clerks, market men, shopkeepers, wholesale merchants, brokers, and their wives and children), who in the nature of things were neither pamphleteers nor editorialists. In the absence of survey research for earlier centuries, one of the few ways to know what the 'silent majority' felt is to examine what they did and then infer from their behaviour the sentiments and hopes that motivated them. Doing so makes it clear that most emancipated Jews did not imagine a future in which they would renounce or transcend their Jewish attachments. While willing, even eager, to redefine what it meant to be Jewish, and to tailor their behaviour and views accordingly, there is no evidence, as we will see, that they viewed their disappearance as desirable, necessary, or inevitable, as the final outcome of their integration and acculturation. Nor is there evidence that they even believed that they must shed their collective social attachments and become invisible outside their synagogues and homes. In this regard, their understanding of what was required of them differed from that of Christian emancipationists, who, however vague their expectations, clearly envisioned a more radical and ruthless break with the Jewish past.

Any analysis of changes in Western Jewish behaviour between the mid-eighteenth and mid-twentieth centuries must begin with the recognition that while these changes were far-reaching and ubiquitous they were not uniformly so in all spheres of life or even within the same sphere. Thus, while the practice of many religious traditions declined, key life-cycle rituals continued to be observed even in families otherwise distant from the world of tradition. In Amsterdam, for example, the circumcision of male children remained almost universal into the twentieth century—though some parents claimed they were doing it for hygienic reasons or for the sake of the

[23] Levenson, 'The Conversionary Impulse in Fin-de-Siècle Germany', 112; id., 'Radical Assimilation and Radical Assimilationists in Imperial Germany', 40.

grandparents. In 1932, 1933, and 1934, the number of boys born to Jewish mothers who were not circumcised was 4 per cent, 8 per cent, and 10 per cent respectively. (Most of those who were not circumcised were from mixed marriages.) Similarly, most marriages between Jews in Amsterdam continued to be solemnized in religious ceremonies: the number between 1901 and 1933 fell only from 97.3 per cent to 91.9 per cent.[24] Jewish economic activity showed similar patterns of continuity. To take another example: while most Jewish families in the West experienced *embourgeoisement* over two or three generations following the removal of disabilities, their overall occupational profile remained skewed. Most heads of families worked in commerce rather than in heavy industry, agriculture, or the liberal professions. Buying and selling continued to be the material pillar on which Jewish life rested. The transformation of the Jews, in short, was incomplete, uneven, and irregular.

How irregular becomes clear when one ceases to speak of the transformation of the Jews as an undifferentiated process of 'assimilation' and views it in terms of its four constitutive elements—emancipation, acculturation, secularization, and integration. Breaking down the analysis in this way brings into focus the unevenness of the changes that Jews experienced and the problems that this created for them when they needed to define their Jewishness in public debate. For the purpose of this chapter, I want to focus in particular on distinguishing secularization from acculturation and then acculturation from integration.

Curiously, the analytical category of secularization is absent from the standard histories of the entry of the Jews into state and society in western Europe (in contrast to its prominence in the history of Christianity in modern Europe, where what is known as the 'secularization thesis' functioned as the master-narrative for decades after the Second World War.[25]) Neither Michael A. Meyer's *The Origins of the Modern Jew* (1967) nor Jacob Katz's *Out of the Ghetto* (1973) discusses the secularization of Jewish life as such. Of course, they chart the abandonment of traditional rituals and beliefs, but they do so in the context of acculturation and integration, the changes in belief and behaviour that Jews embraced in order to make a place for themselves in European life. Even the later, more conceptually nuanced, account of Pierre Birnbaum and Ira Katznelson, their introduction to the collection *Paths of Emancipation* (1995), fails to bring secularization into the equation

[24] Blom and Cahen, 'Jewish Netherlanders, Netherlands Jews and Jews in the Netherlands', 249.

[25] C. G. Brown, 'The Secularisation Decade'; Cox, 'Master Narratives of Long-Term Religious Change'.

as a transformative category in its own right. The word itself is also absent from the index to the volume, so presumably none of its contributors considers secularization qua secularization a critical part of the story. The most recent surveys of modern Jewish history also take no notice of secularization. David Vital's *A People Apart* (1999) views emancipation as the great agent of change, while Lloyd P. Gartner's *History of the Jews in Modern Times* (2001) speaks more broadly of capitalism, the Enlightenment, and the modern state undermining traditional Jewish life.[26]

The conceptual distinction between secularization and acculturation is not pedantic. Much of the decline in Jewish practice (observance of the dietary laws, family purity, synagogue attendance, festival customs) was the result of currents and influences that were not specific to the historical experience of the Jews. In the eighteenth and nineteenth centuries religious indifference, anti-clericalism, impiety, scepticism, and ignorance of scripture and doctrine were to be found in all Western societies, among poor and rich alike. Religious doctrine and sentiment guided fewer areas of behaviour among both Jews and Christians (although there is some evidence that this occurred earlier among Jews than among Christians[27]). Historians of European Christianity attribute the growth of irreligion to the economic and intellectual revolutions of the eighteenth and nineteenth centuries (urbanization, industrialization, technological innovation, materialistic theories of the universe, the scientific critique of religion, Darwinism, and so on) and to the political, social, and intellectual conservatism of state churches, which repelled businessmen, intellectuals, and workers alike, depending on the national context. Max Weber set the rise of irreligion in an even longer time frame. He posited a gradual, millennia-long process of disenchantment (*Entzauberung*) of the world, of increasing rationalization and intellectualization, beginning with the rationalization stimulated by Israelite religious prophecy and continuing, during the Reformation, with the elimination of magical ritual. In the nineteenth and twentieth centuries, science, science-oriented technologies, bureaucratization, capitalism, and political

---

[26] Michael Meyer briefly discusses the relationship between modernization and secularization in his contribution to the Yosef Yerushalmi Festschrift. While acknowledging that Jews expanded 'the secular spheres of their existence' and devoted 'less time and concentration to specifically religious matters', he prefers to describe this change as 'a displacement of the sacred rather than its abandonment'. Thus, when Jews performed tasks to further 'universal progress', he believes that those activities were cloaked in 'the mantle of sanctity' (Meyer, 'Reflections on Jewish Modernization', 372–3). Perhaps. But this interpretative move may also express an unwillingness to confront the decline of Jewish belief and practice in the modern period.

[27] Steven Lowenstein found that in nineteenth-century Germany small-town Jews often embraced a secular outlook before moving to the city. See *The Mechanics of Change*.

centralization accelerated the process, according to Weber, while technical means and calculations banished supernatural, incalculable forces.[28]

Granted, secularization is an elusive concept, the process difficult to describe and even more to explain with precision.[29] As the master-narrative of modern European religious history it no longer enjoys the prominence it once did. Nonetheless, the fact remains that Jews were not immune to the impact of the broad, impersonal currents that fuelled the decline in Christian belief, affiliation, and worship. In the eighteenth and nineteenth centuries, for example, Western Jewish communities became urban communities. It is an axiom that when west Europeans moved from the country to the city they encountered conditions that 'militate[d] against the roots of the familiar and the familial', with which religious beliefs and practices were associated, and that religious institutions were 'adversely affected by the increasing size of urban concentrations . . . and corroded by geographical and social mobility', especially when they led to a relativization of perspectives on the world'.[30] Was Judaism exempt from the impact of urbanization? Hardly. It is no coincidence that impiety and indifference were hallmarks of the London and Amsterdam communities, the two largest communities in the West, in the late eighteenth and early nineteenth centuries.[31]

Of course, it is impossible to know how much the decline of Jewish observance was the result of a general cause (the disenchantment of the world) and how much the result of a particular one (the flight from Jewishness). It is hard to even imagine how to disentangle their respective influences. Nonetheless, it is important to separate them conceptually. Leaving secularization out of the picture suggests that the Jews were immune to general forces of social change and, at the same time, inflates the transformative power of the Haskalah and other programmes of regeneration, leaving the false impression that reason, natural law, and other novel ideas convinced Jews that it was meaningless or unprofitable to separate meat and milk (for example). Owen Chadwick warned against explaining secularization 'by seizing only upon what was expressed in formal propositions, articulately'. There are shifts in sentiment and consciousness that run deeper. 'That is why the problem of secularization is not the problem of enlightenment. Enlightenment

[28] Weber, 'Science as a Vocation', 139.
[29] The best working definition of secularization with which I am familiar is that of David Ellenson: 'If the attitude of the premodern traditionalist is captured in the words of the Psalmist, "I have placed the Eternal before me always", the paraphrase uttered even by the religious traditionalist in a secularized world is, "I place the Eternal before me, but not all the time"' (*After Emancipation*, 239).   [30] Martin, *A General Theory of Secularization*, 83, 160.
[31] I explore this theme at greater length in Endelman, 'Secularization and the Origins of Jewish Modernity'.

was of the few. Secularization is of the many.'[32] Ignoring the impact of broad impersonal currents simply reinforces the old Germano-centric view of the origins of Jewish modernity, in which new ideologies restructured Jewish lives.[33] There is another reason as well to bring in the analytical category of secularization. If one attributes the decline of religious observance solely to the desire to efface Jewish distinctiveness, it is then impossible to explain the survival of Jewish social bonds after this decline, for, if the flight from Jewishness were the key, social cohesion would have declined at the same time as religious observance. But this was not the case. Secularization and integration did not advance in tandem. Social acceptance and mixing lagged behind the decline of belief and practice.

5

The unevenness of the transformation of the Jews was most pronounced at the level of social relations between Jews and Christians. At first glance, middle-class Jews in Berlin, Paris, London, Amsterdam, Vienna, and Budapest were indistinguishable from their non-Jewish counterparts. They wore the same clothes, spoke the same language, visited the same cafés, museums, and concert halls, educated their children at the same schools, and enjoyed the same leisure-time activities. To be sure there were subtle differences between the 'intimate' culture of the Jews and that of their neighbours. In imperial Germany, for example, urban, middle-class Jews read different books and newspapers, voted for different parties, responded to 'Jewish' jokes in a different manner, and raised their children according to different norms.[34] They clung to the humanistic ideal of *Bildung*, to which the age of Enlightenment and emancipation first gave birth, long after irrationalism and nationalism had weakened its hold among educated Germans. They also killed themselves more frequently per capita than either Protestants or

---

[32] Chadwick, *The Secularization of the European Mind*, 8–9.

[33] This is the central theme of Goldscheider and Zuckerman's *The Transformation of the Jews*. For example: 'Religious decline resulted neither from the inability of old ideas to adapt to new conditions nor from the less demanding nature of some of the new religious ideologies, but from transformations in social conditions' (p. 64). More broadly, they argue that 'most—but not all—of the transformations that have occurred among Jews during the processes of modernization relate to general forces of social change' (ibid., p. ix). The problem with their account is that in seeking to undermine explanations that emphasize the unique and the particular in the transformation of the Jews they take an equally unbalanced view and throw out the baby with the bathwater—that is, they fail to give due recognition as well to the transformative pressures that Jews qua Jews experienced as Christendom's quintessential outsiders.

[34] H. Wassermann, 'The Intimate Culture of German Jewry' (Heb.); Volkov, 'Unity and Assimilation' (Heb.); Katz, 'German Culture and the Jews'.

Catholics—which certainly suggests a distinctive sensibility.[35] But, on the surface, to the casual observer, little distinguished Jews from non-Jews in the broad externals of life.

However, while acculturation was well advanced by the turn of the century, integration into non-Jewish social circles and voluntary associations was not. During the nineteenth century Jews in western and central Europe gained access to institutions and organizations that had excluded them in the past: legislatures, municipal councils, the military, the professions, fraternal groups, elite secondary schools, universities, clubs and casinos, charities, and athletic and recreational associations. As a rule, English, French, Italian, and Dutch Jews were more successful in doing so than German, Austrian, and Hungarian Jews, although even the latter made their way, however haltingly, into the associational life of middle-class society. Yet despite these advances in institutional integration and social mixing in public forums, Jews remained a people apart in terms of their most fundamental social ties. Most married other Jews, formed their closest friendships with other Jews, and relaxed and felt most comfortable in the homes of Jewish friends and relatives. Describing his upper-middle-class youth in late imperial Berlin, the fashion photographer Erwin Blumenfeld recalled that his freethinking, atheist parents contentedly lived within 'invisible walls', associating exclusively with other Jews and 'were probably not even aware of it themselves'. Very rarely 'a stray goy happened to find his way into our house' and when one did 'we had no idea how to behave'.[36] The absence of social integration also characterized the home of Gershom Scholem. Despite his father's allegiance to liberal integrationism, 'no Christian ever set foot in our home',[37] not even Christians who were members of organizations in which his father was active (with the one telling exception of a formal fiftieth-birthday visit). The oft-cited autobiographies of famous Jews (musicians, writers, scientists, intellectuals, bohemians), Scholem warned in another context, present a misleading picture. In 'an ordinary middle-class bourgeois home, neither rich nor poor' like his, there was no social mixing between Jews and Christians.[38] Richard Lichtheim underlined the awkwardness that arose when these barriers were transgressed. In the 1890s when he visited the home of a non-Jewish school friend, who lived with his uncle, a general, or when his friend visited him, each was aware of entering 'enemy territory'. No Jew had ever before appeared in the general's house or any

[35] Kwiet, 'The Ultimate Refuge', 140, table 1. On the ideal of *Bildung* in German Jewish culture, see G. L. Mosse, *German Jews beyond Judaism*.
[36] Blumenfeld, *Eye to I*, 52.   [37] Scholem, 'With Gershom Scholem', 5.
[38] Scholem, 'On the Social Psychology of the Jews in Germany', 18–19.

Christian in the Lichtheim house—although the Lichtheims were non-observant and most of his father's relatives converts to Christianity.[39] Reciprocal home visits, Marion Kaplan aptly comments, 'raised the stakes, announcing an intimacy with which most did not feel comfortable'.[40]

The situation was not radically different among the very wealthiest Jewish families. In his exhaustive study of the German Jewish economic elite before the First World War, Werner Mosse concluded that from the late 1870s 'unselfconscious and more or less spontaneous social relations between Jew and Gentile virtually ceased'.[41] While government ministers, upper civil servants, army officers, and diplomats accepted invitations to lavish entertainments in the homes of Berlin's Jewish bankers and industrialists, they rarely reciprocated. Moreover, while social ambition and 'feudalization' (capitulation to aristocratic values) fuelled the cultivation of the high-born, a very bourgeois motive was at work as well: the Berlin business and financial elite, Jews and non-Jews alike, courted the pre-industrial elite for pragmatic reasons. They wanted the government business and privileged information that holders of high office and power brokers dispensed, while hoping to influence economic and diplomatic policy. Contrary to popular belief then and now, the highest goal of wealthy Jews was not social acceptance by and intermarriage with the Prussian nobility. Yes, their patterns of sociability were a defensive response to antisemitism, but they also reflected 'the fact that most Jews of the upper bourgeoisie wanted to associate with Jews'.[42] As Marion Kaplan concludes, 'their starting point was a deep, primary loyalty to their families and a steady allegiance to their religious and ethnic community', both of which 'restrained' social interaction with non-Jews.[43]

[39] Lichtheim, *A Remnant Shall Return* (Heb.), 37.

[40] M. A. Kaplan, 'Friendship on the Margins', 481. Georg Simmel's distinction between 'friends' and 'acquaintances' is helpful in understanding the character of German Jewish social relations. Ties between 'friends' are rooted in the total personality, while mutual acquaintance, such as we find in the German Jewish case, 'involves no actual insight into the individual nature of the personality'. 'Acquaintance' 'depends upon the knowledge of the *that* of the personality, not of its *what*. After all, by saying that one is acquainted, even well acquainted, with a particular person, one characterizes quite clearly the lack of really intimate relations. Under the rubric of acquaintance, one knows of the other only what he is toward the outside . . . The degree of knowledge covered . . . refers not to the other per se; not to what is essential in him, intrinsically, but only to what is significant for that aspect of him which is turned towards others and the world' (*The Sociology of Georg Simmel*, 320). Simmel's own fate—baptized at birth, he, as well as his work, was labelled and scorned as Jewish—likely contributed to the distinction he drew.

[41] W. E. Mosse, *The German-Jewish Economic Elite*, 95.

[42] Augustine, *Patricians and Parvenus*, 240.

[43] M. A. Kaplan, 'Friendship on the Margins', 474.

Outside Berlin the social lines between wealthy Jews and non-Jews were often firmer. In Hamburg, for example, Jews lived entirely in a private sphere of their own. They did business with non-Jews during the day, but at night went their own way.[44] A similar pattern characterized Jewish–Christian interaction in imperial Königsberg. Jews were welcome in all spheres of public life, including the city council and most voluntary associations, but their social contacts with non-Jews were limited to formal civic occasions and business-related dinners and *Kaffeekränzchen*. Informal, private life 'mainly took place in the frame of one's own extended family or within a circle of other Jewish families, with the exception of a small group of Christian and Jewish music-loving families that met regularly'.[45] Till van Rahden finds it remarkable that in Breslau, where friendships between Jews and Christians were perhaps more common and in light of the numerous possibilities there were for interaction, 'there were not even more and that in many of these friendships a residue of social distance remained much in evidence'.[46] In Prague Jewish merchants and professionals were well integrated into the institutional life of the German community (largely in response to Czech nationalism). In the last two decades of the nineteenth century their role as members and officers in the Deutsches Casino and the Deutscher Verein actually increased. But in the most intimate areas of family life Prague Jews remained a group apart. Few married non-Jews before the First World War.[47]

From the 1870s onwards in central Europe even baptized Jews remained immersed in Jewish kinship and friendship networks, in which Jews, converted Jews, intermarried Jews, and Jews without religion (those who had formally withdrawn from the *Gemeinde* (Jewish community) without converting to another faith) mixed. As social discrimination mounted, converts and those without religion were often forced (or preferred) to choose former Jews like themselves as friends and marriage partners. The close male friends of Gustav Mahler, Maximilian Harden, and countless other celebrated central European converts were almost entirely Jews and converted Jews.[48] In *fin-de-siècle* Vienna the poet André Spire wrote that little changed in the lives of converts after their conversion: 'they continued to live apart, in a separate world, among the Jews ... Their sons were able to marry only Jews or the daughters of converts.'[49] And in Weimar Germany, Hannah Arendt

[44] Augustine, *Patricians and Parvenus*, 194–5.
[45] Schüler-Springorum, 'Assimilation and Community Reconsidered', 105–6, 110.
[46] Rahden, *Juden und andere Breslauer*, 132.
[47] G. B. Cohen, *The Politics of Ethnic Survival*, 136, 177–9.
[48] Lebrecht, *Mahler Remembered*, pp. xix–xx n. 53; W. E. Mosse, *The German-Jewish Economic Elite*, 130.   [49] Spire, *Quelques Juifs*, 195.

recalled, the convert 'only rarely left his family and even more rarely left his Jewish surroundings altogether'.[50]

In more liberal states, France and Britain in particular, there was greater social intimacy between Jews and non-Jews, just as there was greater integration at an institutional level.[51] But even in these states Jewish social solidarity remained more or less firm. Like their German counterparts French and English Jews kept Jewish company more often than not. The novelist Julia Frankau, a radical assimilationist who raised her children as Christians, noted the same absence of mixing as the German memoirists above. In her novel *Dr. Phillips* (1887) middle-class London Jews live in social isolation, cut off from intimate contact with Christians. In 'the heart of a great and cosmopolitan city', she wrote, they constitute 'a whole nation dwelling apart in an inviolable seclusion'. 'There are houses upon houses in the West Central districts, in Maida Vale, in the City, which are barred to Christians, to which the very name of Jew is an open sesame.' To their most common form of social intercourse—card playing in each other's homes—'it was decidedly unusual to invite any but Jews'.[52] In seeking to explain the prevalence of marriages between first cousins in late Victorian Anglo-Jewry, the pioneer social scientist Joseph Jacobs cited, *inter alia*, what he termed 'shoolism'—the inclination of London Jews to limit their circle of friends and acquaintances to the members of their own synagogue (*shul*).[53] In France even those high-ranking judicial and administrative officials whom Pierre Birnbaum dubbed 'les Juifs d'état', graduates of the universities and the *grandes écoles*, who zealously served the Third Republic as prefects and subprefects and as members of the Conseil d'État, the Cour de Cassation, and the *cours d'appel*, tended to marry within the fold, retain membership in Jewish organizations, and establish close social ties with other Jewish state functionaries and politicians. If they had become servants of the universal, laicized state in the public arena, they remained Jewish in their private lives.[54] Marcel Proust captured this kind of social cohesion in describing the Jews who vacationed at the seaside resort of Balbec. When they visited the casino, 'they formed a solid troop, homogeneous within itself, and utterly dissimilar to the people who watched them go by and found them there again every year without ever exchanging a word or greeting'. They presented 'a bold front in a compact and closed phalanx into which, as it happened, no one dreamed of trying to force his way'.[55]

---

[50] Arendt, *The Origins of Totalitarianism*, pt. 1, *Antisemitism*, 64 n. 23.

[51] Endelman, *Radical Assimilation in English Jewish History*, chs. 3–4.

[52] J. Frankau, *Dr. Phillips*, 55, 168.   [53] Jacobs, *Studies in Jewish Statistics*, 6.

[54] Birnbaum, *Les Fous de la République*.   [55] Proust, *In Search of Lost Time*, ii. 434–5.

While distinguishing the secular from the religious in Jewish culture is always risky, it would appear that the bonds linking Western Jews in the half-century before the First World War were more secular than religious in character. What made them Jewish was their similar background and descent, common memories and intimate culture, intra-group sociability and endogamy rather than their religious faith, synagogue attendance, ritual observance, or Hebrew learning. Their Jewishness manifested itself in shared social and cultural practices that were rooted more in the immediate circumstances of their recent history than in the religious culture of traditional belief and practice. In this sense, their Jewishness resembled the ethnicity of post-Soviet Russian and Ukrainian Jews, an ethnicity based on biology and sentiment and defined more by boundaries than by content.[56] Their Jewishness was symbolic ethnicity, a 'thin' rather than 'thick' culture, which was becoming progressively thinner with each generation, because high levels of acculturation and secularization weakened its transferability. Unlike secular forms of Jewishness in eastern Europe and the Yishuv (the Jewish community in the Land of Israel before the State of Israel was established), that of central European Jews was not expressed in a distinctive and exclusively Jewish language (Yiddish or Hebrew) nor buttressed by a nationalist ideology (Yiddishism or Zionism) or territorial concentration (the Pale of Settlement or the Land of Israel).

Jacob Katz attributed the persistence of Jewish cohesion after the decline of Jewish observance, to 'the fact—the existential fact, as it were—of Jewish community, which, out of its own inner necessities and traditions, resisted the higher blandishments of emancipation'. For him and other nationalist historians, 'Jewish existence was a fact, a stubborn fact defying regnant ideology and philosophy'.[57] In the early twentieth century Jewish ethnologists and scientists attributed the persistence of Jewishness to the biological ties of race. The Anglo-Jewish geneticist Redcliffe N. Salaman wrote to his fiancée in 1901 that it seemed almost self-evident to him, given the low level of 'religious feeling amongst a large majority of the Jews', that 'racial feeling' was the chief ingredient in Jewish cohesion: 'When I am amongst Christians & the question at all arises of defending one's position as a Jew it is always the racial element that at once appeals—and in that way I feel that the Polish Jew is a brother though we may differ considerably in religion.'[58] For the purpose of this chapter, knowing the source of Jewish consciousness and

[56] Gitelman, 'Jewish Identity and Secularism'.
[57] Katz, 'Emancipation and Jewish Studies', 81–2.
[58] Redcliffe N. Salaman to Nina Davis, 16 July 1901, Redcliffe Nathan Salaman Papers, MS 8171/97.

cohesion in the aftermath of emancipation is less important than recognizing that it was manifested more frequently in secular than in religious ways.

6

That said, it would be misleading to suggest that Jewish social cohesion in the nineteenth and early twentieth centuries remained rock solid, unshaken by drift and defection. The stigmatization of Jewishness in social and cultural life and the persistence of legal and social barriers to integration took their toll, leading tens of thousands of Jews (especially in central Europe) to cut their ties to Judaism through baptism, intermarriage, and other forms of radical disengagement. In Vienna alone, 9,000 Jews formally severed their ties to Judaism (withdrew from the *Gemeinde*, with or without baptism) between 1868 and 1903—a figure that does not include an unknown but considerable number of children who were baptized by their parents, either at birth or later. In Germany between 1880 and 1919, about 25,000 Jews chose either Protestant or Catholic baptism.[59] The German census of 1939 and the Hungarian census of 1941, both of which defined Jews in racial terms, provide evidence about the cumulative effect of communal secessions over several generations. In Berlin 8.5 per cent of the Jews were not members of the *Gemeinde*; in Vienna, 12 per cent; in Budapest, 17 per cent.[60]

Secession figures alone do not express the extent to which the stigmatization of Jewishness eroded its public expression. Among Jews who rejected conversion or secession, for reasons of conscience or otherwise, efforts to mute markers of Jewish difference became increasingly common from the 1870s. The Viennese novelist and satirist Robert Neumann recalled in his memoirs an incident about his mother that encapsulates these efforts. 'To be a Jew [in pre-First World War Vienna] was one thing', he wrote, 'but to discuss it was as much bad form as it was to swear, and almost as bad as mentioning anything with the functioning of the digestive or sexual organs.' Once when his mother had to introduce to her guests a visitor 'with the un-gentile name of Cohen . . . she pronounced his name again and again so unrecognizably and so much as if it were some painful infirmity from which he suffered that in the end he withdrew, red-faced'.[61] To escape the stigma attached to Jewish family names, German Jews tried to change theirs—a

---

[59] Thon, *Die Juden in Oesterreich*, 69–70; Richarz, 'Demographic Developments', 15–16.

[60] Honigmann, 'Jewish Conversions', 5. Honigmann acknowledges that these figures are not precise and 'at best give no more than the order of magnitude' of formal defection. This is because the considerable emigration that occurred after 1933 might have changed the balance between the two groups (Jews by virtue of their formal communal membership and Jews by virtue of their racial background). [61] Neumann, *The Plague House Papers*, 85–6.

move that officials fought tooth and nail. Some changed even their noses, following the development of cosmetic rhinoplasty by the Berlin Jewish orthopaedic surgeon Jacques Joseph in 1898.[62] The pejorative associations of the word *Jude* caused some to avoid using the word in conversation with other Jews, especially in public. Robert Weltsch, long-time editor of the *Jüdische Rundschau*, recalled that in the bourgeois circles of his youth in pre-First World War Prague it was considered tactless for anyone to say that he was a Jew and that 'every Jew of good bourgeois standing avoided doing so', for the word had been 'emptied of all positive content' and 'shriveled up into a mere name of derision'.[63] Ernst Lissauer, author of the First World War 'Hate Song Against England', recalled that in his parents' Berlin house they would not use the word *Jude* if young girls were present and instead would replace it with 'Armenian' or 'Abyssinian'.[64]

Stigmatization and exclusion were not so pervasive, however, that they stifled all informal social mixing. Social relations between Jews and non-Jews—the young above all—increased gradually, especially in the early twentieth century, weakening though not dissolving Jewish social cohesion. The increase in intermarriage from the 1870s through to the 1930s indicates that Jews were not confined entirely to their own social circles. Intermarriage, then and now, presupposes sustained and more or less intimate social contact. In the case of west and central European Jews, the sites of this social intercourse were the workplace, the university, the voluntary association, the political arena, the dance hall, and the promenade—sites where parents could not monitor their children's friendships and sexual relations. In the Netherlands the proportion of Jews marrying who took non-Jewish spouses rose from 6.02 per cent in the period 1901–5 to 16.68 per cent in the period 1931–4.[65] In German cities intermarriage was even more common. In Berlin, in the period 1905–6, there were 43.8 mixed marriages per 100 pure Jewish marriages; in Hamburg, in the period 1903–5, 49.5; in Frankfurt, in the period 1905–9, 24.7.[66] In Breslau the number jumped from 22.8 in the period 1874–94 to 64.5 in the period 1905–20.[67] In Prussia the rate of intermarriage almost doubled in the last quarter of the nineteenth century, rising from 9.8 intermarriages per 100 all-Jewish marriages in the period 1875–9 to 18.6 in the period 1900–3.[68] On the eve of the First World War there were perhaps as many as 10,000 intermarried couples in Prussia. Defection from

[62] Bering, *The Stigma of Names*; Gilman, *The Jew's Body*, 181–8.

[63] Weltsch, Introduction to Buber, *Der Jude und sein Judentum*, p. xv.

[64] Lissauer, 'Bemerkungen über mein Leben', 297.

[65] Boekman, *Demographie van de Joden in Nederland*, 59.

[66] Ruppin, *The Jews of To-day*, 163.   [67] Rahden, *Juden und andere Breslauer*, 149, table 27.

[68] Lestschinsky, 'Apostasy in Different Lands' (Heb.), 5/9 (1911), 4.

Judaism in imperial Germany, whether through intermarriage, conversion, or formal withdrawal from the *Gemeinde* without baptism, was common enough to lead some observers to prophesy that German Jewry was fated to disappear of its own accord. The best-known exposition of this theme was Felix Theilhaber's *Der Untergang der deutschen Juden*, first published in 1911.

Yet even while the number of informal social contacts was rising Jews retained a collective social identity wherever they lived, an identity as we have seen defined less by their religious practice than by their social behaviour. What struck non-Jewish contemporaries was the persistence of Jewish social separatism ('tribalism'), not its breakdown and decay. Despite their seemingly rapid progress in becoming Germans, Englishmen, Frenchmen, and so on, Jews, the argument went, refused to abandon their cultural and social distinctiveness. In the eyes of their critics, their transformation was stalled and incomplete. They still constituted a well-defined, high-profile, social group. Heinrich Treitschke complained that despite their emancipation German Jews rejected 'the blood mixing' (intermarriage) that was 'the most effective way to equalize tribal differences'.[69] To both conservative and liberal critics this was scandalous: was not the purpose of emancipation to eradicate Jewish tribalism, to remove social and cultural barriers? Moreover, the upward mobility of the Jews, their unparalleled economic and cultural achievements after the removal of old regime restraints—along with their refusal to intermarry en masse or abandon their social cohesion—was an affront to Christian sensibility and pride, fuelling fears of Jewish domination and further compounding the scandal. The contrast between their economic and cultural prominence and their marginal demographic status also contributed to anxiety among non-Jews. In rebutting Treitschke's antisemitic articles in the *Preussische Jahrbücher* in the winter of 1879–80, the liberal historian Theodor Mommsen scolded Jews for failing to disappear into German society. Just as they had served as a universal element in the Roman empire, 'a force for cohesion shattering particularistic tribal elements, so now they must as *ein Element der Composition der Stamme*'.[70] To enable them to carry out their historical task of aiding in German unification, Mommsen instructed them to dissolve their own associations with the same goals as non-denominational, integrated ones. In his view the preservation of Jewish identity for secular reasons was an affront to the Christian character of modern civilization. In the following decade the Verein zur Abwehr des Antisemitismus, established by Christian liberals and progressives in 1891 to combat the new racial antisemitism, denounced the formation of Jewish

[69] Quoted in Boehlich (ed.), *Der Berliner Antisemitismusstreit*, 79.
[70] Tal, *Jews and Christians in the Second Empire* (Heb.), 26–7.

fraternities and sports clubs because they encouraged Jewish continuity and survival.[71]

While the German case represents an extreme manifestation of liberal intolerance for Jewish continuity, it embodies nonetheless a broader split in Jewish and non-Jewish understandings of the meaning and scope of the transformation of the Jews. In Victorian Britain, where the revocation of Jewish emancipation was not on the table as it was in central Europe, liberals and radicals still complained about the persistence of Jewish 'tribalism'. The radical crusader Henry Labouchere, editor of the pro-Gladstonian *Truth*, attacked Jews, beginning in 1878, for resisting 'fusion' with Christians. Their endogamy and 'clannishness' and their willingness to employ their resources collectively gave them an unfair economic advantage. 'It would be desirable', he concluded, 'that the state should allow no Jew to marry a Jewess.' If the state failed to act and Anglo-Jewry refused to engineer its own voluntary dissolution, then the latter would be responsible for whatever prejudice they faced.[72] In the outburst of Liberal antisemitism sparked by Disraeli's Eastern policy, the historian Goldwin Smith attributed the persistence of anti-Jewish hostility to a fundamental misunderstanding in the mid-century emancipation debate. Those Christians who supported emancipation saw Jews as simply another dissenting sect, as persons no different than other citizens, except for their theological opinions, and assumed that when toleration was extended to them they would become 'like other citizens in every respect'. The problem was that Jewry was 'not a religious sect, but a vast relic of primeval tribalism, with its tribal mark [circumcision], its tribal separation, and its tribal God'. 'The affinity of Judaism' was 'not to nonconformity but to caste'. It was not Jewish beliefs that were 'the root of the mischief' but the Jews' 'peculiar character, habits, and position', which their endogamy preserved.[73]

7

Non-Jewish criticism of the tribalism of the Jews (that is, their failure to intermarry and fade away) created a dilemma for Jewish spokesmen and apologists in the West. Needing to define the character of post-emancipation Jewish cohesion in public debate, they had few options (unless they were Zionists). Once again they restated the conceptual framework for emancipa-

---

[71] Schorsch, *Jewish Reactions to German Anti-Semitism*, 63, 95–7. Earlier in the century the Abbé Grégoire expressed his frustration with French Jews for refusing to regenerate themselves, like their 'enlightened brethren' in Germany, in the wake of emancipation (Sepinwall, 'Strategic Friendships', 192).   [72] Quoted in Hirshfield, 'The Tenacity of Tradition', 69.
[73] G. Smith, 'The Jewish Question', 495, 497, 499.

tion articulated by Jewish and Christian emancipationists a century before. The Jews were to be integrated into state and society as members of a religious sect who differed from their fellow citizens only in their manner of worship. Their inclusion on this basis meshed with the liberal principle of religious toleration, which first emerged in the wake of early modern Protestant–Catholic violence and then gradually encompassed the toleration of non-Christian faiths as well. Jewish apologists and spokesmen told themselves, their fellow Jews, and the world at large that they were similar to everyone else, except for their religious beliefs and practices. The problem with this strategy was its failure to represent the character of post-emancipation Jewish life accurately.

First, Judaism, even after emancipation, was not a religion in the same way that Christianity was. It retained a collective social dimension and encompassed customs and laws that in Christian eyes were no longer matters of conscience. It regulated behaviour in which Christianity took little interest, for example, matters of diet and sabbath and festival rest. Jewish claims to toleration on the basis of religious difference extended into realms that went beyond conventional Christian understandings of the nature of religion. For example, in Victorian England university entrance and scholarship examinations were administered on Saturdays, causing considerable distress to those who observed the laws of sabbath rest. The Board of Deputies of British Jews repeatedly intervened to make alternative arrangements for Jewish candidates.[74] These met with success in most cases, but communal bodies elsewhere did not seek similar exemptions, knowing full well that officials neither understood nor felt sympathetic towards Jewish religious concerns. In the words of David Landes: 'If you want a lively debate, try to explain to a group of French people, Jewish or non-Jewish, that the institution of Saturday classes is objectively anti-Jewish. Most Frenchmen cannot even understand the issue.'[75]

Second, presenting the Jews as a religious minority misrepresented social reality. When Jewish spokesmen made religion the basis of Jewish difference, they did so as much from necessity as conviction. They were not blind to the social dimension of Jewish group life, as we will see. They knew full well that emancipation had not dissolved the social ties that bound Jews together and that what united most Jews was the synagogue they did not attend. Their problem was that European states (with the exception of the two multi-national empires) endorsed the toleration of religious, not ethnic or national, difference. They conflated citizenship and nationality, leaving no

---

[74] Emanuel, *A Century and a Half of Jewish History*; Itzkowitz, 'Cultural Pluralism and the Board of Deputies of British Jews'.   [75] Landes, 'Two Cheers for Emancipation', 291 n. 4.

conceptual space for Jewish social cohesion and distinctiveness. For them citizenship required more than faithful observance of the laws of the land. They expected that those who enjoyed its blessings would share the same fundamental ethnic or national identity and the habits, values, and tastes that went along with that identity. This meant that Jews were expected to experience an inner transformation that would reorient their sentiments and affections. Of course, states and societies varied in the degree to which cultural heterogeneity preoccupied them. The more secure they were about their own national greatness, the more content with their place in the world, the less obsessive they were about Jewish distinctiveness. German official-dom, for example, worried more about making Jews German than its British counterpart. But, in general, notions of multiculturalism, ethnic diversity, cultural pluralism, and the like were in the future. Political leaders, social theorists, and cultural spokesmen dreamed of national homogeneity, unity, solidarity, fusion, and integration, leaving religion as the sole basis for de-fining Jewish difference. As a result, in the face of cries to revoke emancipa-tion and circumscribe their freedoms (which became widespread from the 1870s), Jews insisted ever more zealously in public debate that they were Germans (or whatever), reducing their Jewishness to a mere matter of con-fessional difference. What they could not do was acknowledge publicly their social cohesion and ethnic distinctiveness. That would have seemed a dan-gerous move, an invitation to disaster—aside from the question of whether they possessed the conceptual wherewithal to do so. And when spokesmen for the nascent Zionist movement began to do just that, to define Jews in national terms, communal leaders in the West reacted with alarm, fearing that this endangered their hard-won legal and social achievements.[76] In his presidential address to the Anglo-Jewish Association in 1898, for example, Claude Goldsmid Montefiore warned that in the long run Zionism would be 'prejudicial and deleterious to the best interests and truest welfare of the Jews themselves'.[77]

It is not clear how conscious Jews (Zionists aside) were of the tension between how they defined themselves in public and how they actually lived their lives in private. To the best of my knowledge, there was no public con-versation about this tension, not even an acknowledgement that it existed. And with the advent of Zionism there was little likelihood that integrationist Jews would pursue the matter. Nonetheless, there is evidence that even those who opposed Zionism were aware that there was a non-religious collective dimension to their Jewishness. This can be inferred from the willingness

[76] S. A. Cohen, *English Zionists and British Jews*, chs. 5–8; Reinharz, *Fatherland or Promised Land?*, ch. 5; P. E. Hyman, *From Dreyfus to Vichy*, 155–69.   [77] *Jewish Chronicle*, 8 July 1898.

of Jews across the political and social spectrums to employ the language of race to describe their collective bonds. John Efron and Mitchell Hart have explained how the pioneers of Jewish social science used the terms and concepts of 'race science' to study the sociology, anthropology, demography, and medical pathology of the Jews.[78] However, I have in mind a broader, less ideologically driven, phenomenon—the widespread, casual, everyday use of racial language to describe the Jews as a social unit. (Most Jewish 'race scientists' were Zionists for whom the racial and national characters of the Jews were fused and perhaps inseparable.) Unable to describe their collective ties as national because of the terms of emancipation, emancipated Jews, observant and non-observant alike, borrowed the notion of race, which was ubiquitous from at least the 1870s through to the 1940s.

French Jews, perhaps the least observant in western and central Europe, commonly and freely spoke of *la race juive*. The Radical politician Alfred Naquet, non-practising and married to a Catholic, declared in the *Univers israélite* in 1886 that he was 'a Jew by race' but no longer a Jew 'by religion'.[79] Proust repeatedly ascribed the behaviour, looks, and health of his Jewish characters to their racial background. Charles Swann, for example, the son (or grandson—it is not clear) of converted Jews, suffers from 'ethnic eczema' and 'the constipation of the prophets'.[80] When Swann aligns himself with the Dreyfusards, Proust attributes his move to a deep, ineluctable force— 'Jewish blood'—that is at work in Swann and others who think of themselves as emancipated.[81] Although these terms were explicitly biological, those who used them were not biological determinists in the main. Their use of the word 'race' was imprecise and often contradictory. By using the word, they wanted to suggest a feeling of community with other Jews, a sense of common historical fate, and a deep emotional bond that transcended religious faith and observance. As Michael Marrus wrote in his analysis of French Jewry at the time of the Dreyfus affair (1894–1906), 'the biological terminology of race provided a semantic framework within which all Jews could express these feelings of Jewish identity'. Although French culture did not sanction this form of belonging and allegiance, it worked well for Jews, especially non-observant ones. 'Only race offered the excuse for a lingering Jewishness among men who had renounced their religion.'[82]

In Britain communal notables, including those who opposed Zionism, freely used the term to describe the non-religious foundations of Jewish

[78] Efron, *Defenders of the Race*; Hart, *Social Science and the Politics of Modern Jewish Identity*.
[79] Quoted in Marrus, *The Politics of Assimilation*, 20.
[80] Proust, *In Search of Lost Time*, i. 571.
[81] Ibid. ii. 643–4.
[82] Marrus, *The Politics of Assimilation*, 26.

cohesion. In 1871 the founders of the Anglo-Jewish Association, in setting forth their motives for creating an organization to aid unemancipated Jews in other lands, stressed the international, cosmopolitan character of Jewishness, using the language of race. Their aim, they wrote, was 'to knit more closely together the bond of brotherhood which united Jew with Jew throughout the world, and which should make its members and fellow-workers sensible of the grand fact that the race of Israel belongs not to England or France alone, but to all the countries of the globe'.[83] The Jewish notables and scientists who supported Jewish participation in the Universal Races Congress in London in July 1911 were not Jewish nationalists (with the exception of Israel Zangwill). The only public objection to participation came from the American-born Cambridge archaeologist and art historian Charles Waldstein, who deplored any manifestation of Jewish separatism and wrote to *The Times* protesting the classification of the Jews as an oriental race in the congress programme.[84] When a reviewer of the memoirs of Lady Battersea (née Constance de Rothschild) implied that she had converted to Christianity, she angrily responded that it was not true, that she was 'a Jewess by religion as well as by race'.[85] Again, as in France, it was possible for Jewish apologists to both emphasize the ability of Jews to adapt to their surroundings and acknowledge simultaneously the ethnic basis of Jewish solidarity. For example, in the opening pages of his apologetic volume *Jews As They Are* (1882), the composer and pianist Charles Kensington Salaman repeated the old integrationist chestnut that Jews differed from country to country since they took on the coloration of their surroundings, even quoting Isaac D'Israeli's words to this effect from his *Genius of Judaism*: 'After a few generations the Hebrews assimilate with the character, and are actuated by the feelings of the nation of which they become part.' But two pages later Salaman asked his readers to reflect on the near-miraculous post-biblical history of the Jewish 'nation' and, in particular, on how modern Jews triumphed over 'so terrible a state of racial adversity and degradation'. He concluded: 'None but a divinely-protected people could have done so.'[86] Thus, in a mere few lines, Salaman managed to describe Jews as a race, a nation and a people under divine protection. This kind of unsystematic thinking, riddled with contradictions and tensions, was typical of 'ordinary' Jews in Britain, who as a rule did not reflect at length on the character of their Jewishness.

In Germany, where defining Jewishness was a more pressing issue, Jews were much less likely to use the language of race in this ambiguous and unfocused way. Nonetheless, by the Weimar period there is evidence that

---

[83] *Report of the Anglo-Jewish Association, 1871–1872*, 8.   [84] *Jewish Chronicle*, 12 May 1911.
[85] *Jewish Guardian*, 1 Dec. 1922.   [86] C. K. Salaman, *Jews As They Are*, 7, 9.

even the staunchest liberals were dissatisfied with the old definition of the Jews as a religious group pure and simple. The leaders of the Centralverein deutscher Staatsbürger jüdischen Glaubens, a liberal, integrationist defence agency dating from 1893, used various neologisms that departed from the strictly religious definition of Jewishness that an earlier generation had invoked in the struggle for emancipation. Recognizing that this definition did not encompass the tens of thousands of non-observant Jews who still felt attached to other Jews (and who supported the work of the Centralverein), Ludwig Holländer, who headed the organization from 1921 to 1933, spoke increasingly of the Jews' *Schicksalsgemeinschaft* (community of fate). Words like *Stamm* (tribe) and *Abstammung* (descent) were invoked in sermons, apologia, and Centralverein publications.[87] In seeking to define what was uniquely Jewish, Rabbi Cesar Seligmann told his Frankfurt congregants: 'It is not Jewish conviction, not Jewish doctrine, not the Jewish creed that is the leading, the primary, the inspirational; rather, it is Jewish sentiment, the instinctive, call it what you will, call it the community of blood, call it tribal consciousness [*Stammesgefühl*], call it the ethnic soul [*Volksseele*], but best of all call it: the Jewish heart.'[88]

8

The willingness of German Jews to coin new terms to describe the basis of their ties, and of Jews in more liberal settings to define them in ambiguous and contradictory ways, was symptomatic of a Europe-wide problem: Jews did not fit into the slot that classical liberalism created for them. Their Jewishness overflowed the narrow framework of religious doctrine and practice to which emancipation theoretically confined it. Liberal and other supporters of emancipation in the late eighteenth and nineteenth centuries envisioned the integration of Jews on the basis of their status as individuals without historical or cultural baggage. During the course of the emancipation debate, Jews agreed with their allies that their integration into state and society required their transformation, especially the differentiation of dimensions of Jewish life that earlier were part of a seamless web of behaviour and consciousness. In hindsight it is clear that both sides were vague, even naive, about what this entailed. It is also clear that, however vague the expectations of Jewish transformation were, the non-Jewish friends of the Jews expected a more radical transformation than occurred following the removal of legal disabilities. Traditional faith and practice eroded, cultural

---

[87] Niewyk, *The Jews in Weimar Germany*, 103–6.
[88] Quoted ibid. 106. See also Pierson, 'German Jewish Identity in the Weimar Republic', ch. 1.

distinctiveness shrank, but social cohesion remained strong (though not intact). To the extent that non-Jewish supporters of emancipation thought in concrete terms, this was not an outcome that they foresaw. Their vision was blinded by a naive faith in human perfectibility and plasticity, in the power of laws, institutions, and circumstances to uproot and replace well-entrenched social and cultural traits. Their understanding of the visceral ties—memories, fears, affections, loathings—that bind historical minorities together was equally shallow. The persistence of Jewish ethnicity long after the weakening of Jewish religion frustrated, irritated, and in some cases enraged them. For their part, Jews had little ideological space in which to respond to this frustration and anger. Emancipation allowed them to define themselves, at least in public debate, only as a religious minority. What other choice was available? Racial discourse was available before the rise of Nazism, at least in those states where Jews avoided constant scrutiny and were able to talk about themselves in contradictory and ambiguous ways. The inadequacy of defining themselves solely in terms of faith and observance was obvious. Even hard-pressed German Jews struggled to find new terms and expressions to describe the reality of what bound them together. In any case, we can be confident that the construction 'German [French, English, Hungarian] citizens of the Jewish faith' neither exhausted their self-understanding nor captured the social texture of their lives.

CHAPTER TWO

The Legitimization of the Diaspora Experience

From the french revolution to the Second World War, the major item on the agenda of Western Jewish leaders was the promotion of Jewish integration into the mainstream of social, political, and cultural life. Communal energies everywhere were devoted to removing legal obstacles to full equality; to combating the bureaucratic discrimination that persisted after emancipation; to countering defamation in the press, in fiction, on the stage, and in other public forums; and to gaining entry to elite social circles and institutions. Even communal tensions between traditionalists and reformers over the modernization of Jewish worship fit into this framework, for one of the chief motives of the reformers, at least in Germany, was to enhance the image of Judaism in order to improve the legal and social status of Jews.[1] Similarly, Western Jewish concern about immigration from eastern Europe from the 1880s on derived in part from the fear that the newcomers, with their alien ways, would fuel antisemitism and thus slow efforts to gain acceptance.

Within leadership circles there was widespread agreement, as I emphasized in the previous chapter, that acculturation and integration were absolutely necessary. Jews who had been emancipated or who wished to be emancipated, it was believed, needed to conform to non-Jewish standards, diversify their occupational structure, and abandon their cultural and social isolation if they wished to survive and prosper in the modern world. When acceptance into exclusive circles came, it was regarded as evidence that old hatreds were waning and more tolerant attitudes taking root. Every appointment of a Jew to a professorship, judgeship, or military post was regarded as Christian recognition of Jewish worth and accordingly hailed in the Jewish press and from synagogue pulpits as a triumph for Judaism and the Jewish people.

Before the rise of Jewish nationalism at the end of the nineteenth century,

---

[1] For a different interpretation of the origins of the Reform movement that subordinates social and political motives to religious and cultural ones, see Meyer, *Response to Modernity*.

there was little dissent from this position. Eager to win acceptance, integra-tionist leaders in the West ignored or remained unaware of the long-term consequences of extensive mixing. Today it is widely recognized that Jews who move in largely non-Jewish social and occupational worlds are more likely to become alienated from Jewish life than those who do not.[2] But in earlier periods Western Jewish leaders were insensitive to this. They failed to see (or did not want to see) that their well-meaning efforts to promote inte-gration unintentionally contributed to drift and defection from the Jewish community—a result they would not have applauded, however strong their desire for acceptance and recognition. For them, after all, 'assimilation' was an honourable project; it did not mean full absorption into the surrounding society and the total loss of Jewish identity, but rather adaptation, adjust-ment, and transformation in the light of new conditions.

The growth of Jewish nationalism from the 1880s launched the first seri-ous discussion of the impact of acculturation and integration on Jewish iden-tity, stimulating, in turn, the first scholarship on the subject. Beginning in the early twentieth century, a handful of young central and east European Zionists, university trained but without university appointments, produced a substantial body of sociological and demographic research on how Jew-ish attachments were actually faring in emancipated communities.[3] Chief among them were Alfred Nossig (1864–1943), Arthur Ruppin (1876–1943), Jacob Lestschinsky (1876–1966), and Felix Theilhaber (1884–1956). On the basis of statistical analysis, they concluded that Jewishness was not faring well and that acculturation, integration, and secularization were as much a threat to the survival of the Jewish people in the West as persecution was in the East. They pointed out that in those states where Jews enjoyed the fruits of emancipation—mixing with non-Jews, pursuing new careers, cultivating secular intellectual and cultural interests—disaffiliation, intermarriage, and conversion were on the rise. The opening paragraph of Arthur Ruppin's *Der Juden der Gegenwart*, first published in 1904 and here quoted in Margery Bentwich's translation, conveys both the substance and the tone of their findings: 'The structure of Judaism, once so solid, is crumbling away before our very eyes. Conversion and intermarriage are thinning the ranks of Jews in every direction, and the loss is the heaviest to bear, in that the great decrease in the Jewish birth-rate makes it more and more difficult to fill up the gaps in the natural way.'[4] That Ruppin and other early Jewish social

[2] See e.g. Endelman, *Radical Assimilation in English Jewish History*; id., *Leaving the Jewish Fold.*
[3] On the origins of social science research on modern Jewry, see Hart, *Social Science and the Politics of Modern Jewish Identity.*   [4] Ruppin, *The Jews of To-day*, 3.

scientists were ideologically predisposed to reach such a conclusion does not necessarily diminish the value of the work they did. (Is not most compelling social-science scholarship inspired by extra-scholarly commitments?) Contemporary historians of modern Jewish communities can still learn much from their work, even if they do not share their worldview.

Unfortunately the themes they investigated—themes essential to understanding Jewish history in the last two centuries—did not find favour with the generation of researchers who, beginning in the 1970s, 'normalized' the writing of modern Jewish history and pioneered its introduction into the American academy. Their work and that of their students tended to focus on other themes: emancipation, Haskalah, religious reform, Wissenschaft des Judentums (the academic study of Judaism), antisemitism and Jewish responses to it, Jewish nationalism and socialism, gender and the family, and the formation of identities. Moreover, when they turned to questions regarding the maintenance of Jewish ties in the modern period, they tended to sound a very different note to Ruppin and his colleagues. Instead of accentuating the widespread dissolution of communal and religious loyalties, they emphasized the opposite: the perpetuation of Jewishness, albeit in novel forms at times, in the face of social and political circumstances overwhelmingly hostile to its continuation.[5] Whether intentional or not, the underlying message of their work has been that Jewishness can thrive outside the State of Israel, that a creative and healthy Jewish life is possible in the diaspora, and that Zionist-inspired scholarship was wrong in predicting the inevitable disintegration of Western Jewry. (David Engel labels them the 'neo-Baronian' school in recognition of their frequent rhetorical use of Salo Baron's reservations about 'the lachrymose conception of Jewish history'. As Engel explains, however, these historians are disciples of Baron in name only, since their use of his critique of lachrymosity mistakenly assumes that he was referring to all periods of Jewish history, rather than the medieval period alone.[6] For this reason the label works only when used ironically.)

It would be facile to attribute this current—the legitimization of the diaspora experience—to the fact that most of the historians identified with it live in the United States. In this light, their affirmation of diaspora vitality was a simple reflection of their unease, perhaps unconscious, at continuing to live

[5] The following are representative of this current: Schorsch, *Jewish Reactions to German Anti-Semitism* (1972); id., *On the History of the Political Judgment of the Jew* (1976); Gurock, *When Harlem Was Jewish* (1979); Moore, *At Home in America* (1981); Rozenblit, *The Jews of Vienna* (1983); N. Cohen, *Encounter with Emancipation* (1984); Sarna, *JPS: The Americanization of Jewish Culture* (1989); id., *American Judaism* (2004); M. A. Kaplan, *The Making of the Jewish Middle Class* (1991); Wenger, *New York Jews and the Great Depression* (1996); Kaufman, *Shul with a Pool* (1999); McGinity, *Still Jewish* (2009).   [6] Engel, 'Crisis and Lachrymosity'.

outside the Land of Israel. (One weakness of this explanation is that the work of some Israeli and German historians—Shulamit Volkov, Michael Graetz, Henry Wassermann, and Till van Rahden, for example—also exhibited this tendency.) Similarly, one could argue that because these historians felt both 'at home' in America and 'comfortable' about their Jewishness, as I wrote in the Introduction, they tended to stress the ability of earlier generations of diaspora dwellers to maintain a sense of Jewishness while actively participating in the life of the surrounding society. Moreover, it is possible that because many of these historians also took part in communal affairs they inadvertently focused their attention on the most visibly committed Jews in the communities they studied, thus leaving the impression that the former were representative of the Jewish population as a whole. This deflected attention from 'ordinary' Jews, those outside the communal spotlight and on the periphery of active involvement, that is, those who were more likely to be absorbed into non-Jewish circles. Alternatively, in a different vein altogether, one could argue that this emphasis was largely a reaction to crude assertions about Jewish 'assimilation' that were the stock-in-trade of an earlier generation of nationalist historians and that, in seeking to revise this imbalance, the new emphasis veered too far in the opposite direction, as is often the case with revisionist scholarship.

I suspect that there is some truth in each of these explanations. However, even taken in tandem they are insufficient, for they fail to illuminate the larger intellectual climate in which this approach to acculturation and integration evolved. Here, as with so many other matters in Jewish life in the second half of the twentieth century, the starting point for understanding the genesis of this trend is the impact of the Holocaust—specifically, in this case, the debate over the character of European Jewish responses to Nazi persecution.

In the first decade and a half after the end of the Second World War, the Holocaust was not a central theme in American Jewish intellectual life.[7] The impulse to come to terms with the mass murder of European Jews was then largely absent. This began to change in the 1960s for a number of reasons. One that was especially important for the scholarly community was the publication of three controversial works early in the decade that raised questions about Jewish resistance during the Holocaust: Bruno Bettelheim's *The Informed Heart* (1960), Raul Hilberg's *The Destruction of the European Jews* (1961), and Hannah Arendt's *Eichmann in Jerusalem* (1963). Their publication ignited a furious debate in Jewish circles, a debate that remains passionate fifty years later. It is unnecessary to enter into the particulars of the

[7] Whitfield, 'The Holocaust in the American Jewish Mind', 32–4.

controversy here. What is important to note is that most critics of Bettel-heim, Hilberg, and Arendt believed that they were indicting European Jews for failing to resist their persecutors and even for actively co-operating in their own destruction.

One consequence of the debate was that historians of European Jewry began examining questions of Jewish behaviour in Nazi-occupied Europe. They initiated research on topics like armed resistance in the ghettos, Jewish participation in partisan units, 'collaboration' of the *Judenräte* (Jewish councils) with the SS, and the availability of information within the ghettos about the Nazis' ultimate objectives. The books and articles that appeared in due time offered a more balanced perspective than that of Bettelheim, Hilberg, and Arendt (none of whom was a historian, incidentally) and were less polemical and accusatory.[8]

Once the question of Jewish behaviour during the Holocaust was on the historiographical agenda, historians who studied the pre-war period (1870–1939) began to ask whether the alleged failings of the Jews during the war years were rooted in earlier patterns of behaviour, patterns that were well established long before Hitler seized power. Both Hilberg and Arendt had argued explicitly that this was the case. In the introduction to his monumental study of the bureaucracy involved in the killing, Hilberg had declared that diaspora Jews 'responded to force in a typical fashion for almost two thousand years'. Preventive attack, military resistance, violent opposition, and armed revenge were 'atypical and episodic'. 'Ghetto Jews' (his phrase) preferred non-violent attempts to alleviate their plight: 'petitions, protection payments, ransom arrangements, anticipatory compliance, relief, rescue, salvage, reconstruction—in short, all those activities which are designed to avert danger, or, in the event that force had already been used, to diminish its effects'. Jews deliberately and calculatingly played along with their enemies in the belief that this policy would produce the least suffering. In Hilberg's view, when the Nazi onslaught again triggered this deeply ingrained pattern of reaction, the results were catastrophic.[9]

Arendt's indictment of pre-war European Jewry was more specific. Years before the Eichmann controversy erupted, in essays that appeared in American Jewish journals in the 1940s and in the antisemitism section of *The Origins of Totalitarianism* (1951), she argued that from the end of the seventeenth century Western Jewish leaders failed to develop realistic political concerns and perceptions that would allow them to see their true position.[10] In her

---

[8] See e.g. Trunk, *Judenrat*; Bauer, *They Chose Life*; Laqueur, *The Terrible Secret*; Gutman, *The Jews of Warsaw*.   [9] Hilberg, *The Destruction of the European Jews*, 14–17.
[10] The essays are collected in Arendt, *The Jewish Writings*.

view, the Jewish people lacked political experience and, with no state of its own, was compelled to forge alliances with the ruling authorities, whoever they might be. In antiquity and later in the Middle Ages this was an effective strategy, but in the modern world, circumstances having changed, Jewish faith in the state was illusory and dangerous. Jewish notables, she argued, 'ignored completely the growing tension between state and society' in the nineteenth century and were 'the last to be aware that circumstances had forced them into the center of the conflict'. Thus, they 'never knew how to evaluate antisemitism' and could not recognize when it ceased to be merely social discrimination and became a political peril.[11]

In the mid-1960s, in the wake of the debate about Jewish behaviour during the Holocaust and in response to accusations about Jewish political ineptitude before the war, historians began for the first time to examine the question of how assimilationist leaders responded to the growth of virulent forms of antisemitism before 1870. Some, like Michael Marrus, Jehuda Reinharz, and Sidney Bolkosky, concluded that the assimilationist response was inadequate and flawed, largely because it rested on fundamental mis-perceptions about the character and extent of the new antisemitism.[12] Marrus, for example, in his study of the French Jewish community at the time of the Dreyfus affair, described its chief spokesmen as 'tragically blind to the implications of the anti-Semitic campaign of which they were the vic-tims'.[13] In his view, they naively swallowed the official optimistic creed of the Third Republic, with its belief that France was leading the world to a higher, more enlightened and progressive stage of civilization, and were 'generally unable to respond except with the most orthodox assertions of patriotism'.[14]

But other historians of west European Jewry, like Ismar Schorsch and Marjorie Lamberti, took a critical view of the Arendtian indictment of Jewish political behaviour. Instead of judging the behaviour in the light of later events, they strove to demonstrate that communal leaders acted reasonably, intelligently, and honourably, given their own previous experience and the political and social assumptions of the time. The very title of Lamberti's important contribution to the debate—*Jewish Activism in Imperial Germany*—declared its revisionist intent. While other historians belittled the liberal defence campaign in Germany as 'the story of ineffectual small deeds and failures' and branded its leaders as politically obtuse accommodationists, fearful of an antisemitic backlash, overly submissive to state authority, in-

[11] Arendt, *The Origins of Totalitarianism*, pt. 1, *Antisemitism*, 23–5.
[12] Marrus, *The Politics of Assimilation*; Reinharz, *Fatherland or Promised Land?*; Bolkosky, *The Distorted Image*.   [13] Marrus, *The Politics of Assimilation*, 1–2.
[14] Ibid. 284. Marrus later modified his views on assimilationist behaviour (see his review essay 'European Jewry and the Politics of Assimilation').

capable of grasping the truly precarious nature of their situation, Lamberti found, to her surprise, a very different set of qualities among this group— 'the qualities of courage, self-confidence, sound political judgment, and political militancy'.[15] Of those historians with a similar outlook, the most influential was Ismar Schorsch. His study of institutional responses to antisemitism in imperial Germany launched, along with Marrus's book, the scholarly investigation of pre-war Jewish political behaviour, while his much-quoted Leo Baeck Memorial Lecture of 1976, *On the History of the Political Judgment of the Jew*, directly challenged Arendt's assertion that diaspora Jewry lacked political experience and judgement. In the latter, Schorsch expanded the parameters of the debate, which until then was confined to the period 1870–1939, arguing that all of Jewish history was 'a vast repository of political experience and wisdom acquired under the most divergent and adverse conditions'.[16] For Schorsch, the very fact that Jews had survived 2,000 years of exile was evidence of 'the intelligence and effectiveness with which they conducted their foreign affairs'.[17]

This re-evaluation of diaspora political leadership set the stage for a long-term, far-ranging reassessment of Jewish fate in western and central Europe and North America in the wake of emancipation. The inclination to defend rather than disparage diaspora Jewry spilled over into accounts of other areas of Jewish behaviour in emancipated communities. A new, more positive image of Western Jewry emerged, independent of the initial debate about the adequacy of Jewish responses to antisemitism. The historians who undertook this re-evaluation celebrated the tenacity of Western Jews in preserving their Jewishness in the face of overwhelming pressures to dissolve it. They emphasized the creativity of Western Jews in meeting the challenges of living in open societies by developing new, frequently secular, forms of Jewish identity and creating new institutional forms in which to express and preserve their Jewishness. They pointed out that despite rampant secularization Jews remained a socially cohesive group with distinctive patterns of behaviour that set them off from the rest of the population. They stressed transformation rather than decline, continuity rather than disjuncture, cohesion rather than dissolution, change rather than crisis. In their work, emancipation, acculturation, and integration were serious challenges rather than fatal blows to the perpetuation of Jewish identity in the West.

From the late twentieth century the growth of two interconnected currents of thinking in the academy at large reinvigorated this by now well-

---

[15] Lamberti, *Jewish Activism in Imperial Germany*, pp. ix–x.
[16] Schorsch, *On the History of the Political Judgment of the Jew*, 12.   [17] Ibid. 19.

established perspective. The first was the belief that nationalism is a destructive but increasingly anachronistic force in human history, called into being by earlier but now disappearing historical circumstances, and that the nation-state is on its last legs, as the history of European integration demonstrated (so it was claimed). Historians and other scholars for whom these were articles of faith encouraged scholarship that transcended the time-bound, ideologically generated category of 'the nation' and promoted the virtues of transnational perspectives. It is not difficult to see how views like these reinforced perspectives emphasizing the vitality of Jewish life outside the Land of Israel, both in the past and at present. In one version of this interpretative current, the historian David Schneer and the sociologist Caryn Aviv argued that globalization, economic prosperity, and political stability created 'a new Jewish map', in which notions of periphery and centre were no longer relevant. Invoking the old binary, they believed, obscured the ways in which Jews craft their identities wherever they make their home. Thus they wrote of 'the end of the diaspora', by which they mean the concept of 'diaspora', with its value-laden implications of centre and periphery, rather than 'the emptying of the diaspora', as in classic Zionist ideology.[18]

The repudiation of the nation-state intersected with a second intellectual vogue—the delegitimization of the State of Israel and the demonization of Jewish nationalism as racist and exclusionary. While these notions were not ascendant in the American academy (in contrast, perhaps, to British universities), they were seductive, especially since they came bundled with postmodernist assumptions that were linked to cutting-edge scholarship in the humanities and the social sciences. For obvious reasons, most Jewish historians were resistant to the lure of this kind of thinking. However harsh their criticism of Israel's occupation of the West Bank, they knew that the assault on Israel's legitimacy was fuelled by more than humanitarian concern for the fate of Palestinian Arabs. On the other hand, in areas of Jewish studies in which the cultural studies project was more welcome, academic anti-Zionism made some inroads. In the work of the brothers Daniel and Jonathan Boyarin, for example, the postmodern critique of the nation and the fashionable anti-Zionism of the academy combined to empower a privileging of the diasporic mode of life—'a disassociation of ethnicities and political hegemonies as the only social structure that even begins to make possible a maintenance of cultural identities in a world grown thoroughly and inextricably interdependent'.[19] Their explicit goal was to replace 'national self-determination' as a 'theoretical and historical model' with the ideal of the diaspora.[20]

---

[18] Aviv and Shneer, *New Jews*.   [19] Boyarin and Boyarin, 'Diaspora', 717.   [20] Ibid. 723.

In the case of Jewish history-writing, however, the impact of these fashions was more subtle and indirect. Their acceptance in the academy functioned to support—even if this was not their intention—a pre-existing emphasis in Jewish historiography that celebrated the tenacity and creativity of Western Jewish communities. By denying the Zionist claim that Jewish life in the diaspora was perpetually vulnerable and that Jewish sovereignty was the only solution to this vulnerability, the demonization of Israel, along with the repudiation of the nation-state more broadly, created an atmosphere in which this celebratory historiographical current was not out of place. This is not to say that those historians who cast the modern Jewish experience in America and Europe in a positive rather than negative light were Israel-bashing fellow travellers. This was hardly the case. I speak, rather, of an unexpected, unwilled convergence of ways of thinking that were rooted in unrelated, dissimilar circumstances.

Significantly, historians who celebrated the diaspora experience devoted little attention to the state of Jewish religious practice—matters like synagogue attendance, observance of the dietary laws and the laws of sabbath and festival rest, and other practices that were historically hallmarks of Jewish distinctiveness.[21] For example, in her study of *fin-de-siècle* Viennese Jewry, Marsha Rozenblit allotted only two paragraphs to the character and extent of Jewish religious practice.[22] In a work devoted to charting acculturation and integration, the question of adherence to—or neglect of—religious traditions was a marginal concern. Similarly, in her study of the formation of a middle-class ethnic identity among second-generation New York Jews, Deborah Moore wrote only briefly about the maintenance of religious belief and practice, even though a major theme of the book was the commitment of the second generation to the preservation of strong communal ties. Moreover, the little evidence regarding observance that she presented weakened rather than strengthened her conclusion about the persistence of Jewishness in America. For example, Moore wrote appreciatively about the creation of multifaceted synagogue centres in new middle-class neighbourhoods to meet the needs of Americanized Jews that immigrant synagogues, based on Old World models, were failing to satisfy. These institutions, she explained, were established 'to nourish the primary contacts vital to Jewish group preservation' and 'to guarantee Jewish structural segregation from American society'. Yet she also noted in passing that they attracted only about 10 per cent of the city's Jewish population in the late 1920s.[23]

[21] One exception to this generalization is Marion Kaplan, whose *The Making of the Jewish Middle Class* stresses the role of Jewish women in preserving religious traditions in the home after their husbands began to neglect them.

[22] Rozenblit, *The Jews of Vienna*, 6–7, 8.   [23] Moore, *At Home in America*, 144–5.

There is no better illustration of the strength of the upbeat model than Jonathan Sarna's much-heralded history of American Judaism. Unlike the historians cited above, Sarna intended to write a history of the Jewish religion, not a history of the Jewish people. He focused on those who joined synagogues and practised their religion publicly—very likely a minority at any time in the past three centuries. He knew full well that his emphasis on innovation, creativity, and revival in the history of American Judaism ran counter to the 'long-standing fear that Jews in America are doomed to assimilate, that they simply cannot survive in an environment of religious freedom and church–state separation',[24] a fear exacerbated from the 1960s on by increasing intermarriage and declining fertility. Invoking Simon Rawidowicz's well-known characterization of the Jews as 'the ever-dying people', Sarna suggested that American Jewish spokesmen in every age, from the colonial period to the present, predicted the imminent decline, if not death, of Judaism. To these doomsayers and handwringers, Sarna responded with Rawidowicz's words (written as consolation in the aftermath of the Holocaust): 'A nation dying for thousands of years means a living nation. Our incessant dying means uninterrupted living, rising, standing up, beginning anew.'[25]

While upbeat, Sarna's account of how Judaism adapted to American challenges was not naive. He acknowledged that intermarriage and fertility statistics at the end of the twentieth century pointed to 'a gloomy future for Judaism in America' and soberly described the contemporary scene as 'bipolar': 'At one and the same time, then, American Judaism seems to be experiencing both revitalization and assimilation.'[26] Some Jews were recommitting themselves, cultivating, enhancing, and deepening their Jewishness, while others were drifting away at an accelerated pace. Fair enough—but what interests me is that, having acknowledged the demographic losses American Jewry was suffering at the turn of the century, Sarna chose to end, literally, with Rawidowicz's article of faith in the eternality of the Jewish people, a declaration in harmony with his message throughout the book but not with the qualifications and reservations noted above. It is not my aim to argue, contra Sarna, that the future looks bleak and gloomy—prophecy is not the historian's métier—but rather to emphasize how strong the need to legitimize the diaspora experience and view it through rose-coloured lenses was and is.

The reason that historians who celebrate diaspora vitality tend to ignore religious practice or, as in Sarna's case, mute the extent to which American Jews express their Jewishness in religious terms is not difficult to fathom.

---

[24] Sarna, *American Judaism*, p. xiii.   [25] Ibid. 374.   [26] Ibid. 365–6.

Religious observance in the Jewish communities of the West declined radically in the eighteenth, nineteenth, and twentieth centuries. On this point there is little disagreement. Historians who celebrated the persistence of Jewishness in the diaspora, however, did not dwell on the decline because doing so would have challenged their optimism about Jewish continuity and cohesion. Nonetheless, they acknowledged in a roundabout way that Judaism (as opposed to Jewishness) ceased to be of much importance to most Jews by stressing the emergence of new forms of Jewish solidarity— secular, ethnic, and associational—to take the place of traditional ones that were in decline. As Rozenblit concluded, the Jews of Vienna 'may have abandoned many of the traditional forms which had typified their communal life for centuries in Central and Eastern Europe', but 'they did not necessarily assimilate fully into the urban society' to which they moved. On the contrary, they 'created new patterns of Jewish behavior which differed from traditional ones but were nonetheless distinctively Jewish'.[27]

From the 1980s this emphasis—highlighting the creation and vitality of new, secular forms of Jewishness—was echoed in some sociological studies of American Jewry. A lively debate emerged in that decade about the interpretation of survey research data concerning the contemporary American Jewish community and its future.[28] The so-called 'pessimistic' school maintained that a declining birth rate and a climbing intermarriage rate, along with a relatively low rate of children of mixed marriages being raised as Jews, was sapping the demographic vitality of American Jewry. (Although the demographers and sociologists in this camp employed more sophisticated analytical tools than the pioneer social scientists of Europe in the early twentieth century, they reached remarkably similar conclusions about the health of diaspora Jewry.) Critics of this perspective—the so-called 'optimistic' or transformationist school—conceded that unprecedented demographic patterns were changing American Jewry, but viewed these developments in a positive or neutral light, as transformation rather than erosion. They argued that the ethnic cohesiveness of American Jewry was much stronger than their opponents portrayed it, despite an increase in intermarriage and a decline in some forms of religious observance. As Calvin Goldscheider, a leading proponent of this view, explained, 'the changes and transformations over the last several decades have resulted in greater ties and networks

[27] Rozenblit, *The Jews of Vienna*, 7.
[28] Calvin Goldscheider (*Jewish Continuity and Change; Studying the Jewish Future*) states the transformationist case. For the 'pessimistic' position, see DellaPergola and Schmelz, 'Demographic Transformations of American Jewry', as well as Goldscheider's response to them and their rejoinder to him in the same volume. For a perspective more or less midway between the two, see S. M. Cohen, *American Assimilation or Jewish Revival?*

among Jews . . . [connecting] Jews to each other in kinship relationships, jobs, neighborhoods, lifestyles, and values'.[29] Like the historians who described the pre-war diaspora experience in positive terms, Goldscheider and his associates downplayed the decline in traditional religious observance in the United States, emphasizing instead the persistence of ethnic solidarity. The extent to which historians who championed the diaspora influenced the 'optimistic' camp—or the reverse, for that matter—cannot be known. All that can be said is that neither group was ignorant of the other's work. Perhaps both were responding similarly to a similar set of external circumstances.

By stressing the persistence of a distinctive Jewish identity in post-emancipation communities, these historians offered a valuable corrective to an older, nationalist-inspired historiography that dismissed Western Jews as rabid assimilationists. That said, the objection must still be raised that stressing social cohesion while downplaying religious discontinuity tended to obscure the extent to which Jewish ties were being loosened, even if the consequences of that loosening were not apparent until some time later. The children of migrants from eastern Europe who settled in New York, London, Paris, Berlin, Vienna, and other urban centres maintained a strong sense of Jewish identity, even when they fled the synagogue and adopted Western ways, because strong countervailing pressures kept them from being absorbed into the surrounding society: their emotional attachment to their parents and their world, their struggle to make a living in a narrow range of occupations, and the hostility of non-Jews to their full incorporation.

Second-generation Jews in the West had few real opportunities for intensive social contact with non-Jews, and thus were in no position to experience the lure of radical assimilation. However, their children and grandchildren —the third and fourth generations to live in an open society—were candidates for disaffiliation because they faced fewer obstacles to their integration and because they encountered fewer reminders of their Old World past. In such circumstances, especially when antisemitism declined and religion lost its hold, ethnic bonds rarely continued to ensure the persistence of strong Jewish attachments. Evidence for this can be seen in the histories of Western Jewish communities in the second half of the twentieth century, in which intermarriage, indifference, and disaffiliation made strong headway among the third and fourth generations. In the case of Britain, the weakening of Jewish identity was so great that the size of the community declined in absolute terms, shrinking from about 400,000 in the years immediately after the Second World War to 300,000 at the end of the

---

[29] Goldscheider, *Jewish Continuity and Change*, 183.

century.[30] (It is more difficult to follow these developments in the Jewish communities on the Continent since the Holocaust abruptly ended the assimilatory process there and the grandchildren and great-grandchildren of earlier immigrants from traditional milieus were either murdered or forced to emigrate.)

The decline in Jewish attachments since the end of the Second World War was not the outcome of improvements in Jewish status alone, however important their role in facilitating intensive social integration. Much of the decline was rooted in acculturation and secularization that was well under way before the war. In most instances the weakening of Jewish sentiments and attachments was a cumulative, multigenerational process, with each succeeding generation more distant from ethnic and religious loyalties. The process was not linear—there were families in which it was halted or reversed, but these were the exception, not the rule. Nor was the process in any sense 'necessary'—it need not have unfolded in the way it did, but nonetheless that was how it happened. Studies that celebrated diaspora vitality failed to take into account the multigenerational character of this process, offering instead a snapshot, frozen in time, of the behaviour of one generation over three or four decades, when in fact what was needed were studies of successive generations. In this light, I would suggest that, were we to extend Rozenblit's study of Viennese Jewry into the interwar years or Moore's study of New York Jews into the post-war years, we would reach different conclusions about the strength of ethnicity in those two groups of Jews. This is not to say that historical hindsight should dictate the standards by which earlier behaviour is assessed, but rather that the outcome of long-term developments has the potential to alert historians to the beginnings of those developments in earlier periods, beginnings that might otherwise be ignored or obscured. Taking the long view might also alert historians to the manifold ways in which contemporary extra-scholarly concerns subtly shape their readings of the past.

The notion that drift and defection are multigenerational processes has implications as well for the heated debate on the meaning of intermarriage in the United States of America that began in the wake of the National Jewish Population Survey of 1990. (The study reported that 52 per cent of Jews who married in the period 1985–90 married non-Jews.[31] Even if methodological flaws overstated the rate, as some critics claimed, the debate was predicated on the assumption that more than half of Jews who were marrying were

---

[30] On the demographic decline of British Jewry since the end of the Second World War, see Endelman, *Radical Assimilation in English Jewish History*, 203–5.

[31] Kosmin and Goldstein, *Highlights of the CJF 1990 National Jewish Population Survey*.

marrying out.) Social scientists who were critical of the alarm generated by the survey data pointed out that the consequences of intermarriage at the end of the twentieth century were not the same as they were earlier in the modern period, when intermarriage (without the conversion of the non-Jewish partner) was the same as disaffiliation.[32] In late twentieth-century America, due to the decline in antisemitism and the public validation of multiculturalism, men and women (in particular) who intermarried did not necessarily sever their ties to Jewish communal organizations. Some even took steps to raise their children as Jews, even when their partners remained Christians. While no one doubted that this was the case, what was unclear was the frequency of the phenomenon. Did the number of children being raised as Jews outweigh the number of children being raised as Christians or (probably more common) without any specific religious identity? For the social historian, for whom numbers count and the typical takes precedence over the exceptional, this question is central. Survey evidence on this point, which was less abundant than evidence on the intermarriage rate, revealed that a minority of the offspring of mixed marriages were being raised in a consciously Jewish environment. This alone seemed to support the 'alarmist' interpretation of the intermarriage rate. However, even if the survey data had shown otherwise—that is, that a majority of the children were being raised as Jews—the debate would not have been settled. The critical question was not whether intermarried Jews were raising their children as Jews, but what that meant and whether these children transmitted a viable Jewish identity (something more than symbolic ethnicity) in turn to their children. The tracking of Jewish continuity in the modern period, whether in Vienna or New York, requires multigenerational data and a long-term perspective, both of which were absent in the debate between 'optimists' and 'pessimists' at the close of the twentieth century.

There was one other way in which the desire to celebrate the tenacity of diaspora communities led historians to underestimate the demographic losses they sustained in the modern period. Many quantitative studies masked their extent by examining disaffiliation in the aggregate.[33] That is, they measured it by tallying the number of Jews leaving Judaism (whether by conversion, intermarriage, or formal secession) on an annual basis and then viewing this number as a percentage of the total Jewish population in a locale. Measuring radical assimilation in this manner yields deceptively low

---

[32] I discuss this more fully in Endelman, *Leaving the Jewish Fold*, ch. 5.

[33] See e.g. Rozenblit, *The Jews of Vienna*; D. Hertz, 'Seductive Conversion in Berlin'; Riff, 'Assmilation and Conversion in Bohemia'. The articles by Hertz and Riff, while not written in the spirit of 'diaspora legitimization', nonetheless employ quantitative methods that minimize the demographic losses resulting from conversion.

rates. For example, in Vienna in 1900, 559 Jews—0.04 per cent of the city's Jewish population—converted to Christianity. Even a cumulative percentage of conversions over a decade, which would have yielded a higher figure, of course, would have represented 'only a tiny fraction of the Jews of Vienna'.[34] In this light, it did not seem that conversion was eating away at the fabric of Viennese Jewish life.

The flaw in assessing the extent of radical assimilation in this way was that the base population to which the number of conversions was being compared was not constant but continually expanding, not from natural increase primarily but from immigration. During the nineteenth and early twentieth centuries successive waves of newcomers—from rural areas in the German states and from the towns and villages of east and east-central Europe—swelled the size of urban Jewish centres in the west, thereby offsetting the losses occurring among 'native' families long settled there. Having lived prior to their migration in communities that were more traditional than the cities to which they moved, the newcomers were not likely to embrace Christianity in order to advance their careers, intermarry, or gain entry into elite social circles (although their descendants were often prepared to do so). Including these new arrivals in the base population of potential converts minimized the inroads radical assimilation was making within long-settled families. A more revealing study would have measured those leaving the Jewish community in terms of the number of Jews in the community whose acculturation was sufficiently advanced that secession would have been a real option for them. Jews who were still religiously observant or emotionally bound to the society in which they had been raised formed 'at best a reservoir from which potential seceders [were] recruited in due course'.[35]

The impact of this celebratory interpretative current on the writing of modern Jewish history in the United States was—and remains—substantial. The classic Zionist interpretation, with its pessimistic perspective on the health of diaspora communities, was more or less dead in academic circles by the 1980s. Indeed in Israel itself it claimed few adherents by the turn of the century. At the same time historians in the United States who wrote more soberly about post-emancipation communities recognized the startling persistence of Jewish ties and sentiments in settings unfavourable to minority group survival. In the early twenty-first century, works like Michael Marrus's *The Politics of Assimilation* and Sidney Bolkosky's *The Distorted Image*, with their consistently bleak view of diaspora efforts to combat antisemitism or manufacture a vital Jewish identity, seemed curiously old-fashioned.

[34] Rozenblit, *The Jews of Vienna*, 132.   [35] Honigmann, 'Jewish Conversions', 26.

This is not to say that the 'pro-diaspora' perspective swept the field. There are those, like myself, who were sceptical then, and are sceptical now, about the claim that the Jews of the West successfully met the challenge that emancipation, acculturation, integration, and secularization posed to their group survival. Most of the essays in Parts II and III of this volume address *inter alia* this question—how Judaism and Jewishness fared in open societies in the modern period—and thus they offer an alternative to the historiographical emphasis that is the topic of this chapter. They do so by casting a wide net, one that seeks to capture the historical experiences of large numbers of Jews, articulate and inarticulate, respectable and disreputable, rich and poor alike. Broadening the scope of Jewish history in this way raises questions about the 'successes' and 'failures' of Western Jewish communities in the age of emancipation and beyond.

CHAPTER THREE

The Englishness of
Jewish Modernity in England

BEFORE THE ASCENT of social history in the academy, most Jewish historians looked to the German Jewish experience as the paradigm for the transformation of European Jewry and to Moses Mendelssohn, the maskilim, the pioneers of Reform Judaism, and the practitioners of Wissenschaft des Judentums as the key actors in this development. Some, in addition to privileging the shifts in thinking they brought about, tied the transformation of communities elsewhere as well to the influence of their ideas. They constructed a model of change in which new ideas radiated outwards from Berlin and slowly diffused throughout Europe, bringing change in their wake. For Jewish historians who looked at developments in Germany from the perspective of liberal states like Britain, France, and the Netherlands, this model was problematic, for by any of the criteria conventionally invoked in discussing the transformation of Europe in this period the German states were not in the vanguard of change. The Prussia of Moses Mendelssohn and David Friedländer was a social and economic backwater, lagging far behind Britain, France, and the Netherlands in those changes associated with the arrival of liberal individualism, religious toleration, and modern capitalism. It lacked an entrepreneurially minded, politically conscious bourgeoisie, representative political institutions, the infrastructure for industrial development, and a liberal–capitalist ethos.

The course of Jewish transformation in central Europe reflected the 'backward' nature of the states in that region. German Jews faced formidable obstacles to their incorporation into state and society; the self-consciously modern programmes they developed to reform Jewish life were rooted in the belief that their social and political exclusion was the result of their outmoded habits and customs. The programmes of the maskilim reflected the absence of toleration and integration, the failure of widespread German–Jewish rapprochement. They did not betoken the path-breaking role of German Jewry in forging new links with non-Jewish society, but rather the opposite: its inability to achieve those links as a matter of course, informally, without public gestures. What Karl Marx wrote in 1844 about the relationship between German social theory and the actual history of the German people describes equally the situation of German Jewry: 'Just as the nations of the ancient world lived their prehistory in the imagination, in mythology, so we Germans have lived our post-history in thought, in *philosophy*. We are the *philosophical* contemporaries of the present day without being its historical contemporaries . . . In politics, the Germans have *thought* what other nations have *done* . . . The abstraction and presumption of its philosophy were in step with the partial and stunted character of their reality.'[1] To paraphrase Marx, German Jews theorized what Jews elsewhere—and in England in particular, as I will argue in this chapter—were already doing.

The ideological programmes of the Haskalah and later Reform Judaism had little impact on the course of Anglo-Jewish history, primarily because they emerged in circumstances that were far removed from those in England. In England acculturation and integration were well advanced before the 1770s,[2] the decade usually designated as the turning point in the transformation of German Jewry. Spontaneously, without recourse to ideological guidelines or rationales, wealthy Ashkenazim in England had begun to abandon marks of Jewish distinctiveness by mid-century. Men shaved their beards and gave up wearing the long caftan-like coat typical of central European Jewry. Women no longer covered their heads nor dressed demurely, preferring instead the fashionable, low-cut gowns of the time that exposed ample amounts of flesh. Jews who were financially able to adopted a style of living not noticeably different from that of other well-to-do Englishmen. They attended the theatre and the opera, gossiped and played cards in the coffee houses of London, had their portraits painted by the best artists of the period, lost money at the faro tables in St James's Square, threw lavish parties and entertainments, took the waters at Bath, and acquired country homes. (When the Palestinian rabbi Hayim Yosef Azulai visited London in the spring of 1755 to collect funds for the Hebron yeshiva, he complained that the wealthy Jews had left the metropolis for their country estates.) Jewish bankers and brokers also adopted a code of sexual behaviour radically freer than permitted by Jewish tradition, conspicuously visiting high-class brothels and lavishly maintaining mistresses. They were lax in observing *kashrut* and attending synagogue on sabbaths and festivals. Among the Sephardim these trends were even more marked, since many of their families had been immersed in the social and cultural life of the non-Jewish world prior to their settlement in England, a theme I discuss at length in Chapter 11.

[1] Marx, 'Contribution to the Critique of Hegel's Philosophy of Right', 49, 51.
[2] Endelman, *The Jews of Georgian England*, chs. 4–6, 8.

A similar process of acculturation occurred among the Jewish poor, although perhaps not at quite such an early date. The street hawkers and old-clothes men of London took to the habits of the urban poor more generally, including irreligiosity, criminal activity, sexual promiscuity, street violence, and prize-fighting.[3] Their adoption of an English lower-class lifestyle, like the adoption of upper-class habits by prosperous Jews, proceeded apace uninfluenced by events in or doctrines from Germany. Anglo-Jewish acculturation was well under way before the appearance of the first journalistic writings of the Berlin Haskalah, such as Naphtali Herz Wessely's *Divrei shalom ve'emet* (*Words of Peace and Truth*, 1782), and before the creation of the first institutions to normalize the profile of Jews such as the Berlin Freischule (1781).

The integration of English Jews into non-Jewish circles also commenced before 1770. At all levels of society and from very early in the eighteenth century, small groups of anglicized Jews began to forge social ties with their Christian peers. Highly acculturated Sephardi brokers, ensconced in their Thames-side homes to the west of London, entered into the social life of the neighbourhood's fashionable set. Well-to-do Sephardim were admitted to Masonic lodges as early as the 1730s; some with scientific interests were elected Fellows of the Royal Society.[4]

Wealthy Ashkenazim appeared in upper-class Christian circles at a later date than their Sephardi counterparts due to their later arrival in England and their previous isolation from broader social and cultural currents. Still, there were a few Ashkenazi families, such as the Franks and the Harts, who moved quite easily into the social life of the English countryside around mid-century. At the lower end of the social scale, intimate and sustained socializing between Jews and non-Jews was far more pronounced than among those higher up. The Jewish poor and petite bourgeoisie of London lived on close physical terms with their non-Jewish neighbours, lodging in the same narrow streets and crowded courts, frequently in the same buildings. They sought entertainment and diversion in the streets, public houses, theatres, and open spaces of the City and the East End, where they mixed

---

[3] In addition to the material on Jewish criminals in Endelman, *The Jews of Georgian England*, see Pfeffer, 'From One End of the Earth to the Other', 56–68, 221–45. The latter includes a remarkable account of the hanging of the burglar Abraham Abrahams. On violent acts committed by Jews against each other and against non-Jews, see Warner, 'Violence Against and Among Jews', 443–7.

[4] Geoffrey Cantor reviews and analyses the engagement of Jews with science in this period in *Quakers, Jews, and Science*. Appendix 3 includes a list of Fellows of the Royal Society who were of Jewish origin.

with non-Jews in settings not governed by the rigid conventions of upper-class socializing.[5]

Clearly, the transformation of English Jewry in its initial stages was autochthonous, the outcome of indigenous conditions rather than trends from abroad. After all, German Jewry in the middle of the eighteenth century was still overwhelmingly traditional in its outlook and behaviour, at least according to the standard accounts of the period, and could not have served as a model for Jews elsewhere. What then of later developments? Did Jews in late Georgian or Victorian England seek to emulate the trailblazers of Berlin, Hamburg, and Frankfurt? Did the Haskalah, Wissenschaft des Judentums, and Reform Judaism shape the course of Anglo-Jewish history from the 1770s on?

In the case of the Haskalah, the earliest programme to reshape Jewish life and thought, the evidence that German thinkers and writers influenced Anglo-Jewry is slim. Cecil Roth, who treated the Haskalah more as a literary phenomenon than a movement for social change in his essay 'The Haskalah in England', discovered only three instances of direct contact between German maskilim and English Jews.[6] The first of these came in 1781, when Moses Mendelssohn sent Robert Lowth, bishop of London, whose book on biblical poetry he admired, his translations of Genesis and Exodus, using Joseph Hart Myers, physician to the Sephardi congregation in London, as his intermediary. In the second instance, when the young Benjamin Goldsmid, later a major figure in London finance, travelled in Germany in the late 1770s, he was in contact with maskilim there. And third, when Michael Josephs, later a communal reformer and Hebraist in London, was a young man he spent five or six years in Berlin, during which time he came under Mendelssohn's influence. There is no reason to believe that these few interactions contributed appreciably to the transformation of English Jewry.

Significantly, the figures whom Roth discussed in his essay were not communal activists, reformers, or modernizers, but Hebrew scholars who were familiar with Western culture and wrote in a modernized Hebrew style, frequently on themes of general cultural interest. However, their concern with the revitalization of Hebrew and their familiarity with non-Jewish literature do not add up to a Haskalah movement. They did not create institutions to modernize Judaism or Jewish life or compose tracts to rouse their fellow Jews from their alleged lethargy. Most importantly, these individuals did not constitute a cohesive circle of intellectuals committed to the transformation of the fundamental values and structure of Judaism.

---

[5] A trove of information about the cohabitation of Jews and Christians may be found in the cases that came before the London Beth Din (rabbinical court) (Pfeffer, *'From One End of the Earth to the Other'*).   [6] Roth, 'The Haskalah in England'.

David Ruderman reopened the question of the significance of this small group of thinkers with the publication of *Jewish Enlightenment in an English Key* in 2000. As the title suggests, Ruderman stressed the Englishness of Jewish thinkers in Britain, revealing for the first time their engagement in debates that engaged English scholarship more generally (for example, the authenticity of the Masoretic text of the Hebrew Bible). While acknowledging that they were few in number and heterogeneous in background and outlook, Ruderman nonetheless identified them with the Haskalah by employing an expansive definition of the term in which the transformation of Jewish life and thought was not a necessary feature. Whatever the merit of using the term in this way, Ruderman agreed that what he called the Haskalah in England was not a socio-cultural movement in the German Jewish sense. More critical to the argument of this chapter, he declared emphatically that it was autochthonous. It would be wrong to assume, he wrote, that 'English Jews required either the cultural image or the philosophical ideas of Moses Mendelssohn and his followers to precipitate their own ruminations on Judaism and general culture'. He concluded that 'the Jewish cultural response to modernity' in England emerged from 'the uniqueness of the English political and social climate'.[7] His conclusion, however, left unanswered the question of the impact of these writers on the transformation of Anglo-Jewry more generally—for which he offered no evidence. In any case, the men of letters whom he featured only began to publish their work in the last quarter of the century, several decades after secularization and acculturation were well under way, and thus could not have influenced these transformations. Their dialogue with English culture and bold defence of Judaism were made possible by changes that occurred *before* they commenced their intellectual activity. To stress this is not to dismiss or belittle what they accomplished but to emphasize once again that social history and intellectual history each register a distinct dimension of change and that both histories are equally 'true' (but not necessarily representative). It is the historian's own orientation—subjective and arbitrary—that privileges one over the other.

The break with traditional practices that was so characteristic of Anglo-Jewry in the late Georgian period occurred largely without recourse to ideological justification. Most English Jews adopted the habits of English men and women because they wanted to feel at home in England and because they lived in a society in which rabbis, synagogues, and other pillars of tradition were less powerful than on the Continent. They quietly abandoned the ways of *ancien régime* Judaism that set them apart from their neighbours and

[7] Ruderman, *Jewish Enlightenment in an English Key*, 20.

interfered with their pursuit of pleasure and profit. Very few felt it was necessary to change the public character of Jewish worship or the fundamental
beliefs of Judaism in order to gain respect and acceptance outside their own
community. Instead, they maintained a nominal allegiance to Judaism as it
was and simply ignored those beliefs and practices that were obstacles to
worldly aims.

Appropriately, the most articulate public critic of traditional Judaism
in the late Georgian period was Isaac D'Israeli (1766–1848), father of the
future prime minister, who quit the Sephardi synagogue in 1817 and made
his children Christians soon thereafter, and whose impact on Anglo-Jewry,
aside from fathering one of its favourite sons (even if he was a convert), was
nil. In his novel *Vaurien* (1797), in an essay on Mendelssohn (1798), which
revealed his ignorance of what Mendelssohn actually wrote and instead
exploited his symbolic importance as a progressive thinker, and in *The
Genius of Judaism* (1833), he developed a critique of rabbinic Judaism similar
to that of the radical maskilim in Germany.[8] D'Israeli rejected the authority
of rabbinic law, which he characterized as obsolete and arbitrary, and called
for a radical reform of Jewish education, which he blamed for the Jews' intellectual inferiority, aesthetic degeneracy, and physical flaccidity. He urged
Jews to reject every 'anti-social principle' in their culture that set them apart
from non-Jews, so that they might fuse socially and politically with their
fellow citizens. Very much the outsider, he evoked no response from other
Jews.

Less peripheral was a small number of moderate reformers at this time
who wished to revive and update Jewish life. Unlike their German counterparts, they did not seek to make sweeping changes in Jewish tradition, nor
did they develop any systematic intellectual framework for their work. They
commented more frequently on the necessity of expanding the intellectual
perspective of Anglo-Jewry than they did on the necessity of changing this
belief or that custom. In particular, they rejected the idea that the study of
rabbinic texts should be the foundation of Jewish learning while other subjects remained peripheral. The printer Levy Alexander and the engraver
Solomon Bennett, for example, criticized Anglo-Jewry for its indifference to
secular letters—Alexander described his fellow English Jews as 'abject slaves
of prejudice and obstinacy'—while praising German Jews for their intellectual enlightenment.[9] Yet the only sphere of communal life in which these
critics acted as agents of transformation was the education of the poor, and
even here it is difficult to say how influential if at all their ideas were. The

---

[8] D'Israeli, *Vaurien*; id., 'A Biographical Sketch of the Jewish Socrates'; id., *The Genius of
Judaism*.   [9] Endelman, *The Jews of Georgian England*, 154–9.

wealthy merchants and brokers who governed the community's schools also shared their objections to traditional Jewish education, but their concerns were more pragmatic.[10]

The absence of a systematic ideology of religious and social transformation in the decline of tradition in Anglo-Jewry is symptomatic of the weakness, more generally, of ideological thinking in its historical development. By comparison with the German Jewish middle class, prosperous English Jews in the eighteenth and nineteenth centuries were ill educated and intellectually unsophisticated and unadventurous. They did not take much interest in the intellectual life of the country, nor did they make any significant contribution to either English letters or Jewish scholarship. The Jewish salons of Berlin and Vienna lacked counterparts in London or any provincial city. Similarly, it would be impossible to find an Anglo-Jewish counterpart to either Heinrich Heine or Karl Marx. Few Jewish youths attended university before the end of the nineteenth century, although there were universities in Britain (Oxford and Cambridge aside) that admitted professing Jews.[11] This indifference to the world of ideas stemmed primarily from the character of Jewish integration into English society rather than, presumably, from any innate lack of intelligence. The path to acceptance was relatively straightforward: acquiring a fortune, purchasing a country home, contributing generously to Jewish and non-Jewish charities, entertaining lavishly, and cultivating genteel manners. Neither a university education nor book-learning played a role in certifying Jews as acceptable, especially in upper-class circles, where there was little enthusiasm for clever intellectuals. Thus, in transforming themselves into English gentlemen and ladies, Jews did not have recourse to ideological thinking either to justify what they were doing in their own eyes or to convince non-Jews of their willingness and ability to reconcile their Jewishness with the demands of citizenship and gentility. Like the aristocracy and gentry whom they emulated, they shunned theoretical systems and philosophical abstractions, preferring instead an empirical piecemeal approach to winning acceptance.

This is nowhere more evident than in Anglo-Jewish efforts to improve the character of Jewish worship.[12] The commercial and financial magnates who controlled the institutional life of the community and who spearheaded efforts to make the synagogue conform more closely to English patterns were primarily motivated by social considerations. In altering traditional forms in public worship, they strove to make their service more decorous

---

[10] Ibid., ch. 7.   [11] Endelman, *Radical Assimilation in English Jewish History*, 77–80.
[12] See the surveys of Kershen and Romain, *Tradition and Change*; Persoff, *Faith against Reason*.

rather than more rational or universal, more genteel rather than more theologically correct. Not surprisingly, rabbis and scholars, who were few and far between in England before the late nineteenth century, took a negligible role in shaping the course of reform. The situation in Germany was, of course, very different.

The earliest move to increase the dignity of Jewish worship in England came in the mid-eighteenth century, when the Great Synagogue ordered its *ḥazan* (cantor) to wear canonicals (a long black robe with a pair of white ribbons at the neck). After this innovation, no further efforts to make Anglo-Jewish worship more genteel occurred until the 1820s, when some of the London congregations introduced (or attempted to introduce) minor reforms, such as limiting the number of *mi sheberakh* blessings when the Torah was read, engaging *ḥazanim* who were able to chant the liturgy in an unadorned rather than a florid manner, prohibiting children from interrupting the reading of the Scroll of Esther on Purim with noisemakers, and slightly abridging the singing of psalms on the sabbath. Some of these reforms were designed to make attendance at synagogue more attractive to congregants who no longer understood Hebrew and who were impatient with the length of the traditional service. But most of them, particularly those initiated by the Ashkenazi congregations, were cosmetic in character, undertaken within the context of traditional Judaism. They were concerned with the appearance of Jewish worship, not with the content of Jewish prayer. None of these reforms could be considered radical. There were no attempts, as in Germany, to tamper with references to the restoration of the Davidic kingdom, the rebuilding of the Temple, and the coming of the messiah, since English Jews, whose legal disabilities were few, did not face pressure to renounce their belief in a separate messianic future.[13]

After 1840, however, religious reform in Anglo-Jewry was a less quiet and modest affair. The creation of a Reform congregation in London (the West London Synagogue of British Jews) that year by a handful of wealthy Sephardim and Ashkenazim who seceded from their respective synagogues provoked considerable communal disharmony, at least initially. There are three interpretations of the secession—none attributes any influence to events in Germany. The older view, most fully developed by Albert Hyamson, sees the breakaway largely as the outcome of an internal split within the Sephardi congregation.[14] According to this interpretation, progressively minded Sephardim took the initiative in founding the Reform synagogue when the privileged members of the congregation refused to sanction the

---

[13] Endelman, *The Jews of Georgian England*, 160–4.
[14] Hyamson, *The Sephardim of England*, ch. 15.

establishment of a branch synagogue in the West End, nearer their homes than the existing building in Bevis Marks, and with it a service conducted in a more decorous manner. The second view, argued by Robert Liberles, shifts the focus from Sephardim to Ashkenazim, making the latter the protagonists, and places the affair in a much broader context.[15] According to Liberles, the financier Isaac Lyon Goldsmid, a champion of political emancipation, was the major figure in the establishment of the Reform congregation. Dissatisfied with the caution of the Board of Deputies (the representative body of British Jewry) in seeking emancipation, he saw the proposed congregation as an alternative institutional platform from which to campaign for full access to political office. In this reading, the aim of the reforms, especially the elimination of the second day of festivals, was to promote political emancipation. (The belief was that eliminating the second day would reduce the number of days on which Jews would not be available for government service.) The third view, most fully articulated by Anne Kershen and Jonathan Romaine, gives little credence either to the notion that reform was driven by strife at Bevis Marks or to the notion that it was tied to the emancipation struggle.[16] According to this interpretation, the founders were more conservative than radical, intent above all on making Jewish worship attractive to acculturated, middle-class Jews like themselves who lived in the West End (and could not or would not walk to the City synagogues). Their aim, above all, was to combat indifference and stem defection by introducing decorum and English-language sermons.

The first interpretation is clearly inadequate, for it accords no importance to Isaac Lyon Goldsmid and his family, who were instrumental in the creation of the synagogue. D. W. Marks, the first minister of the congregation, wrote of the barrister Francis Henry Goldsmid (Isaac Lyon's son) that 'to him more than anyone else we owe . . . that our congregation was brought . . . into being'.[17] However, the second interpretation, which foregrounds the political aims of the Goldsmids and their allies, gives inadequate attention to the *social* ambitions of the secessionists, including the Goldsmids, who desired a decorous Judaism that complemented their social rank and their genuine alarm at the spread of drift and defection. Both Sephardim and Ashkenazim were concerned with winning respect and acceptance outside the Jewish community. Indeed, Isaac Lyon Goldsmid's interest in synagogue reforms pre-dated the first campaign for emancipation by almost a decade. Throughout the 1820s, before Jewish emancipation was on anyone's political agenda in England, Goldsmid worked to make the service at the Great Synagogue

[15] Liberles, 'The Origins of the Jewish Reform Movement in England'.
[16] Kershen and Romain, *Tradition and Change*, 7–28.   [17] Quoted ibid. 11.

more genteel and decorous.[18] These early attempts at reform lacked any political overtones. Sensitive to the Christian perception that Jewish worship was noisy and chaotic, Goldsmid and those who acted with him aimed to make the public face of Judaism more reverent, solemn, and respectable, to bring it closer to well-bred Anglican norms.[19] The third interpretation comes closest to incorporating this mix of motives.

Social motives such as these were still at work in the early 1840s, among both Sephardim and Ashkenazim, when the breakaway occurred. In fact, the social benefits of reform may have been paramount in the minds of the former, since there is no evidence of intense Sephardi interest in pursuing parliamentary emancipation.[20] The character of the reforms instituted at the new synagogue accords with this interpretation. The changes made there did not reflect any politically driven goal to make Judaism less offensive or more attractive to the Tory politicians who were the principal impediment to the relief of Jewish disabilities. Rather, they reflected the bibliocentric or neo-Karaite ideas of D. W. Marks, who compiled the synagogue's first prayer book, and the social needs of the founding members, who shared Marks's views to a large extent.[21] Nothing of a nationalist or particularist nature was eliminated. Prayer in Hebrew was retained, as were specific prayers for the coming of the messiah, the return to Zion, and the restoration of the Temple cult. Most of the reforms were of a moderate, cosmetic nature: the morning service began at a later hour on the sabbath; *aliyot* (calling men to recite blessings before and after the public reading of sections of the Torah) and *mi sheberakh* blessings were abolished, the Musaf Amidah (the central section of the additional prayer service following the morning service on the sabbath and festivals) was shortened, and an English-language sermon was introduced. The one substantial break with tradition was the abolition of the second day of the festivals. This innovation may have been the outcome of Goldsmid's desire to ease the participation of Jews in public life or it may have reflected Marks's anti-rabbinic outlook, which led him to devalue customs without biblical authority—or perhaps both. In any case, it was the only radical reform to be introduced.

---

[18] Roth, *The Great Synagogue, London*, 252–3; Endelman, *The Jews of Georgian England*, 161.

[19] Liberles agreed that some of the reforms introduced at the West London Synagogue of British Jews were 'a response to the critical views of the British public' ('The Origins of the Jewish Reform Movement in England', 141).

[20] See Salbstein, *The Emancipation of the Jews in Britain*; Gilam, *The Emancipation of the Jews in England*.

[21] The Karaites were a medieval Jewish sect which rejected the rabbinic interpretation of the Torah. On the diffusion of neo-Karaite views in Victorian Anglo-Jewry, see Petuchowski, 'Karaite Tendencies in an Early Reform Haggadah'; Singer, 'Jewish Religious Observance'; Feldman, *Englishmen and Jews*, ch. 2.

Even if the example of the Hamburg Temple inspired Isaac Lyon Goldsmid, as is sometimes claimed,[22] it was the idea of establishing an independent synagogue and not the specific character of the reforms undertaken there that motivated him, for the ideology of German Reform cannot be found in any of the changes introduced at the West London Synagogue. Indeed, there is a consensus among Anglo-Jewish historians that the establishment of the congregation did not encompass a radical doctrinal reformulation of Judaism or a wholesale repudiation of traditional practice.

The independence of the English Reform movement from developments in Germany is also visible in the establishment of a second Reform congregation—in Manchester in 1856. Two distinct currents led to the creation of this synagogue. First, local pride and self-confidence created pressure for a greater degree of independence from the authority of the Board of Deputies and the Chief Rabbinate, both of which were under the control of the London plutocracy. Second, some of the wealthiest Jews in Manchester were of German birth and had abandoned traditional belief and practice before their arrival in England. Many of them, as we will see in Chapter 7, became Unitarians, others never affiliated with any religious body, and still others worked for a more decorous Judaism, shorn of customs they considered superstitious. This latter group spearheaded the creation of the Manchester Synagogue of British Jews; twenty-nine of the forty-six founder members were of German birth and sixteen of them were from large cities, where religious modernism was at its strongest. This evidence would seem to invalidate the claim that German influence on the transformation of Judaism in England was slight. In fact Bill Williams argued in his history of Manchester Jewry that reform there primarily represented 'the impact of currents of thought emanating from Germany'. In his view it was 'a foreign import which subsequently gained adherents from local causes'.[23]

Williams's conclusion was undoubtedly correct if he meant that the *idea* of modernizing Judaism—rather than any specific ideology of reform or set of doctrinal and liturgical innovations—was a German import, or that the success of Reform in Germany inspired German Jews in Manchester to undertake their own improvements. But it would be wrong to infer that the Manchester reformers looked to Germany for guidance in matters of doctrine and liturgy. Their model was the West London Synagogue: they adopted its prayer book and its form of public worship. The German-born foreign-language teacher Tobias Theodores, whom Williams treated as the ideologue of Reform in Manchester, appears to have been ignorant of the

---

[22] e.g. Shaftesley, 'Religious Controversies', 94–5.
[23] Williams, *The Making of Manchester Jewry*, 259–60.

historicist developmental framework of German Reform. Moreover, neither he nor any of the other founders showed any interest in denationalizing Judaism. What they wanted, above all, was freedom from the high-handed rule of London's Jewish authorities and flexibility in shaping a service that had become, in their judgement, unseemly and undignified.[24] Thus, by comparison with its ostensible counterpart in Germany, Reform Judaism in England was a tepid affair.

The appeal of Reform in England was very limited. Only three Reform congregations were founded in the nineteenth century—the ones in London and Manchester and in 1873 one in Bradford (where German Reform was influential). Few English Jews, certainly no more than 10 per cent, were attracted to Reform Judaism at any time before the Second World War.[25] Reform's failure to make headway was not due to pious loyalty to traditional standards of personal observance. Most English Jews in the Victorian era were not Orthodox Jews by the standards of Continental Orthodoxy at the time or of British Orthodoxy in the early twenty-first century. Despite this, they did not flock to Reform Judaism, in part because they did not feel any compelling need to change the public face of Judaism, namely its theology and worship service. Political pressure to universalize and denationalize Judaism was weak. English Jews did not feel that Judaism was on trial or that they had to prove their loyalty to the nation by abandoning their ethnic particularism. In addition, well-to-do Jews were reluctant to tamper with inherited patterns of public worship because of the high status that the governing class attached to religious tradition in general. The conservative nature of Orthodoxy, however nominal the Anglo-Jewish bourgeoisie's attachment to it, paralleled the conservative profile of the Church of England, while the liberal character of Reform paralleled that of Nonconformity, which did not enjoy the social status of Anglicanism. Most wealthy English Jews valued religious tradition simply because it was venerable and established. The United Synagogue and the chief rabbinate enjoyed their support because they could claim to be the Jewish counterparts of the Church of England and the archbishop of Canterbury.[26] The barrister Arthur Cohen, president of the Board of Deputies from 1874 to 1894, although not an observant Jew himself, dismissed Reform Judaism with the comment, 'I don't believe in reforms in ritual brought about by merchants and City men.'[27] The London *Jewish Chronicle*, the voice of progressive upper-middle-class Jewry, consis-

[24] Williams, *The Making of Manchester Jewry*, 247–63.

[25] Sharot, 'Reform and Liberal Judaism in London', 222.

[26] For a brief discussion of how the alleged virtues of establishment shaped the development of the United Synagogue, see Finestein, 'The Lay Leadership of the United Synagogue', 32.   [27] L. Cohen, *Arthur Cohen*, 24.

tently denounced the Reform movement in Germany. Marcus Bresslau, a frequent contributor to the Anglo-Jewish press, branded the German reformers as 'infidels, who have thrown off the burden of all religion, who discard the oral law and adopt only a few of the written laws which suit their convenience'.[28]

Despite the absence of much enthusiasm for Reform Judaism, there was interest among London congregations in the introduction of cosmetic reforms to the mode of worship. From the 1840s on, as a result of pressure from the elite who dominated communal affairs, Chief Rabbi Nathan Adler sanctioned a number of changes designed to enhance the tone of the worship service. For example, he banned young children from attending services; he forbade congregants to chatter, gossip, or leave their places during services; he ended the public sale of *mitsvot* (liturgical privileges) and limited the announcement of monetary offerings; he encouraged the introduction of all-male choirs, and in 1880 he approved the omission of most of the *piyutim* (liturgical poems). The most radical innovation he sanctioned was the institution of a divided sabbath and festival morning service to accommodate West End Jews who were inconvenienced by services that customarily began at 8 or 8.30 a.m. Adler ruled that the early service—Shaharit—might be held from 8.30 until 9.30 and that a second service—the Torah reading and Musaf (the additional service)—might follow from 11 a.m. until 1 p.m.[29]

If there was any ideological underpinning to the religious thinking of the community notables who demanded reforms such as these, it was an amorphous belief in the primacy of biblically ordained commandments over rabbinically ordained ones.[30] This bibliocentric orientation, which owed much to the pervasive bibliocentricity of English culture and to the evangelical critique of 'rabbinism', was less a crystallized doctrine than a vague tendency. With few exceptions most Anglo-Jewish notables felt that the Bible was the primary source of divine wisdom and law and that all its commandments were binding, while rabbinic traditions were not fully incumbent on modern Jews. In general they did not openly reject the oral law, but rather downplayed its significance, usually asserting that, while the rabbis of antiquity were wise and holy men, their enactments were not eternally binding and some might have to be changed to meet altered circumstances. They also believed that the chief rabbi, by virtue of his office alone, was authorized to introduce ritual changes, regardless of the halakhic status of the changes, thus investing him with power that no traditional rabbi would have claimed.

---

[28] *Hebrew Observer*, 4 Mar. 1853.
[29] Singer, 'Orthodox Judaism in Early Victorian Britain', 143–65.   [30] Ibid. 52–79.

In their view, the chief rabbi was a Jewish archbishop more than a legal scholar bound by hallowed traditions of judicial interpretation.

The fundamental reason that German Jewish patterns were not duplicated in England was the radically different political and social setting in which English Jews lived. Antipathy to Jews, while not inconsequential in England, was less pervasive and less dynamic. Substantial prejudice and insensitivity still coloured daily relations—this was true everywhere in Europe—but at the same time few Englishmen were sufficiently hostile to Jews to mobilize opposition to their integration. The presence of Jews in English society was not problematic in the way that it was in central Europe, where it served persistently as a lightning rod for social and political discontent.

The absence of well-entrenched, broad-based opposition to the entry of Jews into English society can be seen in the course of emancipation there. In the first place, the term 'emancipation' in the context of English history does not have the same meaning as it does in reference to other histories. It refers to the removal of a much narrower and less significant range of legal disabilities than on the Continent. Jews born in England after the readmission of 1656 became citizens and were entitled to most of the rights of other English men and women who were also not communicants of the Established Church. Being a second-class citizen in this way was not especially onerous. Jews, like Roman Catholics and Nonconformists, were unable to hold public office or take a degree at Oxford and Cambridge. Unlike most central and east European states, Britain lacked statutes that spelled out what was permitted and what forbidden to Jews. There were no laws, for example, barring Jews specifically from the professions or from sectors of the economy. No cities forbade Jewish settlement or limited the number of Jews who might live there. Jews in England were not aliens who had to battle for fundamental citizenship rights. The few obstacles of a legal character that they faced affected only the ambitious and the wealthy among them; they were of no consequence to the great mass of Jews since they in no way interfered with their ability to earn a living, raise a family, observe their religion, or enjoy their leisure.

Before 1829 the leaders of Anglo-Jewry made no attempt to gain full political emancipation, for they had little interest in entering government service, attending the ancient universities, or gaining admission to the Inns of Court. They were content to achieve success in commerce and finance. In the wake of the Catholic Emancipation Act of 1829, which allowed Catholics to sit in Parliament and hold public office (but did not permit them to take degrees at Oxford and Cambridge), a small circle of very wealthy Jews began to press the government to remove similar disabilities, in most cases the requirement to take a Christological oath. These men viewed their second-class political status largely as a stain on their honour, as a stigma marking them off from other propertied Englishmen. As Isaac Lyon Goldsmid told the prime minister Sir Robert Peel in 1845, the Jews 'desired to be placed on an equality in point of civil privileges with other persons dissenting from the established church not so much on account of the hardship of being excluded from particular stations of trust or honour, as on account of the far greater hardship of having a degrading stigma fastened upon us by the laws of our country'.[31] Initially, only a handful of Jewish notables supported the emancipation campaign, but over the years, as the community became more prosperous and more immersed in English life, the movement drew increasing support so that when Lionel de Rothschild took his seat in the House of Commons in 1858 it was widely regarded as a triumph for Anglo-Jewry as a whole.

Emancipation came to the Jews of England in a piecemeal fashion between 1830 and 1871. There was no single legislative struggle to remove in one fell swoop all the civil disabilities from which Jews suffered. Some fell by the wayside without legislative action. For example, in 1833 Jews became eligible to practise as barristers when the benchers of Lincoln's Inn decided that Francis Henry Goldsmid, the first Jew to present himself for admission to the bar, might take the requisite oath in a manner acceptable to his conscience, that is, omitting the Christological phrase in it. Similarly, in 1830 Jews gained the right to be admitted to the freedom of the City of London, which meant they could open retail shops within its boundaries, when the Court of Common Council ruled that they could subscribe the oaths without reference to Christianity. In other instances, legislation was necessary. In 1835, for example, Parliament enfranchised all Jews who were otherwise qualified to vote in elections; in 1845 it permitted Jews elected to municipal office to take the oaths in a form acceptable to them; in 1871 it abolished all religious tests for matriculation and graduation at Oxford and Cambridge, a measure that simultaneously benefited Nonconformists, Roman Catholics, and Jews.

In many cases legislative action followed and confirmed what had already been accomplished in practice. Jews had been voting in municipal and parliamentary elections and holding local offices for at least a decade before Parliament officially affirmed their right to do so. David Salomons and Lionel de Rothschild were each elected several times to the House of Commons (although never seated) before Parliament decided in 1858 that each

---

[31] Quoted in Gilam, *The Emancipation of the Jews in England*, 15.

house should determine the manner for swearing in its own members, a decision that broke the impasse between the Commons and the Lords over Rothschild's right to take his seat. Thus, as was so frequently the case in the history of emancipation in England, the question of Jewish participation in political life was not decided in the abstract, but rather on empirical grounds.

Although emancipation was not completed until 1871, it would be a mistake to view its delay as evidence of widespread resistance to the entry of Jews into new spheres of activity. The timing of emancipation depended in the first place on Jewish initiative, and as noted above Jews did not begin to press for the removal of the few civil disabilities affecting them until the middle decades of the nineteenth century. In most instances they succeeded in gaining what they wanted without too great a struggle. Only one issue provoked noticeable opposition: the right of Jews to sit in the House of Commons. But even in this instance the Commons, which, of course, represented a broader spectrum of public opinion than the Lords, voted to accept Jews as members as early as 1833, but was prevented by the Upper House from actually doing so until 1858.

Opposition to seating Jews in the Commons was led primarily by High Churchmen and diehard Evangelicals, who resented the political circumstances that had forced them to grant Catholics and Nonconformists their rights and were further angered by the increasing intervention of the state in church matters. After Catholic emancipation they were loath to consider any further dilution of the religious character of the state, and they accordingly blocked the entry of Jews into Parliament for almost three decades. Their opposition, however, was not representative of any widespread resistance to Jewish integration. Emancipation did not become a major issue in Victorian politics. Yes, it inspired dozens of pamphlets and editorials, but it was not a divisive or explosive question, as it was in Germany. Lord Ashley noted in 1853: 'The popular voice, to take it in the full extent of the term, is neither upon one side or the other. There is, upon the whole, a general apathy upon the question. Where any feeling is entertained in its regard, that feeling is deep and serious; but that feeling has not, however, pervaded the whole mass of the community.'[32]

Because the course of emancipation and integration in England was relatively smooth—at least by comparison with Germany—most Jews there were not under pressure to renounce traditional beliefs and loyalties. A few wealthy Jews who were active in the establishment of the West London Synagogue may have been willing to pay a price for the removal of their civil dis-

---

[32] Quoted in Salbstein, *The Emancipation of the Jews in Britain*, 235.

abilities, but they were hardly typical.[33] Most never felt called on to sacrifice their beliefs. As Abraham Gilam persuasively argued, emancipation in England was unique in European Jewish history: it was not conditional. There was no emancipation contract, no quid pro quo arrangement in which Jews swapped their particularism for membership in the English nation.[34] Parliament did not expect Jews to reform any of their beliefs or practices as a prerequisite to civic equality; in fact, Parliament took little interest in what Jews thought or how they acted in their shops, synagogues, or homes. 'Their Jewishness was taken for granted', Gilam wrote, 'whether compatible with the modern concept of nationality or not.'[35] Of course, there were pressures to make Jews conform more closely to English standards of respectability, but these were social rather than political. In contrast to Germany, statesmen and intellectuals did not look to the state to revitalize society, to reform its degenerate, wayward elements, and to prepare them for active citizenship. The social arena and the marketplace, to which Jews had access before they applied for parliamentary relief, took precedence over those areas under the tutelage of the state. The social emancipation of England's Jews preceded their legal emancipation by a half-century or more.

[33] See e.g. Francis Henry Goldsmid's remarks on the national character of the Jews in *The Arguments Advanced against the Enfranchisement of the Jews*, 13–17.

[34] I discuss this more fully in Endelman, *England—Good or Bad for the Jews?*, 12–20.

[35] Gilam, *The Emancipation of the Jews in England*, 151.

CHAPTER FOUR

Welcoming Ex-Jews into the Jewish Historiographical Fold

CONTRARY TO EXPECTATIONS, emancipation and enlightenment failed to uproot hoary views about Jewish otherness, neither erasing the stigma of Jewishness nor ushering in an era of unconditional social acceptance. Jews became 'less Jewish', but antisemitism persisted and in some contexts worsened. Some declared that this was because Jews were still 'too Jewish', claiming that their transformation was incomplete and the terms of emancipation unfulfilled. From a later vantage point, however, one wonders whether any amount of change would have sufficed to undo the legacy of centuries of Christian contempt and hostility. Historically Jews occupied a central place in the Christian imagination and, whatever their position in fact, were invariably the imaginative other, the standard by which what was Christian (and good) was measured, the collective embodiment of all manner of unpleasant and even dangerous traits, the readily available screen onto which Christians projected their fears and desires. While the Enlightenment and the scientific and industrial revolutions did much to undermine the doctrinal foundations of Christianity, which had, of course, initiated the tradition of viewing Jews as demonic outsiders, they did not eliminate the stigma attached to Jewishness. The perception that Jews were different in kind from non-Jews was too well entrenched, too rooted in Western culture and sentiment, to disappear when the religious doctrines that had engendered it in the first place weakened.

As a result, Jews everywhere, even in liberal states like Britain, France, and the United States, found that being Jewish remained problematic to one degree or another. In the best circumstances, Jews faced social discrimination and cultural stigmatization; in the worst, legal disabilities and verbal and physical violence. Most Jews in Europe and America, whether observant or not, were able to tolerate the exclusion and stigmatization that accompanied their entry into the modern world, largely because they were still embedded in Jewish social and kinship networks that nourished and satisfied their material and emotional needs. Their sense of self-worth was linked to what Jews, not non-Jews, thought of them. To be sure, the hostility of non-Jews, whatever form it took, was deeply troubling and in the late nineteenth and early twentieth centuries sparked the creation of liberal defence organizations in the West and radical political movements in the East. But, at the end of the day, for most Jews whatever intolerance persisted was tolerable.

Still, there were some Jews everywhere who were unwilling or unable to endure what they experienced as the burden of their Jewishness. Driven by hunger or ambition, in search of fame or status, peace of mind, or even just a roof over their heads, they looked to *radical* assimilation for relief, that is, they ceased to identify themselves as Jews and broke with Judaism and the Jewish community. The most common form of escape was conversion to Christianity, but there were other forms of radical assimilation as well. In liberal states, Jews were able to take Christian spouses and merge into non-Jewish circles without being baptized. In central Europe, it became possible towards the end of the nineteenth century for Jews to secede from the state-imposed *Gemeinde* without joining a Christian denomination and to declare themselves officially *konfessionslos*. Other radical assimilationists took more imaginative paths, burying their Jewishness in the cause of socialism, science, or art. Still others dreamed of or even created universalistic, non-revealed, syncretic religions, of which the Ethical Culture movement in the United States was the most successful example. Common to all these strategies was the desire to shed the taint of Jewishness, to be free once and for all of a highly charged, troublesome label.

Until the late twentieth century Jewish historians in the West wrote little about the flight from Jewishness and certainly nothing in a systematic way. They were not blind, of course, to its presence, but in their eyes it was marginal or even irrelevant to the central currents of modern Jewish history. After all, Jews who did not want to be Jews and distanced themselves from other Jews were on the periphery of communal life, if not altogether outside it. They took no part in communal affairs and stood aloof from religious and political movements to transform the Jewish people, nationalist and integrationist alike. Indeed, they were either indifferent to the future of Jewry or zealous for its demise and disappearance. A few, whom I will discuss in Chapter 6, were rabid Jew-baiters, for whom overt hostility to Jews confirmed their gentile or Christian bona fides. Most blended into non-Jewish society—or at least tried to—and never looked back. Seen from this perspective, radical assimilation falls outside the orbit of Jewish history. At best it is a footnote to the text itself. In addition, those who turned their back on Judaism were not heroic, high-minded persons, whose behaviour was exemplary or inspirational. Indeed, in the view of some antisemites, their behaviour confirmed the truth of charges of Jewish opportunism. At a time when the writing of Jewish history served ideological or apologetic ends, converts and other radical assimilationists were an embarrassment best ignored. The few exceptions were the Heinrich Heines and Benjamin Disraelis of history, whom Jewish writers and spokesmen eagerly embraced and celebrated because they were, in their view, a credit to the Jewish people. Even Heinrich Graetz (1817–91), no friend of radical assimilation, devoted an entire chapter in his multi-volume history of the Jews to Heine and Ludwig Börne, the first two sentences of which read: 'Why should not Börne and Heine have a page in Jewish history? Not only did Jewish blood flow in their veins, but they were imbued with true Jewish spirit.'[1]

When Jewish historians were unable to ignore converts they tended to write about them in morally charged terms. In their eyes, converts were marginal figures whose aberrant conduct bespoke spiritual weakness or national degeneration. Graetz, for example, vilified the salon Jewesses of Berlin, most of whom became Christians, accusing them of losing their virtue (literally) to the Prussian nobles whom they entertained. According to Graetz, the visitors to their salons, whom he described as 'the embodiment of selfishness, licentiousness, vice, and depravity',[2] corrupted and seduced them in the absence of their businessmen husbands. 'If the enemies of the Jews had designed to break the power of Israel, they could have discovered no more effectual means than infecting Jewish women with moral depravity, a plan more efficacious than that employed by the Midianites, who weakened the men by immorality.'[3] In a burst of moral indignation, he concluded that these 'talented but sinful Jewish women did Judaism a service by becoming Christians'.[4] While Graetz's condemnation was unusually harsh, his moralizing and lack of empathy were not atypical, then or now. (Nor for that matter was his misogyny.) Well into the twentieth century much that was written about those who left the fold was more judgemental than analytical. Solomon Liptzin (1901–95), writing under the influence of the total collapse of emancipation in Germany, suggested that the downfall of the salon Jewesses was their passion to be Germans, 'nothing but Germans', a passion that led them to hurl themselves 'madly, hysterically, into the arms of an overidealized German culture'. For him, the damage they did was incalculable: 'Their dangerous experiment unleashed forces that raged with undiminished intensity throughout the nineteenth and twentieth centuries.'[5] The implication was that the salon Jewesses, by virtue of the bad example

---

[1] Graetz, *History of the Jews*, v. 536.   [2] Ibid. 422.   [3] Ibid. 423.
[4] Ibid. 425.   [5] Liptzin, *Germany's Stepchildren*, 26.

they set, were responsible for the thousands of conversions that occurred in Germany in the decades that followed.

In eastern Europe Jewish historians were more attentive to the presence of converts. In the interwar period S. L. Tsitron (1860–1930), A. N. Frenk (1863–1924), Saul Ginsburg (1866–1940), and Matthias Mieses (1885– 1945) published popular, anecdotal accounts of ex-Jews who became famous— or infamous—after converting, as civil servants, industrialists, landowners, writers, intellectuals, academics, and journalists.[6] Their ranks included converts who, not content to quit Judaism, became vicious Jew-baiters, like Jacob Brafman (1825?–79), author of the most successful anti-Jewish text in Russian history, *The Book of the Kahal* (1869). They also included converts who, having won recognition outside Jewish society, used their influence to defend their former co-religionists in the press and before government officials. Here the classic example is the St Petersburg semiticist Daniel Khvolson (1819–1911), who became a legend among Russian Jews for attacking the libel that Jewish ritual required Christian blood.

With their invented dialogue, these tales were at once entertaining and moralizing. They highlighted ironic twists and tragic ends in the lives of famous converts, who came largely from the *shtetlakh* (rural Jewish communities) of the Pale of Settlement. Their message was clear: baptism failed to wash away the Jewishness of the Jew. Again and again they described how converts were unable to escape their past and shake themselves free of old associations and memories, how they carried with them, until the very end, feelings of remorse, regret, and bitterness. Like east European Jewish jokes about converts, these stories implied that the ties that bound Jews were racial and/or national as well as religious. Once a Jew, always a Jew, they suggested. Although these accounts were hostile to conversion, they were not unsympathetic to the converts whose lives they related. They praised those who became defenders of their people and celebrated the achievements of those who rose to positions of influence, claiming in a way their successes as Jewish successes, as tributes to national genius, virtue, and perseverance. However, like earlier writers, none viewed conversion in a larger sociological or historical context as a phenomenon linked to less radical forms of Jewish assimilatory behaviour. For them, as for Graetz, converts were in the end birds of a different feather, their behaviour borderline and deviant, unconnected to the behaviour of Jews who remained Jews.

The first writers to treat conversion in a scholarly way—to analyse rather than exoticize it—were the early twentieth-century founders of Jewish social

[6] Tsitron, *Behind the Curtain* (Heb.); Frenk, *Apostates in Poland in the Nineteenth Century* (Yid.); Ginsburg, *Apostates in Tsarist Russia* (Yid.); Mieses, *Z rodu żydowskiego*. Written in a similar vein but at a later date was Remba, *The Children Have Eaten Sour Grapes* (Heb.).

science—Alfred Nossig (1864–1943), Arthur Ruppin (1876–1943), Jacob
Lestschinsky (1876–1966), Ignaz Zollschan (1877–1948), Jakob Thon
(1889–1950), Bruno Blau (1881–1954), and Felix Theilhaber (1884–1956)—
whose pessimism about the diaspora we encountered earlier. Replacing
anecdotes with statistics, they addressed for the first time the quantitative
dimensions of conversion, secession, and intermarriage, thus highlighting
the experience of the well known and the obscure. Most of these early social
scientists were Zionists, for whom it was an article of faith that diaspora
Jewry was in decline and perhaps doomed to extinction. In their view, emancipation and assimilation, along with 'modernity' more generally, were
weakening the social, moral, physical, and mental health of the Jewish
nation. Intermarriage, conversion, suicide, crime, disease, mental illness,
and infertility were symptoms of this collective decay. The best known
work of this school was Theilhaber's *Der Untergang der deutschen Juden*,
which 'sent shock waves through the German Jewish community' when it
appeared in 1912 and was answered with 'a volley of criticism from all
corners of Jewish institutional life'.[7]

In the work of these researchers, the flight from Jewishness was a sign of
national degeneration. Statistical evidence of increases in conversion served
an ideological end, proving 'scientifically' that emancipation, acculturation,
and integration ('assimilation' in their vocabulary) were corroding the foundations of Jewishness. The essentialist notions of nation and race and the
medicalized tropes of disease, decay, and degeneration that were the hallmark of their analysis were very much a product of *fin-de-siècle* central European culture, and in the wake of Nazism and the Holocaust lost all currency
and disappeared from Jewish scholarship. Yet, however wrong-headed and
potentially dangerous these notions, their employment in this research
should not be allowed to mask or discredit the conceptual leap it made—the
demarginalization of conversion, intermarriage, and secession as objects of
serious study. For the pioneers of Jewish social science, disaffiliation was an
essential element in the history of Jewish responses to emancipation and its
failures. To be sure, they still viewed conversion as aberrational in the sense
that they saw it in a negative light, as a sign of collective decay and illness.
However, since they believed that diaspora Jewry as a whole was in a state of
decline, illness was no longer marginal but central to their story. In their
work, conversion was connected organically to broader assimilatory trends.
It reflected and illuminated the health of the entire nation, rather than the
moral profile of weak, ambitious, or misguided individuals.

[7] Efron, *Defenders of the Race*, 141, 144.

After the Second World War there was no immediate follow-up to this interest in conversion. In the United States, where the writing of modern Jewish history thrived from the 1970s onwards, circumstances rooted in the debate about Jewish behaviour in the Holocaust worked to discourage interest in the subject, as we saw earlier, for drift and defection were unwelcome themes in works that celebrated diaspora resilience. However, the historiographical tide was shifting in another direction as well in the last decades of the twentieth century. The ascendance of social history in the academy at a time when Jewish studies was finding a home on university and college campuses broadened and democratized the historical landscape and created space for studying Jews who did not want to be Jews. Since Jewish historians who did social history no longer saw their task as constructing an uplifting, instructive, or usable Jewish past, the inclusion of uninspiring Jews was not problematic or unthinkable.

More important than the question of how radical assimilation became historiographically respectable is the question of what is gained, from the standpoint of understanding Jewish history, by welcoming converts into the historiographical fold. In 1994, writing in the newly relaunched journal *Jewish Social Studies* about the place of deracinated artists, intellectuals, writers, and revolutionaries in modern Jewish history, Ezra Mendelsohn argued that 'the desire to abandon the physical and spiritual ghetto and to disappear into European society' was 'surely a Jewish agenda, albeit a negative one'.[8] Those who chose radical assimilation, he suggested, carried with them the baggage of their Jewishness—attitudes, values, and needs that took shape when they were Jews and reflected their stigmatized, marginalized identity at the time. Thus Mendelsohn attributed the role of the anthropologist Franz Boas (1858–1942) in combating racial thinking in the early twentieth century—at a time when it held sway in social-science research—to his origins as a Jew in imperial Germany. In this vein, Mendelsohn argued that historians and literary scholars, 'working like archeologists, can reveal "Jewish layers" of vital importance to an understanding of these people's life and work', for their careers were connected 'in certain not unimportant ways to what is called these days the "Jewish experience" '.[9]

Few would disagree with Mendelsohn. However, what he wrote was less a plea for incorporating converts into modern Jewish historiography than for incorporating their Jewishness into narratives about their achievements once they had exited the community. Highlighting Boas's German Jewish background illuminates why he was predisposed to challenge the hegemony of racial thinking. Only secondarily, by stressing the burden of a stigmatized

---

[8] Mendelsohn, 'Should We Take Notice of Berthe Weill?', 23.   [9] Ibid. 34.

identity and its enduring impact, does his approach illuminate aspects of Jewish life in imperial Germany. That is, by highlighting the pervasiveness of German antisemitism and its long-term impact on the emotional life of Jews, attention to Boas's Jewishness returns the discussion to pressures with which all Jews, converted or otherwise, well known or otherwise, contended. This understanding, however, is implicit, not explicit, in Mendelsohn's argument.

The question then remains: why welcome former Jews into the historiographical fold from which they fled? The answer, I propose, is that their flight was not a marginal phenomenon. It was not marginal in terms of numbers, since over two or three generations whole groups disappeared from the Jewish scene, including the moneyed elites who directed the affairs of the Jewish communities of the West in the eighteenth and nineteenth centuries. As I wrote in the introduction to *Radical Assimilation in English Jewish History*:

It does not take a professional knowledge of Anglo-Jewish history to realize that scores of once-prominent Jewish families ceased to be Jewish between the mid-eighteenth century and World War II. Harts, Frankses, Goldsmids, Gompertzes, Montefiores, Cohens, Jessels, Franklins, Beddingtons, and Sassoons, to name only a few examples from the Georgian and Victorian periods, disappeared from the ranks of the communal notability, some over a century ago, others more recently.[10]

While the losses due to radical assimilation in any one year were not dramatic (with a few exceptions, such as the wave of conversions during the White Terror in Hungary[11]), the demographic toll in the long term was catastrophic. To cite three examples from different national contexts. First, in England, between 1750 and 1830, the Sephardi community increased by no more than 200, despite the arrival of 3,000 Conversos from the Iberian peninsula during the eighteenth century. (I explore the reasons for this in Chapter 11.) Second, in France, a century after Napoleon convened the Parisian Sanhedrin, more than half of the descendants of its French members had ceased to be Jewish. And third, in Berlin, 44 per cent of the children of ninety-two traceable subscribers to Mendelssohn's Bible translation (1778–83) either converted or had children who converted.[12]

Nor was defection marginal in terms of its character, since it was at bottom a radical form of behaviour—acculturation and integration—that

---

[10] Endelman, *Radical Assimilation in English Jewish History*, 6.

[11] The counter-revolutionary violence that accompanied the overthrow of Béla Kun's communist government in 1919.

[12] Nordau, 'The Decadence of Judaism in France'; Lowenstein, *The Berlin Jewish Community*, 158, table 7.

was commonplace and indeed normative. True, conversion was aberrant in the sense that it transgressed religious and social norms. What should not be overlooked, however, is that it was also a link in a chain or continuum of assimilatory behaviour (the final link, to be sure). The motives and hopes of converts were neither exceptional nor eccentric, but were shared by Jews who remained Jews. Those who left the Jewish community were responding to the same set of circumstances to which other acculturated Jews were responding. What set them apart was the radical, immoderate nature of their response, their unwillingness to tolerate discrimination and stigmatization however weak or intense, their need to attain total rather than partial incorporation into the surrounding society. Their reaction to exclusion, defamation, and contempt differed in degree, not in kind, from that of other acculturated Jews.

Viewed in this light, conversion acts as an index of how Jews—or rather acculturated, upwardly mobile Jews—experienced antisemitism and obstacles to integration. (Less ambitious Jews were less vulnerable to antisemitism, since they tended to be employed in historically Jewish sectors of the economy and to socialize largely with other Jews.) This may seem at first a modest gain. After all, the history of antisemitism is not virgin territory, untouched by historical scholarship. The very opposite is true: we are 'blessed' with an abundance of articles and books on anti-Jewish discourse and anti-Jewish politics, especially for the period 1870–1939. However, one weakness of this body of work is that it takes little interest in how Jews coped with assaults on their status and character. Jewish historians have addressed this neglect, but their work on Jewish responses has focused almost exclusively on institutional and communal defence activities, the work of groups like the Centralverein deutscher Staatsbürger jüdischen Glaubens, the Anti-Defamation League, the American Jewish Committee, and the Board of Deputies. They have not addressed the critical dimension of how anti-Jewish hostility affected ordinary Jews, those who were not communal spokesmen and activists.[13] They have either ignored their reactions or at best tacitly conflated them with those of communal leaders, leaving unexplored the ways in which antisemitism unsettled everyday life, disrupting careers, derailing hopes, warping self-respect and pride. To understand and gauge the toll it took, it is necessary to address everyday as well as public life. Too often historians forget that their subjects were flesh-and-blood human beings, who were reminded continually that they belonged to a reviled and unloved minority. The indignities, small and large, that they faced, especially

[13] For example, of the twenty-two essays in Reinharz (ed.), *Living with Antisemitism*, two or three, at most, address the responses of ordinary Jews.

their encounter with malicious representations of Jews in the press, in fiction, and on the stage, left their mark on their emotional life. The study of radical assimilation in historical perspective offers access to this facet of antisemitism's impact on ordinary Jews.

It also addresses current debates about the relative strength of antisemitism in various European states. Because conversion and formal disaffiliation (in the case of central Europe) were discrete, measurable acts, comparing their incidence in different contexts reveals differences in how Jews experienced exclusion and stigmatization. Comparison highlights differences in how they assessed their situation, especially their optimism or pessimism about achieving success and happiness while remaining Jewish. Since such assessments reflected, in great measure, the ebb and flow of antisemitism, hegemonic political and cultural values, and the flexibility or inflexibility of the social structures that shaped Jewish lives, the study of radical assimilation illuminates the history of the states in which Jews lived. It identifies those cultural ideals, social structures, and political systems that allowed Jews to participate extensively in civic and social life without having to obscure or jettison their ties to Judaism and the Jewish community. Conversely, it identifies those settings in which this was difficult or altogether impossible. Comparing radical assimilation in Germany, France, Britain, and other Western states in the late nineteenth and early twentieth centuries shows that German Jews were more likely to cut their ties to the Jewish community than Jews elsewhere (the evidence for this is examined in the following chapter). This suggests, I would argue, that German Jews were more pessimistic about their future, and thus more willing to take radical measures to solve their Jewish problem. In this light, the assertion that antisemitism was more pervasive in imperial Germany than elsewhere in the West seems eminently creditable, while the opposite claim, that *fin-de-siècle* France was as antisemitic as imperial Germany, seems unconvincing.[14] After all, if the level of hostility to Jews in the two countries was similar, why was radical assimilation more widespread in Germany?

If the history of converts illuminates the experiences of both Jews and the societies in which they lived, the same is also true of what might be called the post-baptismal history of ex-Jews. Radical assimilationists assumed that

---

[14] Among those who have popularized this claim are Hannah Arendt, George Mosse, Zev Sternhell, Shulamit Volkov, and Geoff Eley. Typical, for example, is the following: 'Massive scholarship on antisemitism in France and Britain has made it abundantly clear that Imperial Germany was entirely typical in this respect [antisemitism], and in many ways provided a more hospitable social environment and political culture for Jewish assimilation or coexistence than, for instance, the France of the Third Republic at the turn of the century' (Eley, 'What Are the Contexts for German Antisemitism?', 122).

their formal break with Judaism and the Jewish community ended their connection to Jewishness and that henceforth they would make their way in the
world unencumbered by their origins. Their hopes, their faith in the efficacy
of baptism or secession, were often but not consistently disappointed. In the
way that the practice of emancipation fell short of the theory of emancipation, so too radical assimilation often failed to provide the escape it seemed to
promise. As Disraeli, Heine, Marx, and thousands of less well known converts discovered, many non-Jews continued to regard them as Jews long after
they became Christians. As Ludwig Börne, who became a Protestant in 1818,
remarked in 1832:

It's like a miracle! I've experienced it a thousand times and yet it remains eternally
new. Some people criticize me for being a Jew; others forgive me for being one; a
third even praises me for it; but all are thinking about it. They are as if caught in
this magic Jewish circle from which no one can escape.[15]

Börne's reflection on this fixation was echoed by countless others. Notions of
Jewish difference were too well established in Western thought and sentiment to be washed away at the moment of baptism. When racial thinking
became respectable in the second half of the nineteenth century, it reinforced these older notions, lending them intellectual stature and scientific
respectability.

   Moreover, as the incidence of conversion varied from country to country,
so too the fate of converts was not everywhere the same. In general, radical
assimilation was more effective in liberal settings than illiberal ones. In
France, Great Britain, and the United States, the Jewishness of former Jews
was not an insurmountable obstacle to advancement, barring their entry
into elite political and social circles. There was no central European counterpart to Benjamin Disraeli, for example. Converts less ambitious than
Disraeli were even more successful in neutralizing or obscuring their background. Who today remembers (or ever knew) that Antony Armstrong-
Jones, first earl of Snowdon and husband of Princess Margaret from 1960 to
1978, was a descendant on his mother's side of the German-born Jewish
stockbroker Ludwig Messel (1847–1915) or that the first husband of Wallis
Warfield Simpson, who married the duke of Windsor (the former Edward
VIII) in 1937, was the son of a Jewish father, whose original name was Salaman, not Simpson?[16] Thus, ironically, in those societies where conversion
was more 'necessary' and more common, it 'worked' less well than in those
societies where greater tolerance made it less 'necessary'. A striking example
of this is the resistance with which Prussian converts with Jewish-sounding

---

[15] Börne, *Briefe aus Paris*, 449–50.   [16] Castle, *Oliver Messel; Jewish Chronicle*, 28 July 1972.

names (Levy, Moses, Cohen) met when they petitioned the Ministry of the Interior to allow them to adopt more German-sounding ones.[17]

Welcoming converts into the historiographical fold is unlikely to be a popular project. For historians who write Jewish history as the story of Jewish thought and consciousness, accounting for radical assimilation is irrelevant, a trivial pursuit, and a waste of time. For those who write Jewish history to make Jews feel good about being Jewish, to inspire and congratulate them, it is irresponsible; for those who do so to celebrate working-class, feminist, or nationalist resistance to oppression, it will be disappointing, even discouraging. And for communal leaders and patrons who look to Jewish studies to make Jews more Jewish and ensure Jewish 'continuity', it is simply embarrassing. While the study of radical assimilation is unlikely to encourage disaffiliation, it is also unlikely to inspire lukewarm Jews to cultivate their Jewishness. Still, if historians wish to understand the linked phenomena of acculturation and integration in all their complexity, along with the forces and pressures that promoted and hindered them, then they must push ahead, even if that means disconnecting the writing of Jewish history from the communal and political agendas that sustained it in the past.

[17] Bering, *The Stigma of Names.*

PART II

COMPARISONS

CHAPTER FIVE

The Social and Political Context of Conversion in Germany and England 1870–1914

WITH FEW EXCEPTIONS, Jews who left Judaism in the decades before the First World War were not attracted by the spiritual truths or ethical values of Christianity. They were on the whole indifferent to religious practices and doctrines before baptism and remained so afterwards. Most had been raised in homes in which Jewish customs were not observed or in which Jewish practice was a pale version of its former self. Others gave up Jewish tradition early in life—at school or university or at the start of a career—believing it to be an unnecessary burden or an embarrassing atavism. At the baptismal font they ceased being nominal Jews and became nominal Christians instead. Their reasons for changing their religion were secular and opportunistic. Some sought to improve their social status by escaping the stigma attached to Jewishness. Others wished to make careers outside the usual range of Jewish occupations and bought their ticket of admission, in the memorable phrase of Heinrich Heine (1797–1856), with baptism. Still others, having already mixed in non-Jewish social circles, passed out of the community through intermarriage, which usually but not always was accompanied by conversion.

Although disaffiliation was a hallmark of modern Jewish history everywhere in the West, the flow out of Judaism was not equally strong in all countries and among all strata of Jewish society. Characteristic patterns of drift and defection emerged in every country or region bearing the impress of larger social and political conditions. The temptation to abandon Judaism increased in the period 1870–1914, when rising antisemitism called into question Jewish integration into state and society with unprecedented intensity. In England and Germany, states with markedly dissimilar political cultures and social systems, Jews responded to the temptation in ways reflecting these larger dissimilarities—so much so that a comparative treatment of disaffiliation in these two settings illuminates the history of state and society as much as the history of the Jewish communities there. For the willingness—or refusal—of elite circles to welcome unconverted Jews into their midst and to allow them to occupy public office testifies to their self-confidence and the elasticity of their social institutions.

At the very outset, it is important to note that in the case of England we can never know the number of Jews who formally left Judaism and became Christians in any period, and thus a straightforward statistical comparison is impossible. In England, as in the United States, membership of a religious body was voluntary, and an individual's religious affiliation was a matter of indifference to the state. The state did not monitor the passage of persons from one religion to another, nor did the Church of England, the Roman Catholic Church, or Protestant Nonconformist groups record centrally the names of Jewish converts. Thus there are no statistics on Jewish disaffiliation in England. Complicating the problem is the absence of a legally mandated, clearly demarcated communal structure (*kehilah* or *Gemeinde*). Knowing the number of Jews in England at any point in their history is itself a problem. Missionary groups occasionally published figures on the number of persons whom they converted, but these are of limited value for several reasons. First, the groups tended to inflate the number of souls they saved. Most of the Jews who accepted Jesus under their auspices were impoverished and many returned to the Jewish fold once they were on their feet again. Second, the groups worked only among the poorest strata of the Jewish community, whom they encountered on the street, in markets, and in public squares, and did not enjoy access to middle-class Jewish homes and workplaces. The figures released by missionary groups do not include conversions that took place without any assistance from them.

In Germany, on the other hand, with its centralized bureaucratic traditions, religious status and civil status were linked. The state mandated membership in a religious community, monitored religious life closely, and required those persons moving from one community to another to register their change of affiliation officially. Even those who chose to withdraw formally from the community of their birth without joining another community (this only became legally possible in 1873) were compelled to register their lack of religion. Nonetheless, even quantitative evidence about conversion in Germany is flawed—first, because conversions of children under 14 were not considered conversions and hence were not registered with the authorities and, second, because some converted adults avoided registering their change in status, despite the legal obligation to do so.[1]

---

[1] Lestschinsky, 'Apostasy in Different Lands' (Heb.), 5/8 (1911), 5; Samter, *Judentaufen*, 74; Ruppin, *The Jews of To-day*, 190.

Still, the absence of quantitative data in the English case and the flawed nature of the data in the German case are not insurmountable barriers to comparing them. Fortunately, there is an abundance of other kinds of evidence to fill out the picture. Memoirs, diaries, correspondence, sermons, newspaper and journal articles, and even novels provide sufficient information to reconstruct the nature and extent of disaffiliation, even in the absence of government data, and permit a fruitful comparison between the German and English experiences.

The most striking dissimilarity between conversion in the two communities in this period is that of magnitude. In Germany conversion was a pervasive feature of Jewish life, an item on the public agenda of communal organizations, and a subject for journalistic enquiry, sermonic condemnation, and fictional representation. In the early 1880s there were nearly 200 conversions a year; twenty years later, over 500. Relative to the size of Germany's Jewish population, which was increasing at this time, there was one conversion a year for every 2,200 Jews in the 1880s and one for every 1,100 Jews in the early 1900s. Significantly, in Berlin, the centre of German Jewry, the ratios were more dramatic: about one for every 600 to 650 Jews in the period 1882–1908.[2] These figures, however, do not tell the whole story, for they do not include converts to Catholicism (likely a small number) and children baptized by their parents (a much larger number). Felix Theilhaber estimated that at the turn of the century German Jewry was losing at least 1,000 individuals a year. While the number of conversions each year may not seem shockingly high, their cumulative demographic impact was substantial. On the eve of the First World War, alongside Germany's Jewish population of 620,000, there may have been as many as 100,000 converts and children and grandchildren of converts.[3]

In addition to those who converted, there were many who considered baptism but in the end held back, either because they did not want to create a rift with their parents, or because they realized that it would bring few benefits (this was especially true for those who were in commerce, where Jewishness was no obstacle to success), or because they considered it, in the words of Gershom Scholem's father, 'an unprincipled and servile act' at a time when antisemitism was on the rise.[4] Walther Rathenau (1867–1922), who loathed his origins and officially withdrew from the Berlin *Gemeinde* in 1895, never became a Christian, since he felt that conversion for opportunistic reasons was degrading as well as an implicit endorsement of

[2] Lestschinsky, 'Apostasy in Different Lands' (Heb.), 5/8 (1911), 5–6; 5/10 (1911), 6.
[3] Theilhaber, *Der Untergang der deutschen Juden*, 117.
[4] Scholem, *From Berlin to Jerusalem*, 11.

Prussia's discriminatory policy.[5] Arthur Ruppin (1876–1943) noted at the turn of the century: 'If numbers of men and women cannot decide to be baptized, it is not so much because of their love of Judaism as of their unwillingness to face the reproach of cowardice and treachery by deserting a minority which is in danger, and is being attacked on all sides.'[6]

One indicator of the scope of conversion was the frequency and vehemence with which communal leaders denounced it. The Centralverein deutscher Staatsbürger jüdischen Glaubens, the chief defence agency and voice of liberal integrationist opinion, mounted a scathing polemic against the *Taufjuden* (baptized Jews), who were in its eyes traitorous cowards, 'renegades who sacrifice their honor and conviction to win recognition'.[7] Committed to fostering pride and self-respect among acculturated middle-class Jews, the Centralverein denounced converts as the most dangerous enemies of Jewish survival in Germany, not only because they depleted the ranks of the community, but also because they substantiated the canard that Jews were devious opportunists. Moreover, the Centralverein leadership believed that the willingness of some Jews to convert in order to obtain public office delayed the attainment of full emancipation, since the government could claim that Jews were not being denied access to public employment at all. To counter the rising tide of baptisms, the Centralverein emphasized in its publications the positive values of Judaism and the importance of the Jews as its bearers and simultaneously how little Jews would gain by converting. In 1910 the organization became sufficiently alarmed that it began to sponsor mass meetings to denounce conversion, one of which attracted several thousand people.[8]

In England, by contrast, conversion—at least among the English-born community, as distinct from the immigrant community—was not a matter of communal concern at this time. Cries of alarm about declining synagogue attendance, neglect of the dietary laws, indifference to Jewish education, and even increasing intermarriage were heard in sermons and editorials, but conversion was not cited as a threat. In 1887 the communal worker Oswald John Simon told a missionary that while, before emancipation, some English Jews had been baptized in order to attend one of the ancient universities or enter Parliament, now when being a Jew involved 'no inconvenience to anybody' English Jews who wanted to make their mark outside the Jewish community no longer converted: 'the most pious, the most learned, the most

[5] Schorsch, *Jewish Reactions to German Anti-Semitism*, 145–6.
[6] Ruppin, *The Jews of To-day*, 194.
[7] Quoted in Schorsch, *Jewish Reactions to German Anti-Semitism*, 139.
[8] Ibid. 139–42; Reinharz, *Fatherland or Promised Land?*, 83.

cultivated, and the most enlightened remain honourably by the Covenant'.[9] The only converts in England, he explained, were recent immigrants from Germany, Russia, and Poland, where Jews grew up under different influences from those with which English Jews were familiar—which was certainly true. (Many middle-class immigrants from Germany in the Victorian period, as I explain in Chapter 7, behaved as if they were still living in Germany, that is, in a society in which Jews were subject to widespread discrimination and defamation.) Ten years later, when interviewed for Charles Booth's survey *Life and Labour of the People in London*, Chief Rabbi Hermann Adler discussed the character and extent of intermarriage but said not a word about conversion, an issue he surely would have raised if it had been a pressing concern.[10]

In his sermons, Hermann Gollancz, rabbi of the Bayswater Synagogue, frequently lamented the tendency of some wealthy Jews to discard 'what they regard as the weight of their former surroundings' and 'to withdraw from the circle of their own people, in order, as they fondly imagine, to enable them to rise yet higher in the social scale'.[11] But it is clear from the context of his remarks that he was referring not to Jews who formally became Christians, but rather to Jews who achieved prominence in English society and then ceased to take part in communal activities. In fact, Gollancz did not raise the question of conversion explicitly in his sermons until 1911, when he denounced Jews who 'leave the brotherhood to which they belong, and label themselves with a religious connexion in which they cannot possibly have any faith'.[12] Yet, in surveying the progress of Anglo-Jewry in the journal *Nineteenth Century* the following year, Lewis S. Benjamin stated confidently that 'the number of Jewish converts is so small as to be immaterial'.[13] Clearly, while conversions did occur in the years before the First World War, they were not numerous enough to be considered a threat to communal solidarity, certainly not in the way they were in Germany, where rabbis and lay leaders publicly bemoaned their increase.

The pervasiveness of conversion in Germany is best viewed against the backdrop of the illiberalism of the imperial period, especially the advance of antisemitism from the mid-1870s and the willingness of the state to ignore constitutional guarantees of equality and tolerate widespread occupational discrimination in the public sector. The impact of discrimination and defamation on the consciousness and behaviour of German Jews cannot be

---

[9] Simon, *Correspondence*, 15–16.
[10] Interview with Hermann Adler, Charles Booth Collection, file B197, 17.
[11] Gollancz, *Sermons and Addresses*, 1st ser., 190.
[12] Gollancz, *Sermons and Addresses*, 2nd ser., 108.
[13] Benjamin, 'The Passing of the English Jews', 502.

overemphasized. Neither affluence nor intellect could spare them the pain of knowing that Jews and Judaism were viewed with contempt and disdain. Walther Rathenau, who belonged to the most privileged stratum of German Jewry and was thus sheltered from the taunts of street-corner Jew-baiters, nevertheless experienced antisemitism in an immediate, personal way. As he wrote in 1911: 'In the years of his youth there is a painful moment for every German Jew that he remembers for the whole of his life—when he is struck for the first time by the consciousness that he has entered the world as a second-class citizen and that no ability and no merit can liberate him from this situation.'[14] For Theodor Lessing (1872–1933), who grew up without any consciousness of his ethnic origins, this moment came one day in school when he joined his classmates in taunting the other Jewish students only to be told that he was one himself. He later recalled that he had become convinced that being Jewish was something evil because he had absorbed all the religious prejudices of his schoolmates and had had no training at home to counterbalance them. He became a Protestant at the age of 23, although later, under the influence of Zionism, he embraced his Jewish origins.[15]

Most converts in Germany were young people whose nominal attachment to Judaism imposed obstacles, immediate or potential, to their social and professional advancement. Men intending to enter occupations outside those in which Jews had traditionally been concentrated were more likely to convert than those who followed their fathers into business. This was particularly the case in the public sector, where discrimination was rife. In Berlin, for example, in the period 1873–1906, university students constituted 36 per cent of converts whose occupational status was known.[16] In some Jewish families in imperial Germany, the son interested in a career in the academy or civil service converted, while the son entering the family business remained Jewish.[17] In many cases, young men deserted Judaism before encountering specific obstacles to their advancement. They acted instead on the reasonable expectation that whatever career path they chose they would fare better as Christians than as Jews. Richard Lichtheim, a prominent figure in Zionism before the Second World War, recalled how when he was 14 his father, a prosperous Berlin grain broker, had asked him

---

[14] Rathenau, 'Staat und Judentum', 188–9.

[15] L. Baron, 'Theodor Lessing', 325–6. Non-Jews also commented on the pervasiveness of antisemitism in imperial Germany. Thus, Nietzsche wrote: 'I have never yet met a German who might have been well disposed to Jews; and however unconditionally all careful and political people may reject real anti-Semitism, even their care and politics are really not directed at the type of feeling per se, but rather at its dangerous extremes, especially if these extreme feelings are expressed reprehensively or tastelessly—we must not deceive ourselves about that' (Nietzsche, *Beyond Good and Evil*, 141–2).   [16] Ruppin, *The Jews of To-day*, 194.

[17] See e.g. Fraenkel, *Lebenskreise*, 97; Baker, *Days of Sorrow and Pain*, 96.

if he wanted to convert. Most of his father's relatives had become Christians—some had been Christians for two generations—but his father had rejected conversion as undignified. (In any case, being Jewish was no obstacle to success on the Berlin grain bourse, where most of the brokers were Jewish.) By the turn of the century, however, his father was less sanguine about the future than he had once been and his diminishing sense of security led him to propose baptism to his son, who after all might want to enter a 'less Jewish' sector of the economy.[18]

In many instances parents who remained Jewish had their children baptized at an early age, without regard to their future prospects, hoping simply to spare them unnecessary unpleasantness later in life. Felix Theilhaber estimated that between 1 and 2 per cent of all Jewish children born in Germany in any year between 1880 and 1910 were baptized.[19] The *Allgemeine Israelitische Wochenschrift* reported in 1898, for example, that of the ten or so Jewish professors at the University of Strasbourg—none of whom were baptized—not one had failed to baptize his children.[20] They, like other German Jewish parents, sought to protect their children, boys and girls alike, from humiliation and insults as they grew up and to ease their way later as adults when they made their way in the world. In Heinrich Graetz's 'Correspondence of an English Lady on Judaism and Semitism' (1883), a Jewish mother who urges Jews to baptize their children asks in anguish:

Should we expose them to the ridicule of their classmates and to the spiteful allusions of teachers who fancy themselves comic with their Jewish intonation? Should our sons be barked at in the army by some coarse sergeant or some insolent boor of a second lieutenant simply because they are Jews? Should they fulfill their military service conscientiously, only to be discriminated against? Should our daughters who attend a public ball, even if graced with physical and spiritual charm and impeccably and modestly dressed, be scorned by geese with crosses on their breasts, avoided by men and forced into a gloomy corner?[21]

In some instances Jewish men already launched on their careers were required to convert in order to obtain posts that would have remained closed to them. Conversions of this kind were especially common in academic life. Government and university officials made it quite clear to Jewish *Privatdozenten* that promotion without baptism was nearly impossible. The organic chemist and Nobel laureate Richard Willstätter recalled that his mentor Adolf von Baeyer repeatedly urged him after his *Habilitation* to get himself baptized in order to advance his career. He refused because he

[18] Lichtheim, *A Remnant Shall Return* (Heb.), 19.
[19] Theilhaber, *Der Untergang der deutschen Juden*, 118.
[20] Samter, *Judentaufen*, 80.   [21] Graetz, 'The Correspondence of an English Lady', 192.

thought that conversion for personal advantage, without religious belief, was improper.[22] When *Privatdozent* Harry Bresslau, a medieval historian, complained to Leopold von Ranke that his religion was hindering his career, Ranke flatly advised him to become a Christian. Bresslau rejected the advice, according to his granddaughter, because 'his pride and dignity would never let him take a step that might seem to have been motivated by expediency'.[23] He succeeded, nonetheless, in obtaining a professorship in 1890—not at a venerable German university, however, but at Strasbourg, which was professionally and geographically on the periphery of German academic life. Like the other unconverted Jewish professors there, Bresslau baptized his children (one of whom later married Albert Schweitzer) in the hope of sparing them the anguish he had endured.[24]

Bresslau's success was unusual. In general, unconverted Jews became full professors less often than baptized ones. At the University of Berlin, in the academic year 1909–10, there were 70 Jews, 31 baptized Jews, and 147 Christians at the rank of *Privatdozent*, while at the rank of full professor, there were no unconverted Jews, 5 baptized Jews, and 80 Christians. The career of the theoretical physicist Felix Auerbach well illustrates the burden that Jewishness posed in university life. Auerbach spent the first ten years of his academic life as a *Privatdozent* at Breslau, where his work brought him considerable attention. When the University of Jena established an associate professorship in theoretical physics in 1889, he was a candidate. Worried that antisemitism might derail his appointment, his sponsors took extra measures to gather supporting materials. Auerbach received the appointment, but was then repeatedly passed over for promotion to full professor until 1923, after the fall of the empire. It took him forty-four years after his *Habilitation* to reach a position that the average full professor reached in less than half that time.[25]

Conversion patterns among Jewish women in Germany were different from those among men, since the latter were more likely to have careers, and thus run head-on into discrimination. Most women, at least before the First World War, remained enclosed in a private network of family and close friends, cut off from the social and occupational temptations that led to conversion. However, some groups of women led lives that took them beyond these confines and chose to leave Judaism. Women in the lower middle class increasingly entered into paid employment in the late nineteenth and early twentieth centuries—as clerks, teachers, domestics, milliners, and dressmakers—and some of them found that conversion aided them in finding a

[22] Willstätter, *From My Life*, 83–4.
[23] Brabazon, *Alfred Schweitzer*, 153.   [24] Meinecke, *Strassburg, Freiburg, Berlin*, 27.
[25] Preston, 'The German Jews in Secular Education', 109–10.

position. Thus, in Berlin, the share of women in the total number of conversions rose considerably in this period. In the decade 1873–82 women accounted for only 7 per cent of those converting; by 1908, 37 per cent; and by 1912, 40 per cent. Since 84 per cent of female converts in Berlin in the period 1873–1906 were from the lowest income groups, the increase in the share of women in the total number of conversions was clearly due to greater numbers of women from the lower middle class leaving Judaism.[26]

At the other end of the social scale, women from the wealthiest German Jewish families were also exposed to the temptation to leave Judaism. Here the yearning of social advancement led parents to arrange marriages for their daughters with Christian noblemen.[27] These nuptials, remarked the English novelist Cecily Sidgwick, who was herself of German Jewish stock and an astute observer of the German scene, 'are just as business-like as if the *Schadchan* [matchmaker] had arranged them and received his commission. The Graf or the Major gets the gold he lacks, and the rich Jewess gets social prestige or the nearest approach to it possible in a Jew-baiting land.'[28] While unions such as these were not as common as anecdotal evidence suggests,[29] when they did occur, inevitably the Jewish wife converted. It was inconceivable that she would remain even nominally Jewish. Her noble husband would not have tolerated it, and she would not have desired it. After all, the rationale for the match was the erasure of her origins. (In England, by contrast, Rothschild and Bischoffsheim daughters married into titled families without changing their religion.[30]) This erasure, which was never complete, of course, was more easily achieved with daughters than with sons. Daughters took their husbands' names and titles, becoming *Gräfin* or *Freifrau*, while sons tended 'to "drag down" their aristocratic wives into embourgeoisement'.[31] Parents who arranged these matches knew that they could do little to improve their own social standing; their Jewish background and milieu were simply too obvious. Instead they hoped to enhance their daughters' long-term chances for success by acquiring for them high-ranking husbands of the Christian faith.

This longing for integration into the feudalized ruling class was most intense at the very summit of German Jewish society. There, Sidgwick noted, 'you have the spectacle . . . of Jews seeking Christian society instead of

[26] Lestschinsky, 'Apostasy in Different Lands' (Heb.), 5/11 (1911), 6; M. A. Kaplan, 'Tradition and Transition', 18.

[27] See the examples in L. Cecil, 'Jew and Junker in Imperial Berlin'.

[28] Sidgwick, *Home Life in Germany*, 80.   [29] M. A. Kaplan, 'Tradition and Transition', 16.

[30] Endelman, *Radical Assimilation in English Jewish History*, 89–92.

[31] W. E. Mosse, *The German-Jewish Economic Elite*, 183. In discussing the marriage strategies of the German Jewish elite, Mosse also stresses intergenerational and regional variations.

avoiding it; and you hear them boast quite artlessly of their *christlicher Umgang* [Christian acquaintances]'.[32] Young men and women whose families had arrived at the top a generation or two earlier usually abandoned Judaism. Perhaps the most notable example in this period can be found in the three generations of the Bleichröder family. The founder of the family banking firm, Samuel Bleichröder (1779–1855), embarked on the road to fortune as a money changer and lottery agent in Berlin during the Napoleonic Wars, expanding only a few years later into merchant banking. Success and prosperity came his way after he became the principal agent in Berlin for the Rothschilds in the 1830s. His son Gerson (1822–93), who became senior partner in the bank on the death of Samuel, built the firm into one of the richest and most important in Germany, largely because of his personal connections with Bismarck. When Gerson died he was the richest man in Berlin and perhaps in Germany, his only rival for the title being Alfred Krupp. Where Samuel's energies and ambitions had been focused almost entirely on the family business, Gerson's were divided. Unlike his father, he aspired to recognition and acceptance in a world beyond the Jewish and banking communities. Yet, while Gerson took little active interest in communal affairs, he remained a Jew. From time to time, reports appeared in the press that he was about to convert, but they always turned out to be false. However strongly he craved entry into aristocratic society, he had sense enough to realize that even as a Christian he would still be regarded as a parvenu Jew. His children, however, who had moved in gilded circles from their youth and been exposed to wider horizons than their father, set their sights even higher: exclusive duelling fraternities, elegant army regiments, smart casinos and clubs, membership in the landed aristocracy. All of Gerson's children became Protestants and married out. His three sons, whom he took into the business, inherited none of his financial acumen and ended up as layabouts and womanizers—decadent, debauched, and useless.[33]

Those groups within German Jewry in which conversion was least common were those with little desire or opportunity for intensive contacts outside Jewish circles. Jewish grain brokers, timber merchants, and leather-goods manufacturers, whose closest associates were Jewish businessmen like themselves, were thus less likely to leave the community than Jewish journalists or civil servants. The latter not only moved in non-Jewish company to a greater degree, but were also more exposed to discrimination and defamation. Similarly, university-educated, upper-middle-class Berliners were more likely to cut their ties to Judaism than provincial shopkeepers and

---

[32] Sidgwick, *Home Life in Germany*, 323.
[33] F. Stern, *Gold and Iron*; Landes, 'Bleichröders and Rothschilds'.

merchants with more limited social horizons. In his memoirs Richard Willstätter highlighted this distinction by contrasting his own attitude towards conversion with that of his teacher, Adolf von Baeyer, whose mother was the daughter of a prominent converted Jew. Baeyer, he pointed out, 'stemmed from the exceptional environment in Berlin, in which, favored by the government, a mingling of Jews and Christians took place to a considerable extent during the last century'. He 'represented the principle of assimilation, the absorption of established and more highly developed Jewry into the State religion and the leading stratum of society'. In contrast, Willstätter, whose father was a textile merchant in Karlsruhe, 'came from a smaller, socially limited provincial circle which was liberal in religion but conservative in its adherence to Judaism'. In his circle the accepted escape from antisemitism for persons 'desiring freer and greater development' was not conversion but emigration to the United States or Great Britain.[34] Here local standards, as well as social expectations and aspirations, influenced patterns of conversion.

Whatever their social background, almost all converts in Germany were motivated by worldly considerations: a desire to improve their social standing, advance their careers, or escape the emotional burden of belonging to a besieged minority. In all but a few cases spiritual issues and doctrinal truths were irrelevant. Nominal Jews became nominal Christians. As Fritz Mauthner noted, while it was not impossible that a Jew might become a Christian out of conviction, he for one had never seen such a case. In his experience, expediency brought the overwhelming majority of adult converts to profess their belief in Christianity.[35] However, because both antisemites and observant Jews accused converts of opportunism and careerism, a few of them, mostly intellectuals, went out of their way to attribute their conversion to lofty, though essentially non-religious, motives. Maximilian Harden (né Felix Ernst Witkowski) claimed that he had adopted Christianity because it had seemed to him 'the way of life corresponding to the higher culture'.[36] The Nobel laureate chemist Fritz Haber also claimed that his conversion, while a student, was essentially a matter of demonstrating his cultural allegiance to the German people. He felt thoroughly German and was alienated from Jewish practices and beliefs; since Christianity in Germany was, in his view, no more than a cultural community and his formal attachment to Judaism the last barrier separating him from other Germans, he became a Christian.[37] Claims such as these are, of course, difficult to evaluate. Without doubt, Harden, Haber, and others sincerely preferred *Deutschtum* to

---

[34] Willstätter, *From My Life*, 18, 83. [35] Mauthner, in Landsberger (ed.), *Judentaufen*, 76.
[36] Young, *Maximilian Harden*, 12. [37] R. Stern, 'Fritz Haber', 88.

Judentum, and were convinced that they were not motivated by ambition, greed, or cowardice. At the same time, however, it is difficult to suppress the feeling that beneath the disinterested rationales they offered there lurked more pragmatic needs, which at a conscious level they may not have been able to face. In any case, they must have known that, whatever motives they cited, baptism would bring in its wake certain concrete advantages.

In Anglo-Jewry during this period there were few parallels to the patterns of conversion that were characteristic of German Jewry. As we have seen, conversion from Judaism to Christianity among native English Jews was infrequent. It would be convenient to attribute this to the superior moral character of English Jews, who by comparison with their German brethren appear to have been less opportunistic and more steadfast in their loyalties. However, there is no reason to believe that English Jews were any less eager to get on in the world than German Jews. What was different was the nexus of social and political circumstances in which they strove to do so.

In England, as I explained in the previous chapter, antipathy to Jews was less virulent than in Germany. The Jewish Question occupied a less prominent place in political and cultural life, in public affairs and social arrangements, in schooling and careers, although in the last ten years or so before the outbreak of the First World War this was beginning to change. In 1913, for example, Claude Montefiore noted that it was less easy for Jews to get into certain clubs than it had been six or seven years earlier. Still, for most of the period 1870–1914, English Jews by and large were spared the pervasive and constant disparagement of everything Jewish that so unsettled German Jews.[38]

This is not to say that antipathy to Jews in England was negligible. Expressions of suspicion and hostility were voiced at all levels of society. Caricaturists, novelists, and dramatists employed unflattering stereotypes of Jews in their work; preachers, politicians, and journalists disparaged Jews as sharpers and cheats, aliens and outsiders, and even as the traditional blaspheming enemies of Christendom. Jewish boys in the best public schools were made aware that they were different from their schoolmates. Jawaharlal Nehru, who entered Harrow in 1905, recalled that although the Jews there 'got on fairly well . . . there was always a background of anti-Semitic feeling'. They were 'the damned Jews'.[39] Charles de Rothschild, who was at Harrow a decade earlier, looked back on his years there with much unhappiness. As he

[38] Montefiore, who was not quick to acknowledge the existence of antisemitism in England, made this remark at an annual meeting of the Anglo-Jewish Association following a lecture on the topic by Morris Joseph (*Jewish Chronicle,* 4 July 1913).

[39] Nehru, *An Autobiography,* 18.

later told a friend, 'If I ever have a son he will be instructed in boxing and jiu-jitsu before he enters school, as Jew hunts such as I experienced are a very one-sided amusement, and there is apt to be a lack of sympathy between the hunters and hunted.'[40] Leonard Woolf, who was at St Paul's in the 1890s, told Malcolm Muggeridge that it was at school that he realized for the first time 'that it wasn't merely that my religion was Jewish and somebody else's was Mohammedan' and that it was there that he developed the carapace that protected him from slights and slurs throughout his life.[41]

In less exclusive circles as well, Jews encountered prejudice. A young Jewish journalist in Leonard Merrick's novel *Violet Moses* (1891) admits that 'there *is* a difficulty about admitting oneself a Jew' because 'one is always afraid the genial faces will harden and the cheery smiles grow chilly, and fade away—we have seen it so often'. Christians might aver that their prejudice had disappeared and Jews might try to persuade themselves that indeed it had, but in the view of Merrick's Jewish journalist 'it is all rubbish'.[42] Woolf captured this kind of casual social antisemitism in his *roman-à-clef, The Wise Virgins* (1914), an account of his courtship of Virginia. The Jewish Davises (Woolfs), newly moved to Richstead (Putney), discover that it is not raw anti-semitism that blocks their inclusion in suburban society, where 'everyone is open-minded nowadays, and liberal-minded too', but rather 'a very natural feeling that people should, like decent Christians, sometimes have a racket in their hands on weekdays and a prayer-book on Sundays'.[43]

In comparison with anti-Jewish hostility in Germany, however, English prejudice was an irritant rather than a cancer. This was certainly the perception of contemporary observers who compared the lot of Jews in both countries. In 1908 Cecily Sidgwick noted that the 'the social crusade against Jews is carried on in Germany to an extent we do not dream of here' in England. 'The Christian clubs and hostels exclude them, Christian families avoid them, and Christian insults are offered to them from the day of their birth.' German girls who wanted to invite a Jewish schoolmate to a dance 'discovered that their Christian friends flatly refused to meet anyone of her race'.[44] On the other hand, noted the travel writer Sir John Foster Fraser in 1915, 'nowhere does the Jew receive better treatment than in Great Britain'.[45] English men and women were hardly free of antipathies, but they did not feel strongly enough about them to translate them into a system of defamation and discrimination. The poet Humbert Wolfe characterized the anti-semitism of the pre-war years as largely a matter of 'exclusion from

---

[40] Quoted in Rothschild, *Dear Lord Rothschild*, 90.
[41] Quoted in Glendinning, *Leonard Woolf*, 35–6.
[42] Merrick, *Violet Moses*, i. 151.
[43] Woolf, *The Wise Virgins*, 123.
[44] Sidgwick, *Home Life in Germany*, 319.
[45] Fraser, *The Conquering Jew*, 114.

garden-parties, refusal of certain cherished intimacies and occasional light-hearted sneers'. The 'easy-going and good-humoured English', he explained, 'couldn't be bothered to carry things to extremes', which is not to deny that exclusions and sneers took an emotional toll.[46] One contemporary summed up the difference between the two countries with the observation that 'the Anglo-Saxon has a more robust confidence than the German in his powers and destiny, and does not feel the need of bolstering up his self-esteem by running down the Jews'.[47]

Comments like these over-egged the pudding. They ignored the role of antisemitism in the anti-immigration agitation of the period, which culminated in the passage of the Aliens Act of 1906, and in Liberal and Radical opposition to the Boer War. Nonetheless, they tell us something significant: the antisemitism encountered by English Jews was more often than not social rather than political or occupational. In most cases it lacked political resonance. It did not breed political parties and pressure groups, or become a permanent feature of conservative political thinking. Critically, it never erupted into a public campaign to cancel emancipation and reverse the tide of integration.

The character of antisemitism in England does not alone account for the weakness of disaffiliation in Anglo-Jewry. The occupational structure of the community also contributed to reducing the pressure to convert. With some exceptions, native English Jews were to be found in commerce and finance, not in the professions, the civil service, the academy, and the arts (although this was beginning to change after 1870).[48] The small number of Jews in these areas was not primarily the result of obstacles to their entry, but rather of the absence of incentives to abandon the activities they had customarily pursued. (Earlier, in the mid-Victorian period, when English Jews attempted to enter professions like the Bar from which the requirement of taking a Christological oath barred them, they found that the resistance to their entry was either easily overcome or conveniently circumvented.) Commerce and finance in England did not suffer the same opprobrium that they did in Germany, where capitalism and Jews, which were consistently linked in the public imagination, were held responsible for all the ills of the modern world. In the absence of this anti-capitalist ethos, Anglo-Jewish sons tended to follow the occupational paths of their fathers and grandfathers. The acquisition of wealth in the City did not preclude social respectability. There was no massive 'hemorrhage of ability', in Martin Wiener's phrase, out of commerce and finance in pursuit of occupations considered more prestigious in other

---

[46] Wolfe, *Now a Stranger*, 125–6.   [47] Simon, 'Anti-Semitism in England', 298.
[48] Pollins, *Economic History of the Jews in England*, ch. 11; Cooper, *Pride versus Prejudice*.

national contexts.[49] Stefan Zweig, who was more German than he thought, claimed that something 'subconscious' in 'the Jew' (that is, in Jews everywhere) sought 'to escape the morally dubious, the distasteful, the petty, the unspiritual, which is attached to all trade, and all that is purely business', and that this explained why 'the impulse to wealth' was exhausted in two or three generations within one family. However, the one English example he cited (Walter Rothschild) undermines his claim that this was the case everywhere. True, the second Lord Rothschild was an outstanding naturalist, but he also spent eighteen years in the family bank in New Court before escaping to his beloved collections at Tring. As a rule, male members of the English branch of the Rothschild clan experienced no 'subconscious impulse to free themselves of cold money-making'.[50] In England, then, most young Jewish men remained in occupations where their closest associates in the day-to-day routine of business were very likely Jews. In such circumstances, not only would conversion have been of little utility, it would have been a distinct liability.

Because most Jewish men remained within the orbit of traditional Jewish occupations, few sought or received a university education before the turn of the century. When the future geneticist Redcliffe Nathan Salaman was an undergraduate at Cambridge in the mid-1890s, he later recalled, there were at most a dozen Jewish students, all sons of well-to-do and generally long-established families. In 1906 the head of Christ Church, Oxford, estimated that there had not been more than half a dozen Jews at the college in the previous ten years. And six years later, according to Basil Henriques, there were only thirty Jewish undergraduates in all the Oxford colleges.[51] This indifference to higher education stemmed from the absence of any significant material or social benefits to be gained from attendance at university. (A public school education was more socially beneficial; most public school boys, however, did not go on to university.) A university degree not only did not prepare English Jews for careers they were likely to follow, it also did not confer status in the way that a degree in Germany did. There the university degree was a passport into the mainstream of national life for young Jewish men. It was both a prerequisite for high-status bureaucratic and professional positions and a testimony to the degree-holders' devotion to and mastery of German culture and science. Since English universities did not perform these functions, the sons of the Anglo-Jewish middle class, with a few exceptions, were

[49] Wiener, *English Culture and the Decline of the Industrial Spirit*, 145.

[50] Zweig, *The World of Yesterday*, 20–1.

[51] R. N. Salaman, *Whither Lucien Wolf's Anglo-Jewish Community?*, 17; Israel Rubinowitz to Herbert Bentwich, 17 Dec. 1906, Herbert Bentwich Papers, A100/7א/20; Rose Henriques, unpublished biography of Basil Henriques, ch. 8, Basil Henriques Papers AJ/195.

spared exposure to cultural and social influences that could have weakened their Jewish attachments.

If conversion from Judaism to Christianity was rare in England, marriages between Jews and Christians (that is, with neither partner converting) were much less so. Although no statistical data exist, it is clear from other kinds of evidence that intermarriage was increasing throughout this period at several levels of Anglo-Jewry. *Jewish Society*, a London weekly that appeared for nine months in 1890, printed during its short life a number of articles and a stream of letters on the causes of intermarriage. In its first number it observed that Jewish parents had become so terrified that their daughters would marry out that they were offering enormous dowries to secure them Jewish husbands.[52] In 1895 Hermann Gollancz deplored the increase of mixed marriages in a sabbath sermon at the Bayswater Synagogue, and in another sermon three years later denounced wealthy Jews who identified themselves so slightly with the Jewish community that their children intermarried while their parents were still alive.[53] Marriages between Jews and Christians are a central feature in novels from the period, such as Julia Frankau's *Dr. Phillips* (1887), Leonard Merrick's *Violet Moses*, and Leonard Woolf's *The Wise Virgins*, as well as Israel Zangwill's drama *The Melting Pot* (1908). Describing Leopold Moses' marriage to Violet Dyas, Leonard Merrick comments: 'Religious scruples did not weigh with him an atom, nor social ones. Maida Vale [an area of middle-class Jewish settlement in north-west London, less exclusive than Bayswater or Kensington] was growing used to mixed marriages.'[54]

Communal leaders considered such marriages a form of apostasy, since the offspring of these unions were almost always reared as Christians, and eventually merged into English society. Although such marriages resulted in the loss to Judaism of the children, and hence might seem to resemble instances in which Jewish couples baptized their children, as frequently occurred in Germany, the circumstances surrounding these two types of radical assimilation differed significantly. In the former instance, intermarriage was the outcome of a high degree of prior social contact between Jews and Christians. Generally, such unions were not arranged by parents, but were rather the consequence of unregulated social mixing—at dances, in drawing rooms, at seaside resorts, and so on. Indeed, one contemporary quipped that it was only in mixed marriages that romance played any part—it was only then that 'Israel worships at the feet of Venus'.[55] In the latter case, the decision to baptize the children was the result of the absence of successful social

---

[52] *Jewish Society*, 31 Jan. 1890.   [53] Gollancz, *Sermons and Addresses*, 1st ser., 99, 190.
[54] Merrick, *Violet Moses*, ii. 79.   [55] *Jewish Society*, 10 Sept. 1890.

integration. As Christians, it was hoped, the children would find fewer obstacles to success when they had to make their way in a society actively hostile to Jews. To put the comparison crudely, Jews in England were ceasing to be Jewish because resistance to their incorporation into society was weak; in Germany, their ties to Judaism were being sundered because resistance was strong.

Yet it would be misleading to suggest that there were no similarities between Jewish behaviour in the two countries. Although less numerous than in Germany, there were at various levels of the Anglo-Jewish middle class religiously indifferent persons eager to move beyond their own community who believed that their Jewishness impeded their social ascent. Simeon Singer, rabbi of the fashionable New West End Synagogue, described such persons in a sabbath sermon in 1905 as:

Those who measure their success in life by the distance to which they are able to withdraw themselves from all Jewish associations, and by the force with which they can attach themselves to those who are not of their own people . . . The highest rung in the ladder of their ambition is reached when they are able to say that they have rid themselves of all Jewish consciousness, and are merged body and soul among the Gentiles, by whom they are surrounded.'[56]

In these instances, it was not the existence of specific barriers that prompted the flight from Jewishness but rather the belief that Jewishness was a burden not worth bearing as long as Jews were viewed with suspicion or contempt by some Englishmen. In other words, there were persons whose social aspirations or emotional make-up could not tolerate even the low levels of hostility directed towards Jews in England. For example, the stockbroker Edward William Meyerstein and his wife, who were not practising Jews, made their children Anglicans when their son was about to enter Harrow, although such a step was not necessary for admission—the sons of several prominent Jewish families were students there at the time. In fact, young Meyerstein's status as a convert made his years at Harrow more unbearable than if he had remained unconverted. Much later he recalled that while a Jewish boy who was proud of his religion and confident that he was as good as his schoolmates could get through school successfully, one who had been baptized, especially if he had a German name, was 'due for hell'. Boys, he concluded, 'like to know what a thing is'.[57] For reasons that I will explain in Chapter 7, conversions like these were more likely to occur in families of German origin who settled in England in the course of the Victorian period than in

[56] Singer, *Literary Remains*, i. 254–5.   [57] Meyerstein, *Some Letters*, 240–1.

families whose roots in England went back to the eighteenth or early nineteenth centuries.

The one other section of the community in which conversion was common enough to attract comment during this period was the rapidly growing east European immigrant population. The motives for conversion among recent immigrants were unrelated to the willingness or refusal of the host society to absorb Jews, as was the case with the native community. When immigrants or their English-born children became Christians—and they did so by the hundreds during this period—it was poverty above all that formed the background to their conversion. Christian missions to the Jews worked almost exclusively among the poorest stratum of the Jewish community (middle-class Jews were beyond their reach). More than a dozen missionary organizations operated in the East End of London, for example, offering a wide range of free social services to the newcomers—medical care, reading rooms, vocational training, youth clubs, and country holidays, as well as food, clothing, and even occasional help with the rent—with the aim, of course, of establishing a relationship that would lead to their baptism.

Thousands of immigrants took advantage of conversionist largesse because the aid that communal agencies provided was inadequate. The free library offered them 'a comfortable, cheerfully warmed and lighted room' stocked with newspapers in Yiddish and other languages, as well as abundant conversionist literature, and was 'presided over by quondam professors of Judaism, who are always at hand and ready to assist "enquirers" '. At the medical mission, they were given prompt attention and not kept waiting for hours; they could speak directly to doctors who understood them and dispensed medicines plentifully and without cost.[58] Most of those who availed themselves of this aid remained Jewish; some, however, became Christians, although whether they remained Christians is difficult to say. There were clearly immigrants who changed their religion largely to obtain aid and later returned to Judaism. A handful even supported themselves in a fashion by repeatedly converting or expressing their desire to do so, such as one unnamed Jew who was described in 1894 by the Reverend J. M. Eppstein (himself a convert) as 'an out-and-out rascal' for running away from the Wanderers' Home for Enquiring and Relieving Jews in Bristol on Christmas Day 'after enjoying a good dinner and taking with him his Christmas presents'.[59]

---

[58] Singer, *Conversionist Activity*, 4.
[59] J. M. Eppstein to Lukyn A. Williams, 29 Dec. 1894, letters of enquiry from Jews to the head of the London mission, 1890–1895, Church Mission to the Jews Collection, Dep. CMJ c. 107.

In Germany Christian missionizing among immigrant Jews was minimal. In part, this was due to the weakness of the missionary impulse there. The Berlin theologian Paulus Cassel, a former Jew, thought that the majority of Christians in the German capital were heathens without any sense of religion. German pastors, he told a group of visiting English clergymen in 1886, had no interest in missions to the Jews. They were content to preach in favour of their conversion, but unwilling to exert themselves in any other way.[60] A representative from the London Society for Promoting Christianity among the Jews who surveyed the state of missionary interest in Germany four years later also concluded that 'German Christians as a whole can hardly be said to take a warm interest in the conversion of the Jews'. He further noted that the German Evangelical Church employed only four missionaries to work among Jews and two of them were not so much actual missionaries as agents and secretaries attempting to arouse public interest in the work. The mission at Hamburg, for example, a major port of embarkation for migrants to the United States, was operated by Irish Presbyterians.[61]

Public apathy about Jewish missions also reflects the absence of a large, concentrated immigrant community, such as developed in London's East End, although Germany was better suited economically and geographically to receive migrants from eastern Europe. The German authorities took active measures to prevent the growth of an immigrant Jewish community, for if they considered Jews born in Germany to be problematic how much more so did they consider Jews born in the half-civilized Slavic East? Accordingly, the imperial and state governments prevented Jewish aliens from settling in the country in large numbers. By discriminating against Jewish applicants for residence permits and naturalization, by harassing immigrants for real and imagined offences, and finally by periodically expelling so-called burdensome Jews, Germany reduced the numbers who attempted to settle there while simultaneously discouraging others from even thinking of doing so.[62]

The larger contrasts in the patterns of disaffiliation that developed in Germany and England grew out of the profound differences in the respective positions of Jews in those lands. As we have seen, conversion in Germany was first and foremost a response to the failure of emancipation and the explosion of ideological and social antisemitism after 1870—just as, decades

[60] Ord-Mackenzie and Chaplin, *Report of Visit to Continental Missions*, 10, 13.

[61] Thomas Chaplin, 'Memorandum with Reference to German Societies for Promoting Christianity amongst the Jews', 23 Jan. 1891, Church Mission to the Jews Collection, Dep. CMJ d. 45. See also the comments of Le Roi, *Judentaufen im 19. Jahrhundert*, 22.

[62] Wertheimer, *Unwelcome Strangers*.

earlier, the recourse to ideology (Haskalah and Reform Judaism) was a response to the slowness with which *ancien régime* privileges and restrictions were being dismantled. In England, on the other hand, few Jews took the conversion path to radical assimilation, largely owing to the more benign conditions there. The relative success of emancipation in England and its ultimately tragic failure in Germany were not, of course, isolated incidents in the histories of these two countries. Their willingness or refusal to allow Jews to retain an inherited, collective identity while simultaneously seeking success in new social and professional arenas was part and parcel of a more general orientation to state, society, and nation. In politically illiberal, only recently unified Germany, unsure of its own national identity and unhappy about the passing of an older social and economic order, there was little room for ethnic or religious pluralism, particularly when those who were to be tolerated were previously despised outsiders who were now competing all too successfully for wealth, status, and honour. In England, by contrast a mature industrial society well before 1870, liberal individualism, while not unchallenged, was sufficiently enshrined and national confidence sufficiently robust that Jewish integration into the mainstream did not appear to threaten the nation's well-being, even if it was not welcomed with much enthusiasm.

CHAPTER SIX

Jewish Self-Hatred in Germany and England

USING THE TERM 'Jewish self-hatred' to describe Jews who experienced their Jewishness as a cruel plight and echoed the antisemitic slogans of the day invites controversy. From its emergence early in the twentieth century, most prominently as the title of Theodor Lessing's polemic *Der jüdische Selbsthass* (1930), the term has been used more often to attack opponents than to understand them. In the late 1940s and 1950s writers like Philip Roth and Isaac Rosenfeld who did not respect communal pieties were frequently accused of self-hatred and betrayal of the Jewish people.[1] In intra-communal debates in recent decades, right-wing circles, both nationalist and religious, have invoked the term to disparage liberals and radicals who support a two-state solution to the Palestinian–Israeli conflict, in the first instance, and who champion progressive Judaism, in the second. On the diplomatic front, ultra-nationalist ministers in Israeli cabinets have denounced Jewish officials in the Obama administration, such as Rahm Emanuel and David Axelrod, as self-hating Jews.[2] The term has also been used to describe Jews who intermarry or who are indifferent to Jewish political and cultural concerns. Even moderate critics of the American Jewish scene, writers and academics who belong to neither of these two camps, have invoked the term in discussing the rise in intermarriage and the decline in Jewish observance and knowledge. Thus Jacob Neusner claims that American Jewry as a whole is self-hating, citing as evidence its 'niggardly support for the cultural, scholarly, and religious programs and institutions that make Jews Jewish'.[3] When used in this fashion, the term is of little analytical or heuristic value. It is, rather, a clumsy term of abuse, intended to foreclose, not open, discussion by branding certain Jews as 'bad' Jews—unstable, inauthentic, and marginal—persons whose views are not to be taken seriously.

To make matters worse, in non-polemical, academic contexts the concept has been used in a less than rigorous, almost careless fashion. Historians,

---

[1] Glenn, 'The Vogue of Jewish Self-Hatred', 95–6.   [2] *Forward*, 14 Aug. 2009.

[3] Neusner, 'Assimilation and Self-Hatred in Modern Jewish Life', 56.

social scientists, and literary critics have used it as a kind of catch-all term to describe Jews who expressed negative or hostile views of Judaism and Jewish life, without regard to the context in which these views were expressed and without regard to the measures (if any) these 'self-hating' Jews took to weaken or erase their ethnic and religious links. In numerous cases they have used the term to describe Jews who did not wish to deny their Jewishness or to cut their ties to other Jews, however bitter or lacerating their self-criticism. This failure to distinguish between self-hatred and self-criticism, between Jews who chastise other Jews and those who abandon them as well, has resulted in the disparaging of nationalists, reformers, and others who took an active interest in the collective future of the Jews. The critic Baruch Kurzweil, for example, describes Franz Kafka (1883–1924), the Hebrew novelist and nationalist Yosef Hayyim Brenner (1881–1921), and the converts Otto Weininger (1880–1903) and Karl Kraus (1874–1936) as 'spiritual soul mates' and self-hating Jewish writers because they viewed Judaism as a burden, stigma, or tragedy that had to be overcome rather than a vital source of faith and values.[4] More recently, in his widely cited *Jewish Self-Hatred*, Sander Gilman enrols Moses Mendelssohn (1729–86) and Sigmund Freud (1856–1939) in the ranks of the self-hating because they internalized non-Jewish constructions of Jewishness.[5]

The careless and polemical uses of the notion of Jewish self-hatred have given it a bad name, leading some to argue that it has no place in academic discourse. Allan Janik, for example, challenges 'the validity of the concept even when applied to the thinker who nearly everyone has taken to represent the very archetype of the self-hating Viennese Jewish intellectual: Otto Weininger'. For Janik, the notion is reductionist, judgemental, and dismissive, obscuring more than it illuminates: 'the real target in Jewish discussions of self-hatred is often assimilation, which continues to be a ticklish subject in many Jewish quarters'. (Janik seems unaware that the term 'assimilation' is as problematic as the term 'self-hatred'.) In his view, it is also tainted to the extent that it is rooted in the ideas of Theodor Lessing (1872–1933), a crude racial thinker who attributed Weininger's self-hatred to his loathing of his Jewish blood.[6] One way to circumvent these objections is to acknowledge, with Janik, that self-hatred is a cultural construct rather than a well-established syndrome or mix of attitudes and behaviours. This is Gilman's strategy in his *Jewish Self-Hatred*. For him, whether Jewish self-hatred exists or not is irrelevant. Since he is writing the history of the notion

---

[4] Kurzweil, *Our New Literature* (Heb.), pt. 3.   [5] Gilman, *Jewish Self-Hatred.*
[6] Janik, 'Viennese Culture and the Jewish Self-Hatred Hypothesis', 75, 80, 87.

not the history of the phenomenon, what matters is that some Jews believed that there was such a thing as Jewish self-hatred. For historians, however, this is unacceptable, since it evades rather than confronts issues that the concept of Jewish self-hatred raises, pre-eminently the impact of antisemitism on Jewish behaviour and emotional states in various historical contexts.

Although the notion of Jewish self-hatred is controversial, I do not believe it to be so hopelessly compromised as to be irredeemable and am unwilling to consign it to the historiographical dustbin. Used with care, in circumscribed, well-defined ways, I believe it can illuminate broader patterns of acculturation and integration in modern Jewish history. But to make it do this, a few ground rules are necessary.

First, whatever the utility of the concept, it would be foolish to apply it willy-nilly to any and all Jews who attacked or derided the habits and manners of other Jews, no matter how intemperate or repellent their words. It would be foolish, because self-criticism was a hallmark of Jewish life in the modern period. Enlightenment-inspired efforts to transform the Jewish community drew on non-Jewish standards of beauty and value and non-Jewish views of Jewish shortcomings. The movements that Jews created to accelerate the transformation of the community—Haskalah, Reform Judaism, Positive-Historical Judaism, Neo-Orthodox Judaism, Zionism, and Bundism —echoed Jewry's critics: the Jewish people was flawed and in need of repair. Self-criticism was a common feature of liberal, middle-class German Jewish life throughout the nineteenth and early twentieth centuries. In 1880 (that is, before Zionism's appearance) the philosopher and psychologist Moritz Lazarus (1824–1903) dubbed the Jews 'the classic people of self-criticism',[7] and the following year Emanuel Schreiber (1852–1932) published an anthology of self-criticism, *Die Selbstkritik der Juden*, to show that the prophetic spirit of moral castigation was alive and well.[8]

With Jewish self-criticism so pervasive in the modern period, it would be ludicrous to view all who censured their fellow Jews as self-hating Jews. Moses Mendelssohn was not a self-hating Jew because he believed that Yiddish was a 'repulsive', 'corrupt', 'deformed' language of 'stammerers' that had 'contributed more than a little to the uncivilized bearing of the common man'.[9] Nor was the maskil Judah Leib Gordon (1831–92), who wrote of the Russian Jewish masses:

---

[7] Lazarus, 'Was heisst national?', quoted in Doron, 'Classic Zionism and Modern Antisemitism', 173.

[8] On Jewish self-criticism in the imperial period, see Schorsch, *Jewish Reactions to German Anti-Semitism*, 47–8, 135–7, 227 n. 98.   [9] Quoted in Gilman, *Jewish Self-Hatred*, 102–3.

The bread of your house has been deceit and usury,
The insults and abuses of your adversaries are justified.[10]

Nor the Yiddish writer Mendele Mokher Seforim (1836–1917), who cursed
and reviled Jews, describing them in his fiction as ugly, dirty, evil-smelling,
unkempt, and ill-mannered.[11] Nor classical Zionists, who, in their unsparing assault on the diaspora, denounced diaspora Jews as parasites, huck-
sters, *shnorrers* (beggars), cowards, cripples, and even vermin,[12] for however
virulent their critique, Zionists who negated the diaspora were seeking to
revitalize the Jewish people, not erase their Jewishness. It makes no sense to
describe them and others who were committed to the well-being and perpetuation of the Jewish people as self-hating Jews.

Second, because most Westernized or acculturated Jews internalized
non-Jewish views of Jews to one extent or another, it is a mistake to treat
self-hatred as a pathological disease, a mental illness that afflicted the mal-
adjusted, the disaffected, and the disturbed alone. While self-hatred was
pathological when it intersected with, gave expression to, or fed existing
emotional problems, it was not always so. Having identified with the societies in which they lived, acculturated Jews saw themselves and other Jews
through Christian spectacles, if not at all times then at least some of the time.
Inevitably, there were occasions when they experienced the behaviour of
other Jews as embarrassing or shameful.[13] Heinrich Bermann, the fictional
voice of Arthur Schnitzler (1862–1931) in his novel *Der Weg ins Frei* (*The
Road into the Open*, 1908), confesses that he is 'particularly sensitive to the
failings of the Jews' because he and other Jews have been raised from their
youth 'to see precisely Jewish characteristics as especially comical or repulsive'. When a Jew behaves crudely or comically in his presence, he is
ashamed: 'sometimes such a painful feeling seizes me that I want to die, to
sink into the earth'.[14] The paediatrician Karl Oppenheimer and his wife
Clara wrote in 1919 that a non-Jew could not possibly understand 'the feelings with which we Jews observe the noisy, tactless behaviour of many of
our co-religionists on journeys or in public places'. They experienced every
visible sign of ostentation and every too loudly spoken word as poisoned

---

[10] Gordon, 'The Way of My People' (Heb.), quoted in Y. Kaufmann, 'The Destruction of the
Soul' (Heb.), 259.   [11] See Aberbach, *Realism, Caricature and Bias*, 48–9, 56–60.
[12] Y. Kaufmann, 'The Destruction of the Soul' (Heb.); Doron, 'Classic Zionism and Modern
Antisemitism'.
[13] In a psychological study of self-hatred among Jews in the Los Angeles area in the 1970s,
Ronald M. Demakovsky found that Jews with various levels of Jewish identification, including
students in rabbinical and communal service programmes, accepted some antisemitic stereotypes of Jews ('Jewish Anti-Semitism and the Psychopathology of Self-Hatred', 124–5).
[14] Schnitzler, *The Road into the Open*, 114.

arrows in their enemies' 'over-full quiver'.[15] A common, mild way of expressing this was to make a distinction between 'good' and 'bad' Jews, between those who knew how to behave correctly and those who did not.[16]

Jews who made this distinction were careful, of course, to avoid acting like 'bad' Jews—speaking loudly, dressing ostentatiously, gesturing volubly, and so on. They monitored themselves, 'covering' (the term is Erving Goffman's), that is, toning down markers of an identity that was widely disparaged to fit more comfortably into the mainstream.[17] Myron S. Kaufmann's novel *Remember Me to God* (1957), which draws on the author's years at Harvard in the early 1940s, captures the dynamics of the phenomenon. When the novel's protagonist, Boston-born Richard Amsterdam, enters Harvard, he labours to distance himself from two kinds of Jewish students whom he finds there—New York Jewish 'types' and 'the mob of unattractive Jewish students who commuted to Harvard every day from run-down neighbourhoods at the other end of the Boston subway', where he had lived as a small child before his parents moved to suburban Newton. The only Jew on the *Lampoon*, the undergraduate humour magazine, Richard begins monitoring 'his own manners, his voice, and his clothing more carefully', learning 'the finer, newer points' by watching in particular a Brahmin colleague on the *Lampoon* 'in order that he might be above reproach'. Some of these 'finer, newer points' he records in a notebook 'in order to clarify his thinking and to keep them for review'. For example, he notes his hesitation about inviting a Yankee friend for dinner because he knows his mother 'will make a whole operation out of it, and spend two days cleaning and cooking too much stuff and worrying and making all kinds of complicated jello molds with whip cream'.[18] Hortense Calisher's short story 'Old Stock' (1950) describes the same emotional dynamic. Having boarded a train for the Catskills, Mrs Elkin, the status-sensitive wife of a not-too-successful businessman, assumed 'that prim display of extra restraint' she always wore 'in the presence of other Jews whose grosser features, voices, manners offended her sense of gentility all the more out of her resentful fear that she might be identified with them'.[19]

Since feelings like these were widespread in Western Jewish communities, what is significant is how their strength varied—over time, from place to place, and among social strata—and even more importantly when and

[15] Karl Oppenheimer and Clara Oppenheimer, 'Der Antisemitismus', quoted in Robertson, *The 'Jewish Question' in German Literature*, 292.

[16] Meyer, *Jewish Identity in the Modern World*, 35–7.

[17] Goffman, *Stigma*, 102. See also the employment of Goffman's concept in Yoshino, *Covering*.

[18] M. S. Kaufmann, *Remember Me to God*, 83, 85, 112.　　　[19] Calisher, 'Old Stock', 263.

where they burst into the public sphere, underwriting and adorning strategies of radical assimilation. The Jewish self-hatred with which I am concerned here is the full-blown variety, the kind that Jews who wished to expunge their Jewishness translated into words or actions, rather than the occasional, half-hearted kind that was part and parcel of the ambivalence that most acculturated Jews felt. By this definition, self-hating Jews were those who severed their ties to Judaism and Jewishness by converting or otherwise disaffiliating, and who in addition were moved to proclaim their distaste for those from whom they wished to dissociate themselves. What set them apart from other radical assimilationists was that, having cut their ties, they were unable to move on and bury, at least in public, their Jewishness. Instead, it became a virtual obsession, a matter to which they returned repeatedly, disparaging their background and cursing their fate. To be sure, ex-Jews who were in the limelight were often not allowed to forget their past. This was certainly the experience of Benjamin Disraeli, who as I explain in Chapters 9 and 10 transformed the stigma of Jewishness into a mark of honour when his political opponents threw his birth in his face early in his career. While few converts in Europe ventured where Disraeli went, most were able to live as ex-Jews without loudly reminding the world how awful Jews were and how far they, who were no longer Jews, had travelled. Despite the claim that 'forgetting one's Jewishness was not an option' in *fin-de-siècle* central Europe (which strictly speaking is correct), speaking or writing repeatedly about Jews, returning again and again to the topic, was.[20] Ex-Jews who acted in this way merit the label 'self-hating' Jews.

One corollary of this use of the term is a reluctance to rely on texts alone to understand how an individual managed his or her feelings about being Jewish. Too frequently scholars of German literature, eager to redeem the reputations of writers conventionally described as self-hating Jews, turn to close textual exegesis and contemporary literary theory to demonstrate that these writers were ambivalent about their Jewishness, rather than hostile to it *tout court*. No doubt they were—ambivalence is everywhere—but that is not the point. Interpreting texts without reference to what their authors did or did not do to distance themselves from the Jewish people takes too narrow a view of how they experienced and navigated their world. Take, for example, Paul Reitter's argument about Karl Kraus's anti-Jewish remarks in his notorious essay 'Heine and the Consequences' (1910). Reitter maintains that Kraus's Jew-baiting functioned in multiple ways, explaining that he worked in more than one register when writing about Jews and that he, an arch-satirist, used antisemitic rhetoric ironically. Whatever the merit of Reitter's interpretation

---

[20] Reitter, *The Anti-Journalist*, 209–11.

of this essay, taking the measure of the man must also weigh Kraus's willingness in the first place to voice 'venomous language in so many of his reckon-
ings with German Jewry' (this alone speaks volumes), his decision to secede
from the Vienna *Gemeinde* in 1899 and then to convert to Catholicism in
1911 (in 1922 he formally reclaimed *konfessionslös* status), and above all his
obsessive concern with Jews, his inability to leave them alone after formally
cutting his ties to them.[21] Or consider Jonathan Hess's reconsideration of
the now forgotten man of letters Ludwig Jacobowski (1868–1900). The conventional reading of his novel *Werther the Jew* (1892) is that it is a call for radical assimilation (the 1898 edition includes a preface specifically urging the
dissolution of German Jewry). Rejecting this reading as too simple, Hess
argues on the contrary that the novel 'pays considerable attention to the
process of carving out a role for Jewish specificity' in German culture and
society, that its vision of assimilation is equivocal, wavering between hopes
for renewal and extinction.[22] The problem is, as Hess admits, that the novel's
sense of Jewishness lacks substance, and Jacobowski himself, taking his life
as a whole into account, never performed his Jewishness in any way that left
a trace (unless we count his burial in a Jewish cemetery). If Jacobowski did
believe that his novel articulated 'a vision of Jewish identity in which the
ethically reformed Jew would be an ideal exemplar of German culture and
humanity', he remained quiet about what that vision was as he pursued a
career in German letters.[23] To reiterate a central theme of the present volume, belletristic and polemical texts do not encompass the fullness of Jewish
historical experience. What Jews did was as important as what they wrote.

Among mental-health professionals there is disagreement about the
aetiology and dynamics of ethno-cultural self-loathing. Summarizing these
differences, Shulamit Volkov writes that it can be interpreted as 'a sign of
excessive aggression, ultimately turned against the self', or 'the result of a
unique combination of inferiority complex and/or sense of superiority,
a manifestation of an unresolved Oedipal complex or of a latent, persistent
fear of castration' or evidence of 'homoerotic, sadomasochistic needs'.[24]
Whatever the diagnosis, agreement about the psychology of self-hatred is
not essential to studying the phenomenon in a historical context, that is, to
addressing the political, social, and cultural conditions that caused self-
hatred to be more common in some historical settings than in others. (It is
also impossible to interrogate the dead in psychoanalytic fashion.) Shifting
the focus from the internal to the external, from psychology to history, is

[21] Ibid. 71.   [22] J. M. Hess, 'Fictions of a German-Jewish Public', 211.
[23] Ibid. 216.   [24] Volkov, *Germans, Jews and Antisemites*, 38.

advantageous in another respect: it de-emphasizes questions about responsibility, morality, and virtue, which becloud earlier accounts of self-hatred, and instead foregrounds historical questions. It shifts the discussion from individuals to the societies and circumstances that made their unhappiness possible.

Self-hatred among Jews—whether in England, Germany, or elsewhere— was an outgrowth of the fundamental transformation that occurred in their political status in the eighteenth and nineteenth centuries. A distinctively modern phenomenon, it became possible when—and only when—Jews ceased to live within the walls of their own cultural ghetto and to believe in the superiority of their inherited way of life. In 'Ḥatsi neḥamah' ('Some Consolation'), an essay published in *Hamelits* in 1892, Ahad Ha'am (1858– 1927) emphasized the peculiarly modern character and dynamics of the phenomenon:

In earlier generations, when our ancestors believed literally in their 'chosenness', the abuse that the nations heaped on them had no impact on the purity of their inner self. They knew their own worth and were not affected by the conventional ideas of the world outside theirs, whose members were, in their eyes, a special kind of alien being, different in essence, with no connection or similarity between them. Thus, the Jew could listen with equanimity to the charges of ethical shortcomings and active sins that conventional opinion directed at him without feeling an inner sense of shame or humiliation. After all, what did he care about what 'strangers' thought about him and his worth? All he desired was that they leave him in peace! But in this generation, matters are no longer like this. 'Our world' has greatly expanded and European views greatly influence us in all branches of life. And since we no longer treat the outside world as a thing apart, we are influenced, against our will, by the fact that the outside world treats us as a thing apart.[25]

As long as Jews viewed themselves and their world within the context of their inherited values, they were immune to what Christians thought of them. Their very alienation protected them from being despised, allowing them to feel (to borrow from Erving Goffman) that they were fully fledged normal human beings and that their persecutors were not quite human. The stigma they bore in Christian eyes was irrelevant to their own sense of worth. But once they incorporated standards from the wider society, they became 'intimately alive' to what others saw as their failings. Concerned with being

[25] Ahad Ha'am, *Collected Writings* (Heb.), 70–1. Max Nordau made the identical point five years later, in 1897, in his address to the first Zionist Congress (see the abridged translation in Hertzberg (ed.), *The Zionist Idea*, 237–9).

accepted, they became self-conscious and calculating about non-Jewish opinion, sensitive to the impression they were making.[26]

This occurred whenever and wherever Jews abandoned the world of tradition. In both England and Germany, from the late eighteenth century on, there were Jews who found the stigma of Jewishness so overwhelming that they came to view it as the source of their unhappiness. Perhaps the earliest description of the phenomenon is Benjamin Disraeli's characterization of his paternal grandmother Sarah (1743–1825), who lived in the village of Stoke Newington, where Jews 'were treated with the greatest coldness and dislike by the other inhabitants of the place, and not visited by any one'.[27] Not fond of Jews, but unable to mix with Christians, she was 'so mortified by her social position that she lived until eighty without indulging in a tender expression', Benjamin wrote in the introduction to a new edition (1858) of his father's *Curiosities of Literature*.

My grandmother . . . had imbibed that dislike for her race which the vain are too apt to adopt when they find that they are born to public contempt. The indignant feeling that should be reserved for the persecutor, in the mortification of their disturbed sensibility, is too often visited on the victim; and the cause of annoyance is recognized not in the ignorant malevolence of the powerful, but in the conscientious conviction of the innocent sufferer.[28]

A generation later the Berlin salonière Rahel Varnhagen (1771–1833) reacted in a similar way to her failure to find a secure place outside the conventional Jewish world in which she was raised and from which she felt alienated. However much the external circumstances of her life differed from those of Sarah D'Israeli, she, too, blamed her Jewishness for her misery and misfortune. In 1795 she wrote to her oldest friend David Veit, then a medical student at Göttingen:

I imagine that just as I was being thrust into this world a supernatural being plunged a dagger into my heart, with these words: 'Now, have feeling, see the world as only a few see it, be great and noble; nor can I deprive you of restless, incessant thought. But with one reservation: be a Jewess!' And now my whole life is one long bleeding. By keeping calm I can prolong it; every movement to staunch the bleeding is to die anew, and immobility is only possible to me in death itself.[29]

She worked hard to transform herself, to become another person, but felt trapped nonetheless, unable to avoid 'defilement' from her 'loathsomely degrading, offensive, insane, and low' background.[30] As she wrote to her

---

[26] Goffman, *Stigma*, 6–7, 14.   [27] Le Breton, *Memories of Seventy Years*, 40.
[28] Disraeli, 'On the Life and Writings of Mr. Disraeli', p. x.
[29] Quoted in Key, *Rahel Varnhagen*, 11.   [30] Ibid.

brother Ludwig Robert (1778–1832) in the summer of 1806 when her salon fell victim to the Prussian defeat: 'I do not forget this shame for a single second. I drink it in water, I drink it in wine, I drink it with the air; in every breath that is . . . The Jew within us must be extirpated; that is the sacred truth, and it must be done even if life were uprooted in the process.'[31]

Rahel Varnhagen was partial to self-dramatization. While no record exists of how Sarah D'Israeli expressed herself, it is unlikely that she did so in the same self-pitying, overwrought way, given the cultural mood of late Georgian England. These differences aside, self-hatred functioned in a similar way for both women, allowing them to voice their sense of alienation from the Jewish people, whose fate they did not wish to share. Once we move beyond this level of comparison, however, the similarities between England and the German states fade. In the age of emancipation (1750–1870), expressions of Jewish self-hatred were rare in England. Most Jews who wanted to leave the tribal fold were able to find a sufficiently comfortable niche for themselves in non-Jewish society to put behind them the issue of their Jewishness.[32] In the literary output (fiction, letters, memoirs, tracts) of English Jews and former Jews during this period, examples of self-hatred are few and far between. For example, while alive to Christian, especially conversionist, constructions of 'the Jew', the early Victorian pioneers of Anglo-Jewish literature—Grace Aguilar (1816–47), Charlotte Montefiore (1818–54), Celia (1819–73) and Marion Moss (1821–1907), and Matthias Levy (1839–1918) —neither dwelled on Jewish shortcomings nor reproduced conventional Victorian stereotypes.[33]

The one notable exception in imaginative literature was Samuel Phillips (1814–54), son of a prosperous London tradesman, who converted to Anglicanism in his twenties and became a successful Tory journalist and literary reviewer. In his only novel, *Caleb Stukeley* (1841), he introduced a crafty, Fagin-like Jewish moneylender, whose person, clothing, and home are notable for their filth. But while this figure embodied characteristic features of the conventional early Victorian literary representation of 'the Jew', Phillips himself was not preoccupied with his background and rarely mentioned Jews, for good or evil, in his other work. Like other converts in England at this time, his conversion was successful (in terms of the opportunities it made possible), and he felt no need to voice repeatedly how different he was from those who remained Jewish. To be sure, authors whose work he failed to praise, like William Makepeace Thackeray, did not forget his Jewish

---

[31] Quoted in Arendt, *Rahel Varnhagen*, 120.
[32] Endelman, *Radical Assimilation in English Jewish History*.
[33] Galchinsky, *The Origin of the Modern Jewish Woman Writer*.

background, alluding to it in print and in private,[34] but these were mere pin-pricks which seem to have had little effect on Phillips. Undoubtedly there were other former Jews or deracinated Jews who experienced their Jewishness as a burden or stigma, but, for reasons to be discussed later, they did not air their views in public.

In contrast, public expressions of Jewish self-hatred in Germany in the age of emancipation were depressingly common. The poet and pamphleteer Joel Jacoby (1807–63), who became a newspaper censor for the police after his conversion to Catholicism, characterized the Jews as a fossilized or corpse-like people, weak, tired, yearning for oblivion and the grave, their radiance and creativity having been extinguished long ago. 'We are not worthy of sitting in the council of the wise and the mighty', he wrote in his *Klagen eines Juden* (1837), 'and we have no desire to partake in the tribunal that determines the weal and woe of peoples'.[35] Friedrich Julius Stahl (1802–55), ideologist of the conservative Prussian Kreuzzeitungspartei after his conversion, posed Jewishness and Germanness as polar opposites in *Der Christliche Staat* (1847): 'In general, the Jews lack a sense of honour, self-esteem and masculine persistence in their rights; they are lacking the beautiful way of life, notably the sense of honour, that forms the natural basis of the Germanic tribe.'[36] Karl Marx (1818–83) was even harsher, equating *Judentum* (Judaism, Jewry, and Jewishness) with those oppressive forces and attributes that prevented human beings from realizing their humanity: capitalism, civil society, egoism, practical need, huckstering, money, self-interest, property. Practical need and egoism were 'the basis of the Jewish religion'; money, 'the jealous god of Israel'; the bill of exchange, 'the real god of the Jew'. Thus 'in emancipating itself from huckstering and money . . . from real and practical Judaism, our age would emancipate itself'.[37] On other occasions, Marx was less abstract, abusing Jews qua Jews in coarse, vulgar terms. The Jews of Poland were 'the dirtiest of all races'. Jewish bankers were 'a curse to the people', backing oppressive tyrants as the Jesuits backed the pope, while ransacking the public purse. Revealingly, he was most abusive when attacking Jews who, like himself, had cut their ties to Judaism. He mocked Joseph Moses Levy (1812–88), founder of the *Daily Telegraph* (whom he mistook for a radical assimilationist), for wanting 'to be numbered among the Anglo-Saxon race' and for seeking to prove his Englishness by

[34] Prawer, *Israel at Vanity Fair*, 290, 342–3.
[35] Quoted in Liptzin, *Germany's Stepchildren*, 52.
[36] Quoted in Sterling, 'Jewish Reactions to Jew-Hatred', 110.
[37] The critical text is the second of his two essays on the Jewish question, from which these quotations are taken (Marx, 'On the Jewish Question', 34, 36, 37).

opposing 'the un-English politics of Mr. Disraeli'. Such efforts were futile, Marx concluded, since 'Mother Nature has written his pedigree in absurd block letters right in the middle of his face'. Marx also projected onto Ferdinand Lassalle (1825–64), who liked Jews no more than Marx but was never baptized, the negative qualities commonly associated with Jews: bad manners, pushiness, sexual aggressiveness, exotic blackness. Lassalle was 'the Jewish nigger'; 'descended from the Negroes who joined in Moses' flight from Egypt', as the shape of his head and the frizziness of his hair testified.[38]

Alongside the Marxes and the Stahls were an unknowable number of 'ordinary' Jews who felt similarly about their Jewishness. There was, for example, a type of Berlin Jew, according to *Der Orient*, who was 'blissfully happy when he is told that there is no longer anything Jewish about him'.[39] There were converts who, desperate to leave their Jewishness well behind, overcompensated, becoming more Christian than the Christians. These Jews 'have drilled themselves into Christianity to such an extent', Heinrich Heine wrote in 1831, 'that they already denounce unbelief, defend the Trinity to the death, believe in it even in the dog-days, rage against the rationalists, creep about the country as missionaries and God's spies, and in church are always the best at turning up their eyes and pulling sanctimonious faces'.[40] In Berlin Ludwig Börne saw 'elderly daughters of Israel upon the street, wearing long crucifixes from their necks, crucifixes longer even than their noses and reaching to their navels', carrying Protestant hymnals and speaking of 'the magnificent sermon they had just heard in the Church of the Trinity'. (Or at least that is what Heine claimed that Börne had seen.[41]) And there were free-thinking, non-observant Jews like the parents and relatives of the young Fanny Lewald (1811–89), who never spoke of the fact that they were Jews in her presence. She grew up thinking that Jews were both 'uncanny and mysterious' and 'attractive and repulsive'. By the time she was 5 or 6, she had learned that 'we were Jews and that it was bad to be a Jew'.[42]

In the seven decades of illiberalism that followed German unification, the stigmatization of Jewishness intensified while barriers to social and professional advancement remained in place. Questions about Jews and their place in state and society were in the limelight, attracting widespread

[38] Quoted in Wistrich, *Revolutionary Jews from Marx to Trotsky*, 37, 39, 40, 41. For more examples of Marx's abusive treatment of Lassalle, see Silberner, *Sozialisten zur Judenfrage*, 136–8. Marx erred, I should add, in portraying Levy as a Jew who was ashamed of his Jewishness and his Jewish features. In fact, Levy was 'extremely proud of his striking likeness to Disraeli', bearer of the most famous 'Semitic' physiognomy of the day (Emden, *Jews of Britain*, 358).   [39] Quoted in Sterling, 'Jewish Reaction to Jew-Hatred', 108.
[40] Heine, 'The Town of Lucca', 177.
[41] Heine, *Ludwig Börne: A Memorial*, quoted in id., *A Biographical Anthology*, 242–3.
[42] Lewald, *The Education of Fanny Lewald*, 29, 59–60.

public and private comment. Jews who had ceased to believe in and observe their ancestral religion and who increasingly viewed their own Jewishness through German eyes became less optimistic about the future. Growing numbers tried to escape what had become for them a social, occupational, and emotional burden. The incidence of conversion and, in Prussia after the *Austrittsgesetz* of 1873, secession from the *Gemeinde* mounted steadily.[43] In the five-year period 1880–4, 199 Jews in Germany converted to the Evangelical Church per annum; two decades later, in the period 1900–4, there were 502 conversions per annum. In Berlin the rate soared from 30 per annum in the period 1872–81 to 149 per annum in the period 1902–6.[44] Even more tellingly, the number of Jews who found life itself unbearable skyrocketed. In Prussia there were 4.6 suicides per 100,000 Jews in the years 1849–55, a rate lower than that of Protestants and Catholics. By 1925 the Jewish rate, which had mounted steadily from the mid-nineteenth century, had soared to 53.2 per 100,000, almost double that of Protestants (27.9) and quadruple that of Catholics (13.5). In Berlin in 1925 it was even higher: 67.8 per 100,000.[45] This is not to claim, of course, that all Jews who killed themselves did so because they felt stigmatized and besieged. On the other hand, the stunning rise in the number of Jewish suicides relative to the population as a whole does indicate that growing numbers of German Jews were pessimistic or depressed about the future. There can be little question that growing hostility to Jews in public and private life contributed to the hopelessness and despair that led them to end their lives.

Even within broader segments of the Jewish population, among those who neither converted nor seceded, Jewishness became associated with unattractive traits and distasteful behaviour. The young Martin Buber (1878–1965), for example, was in the habit of using the phrase *echt jüdisch* as a scornful reproach. A friend from his student days at the University of Leipzig recalled that he was then given to 'the usual Jewish antisemitism'.[46] As a child growing up in early twentieth-century Coburg, Hans Morgenthau (1904–80) 'was told over and over not to do this or that' because 'people will see you are a Jew'.[47] To talk with one's hands, to have a dirty face or hands, or uncombed hair, or bad posture, to be unruly, noisy, and ill-mannered—these were 'Jewish' traits. Mothers and fathers, one memoirist remembered, 'found a child to be prettier if it "did not look Jewish" '.[48] Parents who had cut

---

[43] Honigmann, *Die Austritte aus der Jüdischen Gemeinde Berlin*, 46.

[44] Lestschinsky, 'Apostasy in Different Lands' (Heb.), 5/8 (1911), 5; 5/10 (1911), 6.

[45] Kwiet, 'The Ultimate Refuge', tables 1 and 4.

[46] Mendes-Flohr, 'Martin Buber and the Metaphysicians of Contempt', 136–7.

[47] Rosenberg and Goldstein (eds.), *Creators and Disturbers*, 76.

[48] Memoir of Phillipp Löwenfeld (1887–1963), in Richarz (ed.), *Jüdisches Leben in Deutschland*, ii. 312.

their ties to Judaism, whether formally or informally, were sensitive to these matters. The sociologist Reinhard Bendix (1916–91), whose parents left the Berlin *Gemeinde* in 1919, recalled: 'We children were instructed to shun what were considered "Jewish" mannerisms. Evidently my parents remained conscious of their origins (as we did not) and of the need, as they saw it, to guard their children from identification with Jewishness, *as perceived by the outside world.*' Growing up ignorant of the most elementary aspects of Judaism, all he heard about being Jewish were 'admonishing references about combing my hair properly or not gesturing with my hands while speaking'.[49] For Theodor Lessing, whose parents neither observed Judaism nor told their children they were Jewish and who claimed to have first discovered his background when he met with antisemitism at school, the very word *Jude* 'took on a sinister meaning': 'Since I had childishly absorbed all the patriotic and religious prejudices of the school, and there was nothing to counterbalance them at home, I became convinced that being Jewish was something evil.'[50]

As was the case before 1870, radical assimilationists who were unsure of their success in shedding their tribal features often laboured to establish their Christian bona fides by denigrating and distancing themselves from their origins What was new in the post-1870 German context was the sheer number of expressions of Jewish self-hatred in the public sphere. More and more self-hating Jews felt compelled to vent their loathing for Jewish traits in public—in journals, newspapers, novels, pamphlets—where non-Jewish Germans would notice and admire their repudiation of and contempt for these traits. In some cases this took the extreme form of public denials of the value of all things Jewish and calls for the self-annihilation of the Jewish people. Recall, for example, the words of the Polish-born semiticist Jakob Fromer, whose 1904 essay I quoted in Chapter 1 'Dive under, disappear! Disappear, with your oriental physiognomy, with your ways that contrast with your surroundings, with your "mission" and, above all, with your exclusively ethical worldview.'[51] Also recall the proposal of the Halle lawyer and notary Adolf Weissler in 1900 to dissolve German Jewry through child baptism. Weissler himself never withdrew from the Halle *Gemeinde* and, in the end, found salvation only in suicide. His gravestone bore the inscription: 'He did not wish to survive the humiliation of his people.'[52]

These proposals for the self-destruction of the Jews were not the work of eccentrics and cranks. Published in respectable, widely read, and influential periodicals, they voiced a current of thinking that was gaining ground

[49] Bendix, *From Berlin to Berkeley*, 140–1 (my emphasis), 179.
[50] Lessing, *Einmal und nie wieder*, 112.
[51] Quoted in Levenson, 'The Conversionary Impulse in Fin-de-Siècle Germany', 112.
[52] Levenson, 'Radical Assimilation and Radical Assimilationists in Imperial Germany', 40.

among radical assimilationists at the turn of the century. Nor were they isolated incidents. Theodor Lessing noted an upsurge in articles like these, which he described as 'a powerful movement among German Jews advocating assimilation, mixed marriage and mass baptism', while the work of Alan Levenson has shown that Lessing was not too far from the mark.[53]

More common were public endorsements of the view that Jewishness and Germanness were moral and cultural opposites, the one the antithesis of the other. Jakob Wassermann's autobiography, *Mein Weg als Deutscher und Jude* (*My Life as German and Jew*, 1921), is a classic expression of this phenomenon. In this short, self-pitying account of an unhappy life, Wassermann (1873–1934) consistently stereotyped experiences and characters from his childhood in Fürth. Judaism, observant Jews, and Jewish worship he associated with decrepitude and darkness; Germans, with beauty and light, serenity and spirituality. At the very start, he assured his readers that when he ventured outside the community in which he had been raised he did not encounter malicious stings and thrusts because neither his features nor his manners were typically Jewish: 'My nose was straight, my demeanour quiet and modest.'[54] He remembered his mother, who died when he was 9, in words echoing Germanic ideals—'beautiful, blonde, very gentle, very silent', adding as well that her first love had been a Christian.[55] Observant Jews were secretive, soulless old men whose religion had 'degenerated into mere phrases, an empty shell'.[56] Its teachers were cruel 'bleak zealots and half-ridiculous figures', who 'thrashed formulas into us, antiquated Hebrew prayers that we translated mechanically, without any knowledge of the language, what [they] taught was paltry, dead, mummified'.[57] Its services were 'a purely business-like affair, an unsanctified assembly, the noisy performance of ceremonies become habitual, devoid of symbolism, mere drill'.[58] Even in the modern, progressive synagogue in Fürth, all he found was 'empty noise, death to religious devotion, abuse of great words . . . presumption, clericalism, zealotry'.[59] He found relief only in the German sermons of 'a very stately *blond* rabbi'.[60] In contrast to Jewish darkness was German Christianity's shimmering radiance. Studying the 'Old Testament' as a child, Wassermann decided that it lacked 'true illumination'; it seemed 'rigid, frequently absurd, even inhuman, and was not ennobled by any loftier outlook'.[61] His imagination became enriched only when 'a ray broke through from the New Testament, like a gleam of light through a locked

---

[53] Lessing, *Der jüdische Selbsthass*, 188; see Levenson, 'The Conversionary Impulse in Fin-de-Siècle Germany'; id., 'Radical Assimilation and Radical Assimilationists in Imperial Germany'; id., 'Jewish Reactions to Intermarriage', ch. 4.
[54] J. Wassermann, *My Life as German and Jew*, 11.   [55] Ibid. 9.   [56] Ibid. 7.
[57] Ibid. 12–13.   [58] Ibid. 13–14.   [59] Ibid. 14.   [60] Ibid. (my emphasis).   [61] Ibid. 13.

door'.[62] 'Good' Jews, those whom he loved or admired, were inevitably light rather than dark, like his mother, Fürth's Reform rabbi, and a 'tall, slender' schoolfriend with 'blond curls', 'the head of an Antoniüs' and 'a gentle soul'.[63]

The Jews whom the young Wassermann met after leaving home were unattractive 'bad' Jews whose behaviour 'caused' antisemitism. Those in Lower Franconia, where he did his military service, were 'trade-loving, usurious Jews who still bore the mark of the ghetto'.[64] Those in Vienna shamed and disgusted him. He was provoked by their 'idiom; quick familiarity; mistrust that betrayed the ghetto left not far behind; unshakable opinions; idle meditation upon simple matters; sophistical fencing with words where a seeing eye would have sufficed; servility where pride would have been proper; boastful self-assertion where modesty was in place; lack of dignity, lack of restraint; lack of metaphysical aptitude'.[65] What most dismayed Wassermann in Vienna was Jewish rationalism, which found expression, among the base, in 'worship of success and wealth, in self-seeking and lust for gain, in greed for power and in social opportunism', and, among the noble, in idolatrous worship of science and 'impotence in the ideal and intuitive realms'.[66] Needless to say, Polish and Galician Jews were altogether alien to him; even when they tried to arouse his sympathy for them as individuals (rather than as fellow Jews), they repelled him.[67]

Among the strategies that Wassermann used to set himself apart from other Jews was to belittle Heinrich Heine, the German Jewish poet and the bête noire of German antisemites. In his youth, he recalled, 'Heine was referred to whenever the talk turned to Jewish attainment, Jewish achievement, Jewish eminence'. But Wassermann made it clear that from the very beginning he disliked Heine, 'indeed, abhorred him violently'. He considered his poetry to be 'sweetish, frivolous and crudely sentimental'; his critical and political writings, 'either shallow and superficially brilliant or spurious and vain'. Wassermann was by his own account obsessed with Heine, viewing his influence as 'harmful and destructive'. Moreover, he recognized that 'the underlying cause of [his] irritation was Heine's blood', for the poet was, in his eyes, the archetypal rootless Jewish writer, 'a man without divine ties or true affinities, disastrously isolated, thrown entirely upon his own resources, devoid of mythic and mother elements, with no hold on either heaven or earth'.[68] For Wassermann and other German Jewish writers who accepted non-Jewish representations of Jewishness, Heine was a frequent and convenient target. Attacking his work allowed them to demonstrate that

[62] J. Wassermann, *My Life as German and Jew*, 13.   [63] Ibid. 42–3.   [64] Ibid. 65.
[65] Ibid. 188–9.   [66] Ibid. 189.   [67] Ibid. 196–7.   [68] Ibid. 96–101.

they did not share the tribal loyalties of other Jews. As a strategy for coping with a 'spoiled' identity, it was a form of 'covering', to use Goffman's term again, a way of keeping the stigma (Jewishness) from looming large by repudiating one of its characteristic manifestations. In a similar fashion, Shulamit Volkov explains, Maximilian Harden attacked Dreyfus and his followers. A critic of modernity, capitalism, democracy, and republicanism, 'he felt compelled to express hostility toward them' to demonstrate the depth and fastness of his anti-liberalism.[69] Opposing the Dreyfusards was a sign of his loyalty—just as anti-Zionism may be a sign of allegiance to radicalism for contemporary left-wing Jews, whose origins might otherwise imperil their standing.

Public displays of Jewish self-hatred also multiplied in England between the 1870s and the 1930s. As in Germany, this took place against a backdrop of escalating intolerance and among those whose social position made them vulnerable to hostile non-Jewish opinion (professional men, writers, journalists, well-to-do social climbers). Its most vigorous expression was in the explosion of Anglo-Jewish fiction that occurred towards the end of the century. In the late 1880s and early 1890s, even before anti-alien sentiment, the Boer War, and the Marconi scandal breathed new life into political anti-semitism, Jewish writers with few or weak links to the community introduced 'bad' Jews into their work—in a manner that was unprecedented in Anglo-Jewish literature. In the novels of Julia Frankau (1859–1916), Amy Levy (1861–89), Cecily Ullman Sidgwick (1855–1934), and Leonard Merrick (1864–1939) that appeared in this period (novels that were written, it should be emphasized, for a largely Christian readership), ill-mannered, morally unattractive Jewish characters figure prominently.[70]

The Jews in Frankau's first novel, *Dr. Phillips* (1887), for example, are un-educated, vulgar, and clannish. They live in tasteless over-furnished homes in the Maida Vale section of London where Frankau herself grew up. They talk with their hands and at the top of their lungs, dance ungracefully, and in the case of the women are overweight and too fond of bright colours and blazing diamonds. They are ignorant of politics, literature, and art and in general take no interest in the world beyond their families and friends, businesses and homes. They stick together, inviting few non-Jews to their gatherings, which revolve around card playing. They behave this way, according to

[69] Volkov, *Germans, Jews, and Antisemites*, 116–17.

[70] On Frankau, see Chapter 12 and the sources cited there. On Levy, there is a rich secondary literature: Cheyette, 'From Apology to Revolt'; Rochelson, 'Jews, Gender and Genre in Late-Victorian England'; Beckman, *Amy Levy*; Scheinberg, *Women's Poetry and Religion in Victorian England*, ch. 6. There is no secondary literature on Merrick and Sidgwick other than the few brief references in Endelman, *Radical Assimilation in English Jewish History*, 93, 94, 104, 123.

Frankau, because of their inordinate love of money. 'Gain' is their deity, the tie that binds them to each other.[71]

Frankau and her husband Arthur, whose lives I discuss at length in Chapter 12, were determined to escape the tribal fold. They quit the Reform synagogue after the birth of their first child, the future novelist Gilbert Frankau (1884–1952), when it ordered them to have him circumcised. Although Julia and Arthur remained Jews, at least in name, they had Gilbert and his three younger siblings baptized into the Church of England. They took no part in Jewish affairs and moved in social circles that were neither exclusively Jewish nor Christian. In her conversation as well as in her fiction Julia distanced herself and her husband from their origins. She boasted to Marie Belloc Lowndes once that her husband's fine qualities were due to the German Lutheran stock from which he came and the absence of any Jewish blood. She also enjoyed gossiping to her about 'unpleasing traits' in the character of well-known Jews of the day, as if to demonstrate by her willingness to betray their flaws that she was not really one of them.[72]

What distinguished Frankau's flight from Jewishness from the German examples above was its non-collective or individualistic character. Leaving the Jewish fold required her self-transformation, as well as the transformation of her children, rather than that of the community as a whole. In contrast, in late nineteenth- and early twentieth-century Germany, the stigmatization of Jewishness was so pervasive, so ingrained in the social and cultural fabric of life, that self-hating radical assimilationists were compelled to call on other Jews to follow in their footsteps. Frankau and other Anglo-Jewish writers who distanced themselves from their background did not feel compelled to link their own happiness and salvation to a collective project, be it mass baptism or intermarriage. The closest Frankau came to a programmatic or prescriptive statement was a denunciation of Jews who opposed intermarriage as 'entirely unemancipated' and a description of interfaith romance in rapturous language: 'How wide a vista opened out in the mind of the little Jewish girl, as she lay there in the arms of Christianity [her non-Jewish suitor]. How centuries of bigotry and generations of prejudice melted away in the flame of her passion.'[73] Frankau was not exceptional in this regard. However much she and her fellow novelists pilloried Jewish traits, they and other self-hating English Jews showed no interest in encouraging other Jews to intermarry, convert, baptize their children at birth, or in the case of males keep their foreskins. There were no Anglo-Jewish parallels to the collective proposals of self-hating radical assimilationists in Germany,

---

[71] J. Frankau, *Dr. Phillips*, 5, 15, 55, 168.
[72] Lowndes, *The Merry Wives of Westminster*, 58–60.   [73] J. Frankau, *Dr. Phillips*, 112.

largely because there was less handwringing about being Jewish, a reflection in turn of the lesser importance of Jewish issues in English public life.

A comparison of Jewish writing in imperial Germany and in Victorian and Edwardian England offers further evidence about the relative strength of self-hatred in the two nations. In the much-read 'Jewish' novels of Fritz Mauthner (1849–1923), Ludwig Jacobowski, and Conrad Alberti (1862–1918), a central theme is the heightened tension between Jewishness and Germanness in the imperial period. In exploring Jewish responses to the upsurge in antisemitism, these writers insisted that Jewish behaviour and attitudes were preventing a successful resolution of the *Judenfrage*, thus blaming the victims for their own victimization. In their fiction they introduced stereotyped, despicable Jewish characters, whose behaviour they contrasted with that of 'good' Jews.[74] In Mauthner's *Der neue Ahasver* (1882), for example, the 'good' Jewish physician who treats the Jewish protagonist (also a 'good' Jew—he has been wounded in the Franco-Prussian war fighting for German unification and later converts to Christianity) explains that newly enriched, social-climbing speculators, 'bad' Jews, are poisoning the atmosphere in Berlin and thus endangering all Jews: 'Otherwise we hard-working members of the middle class would have long since been able to forget the whole thing.'[75] Mauthner despised both the wealthy Jews of Berlin's Tiergartenviertel and the recently arrived *Ostjuden*, whom he blamed for delaying the absorption of authentic German Jews. In his contribution to the *Judentaufen* (baptized Jews) symposium that Werner Sombart organized in 1912, he proposed that Germany close its borders to Polish and Russian immigrants in order to accelerate the absorption of its own Jews. He argued that, while contrary to Western notions of freedom, sealing the border would benefit both Germany's antisemites and its Jews. In the case of the latter, it would 'create a sharp dividing line between its cultivated elements and a mass with which the educated German Jew has nothing in common'. Mauthner, who had withdrawn earlier from the *Gemeinde*, now urged the rest of the community to follow his example.[76]

Alberti took the same position, not only blaming Jews for causing antisemitism but also urging them to disappear in order to combat it. In an essay in *Die Gesellschaft* in 1889, he wrote that having lost their faith Jews had lost their right to a separate, collective existence and had become a mere 'clique', marked by its 'superfluousness, harmfulness and rottenness'. Echoing *volkisch* anti-modernism, he denounced Jews for their materialism, branding them as the principal contributors to the degeneration and

---

[74] Roper, *German Encounters with Modernity*, ch. 8.
[75] Quoted ibid. 150.   [76] Mauthner, in Landsberger (ed.), *Judentaufen*, 75–7.

corruption of the age. Nonetheless, he opposed the new antisemitism, believing it to be counterproductive; instead of weakening Jewishness, it strengthened it, forcing Jews to turn inward and thus heightening their collective consciousness. Only if the pressure of antisemitism were to be relaxed would Jews be able to carry out their 'inner, spiritual self-disintegration'.[77] In Ludwig Jacobowski's bestseller *Werther der Jude* (1891), the protagonist is a tortured, self-hating Jew, Leo Wolff, who kills himself at the novel's end because he is unable to live with his Jewishness. As a university student in Berlin, Leo struggles to free himself of Jewish traits and feelings of collective solidarity (*Gemeinsamkeitsgefühl*), but is still viewed and treated as a Jew. Beset with anxiety, headaches, and other ills, he becomes obsessed with antisemitism and its solution, at times envisioning himself as the saviour of German Jewry, the leader of a crusade for its moral regeneration and ultimate integration into German society. However, after the collapse of a family-sponsored stock scheme, he concludes that the Jews cannot be reformed and decides to have nothing more to do with them. But when a young woman whom he has seduced and abandoned kills herself, and an aristocratic fraternity brother tells him he is a despoiler of innocent German womanhood, he becomes in his own eyes no different than his relations: he, like them, is corrupting and betraying the moral order. Consumed with self-loathing, he shoots himself.

Self-criticism was not absent from Anglo-Jewish fiction. However, Anglo-Jewish writers rarely foregrounded what was central to much German Jewish fiction of this period: the binary opposition between the 'good' Jew and the 'bad' Jew, the struggle of the tortured, self-hating Jew to find acceptance and peace of mind, and the emotional toll of living in a society that was obsessed with Jews. It is difficult to name a work of fiction that revolves around the Jewish question or its impact on Jewish life. The Jews who populate Anglo-Jewish fiction tend to be less emotionally overwrought than their German counterparts. They may be eager to leave the tribal fold, but they do not struggle with their Jewishness, let alone kill themselves because of it. If they experience it as a burden or an embarrassment, they are able nonetheless to forget it or leave it behind them as they pursue integration and acceptance. It does not become an obsession, to be confronted repeatedly.

Two possible exceptions come to mind, each instructive in its own way. The first is Amy Levy's short story, 'Cohen of Trinity' (1889), the tale of an unkempt, ungainly, 'desperately lonely' Cambridge undergraduate, with marked Jewish features, who is sent down from the university for academic reasons, writes a bestseller that brings him the fame he craves, and then,

[77] Alberti, 'Judentum und Antisemitismus'.

unable to enjoy his success, puts a bullet through his head.[78] The story is eerily prophetic. It appeared in the same year that Levy, who had also been at Cambridge, ended her own life, two months before her twenty-eighth birthday, having recently won recognition for her fiction, poetry, and criticism. Although it is always difficult to know why a person kills himself or herself, there is a consensus in Levy's case that conflicting feelings about both her sexual orientation and her Jewishness contributed to her unhappiness. Curiously, in the short story that foreshadowed her own death, Cohen is not a self-hating Jew and his Jewishness is not the source of his inability to establish lasting and close personal relationships. All we learn is that he 'volunteered little information' on the subject of his family and his middle-class Maida Vale background. The Jewish question is at most a muted subtext, background rather than foreground. Levy never links Cohen's problems to his Jewishness or antisemitism. Doing so, I suggest, would have introduced a theme that would have seemed out of place to late Victorian readers.

The other exception is Pamela Frankau's portrait of a self-hating London Jewish screenwriter in her novel *The Devil We Know* (1939). Granddaughter of Julia Frankau and daughter of Gilbert and the first of his three Christian wives, Pamela (1908–67) was a believing, practising Christian from birth, which explains in part why her Jewishness left her less troubled. On the other hand, the unhappy protagonist of *The Devil We Know*, Philip Meyer, very much dislikes being a Jew and voices his dislike repeatedly. In fact, he is obsessed with the subject and cannot leave it alone. Tired of listening to him, his part-Jewish cousin Sally jokingly remarks, 'I am going to impose a fine on you for every time you mention the race.' When he asks her if he really mentions it that often, she replies, 'About twice an hour.'[79] He struggles to repress those parts of him that are marked as Jewish, such as talking with his hands. In the mid-1930s, as antisemitism at home and abroad mounts, he suffers a breakdown and becomes a raving paranoid, blaming all his misfortunes on his birth. 'Everyone whom I have ever known has hated me. I am not blaming them. I am only sorry that I was born with the taint at this moment when there is no escape.'[80] In the end, however, he is cured; his self-loathing and paranoia recede (although exactly how this is achieved is not clear).

Does the case of *The Devil We Know* weaken my contention that the theme of self-hatred was more muted in England than in Germany? Perhaps. Yet it may also be the exception that proves the rule, first because Meyer is, however improbably, cured of his self-hatred, and second because he is not an

---

[78] The story is reprinted in Levy, *The Complete Novels and Selected Writings*, 478–85.
[79] P. Frankau, *The Devil We Know*, 143.   [80] Ibid. 367.

English Jew but rather a German Jew, a native of Hamburg, who lived in the German Jewish community of Bradford before moving to London, the same community in which Frankau's lover, the poet and critic Humbert Wolfe (1886–1940), grew up. This is no mere incidental detail, for the most unambiguous examples of self-hatred in Anglo-Jewish history emerge from the biographies of German Jewish merchants and manufacturers who settled in Britain in the Victorian and Edwardian periods. Just as these middle-class immigrants and their children were more likely than native-born Jews to become Unitarians or Anglicans, as I will explain in the following chapter, so too they were more likely to experience their Jewishness as a blemish. Wolfe, who as a boy and young man was bitterly ashamed of being Jewish, commented in his memoirs on the thoroughness with which the Jewish merchant families of Bradford adapted to the English environment. 'They left nothing undone that the strange Island-people practised'—in spite of which, they remained outsiders. 'Was it surprising that, instead of standing on their Jewry, as upon a point of honour, some, if not many, were ashamed of it?'[81] The German Jewish grandparents of the *Daily Telegraph* columnist Michael Wharton ('Peter Simple') (1913–2006), who settled in Bradford in the 1860s, were actively hostile to things Jewish: 'My grandfather was said . . . to have driven the visiting rabbi with imprecations from his door; my grandmother was positively anti-semitic, I believe; at any rate she was so anxious to disavow any Jewish antecedents that she made sure that none of her children, three sons and two daughters, married people with Jewish blood.'[82] Wharton himself believed that his father's surname, Nathan, contributed to his lack of social success at Oxford and changed it in the late 1930s to escape identification as a Jew—to remove a label, as he put it, that had 'immense potency' in the eyes of others (Wharton was his non-Jewish mother's maiden name).[83] To cement his escape from Jewishness, he frequently indulged in antisemitic and racist comments in his column. For example, he wrote in 2002 that Ariel Sharon had 'ended the Jews' virtual immunity from hostility' since the defeat of the Nazis. Antisemitism was stirring, and, Sharon aside, 'the immense influence the Jews have in the world', which he speculated was not 'always, everywhere and in every way an influence for the good', was to blame.[84]

To sharpen the contrast between the German and English experiences, I want to conclude by comparing the lives of two self-hating Jews who achieved political prominence in the early twentieth century—Walther Rathenau (1867–1922) and Edwin Montagu (1879–1924). The two shared

---

[81] Wolfe, *Now a Stranger*, 125–7.
[83] Ibid. 37, 83.
[82] Wharton, *The Missing Will*, 4.
[84] *Daily Telegraph*, 19 Apr. 2002.

much in common. Both were born with silver spoons in their mouths. Rathenau's father, Emil (1838–1915), was a titan of German industry, founder of the Allgemeine Elektricitäts-Gesellschaft; Montagu's father, Samuel (1832–1911), was a bullion broker and foreign exchange banker and Liberal MP for Whitechapel from 1885 to 1900. Both were driven, restless men who achieved high political office—Rathenau as chief of the Raw Materials Division of the Ministry of War from September 1914 to March 1915 and as Minister of Reconstruction and then Minister of Foreign Affairs in 1921 and 1922; Montagu as Parliamentary Private Secretary to H. H. Asquith from 1906 to 1910, Parliamentary Undersecretary of State for India from 1910 to 1914, Minister of Munitions in 1916, and finally Secretary of State for India from 1917 to 1922. Both mixed with the great and the mighty—with different degrees of success, however—and both were troubled by their Jewishness.

Each man chose to make his name in a different field from his father. Rathenau was not content with being a successful industrialist and banker, but aspired as well to be a man of letters, social critic, moralist, and prophet. In his dilettantish, overblown essays and books, he denounced mechanization and materialism, criticizing unregulated capitalism and affecting to despise luxury. (His critics derided him as 'the prophet in a dinner jacket' or 'Christ in evening dress'.) But in life as opposed to letters he was an unabashed social climber. He cultivated the company of the powerful and worshipped the old Prussian elite, attributing to them a nobility of spirit and character that he imagined Jews and middle-class Germans lacked. When the time came for him to do his military service he tried to join a cavalry regiment that reputedly accepted only blonds. Later (in 1908 and 1910) he worked assiduously to receive two royal decorations, this time with success. A passionate admirer of the cool, restrained Prussian architecture of the late eighteenth century, in 1910 he purchased and restored Schloss Freienwalde, a former Hohenzollern estate forty miles north-east of Berlin, furnishing it with period furniture, tapestries, and portraits of the royal family.[85] Albert Einstein, who fruitlessly solicited Rathenau's support for Zionism, noted that 'he was in love with Prussianism, its Junker class, and its militarism'.[86] In social life, in addition to cultivating aristocratic connections, he also struck up friendships with 'very inconsequential people' whose sole distinction was their blond hair, blue eyes, and 'Nordic' racial features.[87] Einstein also recognized that Rathenau was 'a person inwardly

[85] Letourneau, 'Rathenau et la question juive', 532; Loewenberg, *Walther Rathenau and Henry Kissinger*, 4–5; id., 'Walther Rathenau and German Society', 59–61; Felix, *Walther Rathenau and the Weimar Republic*, 44, 50.

[86] Einstein, *On Peace*, 52.   [87] Kessler, *Walther Rathenau*, 72.

dependent on the recognition of men much inferior to him in their human qualities'.[88]

Montagu also struck out in new directions. Although his father represented Whitechapel in the House of Commons from 1885 to 1900, and was a leading spokesman on monetary policy, the focal points of his life were the City and the Jewish community, not Westminster. He entered Parliament because he was first and foremost a successful banker. Edwin, on the other hand, knew and loved high politics alone. He refused to pursue a career in medicine or science or at the Bar, which his father encouraged him to do, and a year after taking his degree at Cambridge he entered politics, standing for West Cambridgeshire in 1906. While he shared none of Rathenau's cultural and intellectual interests, he did share his taste for the prominent and the powerful. As an adult, he spent as little time as possible with his relatives (with the exception of his youngest brother Lionel, known as Cardie (1883–1948)) or other members of the Anglo-Jewish notability, the milieu in which his parents socialized, preferring instead the company of well-connected, well-born non-Jews. Among his two dozen closest friends there was not one Jew.[89]

Politically and socially, Montagu had an easier go of it than Rathenau. Thanks to friendships made at Cambridge, he moved in high political circles from the start. He rapidly became a Liberal insider, being appointed Parliamentary Private Secretary to Asquith, then Chancellor of the Exchequer, in February 1906. He went on to hold a series of high offices. This kind of public career was impossible for a Jew, whether baptized or not, in either imperial or Weimar Germany. Rathenau shunned day-to-day politics and public life before the First World War, even though he was friendly with Kaiser Wilhelm II and two imperial chancellors, Bernhard von Bülow and Theodor von Bethmann-Hollweg. When he attained office it was during a period of extraordinary crisis (the First World War and the early years of the republic), and due to his technocratic expertise rather than his political savvy, experience, or connections. Moreover, at every stage of his public life Rathenau encountered opposition based to a large extent on the fact that he was a Jew. The imperial bureaucracy tried to thwart the awarding of royal decorations to him in recognition of memoranda he had written after touring Germany's colonies in Africa in 1907 and 1908 with Colonial Secretary Bernhard Dernburg. During the First World War, despite the importance of his contribu-

[88] Einstein, *On Peace*, 53. Rathenau's sister Edith, who converted to Christianity after their father's death, shared his admiration for blue eyes and blond hair. She wrote in her diary: 'I am forever grateful that my children have so much light blood and that their children in turn will be yet much fairer, lighter, freer and blonder than they' (quoted in Loewenberg, 'Walther Rathenau and German Society', 192).   [89] Levine, *Politics, Religion and Love*, 100, 324.

tion, securing vital raw materials that the army had neglected to stockpile, the Ministry of War treated him as an interloper and pariah (he was the only Jew and the only civilian in the ministry). 'One day', his friend Harry Kessler recalled, 'his department was isolated by a wooden partition, which had grown up overnight, from those of the other old-established gentlemen in the War Office, as if it had been a cholera station.'[90] As Foreign Minister in the Weimar period he faced vicious antisemitic attacks, which culminated in his assassination on 24 June 1922 as he drove from his home to his office in an open car.

Rathenau's social life was no less troublesome. Although he mixed with non-Jews in government and the arts, his closest friends were 'almost wholly confined to people of Jewish origin'.[91] As Werner Mosse observed, the social climate at the time was 'unpropitious for sustained personal relations across ethnic divides . . . Segregation, whether informal or institutionalized, was the order of the day'.[92] Ironically, because he was homosexual, he did not have to face what would have been a vexing problem: finding a non-Jewish wife. This was an issue for German Jewish bankers and industrialists who wanted to marry outside the fold, since few German families from the aristocracy or *haute bourgeoisie* were willing to contract marital alliances with them, whether they were converted or not. On the basis of his close study of marital patterns among the Jewish economic elite, Mosse speculates that Rathenau would have been forced to look outside Germany for a socially appropriate mate.[93]

While Montagu's integration went more smoothly than Rathenau's, it was not trouble free. At Clifton he and the other Jewish boys were teased. (He told his parents that 'of course' he took no notice of it, which is unlikely.[94]) At Cambridge he was snubbed, which has led one historian to speculate that when he later condemned the prejudice and discrimination Indian students met at Oxbridge he was thinking back to his own experiences.[95] His closest friends and colleagues referred repeatedly to his Jewishness and 'Asiatic/ oriental' background. Asquith and Venetia Stanley called him 'Mr Wu', 'the Assyrian', 'Shem', and 'our Oriental friend' and referred to his home in Queen Anne's Gate as 'the Silken Tent'.[96] In defending Venetia Stanley's engagement to Montagu (they were married in 1915), Raymond Asquith, eldest son of the prime minister, admitted that the bridegroom had 'not a drop of European blood'.[97] When the War Cabinet was negotiating with the

[90] Kessler, *Walther Rathenau*, 181.
[91] W. E. Mosse, *The German-Jewish Economic Elite*, 129.   [92] Ibid. 159.   [93] Ibid. 157.
[94] Waley, *Edwin Montagu*, 5.   [95] Levine, *Politics, Religion and Love*, 57.
[96] See e.g. ibid. 177, 199, 211; H. H. Asquith, *Letters to Venetia Stanley*, 29, 306, 524.
[97] Raymond Asquith to Conrad Russell, 24 July 1915, in R. Asquith, *Life and Letters*, 202.

Zionists in 1917, Asquith's sister-in-law Cynthia Asquith wrote in her diary, 'What fun if Montagu and Venetia are forced to go and live in Palestine!'[98] Some of this took place behind Montagu's back, and we do not know the extent to which he was aware of it—but not all was hidden from view. Margot Asquith, the prime minister's wife, told him face to face in 1913 that 'he had the qualities of his race, which do not include courage', a comment that he took 'quite meekly', according to her report.[99] In politics, Edwardian scandal-mongers on the radical right, as well as some social radicals, made much of Montagu's Jewishness and the Jewishness of other prominent Liberals like Rufus Isaacs (1860–1935) and Montagu's cousins Stuart (1856–1926) and Herbert Samuel (1870–1963), especially during the Marconi scandal of 1912–13 and the Indian silver scandal of 1912. The irony was that Montagu had no direct financial interest in the family firm, which was accused of wrongdoing in the silver affair.[100]

Still, the hostility that Montagu encountered was neither as relentless nor as overt as that directed at Rathenau and other German Jews of his generation. It is difficult to imagine Montagu writing, as Rathenau did in 1911: 'In the years of his youth there is a painful moment for every German Jew that he remembers for the whole of his life—when he is struck for the first time by the consciousness that he has entered the world as a second-class citizen and that no ability and no merit can liberate him from this situation.'[101] Nor is it possible to imagine Montagu confessing, as Rathenau did on his first visit to Bülow: 'Your Highness, before I am worthy of the favour of being received by you, I must make an explanation that is also a confession. Your Highness, I am a Jew.'[102] Nonetheless, being Jewish caused the already gloomy and insecure Montagu further anguish. From his Cambridge years on, he did what he could to escape the tribal fold, although he was limited in how far he could go by his financial dependence on his father, an observant Jew, and after his father's death by the terms of his father's will, which disinherited any child who converted or married outside the faith. He gave up regular synagogue attendance and observance of *kashrut* from the time he entered Cambridge, agreeing only, after protracted negotiations, to be with his family on Rosh Hashanah, Yom Kippur, and Passover.

Montagu's flight from Jewishness was more than a repudiation of his family's faith, however. He wanted to put as much distance between himself and the Jewish community as possible—unlike his cousin Herbert Samuel,

---

[98]   C. Asquith, *Diaries*, 360.
[99]   Levine, *Politics, Religion and Love*, 208.
[100] Searle, *Corruption in British Politics*, 202–3.
[101] Rathenau, 'Staat und Judentum', i. 188–9.
[102] Quoted in Joll, *Intellectuals in Politics*, 67.

who also ceased to believe in the God of Jewish tradition, but continued to participate in communal life and attend synagogue. Montagu, for his part, wanted a full break. He refused to take an interest in the club work his sister Lily (1873–1963) did with Jewish girls, because it was 'sectarian' and strengthening 'barriers' that he wanted to abolish.[103] (That he viewed her Jewish interests as 'sectarian' is ironic, for Lily Montagu was allied with the most radical, universalist wing of Reform Judaism.) He refused to consider marriage to a Jewish woman, telling his mother, 'It is not only that I don't as a rule like Jewesses. It is also that I firmly believe to look for a wife in one set of people is as wrong as it would be to say that you must look for a wife among blue-eyed people.'[104]

Montagu's choice of spouse—Venetia Stanley, daughter of the fourth Lord Sheffield—suggests that for him being married to a well-born non-Jew was the most important of the benefits that marriage bestowed. (Venetia went through a nominal Reform conversion so Edwin would not lose his income). Edwin was besotted with Venetia, but his love was not reciprocated. She was not attracted to him sexually and saw their marriage as one of convenience rather than passion. As his wife, she agreed to have sex with him, but only when she chose. This soon became an issue between them, leaving him feeling angry and humiliated, and despite the urgings of her close friends to 'sacrifice herself' more often she refused, making a shambles of the marriage. She also insisted from the start on her right to have sex outside the marriage. She slept with other men, bore a child that was not Montagu's, and spent his money on travel, high fashion, drink, lavish entertainment, and home decoration.[105] It is hard to know what pleasure he received from the union, other than the deep satisfaction of having done what his mother and father did not want him to do. In this sense, Venetia was a trophy wife, a symbol to be displayed to all the world of his successful escape from the embrace of the tribe—and his parents.

Yet however much Montagu desired to be free of his Jewish ties, he never acted or spoke in public to demonstrate how 'un-Jewish' he was. Perhaps this was because his career and his wife were proof enough that he was an insider not an outsider, or perhaps because the pressure to repudiate Jewishness was weaker than in Germany and elsewhere. (Both reasons are linked in any case.) Whatever the reason, his self-hatred never underwrote a public attack on Jewishness, as it did with Rathenau and other self-hating German Jews. Aside from family and close friends, it seems that no one knew of his inner turmoil and unhappiness.

[103] Waley, *Edwin Montagu*, 11.   [104] Ibid. 58.
[105] Cooper, *A Durable Fire*, 57, 91–3, 96–7, 133; C. Asquith, *Diaries*, 74, 98; Levine, *Politics, Religion and Love*, 275, 386–9.

This was not the case with Rathenau, who made his Jewishness a matter of public record and intruded it into his relations with friends and correspondents. In 1897, he published 'Höre, Israel!', a virulent, nine-page attack on German Jews, in Harden's *Die Zukunft*, using the pseudonym 'W. Hartenau'. (He republished it under his own name in a collection of essays, *Impressionen*, in 1902.) In terms borrowed from the vocabulary of racial antisemitism, he represented Berlin Jews as a strange, self-segregating, malevolent Asiatic tribe:

> Walk through the Thiergartenstrasse at noon on Sunday or spend an evening in the lobby of a Berlin theater. What a strange sight! At the very heart of German life, a distinct tribe of foreigners, resplendently and showily dressed, hot-blooded in their deportment. An Asiatic horde on the sands of Mark Brandenberg. The affected contentment of these people does not reveal how many old, unsatisfied hates rest on their shoulders . . . Mixing intimately with each other, cut off from the world without, they live in a voluntary invisible ghetto—a foreign organism in the body of the Volk rather than a living part of it.[106]

Rathenau was clear about who was responsible for the plight of the Jews. The state had made them equal citizens, allowing them to become Germans, but they had chosen to remain strangers. Blaming the victim, he was unsparing in his criticism of their behaviour, and in his prescription for their reformation. He told them to stop walking about in a loose and lethargic way that made them the laughing stock of a race raised in a strict military fashion. He ordered them to reshape their bodies—their underdeveloped chests, narrow shoulders, awkward feet, and effeminate plumpness. To regain their natural beauty, he urged Jewish women to cease smothering themselves in 'bales of satin, clouds of lace and nests of diamonds'.[107] German Jews also needed to learn to speak correctly, to purge their speech of Yiddishisms, hyperbole, and vocal distortions. They needed to curb their unruly ambition, abandon their pursuit of honours and decorations, content themselves with social ties within their own milieu, repress their cleverness and irony, and cease bragging of their charitableness.[108] Rathenau ruled out mass baptism as a solution, since the converts would generate a more pernicious antisemitism than that which presently plagued Jews. (Did he have the historical experience of the Spanish and Portuguese New Christians in mind?) Conversion, as opposed to secession from the *Gemeinde*, the solution that Rathenau himself chose, was 'too Jewish'. What then was the answer? His response was as vague as most proposals for full assimilation: conscious self-cultivation and absorption of German ways, shedding of tribal attributes rather than superficial mimicry. The goal was to produce 'not imitation Germans but

---

[106] Rathenau, 'Höre, Israel!', 454.   [107] Ibid. 458.   [108] Ibid. 459–60.

Germanly conditioned and educated Jews'—that is, Jews very much like Rathenau's idealized image of himself.[109]

In later years Rathenau was more temperate when writing about Jews. Nonetheless he continued to view Jews and Germans in binary terms, each different in essence from the other, and to behave in ways that made visible his fidelity to Germanness and lack of attachment to Jews. From late 1913 until his death, he cultivated and sustained a close, even intimate, friendship with Wilhelm Schwaner, a *völkisch* publisher and youth organizer and author of a Germanic Bible. He supported Schwaner's work with the considerable sum of 3,000 marks.[110] During the war his racial ideals and blind admiration of the Prussian warrior caste led him to hail General Erich Ludendorff as Germany's saviour and to believe, almost until the very end of the war, that he alone could prevent a German defeat.[111] At the same time, when asked in 1918 to join the fight against antisemitism, he refused. While acknowledging the threat, he argued that a collective Jewish response would confirm in the minds of antisemites the myth of Jewish tribal solidarity.[112] According to his friend the theatre critic Alfred Kerr (1867–1948), when Rathenau was a government minister he went out of his way to treat Jews worse than other people, demonstrating, as it were, his lack of solidarity with them.[113]

The pain that Rathenau and Montagu experienced was emotional, not material. They did not suffer economically or physically because they were Jews (excluding, of course, the circumstances of Rathenau's death); Montagu's Jewishness did not even impede his entry into smart society. This does not mean, however, that the pain they felt was any less real or any less active in shaping their behaviour and outlook. Indeed, the very fact that they enjoyed so many other advantages—wealth, talent, intelligence, charm, influence—made their background loom even larger, magnifying its importance in their eyes, for it alone seemed to stand between them and real happiness. Jews on whom fortune smiled in other ways were especially vulnerable to the lacerating effects of self-hatred. To be sure, both men would have been unhappy whatever their birth or however mild the Jewish question. Antisemitism did not make them tortured, anxious men.[114] Their emotional distress had complex, multiple roots and was overdetermined, the outcome

---

[109] Ibid. 456–7. He offered a more principled refusal to be baptized in 'Staat und Judentum', 189–90.

[110] On his ties to Schwaner, see Loewenberg, 'Antisemitismus und jüdischer Selbsthass', 457–64.　　　　　[111] Loewenberg, 'Walther Rathenau and German Society', 120–2.

[112] Rathenau, *Briefe*, ii. 10.　　　　　[113] Kerr, *Walther Rathenau*, 128–9.

[114] Peter Loewenberg notes: 'Ethnic minority self hatred is in each individual case a later socialized manifestation of a basic self hatred that existed prior to any social awareness of minority status, and that to some degree is a normal component of the human personality' ('Walther Rathenau and German Society', 68).

of inheritance and upbringing as well as the temper of the times. What the stigmatization of Jewishness did was to intensify and structure their unhappiness, providing it with an outlet and shaping the way it expressed itself. The Jewish Question both contributed to their despair, and at the same time provided them with themes for its expression, offering them a vocabulary, a set of grievances, and a way of acting out their inner conflict.

The contrast between Montagu's private self-loathing and Rathenau's public self-confession and self-flagellation points to a profound difference between the Jewish experience in the two nations. In nineteenth- and early twentieth-century Germany, Jewishness had greater political or public resonance than in England. It was a more ubiquitous theme, extruding itself into all manner of activities and discussions. The Jewish question was more alive there than in England, where the emancipation debate focused on access to political office rather than the removal of a broad range of legal disabilities and the reformation of Jewish manners, social habits, and occupational preferences. In other words, with state and society in Germany more resistant to Jewish integration, demanding that Jews prove themselves fit for citizenship by emancipating themselves from their Jewishness, radical assimilationists had to work harder to bury their past. They could less easily forget that they had been born Jews, or persuade others to forget it, because the distinction between Jew and non-Jew was more salient, more charged. It carried greater weight, and thus weighed more on those Jews who did not want to be Jews, forcing them to distance themselves publicly and demonstrably from unconverted Jews, and in some cases even to urge others to follow their example. For the latter, their own salvation was inseparable from the collective salvation of the Jews, so pervasive was the obsession with Jews. In this sense, one may speak of a *Sonderweg* in German history.

CHAPTER SEVEN

German Jews in Victorian England

T HE ENGLISH JEWISH COMMUNITY, like its North American cousin, is the product of successive waves of immigration from the Continent. Of the various migrations that contributed to its growth, the German Jewish settlement of the Victorian period is the least known. In part this is a matter of numbers. Although it is impossible to know how many German Jews migrated to England in the Victorian era—the British Census, while recording the country of origin of persons of foreign birth, did not distinguish between Christians and Jews at a time when there was a substantial German trading colony in England—it is clear that their numbers were not great. At best one can say that several thousand, but certainly not more than 10,000, German Jews moved to Britain during the Victorian period.[1] A more critical reason was the 'respectable' social character of the German Jewish migration. Unlike both earlier and later immigrants, those coming from Germany at this time burdened neither the established Jewish community nor the larger society, and thus attracted little notice. In addition, because their numbers were few and their prior break with Jewish tradition advanced, their integration into English society took place with relative ease.

At the accession of Queen Victoria in 1837 there were no more than 30,000 Jews living in England, approximately half of them in London.[2] They were overwhelmingly Ashkenazim, immigrants or the descendants of immigrants from Holland, the German states, and Poland, who had escaped the poverty and degrading restrictions that embittered Jewish life in most *ancien régime* states. They came with few material resources or craft skills and on arrival took to low-status itinerant trades to earn a living—hawking goods on the streets of London, buying and selling old clothes and other second-hand goods, and peddling notions, gimcracks, and inexpensive jewellery in the provinces.[3] These trades required little capital or prior knowledge of English, and were already familiar to the immigrants before their migration. Some were eventually able to improve their economic situation,

[1] Aronsfeld, 'German Jews in Victorian England', 312.
[2] Lipman, *Social History of the Jews in England*, 6–8.
[3] Endelman, *The Jews of Georgian England*, ch. 5.

and entered the ranks of small shopkeepers, wholesalers, and manufacturers; a fortunate few became overseas merchants and dealers in luxury goods; others remained mired in poverty, dependent on communal relief to make ends meet.

The immigration from central Europe in the Victorian period, in contrast, was largely (though not exclusively) middle-class in character—in part, a reflection of the social and economic transformation of Germany that was under way in the nineteenth century. Those who arrived at this time came with greater resources—a secular education, prior experience in large-scale commerce, access to capital—and a broader cultural outlook than their predecessors, and were thus better positioned from the start to make their way into the English middle class. Evidence of this shift can been seen in the fact that by the middle of the century German Jews no longer figured as objects of poor relief in communal appeals. An editorial in the *Jewish Chronicle* in 1846, for example, in urging readers to contribute generously to Jewish charities, attributed the strain on communal resources to newly arrived immigrants from Russia and Poland,[4] while an editorial in 1854 asking for donations to an East End soup kitchen explained that current funds were unable to handle the great influx of Polish Jews.[5]

Most of the new arrivals from Germany were merchants and commercial clerks with links to or previous experience in large-scale trading ventures who were attracted to England by its unrivalled mercantile and industrial pre-eminence.[6] A number of immigrants who rose to prominence in the textile trade, such as Moritz Rothenstein (1836–1915) and Jacob Moser (1839–1922) in Bradford, served apprenticeships in Jewish merchant houses in Germany before settling in England. Emanuel (1833–1914) and Philip Freud (1835–1911) (half-brothers of Sigmund Freud) were in business in Freiburg before an unfavourable turn in their fortunes led them to migrate to Manchester in 1859. Some were sent to England for the specific purpose of establishing branches of already flourishing ventures. The story of Jacob Behrens (1806–89) is typical. His father, Nathan, headed a firm in Hamburg that imported woollen and cotton goods from England, then the centre of world textile production, and in turn distributed them in northern Germany. Jacob visited England a number of times during the years 1832–4 to buy textiles in Leeds for the family firm. His inability each time to persuade local manufacturers to make up goods to his exact specifications convinced him of the advantage of setting up a permanent branch in England. In 1834 he rented a small factory and warehouse in Leeds; at first he manufactured and shipped

---

[4] *Jewish Chronicle*, 30 Oct. 1846.
[5] *Jewish Chronicle*, 3 Mar. 1854.   [6] Chapman, *Merchant Enterprise in Britain*, 139–49.

woollen goods for the firm in Hamburg, but later he set up as a manufacturer and exporter on his own account, eventually becoming one of the great textile magnates of the region.[7]

England's pre-eminence in textile production was not the only attraction for German Jewish merchants. The emergence of London as the largest domestic market in the world for consumer goods of all kinds—its population at mid-century was over 2.5 million—and as a major international trading centre also served to attract enterprising Jewish merchants in a variety of fields. The history of the Geiger and Frankau families is typical in this regard. Joseph Geiger (1807?–70), son of a Frankfurt stationer (and first cousin of the prominent Reform rabbi Abraham Geiger), migrated to London in the early 1830s and set up business in Goodman's Fields in the East End as an importer of fancy goods. A few years later, with the world of fashion rapidly switching from snuff-taking to cigar-smoking, he became an importer and manufacturer of cigars. At about the same time another young Frankfurt Jew, Joseph Frankau (1813–57), also migrated to London, establishing himself as an importer of leeches, sponges, and cigars, first in partnership with another German immigrant, Lesser Friedlander, and then on his own. He lived in the same street as Geiger (perhaps in the same building) and in 1843 married his sister Amelia (1813–63). Four years later Joseph's brother Adolph (1821–56), who had settled in the United States as a young man, moved to London, where he carried on a successful business as an importer of meerschaum pipes and smoking accessories.[8]

Unlike their predecessors in the Georgian period, most immigrants from Germany at this time had received some secular education before their departure—a reflection, again, of the sweeping transformation of German Jewry in the emancipation era. At a minimum they could read and write German; in many instances they were literate in other European languages as well. A very small number had attended university and acquired professional training. The laryngologist Felix Semon (1849–1921) had completed his medical studies in Berlin; the industrialist Ludwig Mond (1839–1909) had studied chemistry at Marburg and Heidelberg; the journalist Karl Marx (1818–83) had studied history and philosophy at Bonn, Berlin, and Jena. One indicator of the cultural status of the immigrants, whatever the level of their formal education, was their ability to take part in musical, artistic, and political activities outside the Jewish community—either in the company of Christian German merchants or English merchants and professionals. In Manchester, for example, the prosperous calico printer Salis Schwabe

[7] Behrens, *Sir Jacob Behrens*.
[8] For details on the Frankaus and their relatives, see Chapter 12 and the sources cited there.

(1801–53), a convert to Unitarianism, moved easily in middle-class philanthropic and political circles. He took an active part in the anti-Corn Law campaign, became a close friend of Richard Cobden and Elizabeth and William
Gaskell, entertained them and other middle-class notables at his country
home in Wales, served as Chopin's host when he visited Manchester in 1848,
chaired a meeting of German residents at the time of the 1848 Revolution to
express sympathy with the Frankfurt Assembly, and in general made his
mark on liberal philanthropic activity in the city.[9] In Bradford, Birmingham,
and Manchester, where there were large German trading colonies, German
Jews and German Christians banded together to establish social and cultural clubs where they could eat heavy, multi-course, two-hour meals in the
German fashion, read German periodicals, gossip about politics and business in their native tongue, nap, and play cards.[10] The first two chairmen of
the Schiller-Anstalt in Manchester, a library, newspaper-reading room, and
dining club, were Jews, as was much of the membership—a fact that led
Friedrich Engels to refer derisively to the institution as 'the Jerusalem
Club'.[11] In London, the merchant banker Isidore Gerstenberg (1821–76)
and the semiticist Emanuel Deutsch (1829–73) were members of the German Association for Science and Art, founded in 1864 by the political exile
Gottfried Kinkel.[12]

Among those immigrants who participated in the cultural life of the
larger society were a handful of university-trained scholars of Judaica and
semitic languages. Victorian Jewry was not a well-educated community,
either in terms of traditional Judaica or secular culture and science, and did
not produce its own, native-born practitioners of Wissenschaft des Judentums, the new critical scholarship that developed in Germany in the first half
of the nineteenth century. As a consequence, university-educated German
Jewish immigrants were employed in a variety of teaching and research
posts in Britain that required advanced training in Hebrew and other semitic
languages. Joseph Zedner (1804–71) served as librarian of the Hebrew division of the British Museum from 1845 to 1869.[13] Emanuel Deutsch, the
major inspiration for the Jewish themes in George Eliot's *Daniel Deronda*,
worked there as well from 1855 to 1872 in a more subordinate position,
although he was a prominent contributor to learned and popular journals on
Judaism, Islam, and the ancient Near East.[14] Adolf Neubauer (1831–1907)

[9] Endelman, *Radical Assimilation in English Jewish History*, 115.
[10] Priestley, *English Journey*, 180; Stroud, *The Story of the Stroud Family*, 83; Josephs, *Birmingham Jewry*, 234.   [11] Williams, *The Making of Manchester Jewry*, 260, 412 n. 95.
[12] Ashton, *Little Germany*, 164.   [13] *The Jewish Encyclopedia*, s.v. 'Zedner, Joseph'.
[14] Lask Abrahams, 'Emanuel Deutsch'.

was hired by the University of Oxford in 1868 to catalogue the Hebrew manuscripts in the Bodleian Library, a task that took eighteen years. When a readership in rabbinics was established at Oxford in 1884, he was appointed the first incumbent of the post, which he held until 1900.[15] At Cambridge, Solomon Marcus Schiller-Szinessy (1820–90), a German-speaking Hungarian Jew, offered private instruction in Hebrew from 1863 to 1866, was then formally engaged by the university, and in 1876 was given the rank of reader, a post he held until his death in 1890.[16]

German Jews who settled in England in the Victorian era were not typical of German Jewish migrants in general in this period, the majority of whom settled in the United States. Most Jews who left Germany arrived at their destination with far fewer resources of any kind with which to start their new lives than the relative few who came to England. Those arriving in the United States were for the most part poor and uneducated, without prior experience in large-scale commerce, or family connections to established mercantile firms. Many of them, especially those who left in the first decades of the migration, had their fares paid by communal charities at home, eager to be rid of persons who might otherwise become a long-term fiscal burden. Without sufficient capital to start their own businesses, the great majority became pedlars in the cities and the countryside, along the Atlantic seaboard and in newly settled regions of the Mid-West, South, and Far West. However, most did not remain pedlars all their lives, but after ascending the various rungs of the peddling ladder became shopkeepers, wholesale merchants, and occasionally manufacturers, primarily in branches of the clothing trade. Indeed, by the turn of the century German Jews in America had become a solidly middle-class community, their rise from poverty to prosperity being the most rapid of any immigrant group at the time.

Jewish immigrants in Victorian England also differed from their Georgian predecessors in their pattern of settlement. In the eighteenth and early nineteenth centuries, almost all newcomers settled in London, where the bulk of the Jewish population was concentrated, although a small number, after a stay in London and a stint peddling in the provinces, set up as shopkeepers on the south and east coasts or in pre-industrial county towns. In the Victorian period, however, substantial numbers of immigrants settled immediately in what had become the industrial heartland of the country, in manufacturing cities like Manchester, Leeds, Bradford, and Nottingham, having prior trading links with manufacturers and brokers there. Jewish trading houses in Germany were active in importing and distributing

---

[15] *The Jewish Encyclopedia*, s.v. 'Neubauer, Adolf'.
[16] Loewe, 'Solomon Marcus Schiller-Szinessy'.

English textiles and other manufactured goods on the Continent. Many of the newcomers were sent to England to establish permanent branch offices for the purchase and export of textiles to family and business associates abroad, thereby circumventing local brokers and ensuring a steady flow of goods at favourable prices. The Behrens family came to Leeds under such circumstances, as did scores of others. To cite only two examples, Jacob Weinberg arrived in Nottingham at the age of 20 to establish a branch of the well-known Hamburg firm of Simon, May & Co. and succeeded in making it into one of the most flourishing in the city;[17] Isidore Gerstenberg came to Manchester, also at the age of 20, to represent the Hamburg textile merchant Abraham Bauer, although he moved to London after several months, where he continued to work for Bauer, until setting up on his own four years later, first as a merchant and then as a banker and stockbroker.[18] Young men without capital and connections also migrated to the Midlands and the north with the intention of working as clerks and managers in the offices, warehouses, and factories of fellow immigrants. After a number of years they frequently went into business on their own.

Of course, immigrants continued to settle in London as well, certainly in numbers equal to (if not greater than) those who went to the provinces, for it remained a dynamic centre of commerce, finance, and small-scale manufacturing, despite the concentration of heavy industry elsewhere. During the mid-Victorian years it attracted German Jewish antique dealers, toy manufacturers, grain brokers, fancy-goods merchants, timber merchants, importers and exporters of colonial products, boot and shoe manufactures, jewellers, picture-frame makers, and wholesale tobacconists—to cite some of the most common occupations of male immigrants.[19] Less typical but more visible were the representatives of Jewish banking clans who were sent to London to take advantage of new opportunities in government loans, international trade, and railway, mining, and industrial securities. From Frankfurt alone came sons of the Stern, Worms, Erlanger, Speyer, Schuster, and Goldschmidt families.[20]

Given the middle-class nature of the German Jewish migration to Victorian England and the commercial motives fuelling it, it is no surprise that these immigrants, unlike their counterparts in the United States, came from urban rather than rural backgrounds. Before emancipation German Jewry was overwhelmingly a small-town and village Jewry, scattered in hundreds of

[17] *Jewish Chronicle*, 23 Mar. 1900.   [18] Behr, 'Isidore Gerstenberg', 208–9.
[19] See the German Jewish entries, easily identifiable by name, in the annual editions of *The Post Office London Directory*.
[20] Chapman, *The Rise of Merchant Banking*, 45, 50, 54, 136; Dietz, *Stammbuch der Frankfurter Juden*, 377–8.

settlements in dozens of states. In the course of the nineteenth century, as city residence restrictions were lifted and the pace of industrial and commercial life accelerated, Jews began moving to urban centres, but the pace of urbanization before 1880 was slower than is commonly assumed. In 1882, for example, only 17 per cent of the Jewish population lived in the forty-five largest cities (100,000 or more inhabitants).[21] In their geographical origins, German Jewish migrants to the United States were representative of German Jewry as a whole: they were overwhelmingly *Dorfjuden*, primarily from the southern and south-western regions of the country. Most German Jews who settled in Cleveland in the 1840s, for example, were from villages in Bavaria;[22] of the twenty-seven Jewish families who arrived in Columbus between 1838 and 1860, twenty-five were from small communities in the south and south-west.[23] These immigrants were coming from German states in which Jews were still subject to legal discrimination. Bavaria and Württemberg, the two largest states in the region, limited the number of Jews who were permitted to marry and establish families and who were permitted to reside in a certain locale. Jewish traders and artisans in these states were also subject to a maze of ordinances and regulations that hampered their ability to earn a living. (In Prussia and the independent city states of northern Germany and the Rhineland, on the other hand, there were few legal obstacles to economic mobility.)

By contrast, German Jewish immigrants to Victorian Britain were more likely to have lived in a major urban area prior to their departure. For example, over half of the German Jews who were founding members of the Reform synagogue in Manchester (sixteen of twenty-nine) were from large cities—Hamburg, Frankfurt, Leipzig, Cologne, Essen, and Berlin.[24] At the end of the nineteenth century, Alexander Dietz traced eighty-nine Jews from Frankfurt who had settled in England but only fifty-two who had settled in the United States, although the total number of German Jews who went there was at least twenty times greater.[25]

However, the fact that most migrants to England came from urban areas should not be allowed to obscure the possibility that some of them might have grown up in small towns and villages and only later become city dwellers. This was the case, for example, with Joseph and Adolph Frankau, who were born in a Bavarian village, but emigrated to England after living in

[21] Barkai, 'German-Jewish Migrations in the Nineteenth Century', 302.
[22] Gartner, *History of the Jews of Cleveland*, 10.
[23] Raphael, *Jews and Judaism in a Midwestern Community*, 14.
[24] Williams, *The Making of Manchester Jewry*, 260.
[25] Dietz, *Stammbuch der Frankfurter Juden*, pt. 6.

Frankfurt, and with Jacob Behrens, who was born in Pyrmont, Hanover, but whose parents moved to Hamburg when he was a child.[26]

Although the immigrants of the Victorian period were motivated chiefly by economic considerations, they were also moved, if not to the same extent, by the pervasive anti-Jewish hostility of central Europe. Some were in flight from discriminatory statutes that limited freedom of residence and occupation, as were those Jews who migrated to the United States; a handful were refugees from the political repression that followed the abortive revolutions of 1848. But most were not so much attempting to escape this or that obstacle to advancement, many of which emancipation slowly removed, as seeking to flee a society in which Jews were routinely treated with contempt and derision. In his memoirs, Jacob Behrens repeatedly recalled the indignities he suffered while growing up in Hamburg. He described, for example, how he and his father when travelling to fairs would be refused lodging because they were Jews. He also told how his friendship with Ferdinand David (1810–73), a Jewish pupil of the composer Ludwig Spohr (1784–1859), was abruptly terminated when the latter insisted that David convert and sever all relations with Jews in order to boost his career. 'This was typical of the times and such experiences fixed an indelible impression in my mind', Behrens wrote.[27] Felix Semon, who grew up in Berlin several decades later, also cited German intolerance as a motive for moving to England. In his autobiography he recalled the difficulty of choosing a profession when he was a *Gymnasium* student in the 1860s. All the careers he most inclined to —the diplomatic corps, the army, the civil service—were closed to Jews. Commerce held no interest for him; history and natural science did, but a university career without baptism was impossible. Thus, by a process of elimination, he settled on medicine. When he completed his training, he chose to leave Germany, in part because of widespread hostility to Jews.[28] Sigmund Freud considered settling in England several times for similar reasons and never ceased to envy his half-brothers in Manchester, whom he visited in 1875, for being able to raise their children far from the daily indignities to which Viennese Jews were subject.[29] A few months after becoming engaged to Martha Bernays, he recalled for her 'the ineffaceable impression' of his trip to England and asked: 'Must we stay here, Martha? If we possibly can, let us seek a home where human worth is more respected.'[30]

Immigrants in the Victorian period differed from their predecessors in one other important respect as well: they did not grow up in a traditional

[26] Behrens, *Sir Jacob Behrens*, 2.   [27] Ibid. 20–1.   [28] Semon, *Autobiography*, 31–2.
[29] Jones, *The Life and Work of Sigmund Freud*, i. 13, 24.   [30] Ibid. 178–9.

Jewish milieu, segregated socially and culturally from the surrounding population. Although legal emancipation was not complete until 1871, the corporate and national character of Jewish life in central Europe was well on its way to dissolution before then. German Jews were embracing German patterns of thought and behaviour and neglecting religious customs. Old loyalties and allegiances were weakening and new identities were being forged. Thus the new immigrants, especially those from urban, middle-class backgrounds, were accustomed to taking part in spheres of activity outside Jewish social and business networks. Few had received a traditional Jewish education or grown up in homes in which regular synagogue attendance and observance of the dietary laws were the norm. Jacob Behrens, for example, received no Jewish education except for some last-minute preparation for his barmitzvah in the Reform synagogue.[31] Ludwig Mond's upbringing in Cassel in the 1840s and 1850s was similar. He was educated at non-Jewish schools, learned only enough Hebrew to celebrate his barmitzvah, and eventually gave up all religious practices, declaring himself an agnostic.[32]

Once settled in England, the immigrants did not rapidly abandon their attachment to German cultural and social habits or cut their ties to family and friends who remained behind. It was not uncommon for merchants to join German-speaking dining clubs and literary institutes, to return to Germany to find wives for themselves, to send their sons and daughters to Germany to be educated, and to continue to speak German with their offspring. Joseph Frankau, for example, sent his son Arthur from London to be educated at the *Realschule* of the Frankfurt Jewish community. Ludwig and Frieda Mond, who settled in England in 1867, maintained a German atmosphere in their home. Because she disapproved of English child-rearing methods—too lax in her view—she engaged a German governess for her children, who grew up speaking German better than English. Their eldest son, Robert (1867–1938), married into a German Jewish family in Manchester that also maintained links to its origins.[33] Though his wife's relatives were anglicized to the extent of owning country estates, they limited the guests at their house parties largely to persons from the same background. As Ludwig Mond's biographer noted, 'they remained a still unassimilated enclave in a Gentile society, from which they were divided by their love for music, their German habit of family celebrations for which humorous verse was still manufactured in the mother tongue, and by a certain uneasy sardonic humour which jarred on their neighbours'.[34] German Jews in London, according to the novelist Cecily Ullmann Sidgwick (1855–1934), celebrated

---

[31] Behrens, *Sir Jacob Behrens*, 11–13.
[32] J. M. Cohen, *The Life of Ludwig Mond*, 16, 62.
[33] Goodman, *The Mond Legacy*, 34, 39.
[34] J. M. Cohen, *The Life of Ludwig Mond*, 189.

Christmas in the German fashion, 'because the memories and customs of their German homes were dear to them. They grumbled a good deal at the annual cost of it, but they never altered their ways. Every year there was a large and elaborate interchange of presents, and a family gathering in each household; and on Christmas Eve, for the pleasure of the family and relatives only, a Christmas tree.'[35]

This kind of attachment to German ways was selective, however; it would be a mistake to infer from impressionistic comments such as Sidgwick's that the immigrants remained immune to anglicization. On the contrary, most seem to have been eager to find a place for themselves in English society even if they retained old attachments in some areas of life. Many families eager to adapt to the English environment sent their sons to elite boarding schools, like Harrow, Eton, and Charterhouse,[36] and made no effort to raise their children in a German-speaking home. The poet and civil servant Humbert Wolfe (1886–1940), recalling his childhood in late Victorian Bradford, was impressed with the eagerness and thoroughness with which his parents and their friends accepted local habits. In speaking they used Yorkshire phrases, clipped their vowels, and attempted to speak slowly without gesturing with their hands. 'The men at the week-ends smoked unusually large pipes, drank whisky-and-sodas, and wore Norfolk jackets, alarmingly checked, and the thickest of heather-mixture stockings under their breeches.' The women went even further: they tried to develop an English complexion and abandoned 'their natural good taste in dress' in order to adopt 'the drab and clumsy apparel habitual among their Christian neighbours'.[37]

Whatever their attachment to German ways, most immigrants were indifferent or hostile to the Jewish religion. Their acculturation and secularization prior to migration, as well as their exposure to the pervasive antisemitism of Germany, left them unenthusiastic about its perpetuation and in some cases eager to escape it altogether. Many of the new arrivals held aloof from any institutional identification with Judaism, while most of those who did affiliate with a synagogue established a largely formal relationship. (Because the German immigrants were few in number relative to the native Jewish community and congregations already existed in the cities where they settled, with the exception of Bradford, they did not establish synagogues of their own, as did German Jews in the United States.) Most of them either moved away from the Jewish community completely, through conversion or intermarriage, or established such a weak connection to it that their

[35] Sidgwick, *Isaac Eller's Money*, 110.
[36] Their names appear in the published directories of the major public schools.
[37] Wolfe, *Now A Stranger*, 126–7.

children or grandchildren eventually drifted away. To be sure, none of this can be established with statistical certainty, but contemporary testimony, as well as non-quantifiable evidence, makes clear that the majority of immigrants from German-speaking lands in the Victorian period took advantage of their new surroundings to shed or mute their Jewishness.

Contemporaries often commented on the disinclination of the immigrants to identify themselves with Jewish institutions. When the newly appointed chief rabbi, Nathan Adler (1803–90), surveyed the congregations under his authority in 1845, the New Synagogue in Glasgow replied that many 'respectable' German Jews who lived there were not members of the synagogue.[38] The *Jewish Chronicle* noted in April 1859 that there were hundreds of foreign-born, prosperous Jews in the country, especially in London, Liverpool, and Manchester, who neither belonged to congregations nor supported communal charities.[39] In Manchester, in particular, there were numbers of German Jews who were not even known as Jews. When Chaim Weizmann arrived there in 1904, he found that 'the great majority of German Jews . . . were disassociated from their people, and many of them were converts to Christianity'.[40] In August 1865 the *Jewish Chronicle* reported that there were many wealthy Jews in Bradford but no congregation—indeed, not even a burial ground. These German Jews, according to the newspaper, did not want to be known as Jews (although apparently everyone knew they were). They failed to circumcise their sons or to educate them in any way as Jews. They buried their dead in a Christian cemetery and married their children to Christians in church ceremonies. Efforts on the part of the Leeds congregation to stimulate the formation of a synagogue in Bradford in the early 1860s failed. When the chief rabbi himself visited the city in 1865, six Jews showed up at the meeting he called and told him that he was wasting his time in attempting to form a congregation.[41] Five years later, when there were 200 to 300 German Jews in Bradford, the one service held that year— on Yom Kippur—drew only fifteen people. The following year, when services were held on both Rosh Hashanah and Yom Kippur, thirty to forty people attended the latter.[42] When the community's first rabbi, Joseph Strauss (1844–1922)—German-born, German-educated, and Reform in outlook— arrived in 1873, he found the older and wealthier Jewish residents 'indifferent to Judaism'.[43]

[38] Bernard Susser (ed.), 'Statistical Accounts of all the Congregations in the British Empire', 5606/1845, MS 104, Office of the Chief Rabbi, reprinted in Newman (ed.), *Provincial Jewry*.
[39] *Jewish Chronicle*, 8 and 15 Apr. 1859.   [40] Weizmann, *Trial and Error*, 115.
[41] *Jewish Chronicle*, 11 Aug. 1865.   [42] *Jewish Chronicle*, 21 and 28 Oct. 1870, 6 Oct. 1871.
[43] Stroud, *The Story of the Stroud Family*, 83.

Some of those who distanced themselves from Judaism remained equally aloof from Christianity because they loathed religion in general. Jacob Behrens found membership in any religious body impossible because he could not believe in the personal God of organized, dogmatic religion. 'When either Christian minister or Jewish rabbi calls on the inscrutable God with the audacity and familiarity of an old acquaintance, I can see nothing but a hollow lie or an unfathomable depth of stupidity', he wrote in his autobiography.[44] He thus refused to educate his children in any faith. (However, his descendants and those of his brothers Louis and Rudolf drifted contentedly into the Church of England. They were eager to get on in polite society and freethinking anti-clericalism was simply not respectable.[45]) Ludwig Mond also refused to join any religious body or to rear his children as either Christians or Jews. In fact, when his son Alfred (1868–1930) was to marry in 1892, the officiating clergyman almost refused to perform the ceremony when he discovered that the bridegroom was neither a professing Jew nor a professing Christian.[46] Felix Semon, too, espoused similar views and remained outside both church and synagogue, believing that all religions, each with its claim to possess the truth, were too exclusive. Like the deists of the previous century, he blamed institutional religion for much of the suffering and bloodshed that had afflicted humankind in past centuries. Yet he raised his children in the Church of England, in part because his wife was a Christian (although he did not cite this as a reason) and in part because he did not want 'to close many careers open to them, by mere obstinate adherence to the old tradition'.[47]

A principled refusal to join any religious group, however, was not characteristic of German Jews who distanced themselves from the Anglo-Jewish community. More common, at least in the provinces, was membership of a Unitarian chapel. As Solomon Marcus Schiller-Szinessy, then rabbi of the Reform congregation in Manchester, explained in 1859, justifying his decision to preach on the differences between Judaism and Unitarianism: 'Our attention is due to Unitarianism on account of the fortuitous circumstances that it is *that* form of Christianity to which such Jews as feel themselves induced to abandon their brethren and to turn their backs on the religion of their fathers are in the first instances chiefly attracted.'[48] Most of the German Jewish merchants who arrived in Manchester between 1790 and the mid-1830s abandoned Judaism; most became Unitarians.[49] In Nottingham the

[44] Behrens, *Sir Jacob Behrens*, 93.   [45] *Jewish Chronicle*, 21 Mar. and 4 Apr. 1913.
[46] J. M. Cohen, *The Life of Ludwig Mond*, 62; Bolitho, *Alfred Mond*, 44, 92, 358.
[47] Semon, *Autobiography*, 33–4.   [48] Schiller-Szinessy, *Harmony and Dis-Harmony*, 9.
[49] Williams, *The Making of Manchester Jewry*, 82–3, 93.

majority of the new arrivals, most of whom were active in the hosiery and lace trades, joined the Unitarian chapel. The most prominent of them, the lace-shipper and civic leader Lewis Heymann (1803–66), was a regular worshipper at the High Pavement Chapel and served as a warden of the congregation several times.[50]

The tendency of those German Jewish immigrants in the provinces who left Judaism to affiliate with Unitarianism was a departure from the usual pattern of disaffiliation in Anglo-Jewish history. In general, when Jews in England embraced Christianity they joined the Church of England—for obvious reasons. Their motives for becoming Christians were almost always pragmatic. They were seeking to escape the stigma attached to Jewishness and to complete their social absorption, to improve their social fortunes, and, before emancipation, to gain entry to elite institutions, such as Parliament, that were closed to professing Jews.[51] In these circumstances, Jews in flight from their Jewishness naturally joined the high-status Established Church rather than low-status Nonconformist chapels, whose members were themselves frequently objects of contempt and scorn and were also barred from certain offices and honours. If the object of conversion was social advancement rather than eternal salvation, it hardly made sense for Jews to become Baptists or Methodists.

However, in the manufacturing cities of the Midlands and the north, the reference group for upwardly mobile Jews was not the same as it was in London or the countryside. The elite whom the recent arrivals sought to emulate and whose social approval they desired was Unitarian and industrial-mercantile, not Anglican and landed (as it was for Jews who made their fortunes in finance and international trade in the City of London). In Manchester, for example, the membership of the Cross Street Chapel included opulent merchants, affluent professional men, and bankers. Its members played a key role in establishing the major educational and cultural institutions of the new liberal order in the city, such as the Literary and Philosophical Society and the Mechanics' Institute. They were well-educated and culturally sophisticated men and women, not dour philistines, as literary caricatures of dissenters frequently suggest.[52] In the words of a contemporary observer, the Unitarians in Manchester were 'as a body, far away superior to any other in intellect, culture, and refinement of manners, and certainly did not come behind any other in active philanthropy and earnest efforts for the social improvement of those around them'.[53]

---

[50] Aronsfeld, 'German Jews in Nottingham', 9; Church, *Economic and Social Change in a Midland Town*, 182; High Pavement Chapel, *A Biographical Catalogue of Portraits*, 28.

[51] Endelman, *Radical Assimilation in English Jewish History*, chs. 1–3.

[52] Seed, 'Unitarianism'.   [53] Shaen, *Memorials of Two Sisters*, 26.

Yet the attraction of Unitarianism for German Jewish immigrants in the provinces was not entirely social. Although rooted in Calvinist Presbyterianism, Unitarianism had become relatively broad-minded by the early nineteenth century. It was theologically relaxed, spiritually undemanding, and politely rationalistic. Its ministers were frequently men of wide secular learning, intellectually sophisticated, and tolerant of diverse opinions. Most importantly, its anti-Trinitarianism removed what was to Jews the most baffling and objectionable aspect of Christianity and made its sincere acceptance possible. To German Jews critical of traditional religion whatever its form, this was an immense advantage. They could enjoy the social benefits of belonging to a religious body whose members were wealthy, dynamic, and influential without having to accept supernatural theological doctrines repugnant to their own outlook.

In London, where Unitarianism did not occupy the same position it did in Manchester and other industrial cities, German Jewish immigrants did not join Unitarian chapels in substantial numbers. The records of the Rosslyn Hill Chapel in Hampstead, which drew its upper-middle-class membership from neighbourhoods throughout north-west London (where many German Jews lived), show that only four or five families of German Jewish origin belonged to the congregation in the 1860s and 1870s, and only eight or nine families at any one time from the 1880s to the start of the First World War.[54] (Even smaller numbers of German Jews affiliated with universalist ethical societies or churches, unlike in the United States, where the Ethical Culture movement was, in terms of its social make-up, a Jewish project.[55]) If German Jews in London formally abandoned Judaism, they were likely to be baptized—or to have their children baptized—in the Church of England, which was the religious home of the dominant social strata in the metropolis.

The tendency of German Jews to shed their Jewishness after settling in England contrasts sharply with the religious behaviour of their native middle-class counterparts, who did not disaffiliate from the community in great numbers in the Victorian period.[56] To some extent, the high rate of defection can be explained by the fact that the newcomers were leaving a Jewish environment in which religious observance and knowledge were already in decline. In other words, they came to England without a strong prior attachment to home observance and synagogue attendance and, once in new

[54] Rosslyn Hill Chapel, list of members, 1 Jan. 1875, Rosslyn Hill Chapel Records, RNC 38.189; subscriptions, 1886–96, Rosslyn Hill Chapel Records, RNC 38.154; minute book, 1907–22, Rosslyn Hill Chapel Records, RNC 38.132.
[55] Endelman, *Radical Assimilation in English Jewish History*, 123–5.   [56] Ibid., ch. 3.

surroundings, simply carried their disengagement one step further. On the other hand, native middle-class Jews, while perhaps more diligent in their observance of Judaism than Jews elsewhere in the West, were not on the whole pious adherents of their ancestral faith. Yet most were content to remain within the boundaries of the community of their birth, even if they felt little attachment to traditional rituals and beliefs—that is, alienation from Judaism as a system of doctrines and practices did not necessarily lead to estrangement from the Jewish group.

The German environment shaped the behaviour of Jewish immigrants to Victorian England in another, more profound way, however. The new arrivals carried with them attitudes towards Jewishness that bore the impress of conditions quite different from those they found in their new home. In German-speaking lands, Jews remained second-class citizens until the last third of the century and even after emancipation still faced widespread social and occupational discrimination. Ideological antisemitism was virulent, deep-rooted, and far from marginal in high culture or respectable society. German Jews who identified strongly with the majority culture frequently experienced their Jewishness as a misfortune or burden; in some instances, as we have seen, bitterness and resentment at the accident of Jewish birth developed into pathological self-hatred. Those who migrated to England at this time often behaved vis-à-vis their Jewishness as if they were still living in Germany, where conversion was a common response to discrimination and denigration. Once settled, they took advantage of their new surroundings to jettison that part of their past with which they were uncomfortable. Migration became for them not only a means for improving themselves materially but also an opportunity for refashioning their status. To be sure, it is possible that they found integration into their new surroundings blocked by their Jewishness—although there is little evidence that this happened—and that they remained apart from Anglo-Jewry in order to expedite their social amalgamation. However, we know that prosperous native-born Jews were able to enter non-Jewish circles and institutions without shedding communal ties.[57] (The relatively few native English Jews who converted at this time did so largely to escape the emotional burden of belonging to a stigmatized minority, rather than to gain access to offices and circles that in other lands were closed to Jews.) This suggests that the flight of German Jews from Jewishness was fuelled not so much by discrimination in England as by the formative influence of conditions in their country of origin. They were unable to free themselves from the experiences of their early years and assess the character of Jewish status in Britain dispassionately. Thus they

---

[57] Endelman, 'Communal Solidarity and Family Loyalty'.

failed to realize that they could attain worldly success without having to leave the Jewish community.

Even those immigrants who chose to identify with Anglo-Jewish institutions were not, in the main, firmly attached to Jewish practices and beliefs. Their profession of Judaism was lukewarm, frequently limited to being married and buried according to Jewish rites. Their homes were largely devoid of Jewish ritual, and their attendance at synagogue infrequent. Their efforts to provide their children with the learning that would allow them to live as Jews were half-hearted, if not altogether absent. As a consequence, their children, most of whom were educated in English schools (those sent to schools in Germany were a minority), grew up feeling far more English than German or Jewish—even if they retained a fondness for music or heavy meals. In her memoir of Edwardian Manchester, Katharine Chorley described the progressive acculturation of a German Jewish family over three generations:

Our Mr. Rothstein was no longer, like his father, a practising Jew although he was still loosely attached through his private and exclusive pride of race to the faith of his ancestors. He had been educated at Manchester Grammar School and spoke English with a slight Lancashire accent as opposed to his father's German accent. He had sold most of his father's German books, but retained all the well-marked opera scores and sheets of music, for he could read a score as easily as he could read a book . . . He had reduced the groaning German board, or his wife had, to a more English weight, but he still drank half a bottle of claret every evening at his dinner. His sons, who were my contemporaries, had no Lancashire accent and a reduced pride of race. They went to Rugby; his daughter went to Roedean.[58]

Jews like Rothstein mixed with non-Jews in a variety of formal and informal settings and distanced themselves from Jewish social networks. Yet however attenuated their sense of Jewish identity, to the larger society they remained somehow different, not quite English, as Chorley's words suggest. Thus many in the second generation found their Jewishness to be a burden that was not worth bearing and ceased to have any contact with Jewish institutions or circles when they grew up.

Humbert Wolfe described in two volumes of memoirs the difficulty of growing up Jewish in such circumstances in late Victorian Bradford.[59] His father was a prosperous wool merchant, a native of Germany who had met and married his Italian-born mother while working in Genoa. In Bradford, where they moved soon after Humbert's birth, the family maintained a loose attachment to Judaism. They visited the (Reform) synagogue on Rosh Hashanah and Yom Kippur, and Humbert attended religious classes there

---

[58] Chorley, *Manchester Made Them*, 117–18.
[59] Wolfe, *Now a Stranger*, and *The Upward Anguish*.

on Sunday mornings for a number of years, but nothing in his upbringing or education fostered warm feelings towards Judaism. Attendance at High Holiday services left him emotionally unmoved. The rabbi, Joseph Strauss, had no message to impart; the Hebrew hymns made no impression. 'There was nothing here to inspire or excite the young worshipper.' Strauss's position in the community brought home to Wolfe how little his parents and their friends valued religion, for the wealthy merchants who managed the synagogue treated him like a clerk in one of their warehouses, bullying him into 'a state of sullen stupidity'. They brooked no interference with their consciences by someone they considered their paid servant. His business was 'to interpret the ways of God to man in general, but to avoid the particular at all costs'. Their contempt for Strauss was infectious; from them, Wolfe learned to sneer at him.

Although Wolfe felt unmoved by Judaism, he could not forget he was Jewish. At school and university he was acutely sensitive about being set apart from his fellow students by his origins. Regularly taunted by a group of urchins as he made his way to the synagogue on Sunday mornings, he felt bitterly ashamed of being different, envying the church- and chapel-goers on their way to worship. As he wrote of himself: 'Each Sunday the boy ran this gauntlet, hating not his persecutors but the object of their persecution.'[60] Attacks such as these, however, were rare and less destructive of his confidence than a myriad of small signs, not always conscious, reminding him that he belonged to a minority, 'edged on the one side, excluded, different'. That the English were too 'easy-going and good humoured' to carry their antisemitism to extremes only made matters worse, for 'when the taint of Jewry means only exclusion from garden-parties, refusal of certain cherished intimacies, and occasional light-hearted sneers, it is difficult to maintain an attitude of racial pride'.[61] Had he been secure in his faith or taken pride in his Jewishness, he later realized, he would have been better able to accept the sense of being different.

In his last years at school Wolfe developed strong literary interests and simultaneously began to think seriously about religious questions. The 'faint shamefaced Judaism of Bradford' offered him no answers or solace and so he turned to Christianity. He discussed the desirability of being baptized with a friend, George Falkenstein, who had himself become a Unitarian. Falkenstein admitted that Unitarianism was a compromise, 'a sort of half-way house'. To Wolfe, the budding poet and prospective Oxford man, this choice seemed 'well enough for unadventurous or doubtful spirits' but 'a little too mild' for himself.[62] Yet he could not bring himself to take the step.

[60] Wolfe, *Now a Stranger*, 129.   [61] Ibid. 125–6.   [62] Wolfe, *The Upward Anguish*, 46.

He repeatedly slunk in to evening services at St Jude's and found himself pleased with the eloquence of the preacher and the light streaming in through the stained glass windows. He realized that it would be 'comfortable' to feel himself 'numbered among those to whom these spiritual elegances belonged' and 'advantageous' to the career he envisioned. 'But something—probably no more than a mixture of shyness and apathy—had held him back.'[63] He arrived at Wadham College, Oxford, still concerned about the fate of his soul—and his career—but unsure about what religion he was committed to. He had no doubt that Judaism was unsatisfactory but still could not take the plunge into the Church of England—'a step which a desire to be like other men tempted him to take'—for he was concerned about what his mother would think (his father was already dead) and restrained by 'something stubborn in his blood, which remembered Zion'.[64] After Wolfe left Oxford in 1907 he passed by examination into the Home Civil Service and went on to a distinguished career in a number of departments. In 1908 he became a member of the Church of England in order to marry the daughter of an Edinburgh headmaster, who would not have allowed her to wed him otherwise. As an adult he took no part in Jewish life, other than joining a small dining club of Christians and Jews who were interested in intellectual and spiritual revival in Palestine.[65]

Children of German Jewish immigrants who grew up in circumstances similar to those in which Humbert Wolfe was raised tended to detach themselves from Jewish life once they reached adulthood. The ambiguous religious and ethnic character of their home life—part-Jewish, part-Christian, part-English, part-German—left them without a firm inner sense of who they were, and thus unable or unwilling to cope with even low levels of contempt and exclusion. That is, because they did not follow a recognizably Jewish regimen or affirm distinctively Jewish beliefs or mix primarily in Jewish social circles, they were not prepared to endure even modest slights on account of their Jewish origins. Humbert Wolfe, it should be recalled, felt that he had been especially sensitive to the taunts of other children because he had been raised in a lukewarm Jewish atmosphere and lacked the pride that would have allowed him to withstand their contempt. He concluded that a Polish Jew, secure in his faith, was better able to withstand anti-Jewish hostility than a deracinated English Jew, ever alert to the least suggestion of being different, the occasional sneer or jibe.

Wolfe was not the only child of German Jewish immigrants who came to this conclusion. His contemporary, the poet E. H. W. Meyerstein

[63] Wolfe, *The Upward Anguish*, 47. [64] Ibid. 62–3.
[65] Bentwich, 'Humbert Wolfe'; Bagguley, *Harlequin in Whitehall*, 80–2.

(1889–1952), son of a London stockbroker whose parents migrated from Germany in the mid-nineteenth century, felt that he became the target of wounding schoolboy taunts precisely because he was neither fully Jewish nor fully Christian. His parents practised no religion at any time in their lives, but raised their children from an early age in the Church of England, presumably for pragmatic reasons, although they did not take them to be baptized until 1903, just prior to their son's departure for Harrow. There he suffered greatly as a newly minted Christian of German Jewish origin. He later wrote that a boy from a well-established Jewish family who was proud of his religion and believed he was good as anyone else got through school just fine, but a boy of Jewish or partly Jewish antecedents who had been baptized and also bore a German name was 'due for hell'. He felt he would have been much happier had he been able to boast 'I am proud of my race!', and then bashed his tormentors with his fists.[66]

The dynamic that Wolfe and Meyerstein described was noted by non-Jewish observers as well. Sir Lawrence Evelyn Jones, remembering his Edwardian youth, noted the response of George Joseph, a junior counsel in the barrister's chambers where he was a pupil after leaving Oxford. Jones and another Oxford man with whom he shared an office teased Joseph mercilessly.

It was a godsend to two Old Blues . . . to have as stable companion a bottle-shouldered, flat-footed Jew, who had been to neither public school nor University, who had never played a game or walked a mile in his life, and who packed a hot-water bottle when he visited Brighton for the week-end. We left him off nothing, and he in his turn, clever, quizzical and amused, enjoyed trailing his coat for us. *Secure in his pride of race, he could afford to be our butt.*[67]

Although hybridity is much celebrated in academic circles in the early twenty-first century, those who write glowingly about it seem blind to the problems it caused for persons with 'hybrid' identities in other times and places.

Even when shame and embarrassment were not present, disaffiliation from the Jewish community was commonplace in the second and third generations. Indifference to Jewish practice and integration into English social circles promoted intermarriage and the dissolution of Jewish ties. In those instances when children from German Jewish families did marry within the fold (usually within the German Jewish fold) their attachment to Judaism might persist for another generation, but it was an attachment that was largely nominal. The publisher Fredric John Warburg (1898–1981), whose

[66] Meyerstein, *Of My Early Life*, 17–19; id., *Some Letters*, 240–1.
[67] Jones, *An Edwardian Youth*, 178 (my emphasis).

grandfather had migrated to England in the 1860s and made a fortune in financing London's first underground train network, described his family's Jewishness as a matter of inertia. The Warburgs, he wrote, were Jews 'because they were born of Jewish parents and believed themselves to be Jews', but 'their religious feeling was slight and their racial exclusiveness negligible'.[68] They were both too proud and too lethargic to disaffiliate formally from the Jewish group through conversion; thus they remained Jews until something unintended occurred—like marrying a non-Jew—to make them leave their Jewishness behind. 'Then they changed with as little fuss as a man changing from one lounge suit to another of a slightly different colour. So they remained basically the same, substituting for the practice of not going to synagogue the rather similar practice of not going to church.'[69]

The absorption of German Jews and their offspring into English society progressed steadily in the years before the First World War. Although it is impossible to gauge their incorporation in any quantitative way, the available evidence seems to indicate that with every year more and more of them ceased to be identifiable as Jews. Their departure was not a dramatic affair for the most part. This was because their numbers were not great by comparison with the native community and even less by comparison with the new east European immigrant community, which became the focus of widespread public attention from the 1880s. Their absorption also failed to attract notice because English society, which after all determined the pace of integration, put few obstacles in their way, and thus there were no battles to be fought to gain access to English circles and institutions. Then, during the First World War, their integration received an unexpected boost: with anti-German hysteria raging, hundreds of families anglicized their names in order to avoid suspicion of disloyalty. Auerbachs became Arbours; Meyers, Merricks; Rothensteins, Rutherfords; Schlosses, Castles; Waldsteins, Walstons; and so on.[70] Although the immediate motive for these name changes was the desire to obscure German rather than explicitly Jewish origins, the effect was the same. Stripped of their foreign-sounding names, the children and grandchildren of the immigrants were able to blend even more easily into England society.

The wholesale name-changing of the war years made possible the virtual disappearance of the German Jewish group in the 1920s and 1930s. Individual families here and there continued to identify as Jews, of course, but they

---

[68] Warburg, *An Occupation for Gentlemen*, 31–2.　　　　　　　　[69] Ibid.

[70] The genealogist Sir Thomas Colyer-Fergusson included scores of change-of-name notices from *The Times* in the volumes of newspaper clippings about Anglo-Jewish families that he compiled. They are housed today in the Anglo-Jewish Archives at the University of Southampton.

were the exceptions. When J. B. Priestley returned home to Bradford in 1933 he discovered, to his regret, that there was 'hardly a trace now of the German Jewish invasion' of the previous century.[71] That same year, when Jewish refugees from Nazi Germany began arriving in Britain, they found no circles or associations of Jews of German origin to help them in their resettlement. Indeed, anti-Jewish agitation and discrimination in the interwar period discouraged persons of Jewish origins without strong Jewish commitments from asserting their links with Jewry. Stephen Spender, whose maternal grandfather, Ernest Joseph Schuster (1850–1924), came from a Frankfurt Jewish banking family, recalled that when he was in his teens and twenties both his German and Jewish origins were 'passed over in silence or with slight embarrassment' by his family. As a child, he had no idea that he was 'a quarter Jewish'. From the conversation of nurses and governesses, he had gathered the impression that Jews were 'a strange race with hooked noses' and 'avaricious manners', with whom he had no reason to imagine that he had any connection.[72]

Because most German Jewish immigrants in the Victorian era were lukewarm in their attachment to Judaism and because so many of them and their offspring failed to affiliate with communal institutions, they had no significant long-term impact on Anglo-Jewry. Of course, there were individual families here and there who were observant before their migration and remained so afterwards, and they in their own small way helped to strengthen Jewish practice in England. The Nottingham lace-shipper Jacob Weinberg, for example, was meticulous in his observance of Judaism. He shut his office on the sabbath and festivals and maintained a private synagogue in his own home. He took no part in political or civic affairs, but instead devoted his leisure time to Jewish learning.[73] But he was not typical. Nor was the small group of strictly observant followers of Samson Raphael Hirsch's Neo-Orthodoxy who lived in Canonbury and founded the North London Beth Hamedrash in 1889. A number of prominent businessmen, like Raphael Tuck (1821–1900), the greeting-card publisher, and David Gestetner (1854–1939), the pioneer of office duplicating equipment, belonged to this group, but its total membership was not large relative to other congregations. Moreover, because it pursued the Hirschian strategy of sectarian independence, refusing to co-operate with or participate in mainstream Orthodox initiatives, its impact on communal life was minimal.[74]

At the liberal end of the denominational spectrum, as well, German Jews contributed little to the religious complexion of the community, despite the

[71] Priestley, *English Journey*, 160–1.
[72] Spender, *World Within World*, 13.
[73] *Jewish Chronicle*, 23 Mar. 1900.
[74] Homa, *A Fortress in Anglo-Jewry*, 7, 10–11.

fact that Germany was the home of the Reform movement. As we saw in Chapter 3, the first and largest Reform congregation—the West London Synagogue of British Jews—was established by Sephardi and Ashkenazi families long settled in the country, not by recent arrivals from Germany. In Manchester, where recent German immigrants were prominent in the establishment of a Reform congregation in 1856, the influence of German Reform was limited. The model on which they drew was the West London Synagogue, whose prayer book and form of worship they adopted. Only in one minor provincial community, Bradford, where German immigrants were the dominant element before the arrival of east Europeans late in the century, was the influence of German Reform substantial. When the German merchants there decided in the early 1870s to establish a non-Orthodox congregation, they wrote to Germany to find a Reform rabbi.

Although German immigrants failed to leave a collective mark on the character of Victorian Jewish life, German-born individuals were conspicuous as religious functionaries and Hebrew scholars. For reasons that I have explained at length elsewhere,[75] the native-born Anglo-Jewish community of the nineteenth century failed to produce the rabbis, cantors, ecclesiastical judges, and educators it needed. It was thus dependent on persons born and educated abroad to fill both minor and major posts. Since east Europeans lacked the social polish and Western education thought necessary to serve English congregations, the community looked to Germany, whence came the most notable religious leaders of the period: Nathan Adler, chief rabbi from 1845 to his death in 1890; Gustav Gottheil (1827–1903), rabbi in Manchester for thirteen years before his departure to New York City in 1873; Michael Friedlander (1833–1910), principal of Jews' College for more than forty years; Samuel Marcus Gollancz (1819–1900), officiant at the Hambro Synagogue, London, and progenitor of an intellectually distinguished Anglo-Jewish family; Benjamin Henry Ascher (1812–93), funeral preacher at the Great Synagogue, London, for forty years and noted Hebraist; Albert Lowy (1816–1908), rabbi at the West London Synagogue for fifty years and secretary of the Anglo-Jewish Association from its founding in 1871 to 1889. Yet, however distinguished their careers, these men did not collectively influence the institutional structure or religious temper of Anglo-Jewry. In particular, they were not successful in imparting to their adopted community the scholarly standards and intellectual tone that characterized the communities where they had been educated. Either they succumbed to prevailing Anglo-Jewish standards or they found their position too weak to exert much influence beyond small circles of similar-minded persons.

[75] Endelman, *Radical Assimilation in English Jewish History*, 187–9.

In light of the negligible impact of German Jewish immigration on the Victorian community, it is not surprising that historians have devoted scant attention to it. Had German Jews in England preserved a distinctive collective identity over several generations, as did the much less numerous Sephardim, then the matter might have been otherwise. The same would be true if the immigrants had successfully transplanted Reform Judaism or Wissenschaft des Judentums, or if they had created lasting communal structures, as did their counterparts in the United States. But few in number and indifferent to Judaism, they and their descendants took advantage of the relatively benign climate to weaken their ties to the Jewish community and move on, attracting little comment from friendly or hostile observers along the way. Because their behaviour contrasts so sharply with that of middle-class, English-born Jews, themselves mostly the offspring of an earlier migration from Germany, and with that of German immigrants to the Unites States, their history, even to those for whom it is neither laudable nor inspiring, merits greater attention than it has received.

PART III

MARGINAL JEWS

CHAPTER EIGHT

The Chequered Career of 'Jew' King

I

MORE THAN most European cities, Georgian London offered exceptional opportunities for advancement to ambitious Jews who had shed
the discipline of traditional Judaism. There were few legal barriers to social
integration and economic mobility. The Jewish community, a network of
voluntary associations rather than a state-backed corporate body as on the
Continent, exercised no police authority over individual Jews. London itself
was the largest city in Europe, with a population of over 900,000 in 1800
—almost twice that of Paris. Its complex and largely unregulated patterns
of urban life allowed those with ambition and drive ample room for man-
oeuvre. Social relations between various groups were not rigidly fixed, but
within certain bounds they were remarkably fluid. There were fortunes to be
made, social heights to be scaled, sexual favours to be won. English landowners, the governing class, flocked to London to enjoy its pleasures and entertainments. Their hedonistic ethic of consumption and expenditure, as well
as their healthy regard for the pursuit of wealth in a variety of fields (urban
and rural real estate; mining, fisheries, timber; stocks and bonds), made
London a haven for adventurers and climbers who knew how to satisfy aristocratic needs and exploit aristocratic weaknesses.

John King—who was born Jacob Rey and known popularly as 'Jew'
King—was a moneylender who flourished in the freewheeling atmosphere
of late Georgian London. Although his links to other Jews—and certainly to
communal bodies—were tenuous, he was one of the best-known Jews in
London between 1780 and 1820. Like Moses Mendelssohn, he was a trail-
blazer, moving in new directions, but in his case in the realm of social relations rather than intellectual activity. His behaviour was often scandalous
and outrageous, and does not fit comfortably into the usual categories for
discussing the transformation of European Jewish society at this time. In
one sense, however, his career was more representative than that of the
much better known Mendelssohn (or any of his disciples, for that matter)—
if for no other reason than that scoundrels always outnumber philosophers.

2

Jacob Rey was born around 1753, presumably in London, although he may have been born abroad and brought to England as a young child. His father, Moses Rey, was a humble street trader, undoubtedly of North African or Gibraltarian origin, judging by the persona he assumed to do business. According to one anonymous account, Moses Rey called himself 'Sultan' and dressed in 'Turkish' garb as he hawked cane strings, condoms, sealing-wax, and bawdy books in the streets and coffee houses of London. Another source, also anonymous, described Moses as a 'Turkish' Jew who had squandered his money in speculations and high living and consequently was forced to spend his last years travelling as a pedlar in the countryside from Monday to Friday.[1] Since Jewish hawkers of Gibraltarian and North African origin commonly wore Levantine costume, it seems likely that Moses Rey was part of this stream of Jewish migration to London.

Moses Rey differed from the mass of Jewish street traders in London in one important respect: he was sufficiently 'successful' to dispense with the potential earnings of his 11-year-old son Jacob, who was thus able to continue his education into his adolescent years, an advantage that served him well when he later mixed with persons of higher social rank. In 1764 Rey was admitted to the charity school of the Spanish and Portuguese Jews. Unlike the schools of the Ashkenazim, this school offered instruction in both religious and secular subjects, with a marked emphasis on the latter. (It was found in 1779 that most of the boys could not read even the daily service in Hebrew.[2]) When Jacob Rey left the school in 1771, the wardens paid a premium of £5 to apprentice him as a clerk in a Jewish business house in the City, again an advantage that few Jewish youths at the time enjoyed.[3]

No doubt Rey was an ambitious young man. Within a few years of leaving school he anglicized his name, and was known thereafter as John King.[4] Since his birth name was hardly difficult to pronounce or spell, his decision was likely a conscious effort to avoid the popular odium attached to Jews. The fact that it was common in mid-eighteenth-century England for stage Jews and fictional Jews to bear extravagant Spanish-sounding names provided an additional incentive for Rey to rid himself of his Iberian Jewish pedigree.

---

[1] *Authentic Memoirs*, 27–8; 'John King', 1.

[2] Picciotto, *Sketches of Anglo-Jewish History*, 162.

[3] Solomons, *Notes and Queries*, 10th ser., 9 (1908), 428.

[4] In 1775, in a letter in Portuguese to the wardens of the Sephardi school, he signed his name 'Jacob Rey', but the English translation of the letter, which was inserted in the records at the same time, was signed 'John King' (ibid.).

Such name changes, however, were not common in Georgian England. Even wealthy Sephardim who had severed their ties with the community, such as Samson Gideon, David Ricardo, and Manasseh Masseh Lopes, did not trouble to anglicize their names. Thus Rey's decision should be seen as a conscious move to de-emphasize his Jewish background.

After completing his clerkship, King was articled to an attorney for a short period—presumably to learn about the property and financial transactions that were the mainstay of an attorney's business. At the time these low-ranking legal functionaries were much-despised figures, although their services were essential for the transaction of important legal matters. They routinely drew up wills, other property settlements, bills of exchange, and mortgages, for example. In addition, their knowledge of men and money enabled them to operate an informal credit system that brought together creditors and debtors who had not previously been acquainted. In the absence of well-developed credit and investment institutions, they assumed a financial role similar to that later performed by bankers, matching persons possessing idle savings with persons needing ready cash.[5]

By the time he was 21 King was active as a moneylender. The actress, writer, and courtesan Mary Robinson recalled in her memoirs that her husband was borrowing money from him from the time they married (12 April 1773). 'About this period I observed that Mr. Robinson had frequent visitors of the Jewish tribe; that he was often closeted with them and that some secret negotiation was going forward to which I was a total stranger. [This was not true, as we will see.] Among others, Mr. King was a constant visitor.' The parlour of their house, she added, 'was almost as much frequented by Jews as though it had been their synagogue'.[6]

King's choice of employment appears puzzling at first. The association of Jews with moneylending was hoary, dating back to the High Middle Ages, when it was the single most important economic activity in the Jewish communities of England, northern France, and Germany. Long after moneylending had ceased to play a critical role in the Ashkenazi economy, the myth of the Jews as grasping and rapacious, hard-hearted and hard-dealing, remained alive. Even in so commercially sophisticated a society as Georgian England, critics of the Jews continued to view them *en bloc* as usurers, sometimes literally but more often in the sense that they brought a usurious spirit to all their economic activity. As Captain Rees Gronow, a chronicler of the comings and goings of the upper class in the Regency years, wrote in his memoirs while discussing Jewish moneylenders, if the Jew 'can become the

---

[5] *Authentic Memoirs*, 28; 'John King', 2; *Gentleman's Magazine*, 94/1 (1824), 184.
[6] Robinson, *Perdita*, 60.

agent of any dirty work, [he] is only too happy to be so, in preference to a straightforward and honest transaction'. Collectively, Jews constituted 'a class of traders who in all parts of the world are sure to embrace what may be termed illicit and illegitimate commerce'.[7] The association between Jews and a usurious sensibility found expression in a quip attributed to Charles James Fox, who was infamous for his gambling and his indebtedness to Jewish moneylenders. Thomas Townshend, so the story went, was talking with Fox and other parliamentary colleagues of the debates the preceding winter in the House of Commons and observed that 'Fox had never been oftener *on his legs* in any one session. "True", answered Charles, who loved to joke on his own misfortunes, "for the Jews left me not a chair to sit on."'[8]

The attribution of a usurious outlook to Anglo-Jewry as a body reflected not only old myths about Jews but also the persistence of Jews in the personal money trade into the Georgian period. These moneylenders did not bankroll industrial and commercial expansion but rather provided personal loans to members of the upper class who lived beyond their means. The mania for gambling in the late eighteenth and early nineteenth centuries, fuelled by the agricultural prosperity that swelled the rent rolls of the aristocracy and gentry, sent well-born young men to Jewish moneylenders to raise funds. According to a censorious pamphlet of 1784, heavily capitalized, lavishly appointed gaming-clubs 'seduced' and 'ruined' the young inexperienced gentleman, whom older associates consequently introduced 'to Jews, to annuity brokers, and to the long train of money lenders' who were prepared 'to answer his pecuniary calls'.[9] Fox, the Prince of Wales, the third earl of Orford, the fourth earl of Sandwich, and Lord Byron were among the better-known clients of Jewish moneylenders at this time. Fox facetiously referred to the antechamber in his house in St James's Place as the Jerusalem Chamber 'because it was the theatre of his negociations with the children of Israel relative to the raising of occasional supplies'.[10]

Critics of gambling fastened on the role of Jewish moneylenders in sustaining the mania. While Captain Gronow admitted that the 'Hebrew moneylenders could not thrive if there were no borrowers: the gambler brings about his own ruin', he also shrewdly noted that 'the mildness and civility with which the Christian in difficulties always addresses the moneyed Israelite contrast forcibly with the opprobrious epithets lavished on him when the day for settlement comes'.[11] Thomas Erskine, the future Lord

---

[7] Gronow, *Reminiscences*, 183.
[8] Walpole, *Life of the Late Right Honorable Charles James Fox*, 29.
[9] Steinmetz, *The Gaming Table*, i. 114–17.
[10] Walpole, *Life of the Late Right Honorable Charles James Fox*, 28–9.
[11] Gronow, *Reminiscences*, 182.

Chancellor, suggested that moneylending should be curbed to dampen the enthusiasm for gambling: 'When the oil is spent, the lamp will go out of itself without an extinguisher; draw off the water from a man of war, and it is as great a victory as to blow her up or sink her. A gamester without his Jew is this very lamp without oil or this ship without water.'[12]

Given its disreputability, why did King choose to make his way in the world by moneylending? The answer, surely, is that his options were limited. An ambitious young Jew without capital and connections had few choices. Military, legal, clerical, and parliamentary careers, which frequently allowed clever young men without the advantages of good birth to improve their status, were closed to unconverted Jews—if not legally in every case, at least in practice. Overseas commerce was not a likely choice because King was not connected to any of the wealthy Jewish clans who made their fortunes in this way. Moneylending, on the other hand, was very profitable if the lender was both shrewd and lucky. Moreover, there was a well-established tradition in Anglo-Jewry of pursuing trades that respectable Englishmen considered marginal or insalubrious. As stigmatized newcomers, Jews gravitated to the periphery of well-developed occupations and trades, establishing themselves in low-status areas of the economy. This, of course, is only speculation, for King left no account of his early years.

Whatever determined his choice, King rapidly left behind the world of hawkers and pedlars into which he had been born. In 1775, only a few years after setting out on his own, he sent £100 to the trustees of the Sephardi charity school in gratitude for the education he had received,[13] and in spring 1776 (19 Iyar 5536) he married Sara, the daughter of Benjamin Nunes Lara and sister of Moses Nunes Lara, future benefactor of the Bevis Marks Synagogue.[14] Both were unmistakable signs that King had become a man of substance, if not standing, within a short time.

The lending transactions in which King engaged differed markedly from those of government loan contractors in the Sephardi community such as Samson Gideon and Joseph Salvador. Lending money to dissolute womanizers and compulsive gamblers in upper-class society was a high-risk business, plagued by uncertainties and irregularities. Georgian gentlemen were not known for their probity or fair play. The aristocratic ethos disdained money matters. Contracts were not to be taken seriously, because money itself was a scornful subject. Cheating in sport, business, gambling, and marriage was widespread and boasted of openly. As the biographer of William Crockford, the upstart gambling-house proprietor, wrote: 'Gentlemen of the

---

[12] Erskine, *Reflections on Gaming*, 14.
[13] Solomons, *Notes and Queries*, 10th ser., 9 (1908), 428.   [14] *Bevis Marks Records*, ii. 103.

Georgian era were not sportsmen; they lied and cheated outrageously . . . even an aristocrat would stoop to the lowest forms of trickery and down-right dishonesty such as were practiced by the rogues who infested Newmarket Heath.'[15] In a 1783 pamphlet King complained bitterly about young men fresh from Eton who rapidly learned 'all the mysteries of borrowing at high interest' and then just as quickly learned 'the mode of cancelling the obliga-tion afterwards'. He surmised that more money was made in one year by well-born 'sharpers' who failed to pay their debts than by Jewish and Chris-tian usurers in ten and singled out Charles James Fox as particularly untrust-worthy. 'There is not a usurer in London, Jew or Gentile, but shudders at your name; and the whole army of money-dealers fly at the first glance of your eye.'[16]

Lord Byron's connection to King and other Jewish moneylenders illus-trates the high-risk nature of the business. When Byron first borrowed money from King he was in no position to repay him, and was likely unconcerned about it. Byron had entered Trinity College, Cambridge, in October 1806, with an annual allowance of £500, and was in debt by the end of the first term in December. He was in need of money, he explained to his half-sister Augusta, because 'like all other young men just let loose, and especially one as I am freed from the worse than bondage of my maternal home', he had been 'extravagant'.[17] He saw King's newspaper advertisement, applied to him, and in January 1806 borrowed several hundred pounds. Through King he came to know other Jewish moneylenders, from whom he also secured loans. Byron was 18 years old when he first did business with King, and as a minor was legally unable to enter into a money contract. He persuaded his landlady in Piccadilly, Mrs Massingberd, and her daughter to co-sign the loan, presumably having convinced them that his fortune, even if not firmly in his grasp, was greater than it really was. In 1809 he left England, owing about £10,000 to his creditors, for a two-year tour of the Mediterranean. When he returned to London Mrs Massingberd was 'in the usual dilem-ma'—facing the threat of jail. Byron asked the solicitor who managed his 'Israelitish accounts' to renegotiate the debts, taking them entirely on him-self and sparing Mrs Massingberd. However, he was unable to extricate himself and in December 1812 complained to his solicitor that, should his creditors continue to hound him, 'I must quit a country which my debts ren-der uninhabitable notwithstanding every sacrifice on my part'.[18] In 1816 his

[15] Blyth, *Hell and Hazard*, p. iv.   [16] J. King, *Thoughts on the Difficulties and Distresses*, 2–5.
[17] George Gordon Byron to Augusta Byron, 27 Dec. 1805, in Byron, *Letters and Journals*, i. 86.
[18] George Gordon Byron to John Hanson, 17 Dec. 1808, 15 Dec. 1811, 16 Jan. 1812, 14 Dec. 1812, in Byron, *Letters and Journals*, i. 182, ii. 147, 154, 255.

debts, along with the scandal of his incestuous relationship with his half-sister Augusta, drove him permanently from England.

In such a milieu a young man like King, without connections, had to have sharp wits and a dull conscience to prosper. Debts were contracted in an atmosphere that encouraged borrower and lender to exploit each other's weaknesses. Honesty in such circumstances was an extravagant liability. In using unsavoury means to secure his fortune, 'Jew' King was replicating the standards of the well-bred wastrels whose needs he supplied. While we have no record of what went through his mind, his daughter Charlotte, who published Gothic novels under the pseudonym Charlotte Dacre, ascribed to the title character in *Zofloya, or The Moor* (1806) thoughts that could have been her father's. Zofloya asks the anti-heroine Victoria why she hesitates to seek the death of her husband: 'From whence then arises this unexpected demur? Is not self predominant throughout animal nature? and what is the boasted supremacy of man, if, eternally, he must yield his happiness to the paltry suggestions of scholastic terms, or the pompous definitions of right and wrong?'[19] At a minimum, the unregulated, limitless pursuit of self-interest (emotional and erotic rather than material) that drives Dacre's characters owes something to the ethical laissez-faire of her father's world.

Much of the time King functioned not as a moneylender, strictly speaking, but as a money broker—that is, as a middleman who negotiated loans for others, taking a fee for himself, without risking his own funds. Money-dealers like King existed because men of property wanted to enjoy a high rate of return on their money (a rate frequently well above the legal rate of interest of 5 per cent) but did not want their willingness to lend to be known publicly, for usury was regarded as contemptible and odious—a calling associated with Jews.[20]

In addition, employing a broker saved the lender the task of locating clients. A money broker's expertise consisted in large part of his knowledge of and access to persons frequently in need of ready cash. In pursuit of his trade, King actively cultivated the acquaintance of high-living men and women of fashion. According to the *Scourge*, a journal devoted to exposing corruption, King first became familiar with London's *haut monde* at the time of his marriage, when he met 'many dissipated noblemen and ruined gamblers' among the visitors at his father-in-law's.[21] When he himself had

[19] C. King, *Zofloya*, 155.
[20] J. King, *Thoughts on the Difficulties and Distresses*, 4; Erskine, *Reflections on Gaming*, 31. Between 1714 and 1833 the rate of interest was fixed by law at 5 per cent, but, according to Jeremy Bentham, writing in 1787, no one lent at that rate. The lowest usual rate, on the very best security, was 8 per cent, with 9 and 10 per cent even more common. Interest frequently went as high as 13 or 14 per cent (Bentham, *A Defense of Usury*, 52–4).   [21] 'John King', 3.

become prosperous, he entertained lavishly and frequently. The *Gentleman's Magazine* noted in his obituary that 'he lived in a very splendid style, keeping an open table everyday, to which such company were invited as were likely to prove profitable, either by wanting, or by lending, money on annuities'.[22] So common was the belief that his hospitality was merely mercenary that the journalist John Taylor, a friend of King's for over forty years, specifically denied the accusation in his memoirs: 'From all I could observe of Mr. King, I had never the least reason to believe that any of his invitations were for pecuniary purposes.'[23]

Taylor's defence of King was beside the point: no money broker who operated in the world of fashion could forgo personal links with its denizens, especially its most free-spending and raffish denizens, or do without the financial information about the aristocracy and gentry that such ties yielded. Money brokers needed to know about the rent rolls, mortgages, debts, and wills of their clients' families. In this regard, King himself admitted that from 'the peculiar circumstances of my life, I had peculiar means of learning secret histories'.[24] What Captain Gronow wrote of King's son, Charles—a money broker in his own right, also known as 'Jew' King—applies equally well to the father: he 'had made the peerage a complete study, knew the exact position of everyone who was connected with a coronet, the value of their property, how deeply the estates were mortgaged, and what incumbrances weighted upon them'.[25] ('Jew' King the younger was also known for the excellent dinners he gave at his house in Clarges Street, Mayfair, and at his Thameside villa, Craven Cottage, at Fulham.)[26]

King's business was not limited, however, to the well-born and the well-connected. At various times he operated moneylending offices and advertised their services in the London press, usually with others fronting for him. Early in his career, for example, he opened an office in Three Kings Court, Lombard Street, in the City, under the name Messrs John Dear and Company. As his notoriety spread, the need to hide his involvement in a venture behind a facade of Christian names and Christian clerks increased. By the early 1780s he found it difficult to rent space for his operations. On several occasions when his role in a moneylending operation became known he was forced to shut it down.[27]

King gained a reputation for unsavoury dealings early in his career and was never able to lose it. Although he always maintained that his name had been unfairly blackened, evidence suggests that he was as willing as the next

---

[22] *Gentleman's Magazine*, 94/1 (1824), 184.   [23] Taylor, *Records of My Life*, ii. 341.
[24] J. King, *Fourth Letter from Mr. King to Thomas Paine*, 6.
[25] Gronow, *Reminiscences*, 183–8.   [26] Feret, *Fulham Old and New*, iii. 91–2.
[27] 'John King', 14; *Authentic Memoirs*, 35–6, 86–7.

moneylender to take advantage of clients when the opportunity presented itself. One well-publicized case involved the millenarian prophetess Joanna Southcott. In 1806 three of her chief disciples—William Sharp, Major Robert Eyre, and John Wilson—turned to 'Jew' King for money to promote her mission. They gave him bills of exchange, bearing their signatures, for over £2,000. King was to raise money for them on these bills by circulating them to third parties, but in the end he provided them with only a fraction of what they expected. King claimed that he had been instructed to raise the money at all risks and on any terms, and that he had supplied them with cash when they could not obtain it elsewhere. At the end of the year, when they refused to repay the full amount of the bills, King took them to court. They claimed in their defence that they had never received true value on the bills, and that they had been arrested on bills for which they had never received a penny. Whether this is true or not, Southcott's disciples were not acting in good faith on their part: at the trial it emerged that they were expecting the coming of the millennium before the bills came due, and thus were not intending to repay King.[28]

King also became entangled in numerous legal disputes arising from his business activities. In 1777, for example, Isaac Shannon, who had advanced over £900 to the husband of Mary Robinson on the (illusory) security of furniture and a landed estate, and who had received little or nothing of what he was owed, summoned King, who had brokered the loan, before the *mahamad* (executive committee) of the Sephardi community. King offered to pay Shannon £50 out of his own pocket on account of his 'great loss', on the condition that Shannon 'write him a letter recanting the gross aspersions he had thrown out against his character'—which Shannon refused to do. (King had no doubt misrepresented Robinson's worth.[29]) On two occasions, once in 1784 and again in 1802, King fled abroad to avoid imprisonment. On Christmas Day 1790, *The Times* described King, with heavy-handed sarcasm, as:

Without any matter of doubt one of the most respectable characters in this country; and until the later attack on him, the breath of infamy never blew on his reputation. In all his dealings with mankind he has been the strict, upright, honest man. He never took advantage of the distresses of a fellow creature, in order to rob him of his property—he never exacted exorbitant interest for discounting a bill—he has justly paid every debt he contracted to the uttermost farthing, and in a domestic line of life has proved himself a fond—faithful—loving husband—a tender affectionate and praiseworthy parent, and a feeling, steady and sincere friend. Chaste in

[28] Southcott, *An Account of the Trials on Bills of Exchange*; Harrison, *The Second Coming*, 128–9.   [29] Samuel, 'The *Mahamad* as an Arbitration Court', 14.

all his actions—virtuous in every sentiment—and unsullied in his reputation as a Man, a Money Lender, a Jew, and a Christian.[30]

Twenty years later the pro-Tory *Scourge* singled out King and his son Charles as the most unscrupulous moneylenders in London. It believed 'their influence to be more extensive and their plans more dangerous than those of all the other money-lenders collectively'.[31] In 1824 the radical tailor Francis Place remembered King as 'an atrocious villain', claiming that if an account of his exploits were written no one would believe it: 'It could not be believed that any man would ever have attempt [sic] to do so many things which he did, without incurring punishments which would put it out of his power to commit other offences.'[32] A thinly veiled portrait of King in one of Pierce Egan's popular accounts of London high- and low-life, published in 1830, described him as 'an old scoundrel—a swindler—a rogue—a money lending vagabond'. Old Mordecai, as Egan named him, 'was so strongly aimed at all points respecting the quirks, quibbles, and the chicanery of the law, that any connexion with him in money matters was truly ruinous. His plans were well laid—he was cold, systematic, deliberate.'[33] Indeed, his reputation was such that it was possible for a hack writer some years after his death to link him with the notorious fence Ikey Solomons, an Ashkenazi Jew thirty-five years younger than King, whom he probably never met, let alone did business with. Yet, according to this chronicler of Ikey Solomons' exploits, King and Solomon joined forces for a time to defraud young noblemen in need of ready money.[34]

Despite the notoriety that clung to King throughout the years, he never suffered from a shortage of clients. There were always young gentlemen in need of money who were willing to take their chances with him. From their perspective, he probably seemed no more dangerous or unreliable than London's other money-dealers, and in any case they were often fortunate to find anyone, whatever his reputation, to advance them money. Gullibility, naivety, ignorance, and stupidity were also important in keeping King in business. As Francis Place noted in his autobiography: 'It would not be believed that people could be found who were so foolish as to be imposed upon and robbed to the extent they were robbed by King, much less would it be believed that such persons abounded to the extent his practices shewed they did.' (Place himself refused to borrow money from King even when he desperately needed it and could obtain it nowhere else—'to have accepted

[30] *The Times*, 25 Dec. 1790.   [31] 'Charles King', 457.   [32] Place, *Autobiography*, 238.
[33] Egan, *Finish to the Adventures of Tom, Jerry, and Logic*, 179.
[34] Hebron, *The Life and Exploits of Ikey Solomons*, 6–9.

any thing from him would have been downright baseness, so I remained in poverty, sometimes wanting food'.[35])

Surprisingly, King's Jewishness did not feature prominently in public attacks on his character. That he was a Jew was well known. But that his Jewishness or his Judaism was the source of his roguery was not a central claim of any of his detractors. Similarly, attacks on King did not degenerate into condemnations of Anglo-Jewry as a whole, nor did they include calls for the imposition of special laws to restrain Jews as a body, as had happened earlier in the century.[36] His misdeeds, of course, reinforced the popular image of Jews as untrustworthy in money matters, but they did not provoke broader discussion of Jewish avarice or misanthropy. This was due, in part, to the relatively high degree of toleration that English Jews enjoyed, at least relative to Jews elsewhere in Europe, and in part to the absence of a rigorous code of commercial ethics at most levels of English society. In short, King may have been seen as one rogue among many, and his Jewishness as incidental to his roguery.

3

King's notoriety was also linked to his social ambition. Like Isaac D'Israeli, a near-contemporary, and many other Sephardim of his generation, King was not content to remain within the social boundaries of Anglo-Jewry and seek companionship and respect there. English in his dress, speech, and tastes, he laboured to make a place for himself in a non-Jewish world far removed from the society of street traders into which he had been born. In one sense, of course, all well-to-do Jews in this period were parvenus or the sons of parvenus (despite Benjamin Disraeli's claims, which I discuss in Chapter 10, to the contrary). Some, like King, were inclined to break their ties to the Jewish community. Most were content to achieve a measure of social integration while maintaining their closest and most intimate ties with other Jews of similar rank.

The most significant step taken by King in his journey was the long-term liaison he established with Jane Isabella, countess of Lanesborough, the only daughter of the first earl of Belvedere, a Protestant with considerable estates in Ireland. Born in 1737, and thus about fifteen years the senior of 'Jew' King, she was a beauty as a young woman and had had many suitors, but in accordance with her father's wishes had married in 1754 Brinsely Butler, a man of modest fortune who served as MP for Cavan from 1751 to 1768. For his loyal parliamentary service, the government rewarded Butler with a

---

[35] Place, *Autobiography*, 174, 238.   [36] Endelman, *The Jews of Georgian England*, 110–11.

commissionership for revenues and in 1756 with an earldom in the peerage of Ireland. He had few emotional or physical qualities to recommend him to an attractive and spirited young woman (she was 17 when they married); they quarrelled frequently, and she left him in the late 1770s and moved to London, her husband dying soon after in 1779. In the metropolis she lived extravagantly. The settlement that her husband had made for her was insufficient to cover her expenses. In financial distress, besieged by tradesmen and shopkeepers to whom she owed money, she applied to King for assistance in 1783.[37]

When King first met Lady Lanesborough, she still retained much of her earlier beauty. 'Though past forty, a considerable share of the extraordinary beauty of her youth has escaped the ravages of time and withstood the blights of a dissolute and profligate life.'[38] King's detractors claimed that he took advantage of her financial distress to extract sexual favours. A gossipy portrait of the couple in the *Town and Country Magazine* in 1787 suggested that he supplied her pecuniary wants 'for a premium which at once indulged his sensuality and pride'.[39] This would have been consistent with his behaviour earlier in regard to another beauty, Mary Robinson, whom he tried to seduce (we do not know whether he succeeded), and who goaded him on with professions of love on her part, undoubtedly to encourage him to arrange the loan her husband was seeking. Indeed, she may have acted with the connivance of her husband, whom gossip cast as her pimp.[40]

If sensuality motivated King and financial need Lady Lanesborough when they first encountered each other, their relationship matured into something less squalid over time, and they remained a couple for the next forty years. John Taylor, noting the shifts in fortune King experienced, recalled, 'I have sometimes seen him riding in his carriage with Lady Lanesborough and his family [his children by his wife Sara], and other times trudging through the streets arm in arm with her in very indifferent weather.'[41] When King had to flee England in 1784 to escape imprisonment, she went with him, and they lived together in Italy for five or six years on her jointure and, one imagines, his wits. When he had to find refuge on the Continent again, in 1802, to avoid debtors' prison, she again joined him, although this time they were abroad only for a year or two. In 1814 she inherited the income from the Belvedere family estates on the death of her brother, the second and last earl of Belvedere, and some time after 1817 they retired to

---

[37] *Gentleman's Magazine*, 98/2 (1828), 82; *Town and Country Magazine*, 19 (1787), 297–8; *Authentic Memoirs*, 233–4.　　　　　　　　　　[38] *Authentic Memoirs*, 233–4.

[39] *Town and Country Magazine*, 19 (1787), 298.

[40] Byrne, *Perdita*, 31–7.　　　　　　　　　　[41] Taylor, *Records of My Life*, ii. 344.

Italy, where they lived in comfort until his death in Florence in August 1823. (Four and a half years later she also died in Florence, in January 1828.)[42]

King's relationship with the countess of Lanesborough began while he was still married to Sara Nunes Lara. Extramarital relationships like this were not uncommon among acculturated English Jews at the time. Wealthy brokers and merchants openly kept mistresses and entertained courtesans. Some years before meeting Lady Lanesborough, King had a long-standing relationship with a Scots woman, Miss Mackay, by whom he had several illegitimate children.[43] Within a year or two of meeting Lady Lanesborough, King abandoned his wife, and when he fled abroad in 1784 made no provisions for supporting her or their children. She followed him to Livorno, however, and there, before a rabbinical court, obtained a divorce. Whether King married Lady Lanesborough before or after the divorce proceedings in Livorno, or indeed ever, is unclear. Despite rumours to the contrary, King never converted to Christianity, and thus could not have married Lady Lanesborough in the Church of England, at least according to the accepted practices of the Church. However, it was not unheard of for an Anglican clergyman to perform the marriage ceremony for a Jew and a Christian without requiring the Jew to convert. What little evidence there is, however, points in the opposite direction. Writing in the early 1830s, John Taylor recalled that people had said that Lady Lanesborough had not really been married to King but only appeared as his wife. More significantly, when King referred to his companion in a pamphlet from around 1804, he never once wrote of her as 'my wife' but always as 'Lady Lanesborough'.[44]

Whatever the legal status of King's 'marriage' to Lady Lanesborough, it gained him entry to social circles that otherwise would have been closed to a Jew. She was not, of course, an intimate of the most elegant or most fashionable aristocratic society, but she undoubtedly made a wider circle of acquaintances available to King than he had previously had access to. In the 1790s among the frequent visitors to his home were the eighth Lord Falkland; his sister Lucia (the Hon. Mrs John Grattan), a prominent figure in faro circles; his brother the Hon. Charles Cary (later the ninth Lord Falkland), a captain in the Royal Navy; the fourth earl of Sandwich, inveterate seducer, flagellist, and one-time member of Sir Francis Dashwood's Medmenham Monks;[45]

[42] *Gentleman's Magazine*, 98/2 (1828), 82; Cokayne (ed.), *The Complete Peerage*, vii. 425.

[43] *Authentic Memoirs*, 59–60, 73–6, 80–3; 'Characteristic Portrait of a Modern Apostate', 219.

[44] 'Characteristic Portrait of a Modern Apostate', 219; *Gainer vs Lady Lanesborough*, I Peake, 25–6; Taylor, *Records of My Life*, ii. 342; J. King, *Oppression Deemed No Injustice towards Some Individuals*.

[45] The Medmenham Monks were upper-class libertines and freethinkers who met from 1749 to 1760 (or possibly 1766) to eat, drink, fornicate, and mock Christianity.

Delves Broughton, son of Sir Thomas Broughton, Bt; and Henry Speed, banker and MP for Huntingdon (1790–6).[46]

King's visitors also included political radicals, both 'respectable' and 'rough', drawn from the ranks of artisans, craftsmen, and shopkeepers. In the 1790s he cultivated the friendship of leading members of the London Corresponding Society (which championed parliamentary reform), including John Ashley, Alexander Galloway, Richard Hodgson, Thomas Hardy, Thomas Holcroft, and Francis Place, as well as the utopian anarchist William Godwin, the Jacobin poet and journalist Robert Merry, and the opposition journalist the Reverend Charles Este. He purchased their products, entertained them at his house, and offered them loans and gifts. John Taylor recalled in his memoirs that he had 'enjoyed many pleasant hours' among 'accomplished and intelligent society . . . at his hospitable mansion' and that King was fond of having men of talent at his table.[47] King may have been a parvenu, but he was a literate, shrewd, and intelligent one.

Like most parvenus, King worked assiduously to expand his circle of acquaintances. His relationship with William Godwin, a frequent guest at his table between January 1795 and March 1807, captures the difficulties that he encountered.[48] When Godwin first began dining at King's house, he found himself subject to criticism from his friends. He defended himself by claiming that he had accepted King's hospitality for anthropological reasons:

My motive was simple—the study to which I had devoted myself was to man, to analyse his nature as a moralist, and to delineate his passions as an historian, or a recorder of fictitious adventures; and I believed that I should learn from this man and his visitors some lessons I was not likely to acquire in any other quarter.[49]

This was certainly true, even if it was condescending. Coming from a Calvinist home, Godwin would have learned much about the seamy side of life through his friendship with King. However, in 1796, when King asked Godwin to appear as a character witness for him in a coming trial, Godwin angrily declined, accusing King of using his dinners as a kind of bribe and reminding him that the frequency of his visits was due to King's initiative. He told King point-blank that many of his friends objected to his visits to a man 'of whom, to say the least, the world entertained a very ill opinion'. Godwin explained that he answered them by saying it was absurd to associate only with 'immaculate persons', adding patronizingly that the errors of the 'vicious' could not be corrected if honest men deserted them.[50] His refusal

46 Taylor, *Records of My Life*, ii. 341.   47 Ibid. 345; McCalman, *Radical Underworld*, 36.
48 Scrivener, 'The Philosopher and the Moneylender'.
49 Quoted in Paul, *William Godwin*, i. 146–7.   50 Quoted ibid. 155.

failed to cool the ardour of King, who continued to seek Godwin's company, assuring him in one letter that Godwin would like him better if he got to know him more intimately. The two remained in touch, even after Godwin's dinner visits ceased in 1807, and when Godwin faced total financial collapse in 1812 King, along with Godwin's future son-in-law Percy Bysshe Shelley, helped to restructure his debts and stave off disaster.[51] The novelist and dramatist Thomas Holcroft was less amenable to King's entreaties. He noted in his diary that when he met King by chance in the street in November 1798 the latter 'again invited me to renew my visits, which I do not intend, and spoke of the frequency of those of Godwin, as I suspect with exaggeration'.[52] Francis Place accepted an invitation 'with much reluctance' once and re-called many years later: 'He gave us a sumptuous dinner of three courses and a dessert all served on plate, the table was attended by men in livery and one in plain cloaths. This disgusted me utterly.'[53]

King was sensitive to the slights and disappointments with which he met, even if they failed to dampen or redirect his ambition. He knew that there were limits to the acceptance and absorption of upstarts like himself, and lashed out at those who closed their ranks to new men whose fortunes were earned exclusively in commerce and finance. Men of rank, he observed, 'view with a jealous eye opulence and splendour that is not derived from inheritance, as if there was intrinsic and superior merit in adventitious birth'.[54] They believe it 'more credible to be a member of a fashionable assembly than director of a trading society; and more honourable to inherit a fortune bequeathed from success at cards than from the honest earnings of traffic'.[55] What King omitted to say was that his Jewishness and his scurrility counted against him as much as the obscure origins from which he had raised himself. He was also unclear about what 'the honest earnings of traffic' included.

4

King's status as an outsider, along with his experience of poverty, are the keys to understanding his long-term immersion in radical underground politics. His interest in anti-ministerial political ideas, unheard of among accultur-ated Jews in Britain at the time, dated to his school years. While still a student at the Sephardi charity school, he came to know the young Tom Paine, who in 1766 was teaching reading and writing at a private academy in Leman Street, Goodman's Fields. Many years later Paine recalled that he had seen in King 'young as you was, a bluntness of temper, a boldness of opinion, and

---

[51] Scrivener, 'The Philosopher and the Moneylender'.   [52] Holcroft, *Life*, ii. 202–3.
[53] Place, *Autobiography*, 237.   [54] J. King, *Mr. King's Apology*, 43.   [55] Ibid. 45.

an originality of thought that portended some future good . . . You used to complain of abuses . . . and wrote your opinions on them in free terms.'[56] Unfortunately, this is all that we know about King's political education.

In 1783 King made his political debut with the publication of an indictment of ministerial policy, *Thoughts on the Difficulties and Distresses in which the Peace of 1783 Has Involved the People of England*. In this short pamphlet he contended that trade was languishing and population decreasing because the government was incompetent and corrupt and its policies harmful to the well-being of the 'middling people'. During the war with the American colonies (1775–83) he charged ministers, generals, commissioners, and 'a whole list of greedy vermin' with exploiting the country's distress to increase their own fortunes. Government monopolies and restraints on trade retarded the economy. Mass emigration to India or North America was no solution to Britain's economic distress, since India was governed by rapacious colonial administrators and had become a refuge for bankrupts and adventurers, while the American climate was unhealthy, its uncleared and uncultivated soil not suitable to 'the dainty sons of England'. What was to be done? Disinterested and sincere patriots had to drive out the designing sophists running the government. Tariffs and taxes had to be lowered, sinecures and pensions abolished, the monopoly of the East India Company broken.[57]

King addressed his first intervention in politics to Charles James Fox, whom he attacked for his avarice, extravagance, and dishonesty. He was particularly severe about the hypocrisy of upper-class gamblers and womanizers (like Fox), lashing out, as we have seen, at those who borrowed at high interest, never intending to repay the debt, and then defamed those who made them the loan in the first place. For King, such hypocrisy was symptomatic of the corruption and immorality that reigned among the landowning class that monopolized government offices, milking them for their own benefit. In his view, personal behaviour and political conduct were closely linked. Thus he introduced his account of the 'difficulties and distresses' besetting the English people with an attack on Fox's duplicity in his dealings with moneylenders.

There was more to his choice of Fox as addressee, however, than Fox's failure to pay his debts. King's anger was linked no doubt to Fox's recent sexual conquest of Mary Robinson, by now a well-seasoned courtesan, whom King had tried to seduce (possibly successfully) a decade earlier. In July 1782, after resigning from the government, Fox had started an affair

---

[56] J. King, *Mr. King's Speech at Egham*, 8–9.
[57] J. King, *Thoughts on the Difficulties and the Distresses*.

with Robinson, whose beauty was widely acknowledged and whose string of conquests included the Prince of Wales. Although King did not refer to Robinson in his address to Fox, she could not have been far from his mind, for in the previous year he had tried to blackmail her, using letters they wrote each other in 1773.[58] The episode was sordid (blackmailing usually is), but also important to King's *political* education, for blackmailing, as we will see, was to become a staple weapon in the radical underground's war on the upper-class establishment in the decades ahead.

The episode began with an extortion attempt by Robinson. When her liaison with the Prince of Wales ended in late 1780, she was deep in debt. To pressure her ex-lover into providing her with a comfortable settlement, she began circulating rumours in January 1781 that she intended to publish her intimate correspondence with the prince. The press reported the threat, as she intended, as well as gossip about the unfolding rivalry between her and the prince's new mistress. Her willingness to use the love letters in her possession seems to have triggered King's decision to profit from his correspondence with Robinson, which dated from the earliest days of her marriage. According to one account, he first tried to sell the letters to her and only published them when she refused. The publication in March 1781 of *Letters from Perdita to a Certain Israelite* (Perdita referred to her most famous dramatic role, as one of the heroines in *The Winter's Tale*) was not a commercial windfall, however. Some scholars believe that the work is a malicious fabrication either in whole or in part. However, there are details in the letters about their time together that only she and King could have known and that harmonize with details in her *Memoirs*, which she wrote at the end of the century. One recent biographer concludes that while King may have 'spiced up the text' for publication' *Letters from Perdita* 'gives us the very voice of the young Mary with an immediacy that is altogether lacking in the carefully self-censored retrospective narrative of the *Memoirs*'.[59]

The content of King's first political publication is unremarkable and typical in most ways of anti-ministerial sentiment prior to the French Revolution, being reformist rather than revolutionary. What is remarkable about this foray into political pamphleteering is that it marks one of the earliest occasions that a Jew anywhere in Europe sought to participate in national political life in pursuit of goals unrelated to Jewish communal needs. In the 1760s and 1770s the French-born Amsterdam merchant Isaac de Pinto addressed matters of economic policy, statecraft (including the rebellion in North America), and philosophy in a number of books and pamphlets (some of which were translated into English and published in London), but his

---

[58] Byrne, *Perdita*, 32–7, 137–9.   [59] Ibid. 32.

interventions were those of a *philosophe* not of one who actually dirtied his hands in politics.[60] In Britain, the maskil Abraham ben Naphtali Tang commented on the John Wilkes affair in 1770 in the anonymously published anti-ministerial tract *A Discourse Addressed to the Minority*. David Ruderman regards the pamphlet as a demonstration of 'the radical potential of English Jewish self-consciousness' and contrasts Tang's 'brazenness' with Mendelssohn's 'public meekness'.[61] There is an important difference, however, between Tang and King that this characterization blurs. Tang's observations on English politics in 1770 were a one-off foray into public life, as far as we know. King's pamphlet of 1783, in contrast, marked the start of three decades of radical political activity. His ongoing involvement reveals the extent to which he identified with the English rather than the Jewish nation at this time in his life. Most well-to-do English Jews in the Georgian period probably thought of themselves primarily as Jews and only secondarily, if at all, as Englishmen; almost certainly most were apolitical. Public life in general mattered little to them unless it affected their status as Jews or their specific economic interests. Still others were reluctant to engage in political activity for fear of endangering the status of the community as a whole.[62] Since the legal basis for Jewish settlement rested on vague, unspecified grounds, they thought it prudent to avoid antagonizing any political faction, especially during the turbulent years of the American War of Independence, the French Revolution, and the Napoleonic Wars. 'Jew' King was among a handful of Jews who broke with this apolitical stance.

In the 1790s King was closely allied with radical groups calling for the democratization of politics and an end to ministerial corruption. This was the decade when he cultivated the friendship of Godwin, Place, and Holcroft (among others). In the early years of the decade, he spoke frequently at a debating club in Carlisle Street, espousing views more radical than those he had expressed in 1783. For two or three years (*c*.1790–2), he served as an editor of *The Argus*, a radical newspaper scathingly critical of William Pitt and his ministers and ardently supportive of Tom Paine and the London Corresponding Society. As I noted earlier, he entertained leading members of the group in his home near Manchester Square. When Thomas Hardy, John Horne Tooke, and John Thelwall were tried for treason in 1794, he contributed to the fund for their support, as he did when John Binns was tried for using seditious words in 1797.[63]

60 Hertzberg, *The French Enlightenment and the Jews*, 142–53.
61 Ruderman, *Jewish Enlightenment in an English Key*, 144.
62 Alger, *Napoleon's British Visitors*, 102; Werkmeister, *A Newspaper History of England*, 32–3; J. King, *Mr. King's Apology*, 36–7.
63 Thale (ed.), *Selections from the Papers of the London Corresponding Society*, 405.

The government considered him a sufficient irritant at one point in the early 1790s that it tried to silence him. Its tactics were devious but typical of the time (in this sense King's conduct was no better or worse than that of his detractors). A common practice of London newspapers in the late eighteenth and early nineteenth centuries was the extortion of 'hush money' from prominent figures to prevent the publication of embarrassing or abusive material about them. *The Times*, for example, regularly composed unflattering letters about the morals of individuals, pretending that the letters had come to the paper with money for their insertion and demanding payment for their suppression. In the late autumn and early winter of 1790 *The Argus* published a number of articles exposing the extortionate practices of *The Times*, while in December King sued the proprietor of *The Times*, John Walter, for libel, charging *The Times* with falsely accusing him of swindling a goldsmith in Pall Mall of large sums of money. King claimed that Walter had told him that he had printed the allegation because it was accompanied by three guineas but had offered to publish a retraction for five guineas. King's libel case against Walter was tried on 23 February 1791, and the proprietor was convicted. The government, however, intervened to save Walter, who at the time was already in Newgate Prison for having supported the Prince of Wales during the Regency crisis of 1788 when George III was mentally incapacitated. On the understanding that the paper would resume its firm support of the ministry, Walter was released from prison with a full pardon, the Treasury paying his fines. In addition, the government prevented King from pressing for judgment and may also have assured Walter that it would retaliate against King.

The evidence that the government exerted pressure on King is largely circumstantial. In July 1792 two prostitutes appeared at the Bow Street magistrate's office to charge him with assault. They claimed that, while engaging in sadistic sexual activity with him, they had been whipped with 'more than customary severity'.[64] In all likelihood Walter or others acting on behalf of the government had paid the women to accuse King. Although they recanted every word of their story the following day and did not testify against him at his trial, he was convicted all the same and fined £3,000. King unsuccessfully appealed the case to the Court of King's Bench and published a protest in *The Argus*. The fine was then increased to £15,000, an enormous sum at the time, which he probably could not have paid. At the same time, the ministerial press launched a campaign to inflame those who had done business with him and harboured grievances of their own. Faced with a

[64]   J. King, *Mr. King's Apology*, 5.

concerted effort on the part of the government and its friends to silence him, King retreated and dropped his association with *The Argus*.[65]

In a speech at Egham, which was published in the ministerial *Morning Herald* on 12 December 1792 and later republished as a pamphlet, King defended the English constitution and attacked the violent turn that the French Revolution had taken. Although he did not completely reject the need for reforms, he now argued that they had to come about in a constitutional manner through proper parliamentary channels. It would be folly, he felt, for the English to seek political guidance across the Channel. The revolution had come under the sway of men lacking either merit or genius; its furious and uncontrollable momentum was consuming those who had brought it into being. When Paine expressed surprise at King's apparent about-face, King replied that his initial sympathy for the revolutionaries had evaporated when they became dictatorial and oppressive, unleashing 'a second carnage on those who differ with them in opinion'. He denied, however, that he had abandoned the cause of political reform: 'When it is the proper season, I shall again exclaim against the twenty millions of annual taxes, against pensions, sinecure places, and unequal representation; but, instead of exclaiming against the King as you [Paine] have done, I look to him to assist in the reformation.' As for Paine's hopes for the 'equalization' of society, which King had never found attractive, they were illusory: under every form of government, there always had to be labourers, just as there always had to be governors to restrain the bad and guide the ignorant. Paine's equality was a prescription for anarchy.[66]

King's defence of the English constitution, including some warm words for George III and property rights, marked a softening of his earlier radicalism. His retreat, however, was temporary and incomplete, for he remained committed to the legislative reform of political abuses. In an open letter to Paine published in the *Morning Herald* of 17 April 1793, he argued that although there were few radical evils in the English system there were many abuses. However, he insisted that their reform had to wait until such time as England's overseas enemies (France and her allies) were no longer seeking to destroy what Englishmen were striving only to amend.[67] He remained in touch with the non-violent reformers of the London Corresponding Society, and, as we have seen, supported those whom the government brought to trial. By 1795 his tone was sharper. In another open letter to Paine, first published in the *Morning Post* of 13 March 1795, he again charged him with

[65] Werkmeister, *A Newspaper History of England*, 24, 32–3, 113–15, 146.
[66] J. King, *Mr. King's Speech at Egham*.
[67] J. King, *Third Letter from Mr. King to Mr. Thomas Paine*.

breeding confusion, disorder, and anarchy among the common people, but he also strongly condemned the government's repressive measures—the use of spies and informers, the suspension of habeas corpus, heavy taxes, and ruinous loans. Under the pretence of securing the constitution, he argued, the ministers had violated many of its fundamental laws. Moreover, by oppressing and exasperating the people, the government pushed them to seek redress, paradoxically, in insurrection and violence.[68]

To some reformers, however, King's change of heart was suspect, perhaps because he was a Jew and a moneylender. The priggish Francis Place did not trust him and 'always suspected that he contemplated some iniquity'—that is, that he was a government spy.[69] But Place did admit that some reformers were willing to credit King with honest opinions and good intentions. King himself noted that his motives were called into question when he had sub-scribed to the defence fund for the radicals arrested for treason, and that rumours circulated that he had been providing intelligence to Pitt and the duke of Portland, the Home Secretary. For King, such accusations were part and parcel of the blackening of his reputation by a sensationalist press.[70]

Early in the new century King's radicalism returned in full force, mesh-ing now with criminal activity in novel ways. He began to work with, perhaps even head, an underground group of 'rough' radicals who used extortion, blackmail, and pornography for political ends and personal profit. Govern-ment prosecution records in the National Archives at Kew show that be-tween 1805 and 1811 King and his associates extorted money from what one document called 'persons of the first distinction and character in the coun-try', including the Prince of Wales, his brothers the duke of Cumberland and the duke of York, Spencer Perceval (Chancellor of the Exchequer from 1807 to 1809 and prime minister from 1809 to 1812), senior law officers, govern-ment and admiralty officials, and other prominent well-born persons. He acted in concert with other radicals who were linked to the London criminal underground—for example, Patrick William Duffin, a former United Irish-man (republican revolutionary), who ran a low gaming house for King in Denmark Court, the Strand, in 1805 and 1806. In 1806 Duffin and Henry White co-founded the *Independent Whig*, probably with financial support from King, and around 1811 King bankrolled the *British Guardian*, a Sunday newspaper. Both newspapers featured ferocious anti-establishment exposés of upper-class corruption, debauchery, and state parasitism. In their pages, sensationalism, scandal-mongering, and muck-raking combined with seri-ous political criticism.[71]

---

[68] J. King, *Fourth Letter from Mr. King to Mr. Thomas Paine*.   [69] Place, *Autobiography*, 236.
[70] J. King, *Mr. King's Apology*, 36–7.   [71] McCalman, *Radical Underworld*, 34–9.

King and Duffin took a prominent role in the well-orchestrated radical campaign against the duke of York in 1808–9 for allowing his mistress, Mary Anne Clarke, to sell military preferments; one pro-Clarke account even claimed that King was the *éminence grise* behind the campaign. Later, in the scandal following the death of Joseph Sellis, valet to the duke of Cumberland in 1810, King, Duffin, and others tried to blackmail Francis Place, who was foreman of the jury that returned a verdict of suicide on the valet's death. The duke was widely disliked and the jury verdict viewed with suspicion. Rumours circulated that the duke had been surprised in a homosexual act with Sellis, had aroused the jealousy of Sellis by taking a new manservant/ lover, had fathered a child by Sellis's wife, and was being blackmailed by Sellis, an ardent Jacobin—in other words, that he had a motive to want Sellis dead. Whatever the truth of the allegations, King and his associates took advantage of the situation to try to extort money from Place, whose turn towards moderation and respectability they rejected. Between August 1812 and March 1813, the *Independent Whig* published a string of pseudonymous letters implying that Place had been a government spy in 1798 and had accepted money from a Treasury official to quash a murder verdict in the Sellis case.[72] Some time after this King wound down his involvement in radical politics, and around 1817 he and Lady Lanesborough left England to settle permanently in Italy.

King's combination of criminality and radicalism strikes a discordant note; it does not harmonize with conventional expectations and standards. We prefer our radicals to be saints, not sinners. To dismiss King only as a criminal, however, is to do him a disservice and to misapprehend the meaning of his career. Iain McCalman, the first to make sense of the intersection of crime and politics in the London radical underworld, reminds us that definitions of acceptable and unacceptable political conduct change over time. In the late Georgian and Regency period, blackmail was a tacitly accepted, widely practised political strategy. 'Where politics was still conducted on an intimate personal scale, scandal gave the powerless (as well as the powerful) a purchase with which to "coerce" their enemies and enrich themselves.'[73] King may have enjoyed wealth at times and hobnobbed with upper-class rakes and libertines, but his political sympathies were always with the 'powerless'. He never forgot that he was a self-made man from lowly, Jewish origins whose social position was ambiguous. This explains much of his bitterness towards the established order; whether it morally excuses his recourse to crime is another matter.

---

[72] McCalman, *Radical Underworld*, 34–5.   [73] Ibid. 41.

5

King's entry into non-Jewish spheres of activity diminished his ties to other Jews, making Jewishness less central to his own sense of who he was. This does not mean that he replaced his old 'Jewish' identity with a new 'English' one and that all traces of his former 'Jewish' self vanished. Human personality is not a malleable lump of clay that can be moulded into new forms at will. Acculturation, integration, and secularization reshaped and attenuated his Jewish identity, but they did not extinguish it. Even converts to Christianity, seeking to wash away their Jewishness in the waters of the baptismal font, usually failed to loosen completely the hold of their Jewish past (although their children or grandchildren were frequently able to do so). At a minimum, the non-Jewish world rarely allowed even the most deracinated Jews to forget their origins. This was certainly the case with 'Jew' King, whose nickname testifies to the inability of non-Jews to forget his background.

As a pupil at the Sephardi charity school, King had received a basic introduction to the fundamentals of Jewish tradition. He had learned to read the Hebrew prayer book and possibly some biblical passages as well. He had also regularly attended services at the Spanish and Portuguese synagogue in Bevis Marks, as did all charity pupils. After leaving school he apparently ceased to observe even the most rudimentary of Jewish traditions. There is no indication that he continued to attend services at Bevis Marks, although, as we have seen, he willingly appeared in 1777 before the *mahamad* for arbitration of a business dispute. (He was still a young man then.) In externals he lived as a non-Jew and if we accept his testimony at a later date he even started to think of himself as a Christian in a vague sort of way. Thus in 1795 when he testified as a witness in the Court of King's Bench, he was sworn on the New Testament. After he began testifying, the defence attorney stopped him and raised questions about whether he was a Jew, and if so whether his oath was binding since he was sworn on the New Testament. King told the court that he had considered himself a member of the Church of England since he had been old enough to judge such matters for himself. However, when questioned further, he admitted that he had been married according to Jewish rites, had never been baptized or admitted to the Church, and had never formally renounced Judaism.[74] Perhaps the best way to interpret King's statement about being a member of the Church of England is to view it as a measure of his desire to be seen as an Englishman rather than a Jew.

---

[74] *Rex* vs *Gilham*, I Espinasse, 285–6. Lord Kenyon ruled that King's testimony was admissible since he now considered himself a member of the Church of England and bound by its precepts.

It was certainly not a statement of his commitment to Christian doctrine and worship.

King's testimony in 1795 raises the question of why he did not formally embrace Christianity, given his distance from Judaism and the Jewish community. When he went abroad for the first time with Lady Lanesborough in the 1780s, it was rumoured that he had converted in order to marry her. Although untrue, the rumour testifies to how widely it was believed that conversion was the obvious thing for someone in his position to do. As we will see in Chapter 11, at this time dozens of Sephardim whose links with the Jewish community were as weak as King's did precisely this in order to advance their careers or their social fortunes. King's unwillingness to take this step suggests that even at this early date radical assimilation did not necessarily lead to conversion, at least in states where religious identity and civil status were not linked. Unquestionably one major reason why he did not become a Christian was the indifference or hostility to religion of those with whom he consorted. Conversion would not have enhanced his standing in the eyes of either dissolute nobles or 'rough' radicals. Conversion certainly would not have brought him greater material success or even improved his civil status much.

Equally decisive in King's case—and surely in many others—was a deeply rooted ambivalence about being Jewish. His testimony in 1795 was meant to give the impression that he was no longer a Jew, but this declaration can hardly be taken at face value. It is difficult if not impossible for a member of a self-conscious, stigmatized minority to shed his or her past like an unfashionable suit of clothing. King had ceased to live as a Jew in a religious or ceremonial sense and was certainly eager to break out of the social confines of Anglo-Jewry, but it is unlikely that he had suppressed all memories, sentiments, and attachments of his Jewish past. Perhaps he retained a muted pride in Judaism, for later in life, when attacked, he proclaimed his Jewishness in proud, almost defiant terms. In defending his character in a pamphlet published in 1798, he noted that his faith was often called into question. It is unclear whether he meant that he had become the object of anti-Jewish animadversions or simply that his own attachment to any religion was being called into question. In any case, King answered his detractors by defending Judaism. In common with other European Jews who had been exposed to Enlightenment thinking, he first defined Judaism in highly rationalistic terms. The 'transcendent object' of his 'adoration' was 'not profaned by mythological fantasms, or incarnated like heathen Deities'.[75] King believed that a superior intelligence or divine intellectual power had formed

---

[75] J. King, *Mr. King's Apology*, 38.

the world and that Judaism divested of its ceremonies was a deistic religion. However, not being a systematic thinker, he also defended Judaism on traditional grounds as well. He argued that Judaism's antiquity gave it an advantage over other religions. Furthermore, the very survival of the Jews over the centuries was evidence that Divine Providence was guiding their fate in history. Their conquerors had perished while they had remained, 'firm in their faith, steady in their religion, and numerous as ever'.[76] Not only did King defend Judaism, but he went on the attack as well. He accused Christians of failing to obey the morality of the Gospels, citing the 'uncharitable temper' of Protestants and the 'intolerant spirit' of Catholics, as well as negative Christian attitudes towards Jews. Anticipating Benjamin Disraeli, he reminded his adversaries that Jesus had been a Jew and that Christian persecution of Jews made it seem as if Christians regretted Jesus' origins.[77]

King's apology for Judaism was not learned, but it was unfettered, spirited, and combative. Unlike communal leaders, who were cautious about openly challenging Christian beliefs and discouraged public polemics and debates,[78] King was not hesitant about bruising Christian sensibilities. He obviously felt that he could write freely in this way without serious consequences for himself or the community. His defence of Judaism was also notable in that it signalled his public acceptance of his Jewishness. By this I do not mean that he had become an observant Jew in any sense, but that he had stopped trying to bury his past and had become reconciled to it. Earlier attachments, seemingly withered, reasserted themselves. Perhaps he had concluded that radical assimilation was futile (at least in his case) or perhaps he wished to spite his enemies. No doubt the mounting press attacks of the 1790s left him feeling besieged and harassed; in the circumstances would not falling back on an older sense of identification be a way of reasserting his integrity?

From this point, King became even more assertively Jewish. When he testified in court in the Southcott bills of exchange case in June 1807, he took the oath on the Hebrew Bible. Questioned about his religion, he acknowledged that earlier in his life he had taken the oath on the New Testament, but asserted that now he was a Jew, not a deist, and 'performed this solemnity according to the Mosaic creed, although he did not observe all the ceremonies of the modern Israelite'.[79] Some time after this King also reestablished contact with the Sephardi community. In 1812, in a number of letters to the *mahamad* criticizing the state of the worship service, he

[76] Ibid. 40–1.   [77] Ibid. 41.

[78] Endelman, *The Jews of Georgian England*, 282–4.

[79] Southcott, *An Account of the Trials on Bills of Exchange*, 32.

mentioned that his infrequent attendance at Bevis Marks was due to the lack of devotion there, a criticism made by a number of writers at this time. He attributed the small attendance to the absence of decorum in the service, targeting in particular the unruly conduct of the charity-school boys. He even proposed a number of reforms to achieve greater decorum and offered his help in implementing them.[80] King's letters leave the clear impression that he was once again a member of the Bevis Marks congregation and that he attended services there, if only infrequently. More significantly, his letters demonstrate a concern with the character of Jewish worship and life in England, although the depth of his concern is unknown. Still, that he bothered at all to address the problem is significant. Jews who were thoroughly alienated from the community rarely troubled themselves about abuses in Judaism; for them, Judaism, reformed or otherwise, was no longer a matter of concern.

King's most forthright statement of his renewed adherence to Judaism and the Jewish community came in an introduction he wrote in 1817 to a new edition of David Levi's apology *Dissertations on the Prophecies of the Old Testament*, which was first published in three volumes between 1793 and 1800. Levi, a learned hat-dresser, was one of the few Jews in late Georgian England to answer Christian polemicists.[81] The work was a refutation of Christian interpretations of prophetic passages pertaining to the fate of the people of Israel. King republished Levi's polemic in 1817 in response to the missionary work of the London Society for Promoting Christianity among the Jews. For the new edition, he wrote a sixty-page introduction, dedicated to Raphael Meldola, head of the Sephardi community, in which he offered a surprisingly traditional defence of rabbinic Judaism. The integrity of Judaism, King asserted, rested on the fact that God delivered the law, both written and oral, to Moses on Mount Sinai in the presence of 600,000 people rather than in a private act of revelation. Those who were witnesses to the events on Sinai transmitted the text of the Mosaic law to the next generation, and thus from generation to generation it was handed on, unaltered, unperverted, and eternally binding. Everywhere in the world Jews observed their religion in precisely the same way that they had in the time of Moses, while Christianity had experienced many mutations and schisms. Jesus himself, who was born and died a Jew, had never abolished any part of the law or expressed any intention of founding a new religion but had continued to observe the commandments all his life. King pointed out that Scripture nowhere asserted or

[80] Hyamson, *The Sephardim of England*, 270.
[81] Ruderman, *Jewish Enlightenment in an English Key*, chs. 2, 4; Popkin, 'David Levi'; Scrivener, 'British Jewish Writing of the Romantic Era'.

even intimated that Jewish law was the adumbration of another law. The messiah of the Jews would support, not destroy, the Mosaic code. King also argued, as he had in 1798, that Jewish survival was itself both consequence and proof of chosenness: the Jews were God's peculiar people, their preservation an act of divine providence. He also mocked the pedigrees of the nations of Europe, pointing out that they were unable to trace their origins back into the distant past and they were each a hybrid mixture of many peoples while the Jews could deduce their genealogy from the beginning of the world.[82] Here too he anticipated Disraeli's celebration of the Jewish people.

King's republication of Levi's work was a response to increasingly aggressive missionary activity and at the same time a public affirmation of his Jewishness. Some historians also link it—and King more generally—to the millenarian restorationism that flourished in English Dissent at the time of the French Revolution and the Napoleonic Wars.[83] They do so on the basis of King's immersion in radical political circles that intersected, at times, with prophetic restorationist circles. The problem with making this connection is that King never wrote anything in support of the view that the turmoil of the time, especially Napoleon's campaign in Egypt (1799) and summoning of the Parisian Sanhedrin (1806), was a sign that the exile of the Jews was drawing to a close and their return to Zion imminent. At best, the evidence is circumstantial—that is, King perhaps knew radicals who interpreted world events in a prophetic way. Levi, on the other hand, did address such views in the third volume of his *Dissertations on the Prophecies*, first published in 1800 when restorationist prophecy burned brighter than it did in 1817, the date of its republication by King. But Levi's attitude towards the millenarian excitement was confused. At one point he reiterated the conventional rabbinic position, rooted in the experience of disillusionment and disaster that followed the collapse of failed messianic movements, that God alone knew the time of the Jews' redemption. Yet he also wrote that the sight of 'so many nations engaged in a war, carried on with almost unparalleled violence, desolating so many countries, and producing such extraordinary Revolutions' was an indication of 'the near approach of the redemption of the nation'.[84] It is impossible to reconcile the two statements. In any case, it is mere

---

[82] Levi, *Dissertations on the Prophecies*. The *Bibliotheca Anglo-Judaica* of Joseph Jacobs and Lucien Wolf, published in conjunction with the Anglo-Jewish Historical Exhibition in 1888, lists two other theological-exegetical works by King on p. 202: *Derekh mosheh* (Dissertation on the Book of Esther, 1817) and *Derekh selulah* (Dissertation on the Prophecies, 1819). I have been unable to locate either of them.

[83] McCalman, 'New Jerusalems'; id., 'The Infidel as Prophet'; Ruderman, *Jewish Enlightenment in an English Key*, 136–9.   [84] Levi, *Dissertations on the Prophecies*, iii. 138–40.

speculation to infer from King's republication of the entire work that he shared the second of Levi's contradictory views.

When King republished the *Dissertations* in 1817 he was an old man by the standards of the day, being over 60. I do not view his decision to republish the work with a lengthy introduction of his own as a theological or political statement. I prefer to interpret it as the defiant gesture of an old, much-abused Jew seeking revenge on a world that had treated him contemptuously. By asserting the superiority of his ancestral faith over the Christianity of his detractors, King was both justifying his return to Judaism and settling scores with the non-Jewish world that he had tried variously to conquer and subvert. When he died in Florence in 1823 he did so unquestionably as a Jew: in his will he left £20 to the Sephardi congregation in London—half to discharge part of his debt to the synagogue and half to be remembered in an annual memorial prayer.[85]

6

'Jew' King was not an 'ordinary' Jew. His notoriety was extraordinary, and perhaps his villainy as well. His commitment to radicalism was also atypical, as was his 'return' to Jewishness late in life. Yet none of the conventional categories for discussing the origins of Jewish modernity in Europe encompasses the ways in which he broke with the world of tradition. He did not campaign to make Jews more equal or productive members of society or to reform synagogue worship. He did not sit on the board of any communal organization or associate with Jews who did. He did not contribute to the debate within European Jewry over the shape of Judaism and the character of Jewish identity in the age of emancipation. He did not amass a fortune in government finance or overseas trade and buy his (or his children's) way into upper-class society. In this sense 'Jew' King was typical, for most Jews never did any of these things.

Yet the career of 'Jew' King is not simply a colourful footnote to the main text of modern Jewish history—unless its proper subject is defined as the activities of that handful of Jews who conducted or commented on communal affairs. If acculturation, integration, and secularization are major themes in modern Jewish history, then the experiences of a 'Jew' King are no less critical to understanding this period than those of a David Friedländer, an Abraham Furtado, or a Benjamin Goldsmid. Regardless of their wealth, intellect, or respectability, all Jews living in the West at this time had to adjust

---

[85] Entry for 1 June 1824, Archives of the Spanish and Portuguese Synagogue, London, MS 111.

to a set of political and social conditions radically different from those that existed half a century or a century before. They did so in a multitude of ways. They did not enter the modern world like a well-disciplined army, tramping faithfully in the footsteps of Mendelssohn and the maskilim. The processes of acculturation and integration were acted out in countless thousands of private acts and encounters, mostly but not entirely unrecorded and unobserved, far from the discursive world of Haskalah, emancipation, Reform, and Wissenschaft des Judentums. The life of 'Jew' King is part of this history. His career suggests that the scope of modern Jewish history remains too narrowly delimited and that understanding its beginnings requires the reconstruction of more Jewish lives outside the groups that continue to monopolize historiographical attention.

A NOTE ON DATES

The exact date of Jacob Rey's birth is unknown. According to Israel Solomons, Rey was admitted to the charity school of the Spanish and Portuguese Jews in 1764 and was about 11 years old at the time.[86] Solomons made this statement on the basis of a minute book of the charity school that was in his possession in 1908 and that he sold subsequently to the library of the Jewish Theological Seminary of America, which is now unable to locate it. A birth date of 1753 would fit well with other clues we have about King's age at different dates. Thus around 1804 he wrote that he was 'in the evening of his life'[87]—that is, about 50 years old if we assume that he was born around 1753. As to the place of his birth, there is a list of aliens in the Mansion House Sessions Book for 1796 (a time of intense xenophobia and invasion hysteria associated with the revolutionary wars on the Continent) in which the name John Rey appears.[88] No address, occupation, age, or place of birth is indicated. Perhaps this John Rey was the same person as Jacob Rey.

There is also confusion about the dates of birth of his children, especially his daughters Charlotte and Sophia, whose poetry and novels began to attract scholarly attention in the last quarter of the twentieth century. The date of King's marriage (1776) to Sara Nunes Lara, the mother of Charles, Charlotte, and Sophia, is not in question. It appears in the records of the Sephardi congregation that Lionel Barnett published in 1949. Despite this, studies of the work of Charlotte and Sophia, as well as various websites, state that they were born in the early 1770s. According to Michael Scrivener, the

---

[86] Solomons, *Notes and Queries*, 10th ser., 9 (1908), 428.
[87] J. King, *Oppression Deemed No Injustice towards Some Individuals*, 27.
[88] Lipman, 'Sephardi and Other Jewish Immigrants', 61.

error is attributable to Charlotte's husband, Nicholas Byrne, editor of the *Morning Post*, who was about twenty years older than his wife and wanted to make the gap between their ages appear less at the time of her early death (1825).[89] No doubt his reason for doing so was linked to the irregularity of their relationship: he and Charlotte had become lovers when she was in her early twenties and he was still married to the first Mrs Byrne. They had had three children out of wedlock—in 1806, 1807, and 1809—but were married only in 1815. Scrivener believes that Charlotte and Sophia were born some time between 1777 and 1780. Neither birth is recorded in the birth register of the Spanish and Portuguese congregation. The dates of their brother Benjamin's birth and circumcision are recorded—12 and 19 April 1783.[90]

[89] Michael Scrivener, personal communication, 1 Sept. 2009.
[90] *Bevis Marks Records*, v. 129.

CHAPTER NINE

The Emergence of Disraeli's Jewishness

B ENJAMIN DISRAELI, the man and his policies, elicited strong reactions. For some, he was a vulgar, cynical careerist; for others, a visionary, patriotic statesman. Few were indifferent. Amid the welter of conflicting assessments, however, there was one point on which both admirers and detractors agreed: Disraeli was a Jew and being Jewish was central to his self-understanding—despite having been baptized at the age of 12. As one of his earliest biographers, James Anthony Froude, concluded, 'at heart he was a Hebrew to the end'.[1] But to conclude that being Jewish mattered to Disraeli does not speak to the question of how it mattered or in what sense 'he was a Hebrew'. It does not explain the meaning or content of Disraeli's Jewishness and its function in his emotional and political life.

In accounts of Disraeli's Jewishness there has been little consensus. Historians and biographers have labelled him variously a proto-Zionist, a Marrano, a racist, a proud Jew, or a self-hating Jew. The truth is that none of these labels captures the complex, ambivalent character of what being Jewish meant to Disraeli at different times in his life. Indeed, it is this last point—the changing rather than consistent character of his Jewishness —that needs to be stressed. For Disraeli's consciousness of being a Jew changed over time. It was not a fixed cultural or biological inheritance, but rather an awareness and understanding that emerged and evolved over several decades in response to external changes in his life and stabilized only when he was in his forties. It drew on Enlightenment deism, Romanticism, racial ideas, Christian doctrine, Sephardi pride, family traditions, and even normative Jewish belief, mixing notions from these diverse sources into an odd, eccentric melange.

Disraeli's views about Judaism owed much to his father, as did his political views. London-born Isaac D'Israeli (as he spelled the family name) was a successful but minor man of letters, who moved comfortably in bookish,

---

[1] Froude, *The Life of the Earl of Beaconsfield*, 262.

non-Jewish circles.[2] Like many of his kinsmen, he was not an observant Jew. Although he married within the fold, had his four sons circumcised, and maintained membership in the Spanish and Portuguese synagogue in Bevis Marks, his allegiance to Judaism was more a matter of familial and ethnic sentiment than belief and practice. He did not observe its domestic rituals nor attend worship services. In 1817 he quit the synagogue over a dispute that had been brewing since 1813 when he was elected *parnas* (warden) and had refused either to serve or to pay the usual fine for declining to do so. (This was, it should be added, a standard procedure for raising revenue for the congregation.) But, as he explained to the synagogue authorities when he first declined the office, he was willing to continue his membership if they withdrew the fine since he felt bound to them by friendship and 'something like the domestic affections'.[3]

Isaac D'Israeli's secession from the Bevis Marks congregation was in no sense remarkable. In well-to-do Sephardi families that had become rooted in English social and cultural life, indifference or even hostility to the Jewish religion was becoming common in the late Georgian period.[4] As these families drew closer to non-Jewish circles, the number of secessions, intermarriages, and conversions rose—to the extent that the Sephardi population grew little if at all between 1750 and 1830 (see Chapter 11). When the Sephardim who participated in the establishment of the Reform synagogue in 1841 offered a rationale for the introduction of religious reforms, they cited defections from the community. They were convinced that improvements in worship would 'arrest and prevent secession from Judaism', which was 'widely spread' among 'the most respectable families' in the community.[5]

Where Isaac D'Israeli differed from other Sephardim who cut their ties to Bevis Marks was in his long-standing espousal of a Voltaire-like, deistic critique of traditional Judaism. Early in life Isaac fell under the influence of the *philosophes*, whose views on religion in general and Judaism in particular he embraced. For him, Judaism had become a repository of the prejudices of earlier, barbarous eras. The Talmud was a mass of superstitions, contradictory opinions, rambling oriental fancies, and casuistic glosses. The rabbis of old were dictators of the human intellect who tricked the Jews into accepting their decisions as divine law, thereby casting the people into the bondage of ridiculous customs. The system of dietary laws was the cruellest curse of

[2] The best introduction to his life and work is still Ogden, *Isaac D'Israeli*.
[3] His letter of resignation is printed in full in Picciotto, *Sketches of Anglo-Jewish History*, 289–90.   [4] Endelman, *Radical Assimilation in English Jewish History*, ch. 1.
[5] These comments were made in a letter to the elders of the Spanish and Portuguese Jewish congregation. It is reprinted in Roth (ed.), *Anglo-Jewish Letters*, 281–6.

all, for it estranged the Jews from sympathetic fellowship with other members of the human race, and along with other particularistic customs contributed to Christian prejudice against them. Isaac expressed these views in print on more than one occasion: in entries on the Talmud and rabbinical stories in his *Curiosities of Literature* (1791 and numerous editions thereafter), in his anti-revolutionary novel *Vaurien* (1797), in an article on Moses Mendelssohn in *The Monthly Magazine* (July 1798), in his discussion of Mendelssohn's self-education in his *History of Men of Genius* (1818), and in his *Genius of Judaism* (1833).

Although influenced by Enlightenment views, Isaac D'Israeli was not a disciple or follower of Moses Mendelssohn, as is often claimed.[6] Close examination of what he wrote about Mendelssohn suggests that he had not read his work, most of which was inaccessible to him at the time, having appeared in German and Hebrew but not having been translated into English. Instead, D'Israeli formed his view of Mendelssohn on the basis of second-hand accounts. He owned none of his writings, with the exception of a French edition of correspondence and essays by Mendelssohn and others related to the so-called Lavater affair, and Moses Samuel's *Memoirs of Moses Mendelssohn*, which appeared only in 1827 long after his view of Mendelssohn had taken shape.[7] As a result, he turned Mendelssohn into a much more radical thinker than he really was. While Mendelssohn championed the broadening of Jewish cultural horizons and the inclusion of secular studies in the Jewish curriculum, he never abandoned observance of the commandments, which he believed were binding on the Jewish people until such time as God told them otherwise.

But it is also wrong to see Isaac D'Israeli as indifferent to or unconcerned with Jewish issues, as is also often claimed.[8] As we have seen, he was not dispassionate when he wrote about Judaism. Some of this is attributable to the influence of Voltaire and other Enlightenment writers, some to the influence of Isaac's mother, Sarah, whom Benjamin described in terms similar to those used to characterize self-hating Jews. In a biographical sketch of his father, written as an introduction to a new edition of *The Curiosities of Literature* (1858) and quoted in Chapter 6, Benjamin reported that his grandmother had absorbed her neighbours' 'dislike for her race'. Proud, beautiful, and ambitious, Sarah 'never pardoned [her husband] for his name' and 'resented upon her unfortunate race the slights and disappointments to

---

[6] Ogden, *Isaac D'Israeli*, 195–7; Weintraub, *Disraeli*, 141–2, 278; Ridley, *Young Disraeli*, 13.

[7] For my reconstruction of the Judaica in Isaac's and later Benjamin's library, see the appendix to this chapter.

[8] Jaffe, 'A Reassessment of Benjamin Disraeli's Jewish Aspects', 116; Berlin, 'Benjamin Disraeli, Karl Marx, and the Search for Identity', 261–2.

which it exposed her'. She was 'so mortified by her social position that she lived until eighty without indulging in a tender expression'.[9] It is most unlikely that Isaac remained untouched by his mother's contempt for her own Jewish origins.

Isaac in turn communicated his negative views about Judaism to his children. Benjamin wrote to his benefactor Sarah Brydges Willyams (1780?– 1863), a childless widow of Sephardi ancestry whose fortune he inherited: 'I, like you, was not bred among my race, and was nurtured in great prejudice against them.'[10] This recollection, however, cannot be taken at face value. Isaac's attitude to Judaism was not unrelentingly hostile. It should be recalled that he maintained his membership in the Spanish and Portuguese synagogue until he was in his fifties and repeatedly took up Jewish themes in his writing. In addition, he arranged for his son Benjamin to receive weekly Hebrew instruction when he was at boarding school at Blackheath.[11] Moreover, on the basis of the Judaica titles in his library (see pp. 221–4), I would conclude that Isaac had a more than casual interest in Jewish history and literature, whatever his hostility to rabbinic tradition. An avid book collector, he acquired fifty to sixty Judaica titles—histories, apologetics, and polemical works in the main, with a smattering of books on philosophical and theological themes. Because he did not read Hebrew, his own Jewish education having been rudimentary, his acquisitions were limited to English and Romance-language works and did not include modern or classical Hebraica. On his shelves were several works of Menasseh Ben Israel and the learned Anglo-Jewish hat-dresser David Levi, the Latin translation of David Ganz's history *Tsemaḥ david*, the Abbé Grégoire's book on the regeneration of the Jews, Leon Modena's account of Jewish customs, Moses Samuel's biography of Moses Mendelssohn, and the English translation of Diogene Tama's transactions of the so-called Parisian or Napoleonic Sanhedrin.

Thus Benjamin did not grow to manhood in a household in which Jewish concerns and interests were treated with either complete indifference or contempt. It would be more accurate to say that his family was neither fully in the Jewish fold nor fully without it, but occupied a place somewhere between these two alternatives. While this does not seem to have disturbed Isaac or to have impeded his career, it was a problem for his eldest son, as it so often was with talented, ambitious sons from well-acculturated families. At school, because his social status and identity were open to question, Ben-

    [9] Disraeli, 'On the Life and Writings of Mr. Disraeli'.
    [10] Benjamin Disraeli to Sarah Brydges Willyams, 28 Feb. 1853, quoted in Jaffee, 'Benjamin Disraeli's Jewish Aspects', 116.
    [11] Monypenny and Buckle, *The Life of Benjamin Disraeli*, i. 19.

jamin was especially sensitive to being seen as different or marginal. He and another Jewish boy were compelled to stand in the back of the classroom during school prayers, for example; a well-intentioned practice that troubled Jewish children with an ambiguous sense of their own Jewishness nonetheless.

The confused nature of his Jewishness also made Disraeli vulnerable to anti-Jewish taunts from his schoolmates. Although the legal and social status of English Jews was better than that of most European Jews, slurs and slights rooted in age-old myths about Jewish difference and malevolence were a well-entrenched feature of cultural and social life.[12] While Disraeli never recounted having endured antisemitism while at school either before or after his baptism, he would have been exceptional to have escaped it given the cruelty of children in general and the prevalence of popular prejudices against Jews in particular. The best evidence we have that he suffered because of his Jewishness while at school is indirect but nonetheless compelling. According to Charles Richmond, unpublished diaries and memoranda written by Disraeli in 1821 (he had left school in summer 1820) reveal that he was concerned with religious persecution. In one passage he denounced the exclusion of 'the follower of another faith' from 'the benefits of the constitution' because of fears that he might change it and the legislature.[13] In addition, in two early novels, *Vivian Grey* (1826) and *Contarini Fleming* (1832), both of which are now recognized as rooted in personal experience, the eponymous heroes experience rebuffs at school. Self-conscious about his 'Venetian countenance', Contarini Fleming, whose very name proclaims his mixed background, feels he is an outsider. 'Wherever I moved I looked around me, and beheld a race different from myself.' In adulthood, he recalls his youth not with fondness but bitterness: 'I was a most miserable child; and school I detested more than ever I abhorred the world in the darkest moments of my experienced manhood.'[14] Both protagonists, it should be added, fight and thrash boys who insult them.

As these autobiographical fragments suggest, Disraeli's baptism—at St Andrew's, Holborn, in July 1817—did not have an immediate, positive impact on his relations with his schoolmates. In the long run, of course, it made possible his political career, since professing Jews were not allowed to sit in Parliament until 1858. But since it failed to alter his un-English looks and name or erase knowledge of his Jewish origins, he was still regarded as a Jew whatever his civil and religious status. In fact, in the short run, his baptism might have made his situation at school even more intolerable. Newly

---

[12] Endelman, *The Jews of Georgian England*, ch. 3; Felsenstein, *Anti-Semitic Stereotypes*.
[13] Richmond, 'Disraeli's Education', 17–19.   [14] Disraeli, *Contarini Fleming*, pt. I, ch. 2.

minted Christians, especially those with marked Jewish features, often fared
worse than unconverted Jews whose Jewishness was unambiguous.[15] In
general, the hybrid character of acculturated, 'non-Jewish' Jews troubled
contemporaries, since it blurred differences seen as essential. In an essay
written in the early 1820s, Charles Lamb vented his unease about 'the
approximation of Jew and Christian which has become so fashionable'. Exas-
perated, he confessed: 'I do not understand these half-convertites. Jews
Christianising—Christians judaising—puzzle me. I like fish or flesh.'[16]

We know nothing about how the young Disraeli viewed his baptism. In
any case, the decision to become a Christian was not his, but that of his
father, who remained an unconverted, Jewish deist. Although Isaac left no
record of why he decided to have Benjamin and his other children converted—a decision made easier by the death of his own father in November
1816—his motives are not difficult to infer. That religious conviction was no
consideration is clear from Isaac's own repudiation of revealed religion and
disinterest in becoming a Christian himself. His close friend the historian
Sharon Turner, author of the multi-volume, best-selling *History of the Anglo-
Saxons*, apparently urged him to take the step, but it is doubtful that Isaac
needed to be convinced of its wisdom. Dozens of Sephardim similar to Isaac
in background and outlook, including his brother-in-law George Basevi,
were doing the same thing, hoping to advance their own or their children's
worldly happiness. Not content to remain within commercial and financial
spheres, where Jews faced no barriers to success, they saw baptism as a
means to escape the popular stigma attached to Jewishness and gain un-
impeded access to professional, bureaucratic, artistic, and social circles from
which Jews had previously been excluded. In the words of the pioneer Anglo-
Jewish historian James Picciotto, who wrote from first-hand knowledge of
the period: 'The mart, the exchange, the Synagogue, the domestic circle, did
not suffice for their aspirations.'[17]

In his earliest stabs at making his way in the world—as fop, man-about-
town, lover, speculator, journalist, and novelist—the young Disraeli made no
mention of his Jewish origins. His conversion, on the face of it, appeared to
have been a strategic success, even if his career at the time was not. (His
repeated failures to launch himself and to fulfil his ambitions were not due
to his origins but rather his ineptitude.) He seemed to be indifferent to his
Jewish background, at least before the winter of 1829–30 when he started
work on his novel about David Alroy, the leader of a messianic movement in
twelfth-century Kurdistan. If it did concern him in the 1820s it remained a

---

[15] Endelman, *Radical Assimilation in English Jewish History*, 128–9, 138–9.
[16] Lamb, 'Imperfect Sympathies', 75–6.   [17] Picciotto, *Sketches of Anglo-Jewish History*, 187.

private, unarticulated concern. Perhaps he was unaware that it was or could be a source of discomfort. Whatever the case (and we can never know for sure), his Jewishness was not something to which he called attention or upon which he reflected in conversation or writing. It was not an obsession, as it would later become. There are few references to Jews in his letters or novels before the publication of *The Wondrous Tale of Alroy* in 1833.

Moreover, even after he started to read Jewish history in earnest in preparation for writing *Alroy*, he exhibited few public signs of a reawakened sense of Jewishness. The most telling evidence of this can be seen in the letters he wrote during the sixteen-month tour of the Mediterranean and the Near East that he made in 1830–1.[18] What is striking about these letters, in light of his later racial chauvinism, was how little interest he showed in the Jews and Jewish sites he encountered in Jerusalem and other Ottoman cities. When he wrote to his sister in March 1831 from Alexandria about his visit to Jerusalem, he made no mention of the Jewish population or the Western Wall, already an object of veneration and pilgrimage.[19] On the few occasions when he did mention Jews, it was in a formulaic way, as one of several 'exotic' peoples who made Levantine cities colourful in the eyes of Western travellers. For example, he wrote to his father from Gibraltar in July 1830: 'This rock is a wonderful place with a population infinitely diversified—Moors with costume radiant as a rainbow or an Easter melodrame, Jews with gabardines and scull caps, Genoese, Highlanders, and Spaniards, whose dress is as picturesque as that of the sons of Ivor.'[20] (In fact, it would have been surprising if the Jews he saw on Gibraltar were wearing 'gabardines', the stereotypical costume of Polish Jewish immigrants in western Europe; in all likelihood, they wore North African garb.) Similarly during his earlier tour of Italy in 1826, which included visits to Venice, with its famous ghetto, and Cento, birthplace of his paternal grandfather, he mentioned Jews only once in his letters home. He told his father that the only ghetto he visited was that of Ferrara. Without affect, in a manner best described as matter-of-fact, he wrote that it was 'a tolerably long street enclosed with red wooden gates and holding about 3000 Jews'.[21]

Although Jews and Judaism were not then central to Disraeli's sense of identity, his visit to the Near East, especially Jerusalem, was critical. In tandem with his work on *Alroy*, it initiated a period lasting some ten to twelve years during which Jewish themes came to occupy an increasingly prominent place in his thinking. Although his stay there did not transform him at

[18] The tour is described in Blake, *Disraeli's Grand Tour*.
[19] Benjamin Disraeli to Sarah Disraeli, 20 Mar. 1831, in Disraeli, *Letters*, i. 188.
[20] Benjamin Disraeli to Isaac D'Israeli, 1 July 1830, ibid. 128–9.
[21] Benjamin Disraeli to Isaac D'Israeli, 29 Sept. 1826, ibid. 86.

once into a champion of the Jews, it made an immediate impression nonetheless. When he first saw the city from the Mount of Olives, he wrote home that he was 'thunderstruck'. But his reaction, significantly, was that of a European Romantic rather than a Jew: his words make no reference to Jerusalem's Jewish significance as the site of the Temple and the Davidic monarchy.

I saw before me apparently a gorgeous city. Nothing can be conceived more wild and terrible and barren than the surrounding scenery, dark, stony and severe, but the ground is thrown about in such picturesque undulations, that the mind is full of the sublime, not the beautiful, and rich and waving woods and sparkling cultivation would be misplaced.[22]

One year after his return to England, Disraeli stood for Parliament for the first time, driven by the desire, in Robert Blake's words, 'to create a sensation, to occupy the limelight, to act a part on the greatest stage in the world'.[23] He lost the contest (a by-election at Wycombe in June 1832) and three subsequent elections, before winning a seat at Maidstone in July 1837. It was this experience, his plunge into electoral politics, more than his visit to Jerusalem, that forced his Jewishness to the fore and led him to rethink its relevance. Standing for election gave a public dimension to his origins that they had not had earlier. He had met with slights and slurs before this as he worked to cut a dash in fashionable London circles, but electioneering—and later the rough and tumble of national politics—exposed him to a level of anti-Jewish abuse that was (for him) unprecedented. As he entered Taunton in April 1835, for example, boys called out 'Old clothes!' and offered to sell him slippers and sealing-wax, references to low-status street trades with strong Jewish associations.[24] In a speech in Dublin several days later, Daniel O'Connell attacked Disraeli for remarks he made at Taunton, describing him as a Jew of 'the lowest and most disgusting grade of moral turpitude' with 'the qualities of the impenitent thief on the Cross' from whom, he claimed, Disraeli was descended.[25] Speaking to the people of Maidstone at the general election of July 1837, Disraeli was interrupted repeatedly with cries of 'Shylock!' and 'Old clothes!' and offers of ham and bacon, while his opponent mocked his foreign-sounding family name.[26] At Shrewsbury in June 1841 hostile members of the crowd waved pieces of roast pork on sticks, taunting him with the cry, 'Bring a bit of pork for the Jew', while one heckler

[22] Benjamin Disraeli to Sarah Disraeli, 20 Mar. 1831, in Disraeli, *Letters*, i. 188.
[23] Blake, *Disraeli*, 84.
[24] Sydney Smith to Mrs Holland, 3 June 1835, in S. Smith, *Letters*, ii. 614.
[25] *The Times*, 6 May 1835.   [26] Ridley, *Young Disraeli*, 202.

drove up to the hustings in a cart announcing, 'I come here to take you back to Jerusalem.'[27] When Disraeli became a national figure in the 1840s, on his way up 'the greasy pole', his Jewish origins attracted even more attention. Cartoonists in *Punch* and other illustrated magazines regularly depicted him as a Jewish old-clothes man, his head crowned with a stack of top hats, or as an importuning secondhand clothing dealer.[28]

Disraeli's initial response to the Jew-baiting that greeted his entry into electoral politics was to ignore it. His letters, speeches, and novels from the 1830s do not dwell on Jewish matters, with the one, curious, exception of *Alroy*. For a converted Jew like Disraeli, whose Jewish education was minimal, this was an unusual choice of subject to say the least. David Alroy was an obscure figure, little known if at all even to professing Jews in Victorian England. In Disraeli's hands he became a larger-than-life conqueror, wielding both kabbalistic lore and a mighty sword, who in the end is distracted from his mission to reclaim Jerusalem by his love for and eventual marriage to a daughter of the caliph of Baghdad. As in much of his writing, Disraeli's own passions and needs are close to the surface: in this case his desire to be a powerful leader in an alien land and his urge to validate the primacy of imaginative experience, as opposed to worldly, rational calculation, in human affairs. That he chose a Jewish military leader (and lover) to make these points is no coincidence. It reflected his own sense of being an outsider, as well as the impact of his visit to Jerusalem. In the preface to a new edition of *Alroy* in 1845, he claimed: 'Being at Jerusalem in the year 1831, and visiting the traditional tombs of the Kings of Israel, my thoughts recurred to a personage whose marvellous career had, even in boyhood, attracted my attention, as one fraught with the richest materials of poetic fiction.'[29] While this may not be the literal truth, it has to it the ring of emotional truth.

Still, it is possible to read too much into the oriental fantasies in *Alroy*. In the early 1830s Disraeli was no champion of the Jews, exulting in their antiquity, nobility, racial purity, and creative genius—nor had he yet stood for election and had his Jewishness thrown in his face. Whatever the impact of his visit to the Land of Israel, the claim that it stimulated 'fantasies of revived Jewish hegemony'[30] exceeds the evidence. It makes Disraeli a proto-nationalist or Zionist *avant la lettre*, which does not fit with what else is known about his thinking in the 1830s. In fact, there are passages in *Alroy* that are hostile to the Jewish religion, if not the Jewish people, passages that

[27] Fraser, *Disraeli and his Day*, 473–4; Weintraub, *Disraeli*, 197.
[28] See e.g. the illustrations reprinted in Weintraub, *Disraeli*, 222, 291, and following p. 274; Ridley, *Young Disraeli*, following p. 278; Cowen and Cowen, *Victorian Jews through British Eyes*, 24–5.   [29] Disraeli, 'Preface to Alroy', p. v.   [30] Schwarz, *Disraeli's Fiction*, 43.

echo his father's deistic critique of rabbinic tradition. A 'learned' exchange between Rabbi Zimri and Rabbi Maimon early in the tale mocks talmudic discourse and the rabbinic penchant for aggadic (non-legal) hyperbole.[31] Later Alroy explodes in anger when he learns that zealous soldiers have plundered a mosque in fulfilment of the biblical commandment to destroy utterly 'all the places where the nations . . . served their gods' (Deut. 12: 2). 'Come I to a council of valiant statesmen or dreaming Rabbis?', he demands to know. His meaning is clear: the laws of Moses are no 'school for empire'; they will not 'establish the throne of Israel'; their time has passed.[32]

Disraeli's obsession with Jewish themes took hold only in the 1840s, that is, after he entered politics. Early in his parliamentary career, he remained silent when bills to remove Jewish disabilities came before the House of Commons. In 1837, soon after taking his seat, he voted with the majority against emancipation. He wrote to his sister after the division, 'Nobody looked at me and I was not at all uncomfortable, but voted in the majority (only of 12) with the utmost sangfroid.'[33] During the 1841 debate on a bill to enable Jews to hold municipal office he was silent. He also said nothing in 1845 when his own party sponsored and successfully guided through the Commons another emancipation bill, despite having voiced Jewish concerns, as well as eccentric views on emancipation, in *Coningsby*, which had been published the previous year. (He first spoke in Parliament in favour of Jewish emancipation in 1847; his speech was not well received, provoking angry responses from both Tories and Liberals.[34])

In *Coningsby*, which he began writing in September 1843, Disraeli voiced publicly for the first time the sentiments that came to form the core of his Jewish identity, sentiments to which he returned repeatedly in subsequent publications, speeches, conversations, and letters. In this novel, the first of his celebrated political trilogy, he introduced the mysterious Jewish banker Sidonia, his alter ego, the embodiment of his desires and fantasies, and spokesman for his most cherished beliefs. Sidonia is cultivated, cosmopolitan, wise in the ways of the world, able to influence world events with a word or two to princes and ministers.[35] He informs the aspiring politician

---

[31] Disraeli, *Alroy*, pt. 6, ch. 3.   [32] Ibid., pt. 8, ch. 5.

[33] Benjamin Disraeli to Sarah Disraeli, 5 Dec. 1837, in Disraeli, *Letters*, ii. 323–4.

[34] Gilam, 'Benjamin Disraeli and the Emancipation of the Jews'.

[35] It is often stated that Disraeli modelled Sidonia on Lionel de Rothschild, but, according to Richard Davis, this is unlikely. The head of the Rothschild bank and the young politician were not close friends at the time Disraeli wrote the book, while Lionel's personality bore little resemblance to that of the fictional Sidonia. Davis adds, however: 'There can be little doubt that the fabulous financier with his mysterious international connections was Rothschild-inspired (though not by any particular Rothschild). This is as far as one can safely go' (*The English Rothschilds*, 87).

Coningsby that the Jews are a powerful race, masters of the world's money markets, arbiters of European thought and sensibility, lords of secret diplomacy and explosive revolution. Their pre-eminence, he explains, derives from their racial purity, their refusal to intermarry with other nations. In his words, 'the Hebrew is an unmixed race' and 'an unmixed race of a firstrate organisation are the aristocracy of Nature'.[36] Wherever Sidonia looks, he sees Jewish power and influence. For example, he tells Coningsby:

There is not a company of singers, not an orchestra in a single capital, that is not crowded with our children under the feigned names which they adopt to conciliate the dark aversion which your posterity will some day disclaim with shame and disgust. Almost every great composer, skilled musician, almost every voice that ravishes you with its transporting strains, springs from our tribes.[37]

Sidonia also makes an unorthodox case for emancipation. Eschewing what he calls 'political sentimentalism' (the liberal argument for religious toleration), he reasons that as the Jews are allowed to accumulate property—the basis of power—they have become a force and should be incorporated into the political nation rather than forced into permanent opposition to its establishment. (Thomas Babington Macaulay, who shared little else with Disraeli, made the same argument.[38]) The Tory refusal to grant them emancipation has pushed them temporarily into the ranks of levellers and latitudinarians. 'The Tories lose an important election at a critical moment; 'tis the Jews come forward to vote against them.' With each generation, they acquire more power, thanks to their racial purity and accumulation of property, and thus become increasingly dangerous to the establishment. 'It is a physiological fact; a simple law of nature . . . No penal laws, no physical tortures, can effect that a superior race should be absorbed in an inferior, or destroyed by it. The mixed persecuting races disappear; the pure persecuted race remains.' But, Sidonia adds, the English have little to fear, for the Jews are at heart Tories, essentially monarchical, deeply religious and thus, if allowed to enter political life, will strengthen the ranks of conservatism, where by nature they belong.[39]

Sidonia adds one further reason for England to remove the Jews' political disabilities: gratitude for their fundamental contributions to Western, Christian culture. He tells Coningsby that Europe owes to them 'the best part of its laws, a fine portion of its literature, all its religion'. He asks him, 'What are all the schoolmen, Aquinas himself, to Maimonides? And as for modern philosophy, all springs from Spinoza.'[40]

[36] Disraeli, *Coningsby*, bk. 4, ch. 10.
[37] Ibid., ch. 15.   [38] Macaulay, *Critical and Historical Essays*, ii. 141–3.
[39] Disraeli, *Coningsby*, bk. 4, ch. 15.   [40] Ibid.

Three years later in *Tancred*, the romantic tale of a young English lord's spiritual quest in the Holy Land, Disraeli carried this racial boastfulness even further. He first stressed Europe's cultural indebtedness to the Jews and its spiritual roots in the Near East. On a pilgrimage to Mount Sinai, Tancred asks himself why he, 'the child of a northern isle', has come to this 'great and terrible wilderness' and what his connection to it is. He concludes that there is an indissoluble, profound link: 'words had been uttered and things done, more than thirty centuries ago, in this stony wilderness, which influenced his opinions and regulated his conduct every day of his life, in that distant and seagirt home'.[41] The sublime laws of Sinai protect the life and property of Englishmen and guarantee working people a day of rest in every seven. The most popular poet in England is not Wordsworth or Byron, he realizes, but 'the sweet singer of Israel'. The heroic history of ancient Israel animates and inspires the English in their pursuit of liberty. Above all, his countrymen owe a debt to the Jews for knowledge of the true God and for the means (Jesus) through which they find salvation.[42] On this last point, Disraeli gave a novel twist to Jewish apologetics about the crucifixion. Instead of denying eternal, collective Jewish responsibility, he affirmed their role, for which he believed Christians should be forever grateful, since Jesus' death gave them the means to be redeemed. The Creator having preordained the crucifixion since the start of time, the Jews were simply carrying out one more divinely appointed task. 'Where then was the inexpiable crime of those who fulfilled the beneficent intention? The holy race supplied the victim and the immolators. What other race could have been entrusted with such a consummation?'[43]

However muddled his thinking, Disraeli's intentions were serious. His message was twofold: first, England's civilization, with its worship of progress, 'its false excitement, its bustling invention, and its endless toil'[44] was tired and superficial, its politics meaningless and futile; second, to save itself, to find inspiration, imagination, and faith, it had to look to the Near East, to the sources of its religion and values. 'A great thought', such as had gone forth before 'from Mount Sinai, from the villages of Galilee, from the deserts of Arabia', could revive England and its people; it could 'remodel all their institutions, change their principles of action, and breathe a new spirit into the whole scope of their existence'.[45] In Disraeli's imaginative universe, civilization came from Mediterranean nations, to which of course he traced his own roots.

---

[41] Disraeli, *Tancred*, bk. 4, ch. 4.   [42] Ibid.   [43] Ibid., bk. 3, ch. 4.
[44] Ibid., bk. 4, ch. 9.   [45] Ibid.

All the great things have been done by the little nations. It is the Jordan and Ilyssus that have civilised the modern races. An Arabian tribe [the Jews], a clan of the Aegean, have been the promulgators of all our knowledge; and we should never have heard of the Pharaohs, of Babylon the great and Nineveh the superb, of Cyrus and of Xerxes, had it not been for Athens and Jerusalem.[46]

Jerusalem, moreover, ranked higher than Athens, for it was in the Land of Israel alone and nowhere else that God revealed himself, which is the reason that Tancred journeys there. 'I know well, though born in a distant and northern isle, that the Creator of the world speaks with man only in this land.' But after pouring forth his prayers at all its holy places and receiving no heavenly sign, Tancred realizes another 'desolating' truth: God does not speak to Europeans. Much to his regret, he discovers 'that there is a qualification of blood as well as of locality necessary for this communion, and that the featured votary must not only kneel in the Holy Land but be of the Holy Race'.[47] God, it seems, speaks only to Jews.

Disraeli's embrace of Jewish chauvinism in the 1840s seems at first to make little sense. Born an outsider, he had had some success by the mid-1840s in overcoming the obstacles his non-aristocratic, 'alien' origins posed. He had become a well-known figure in national politics, having played a central role in the break-up of the Conservative Party and the fall of Sir Robert Peel in June 1846. With Lord George Bentinck, he was leader of the protectionist faction in the House of Commons and sat with Bentinck on the opposition front bench when Parliament convened in January 1847. But he was still consumed by ambition, driven to shine ever more brightly, eager to take the lead, to hold national office. To trumpet his origins and spout racial claptrap about Jewish superiority were unusual steps for someone in his position. Did he believe that this was the best method to win the affections of the well-born Christian landowners whose leader he wished to become? A more obvious strategy would have been to muffle his Jewishness, avoiding constant mention of it, minimizing its relevance, perhaps even expressing contempt for it in order to prove that he had transcended it. This is what other converted or deracinated Jews in similar circumstances did, figures as diverse as Ferdinand Lassalle, Edwin Montagu, Walther Rathenau, Victor Adler, Leon Trotsky, and Bruno Kreisky. When reminded of their Jewish origins, they became even more reticent to dwell on their Jewishness or even more contemptuous of Jews and their concerns. Rosa Luxemburg's response to her friend Mathilde Wurm from her cell in the Wronke fortress in 1917 was typical:

[46] Ibid., bk. 3, ch. 7.   [47] Ibid., bk. 4, ch. 3.

What do you want with this particular suffering of the Jews? The poor victims on the rubber plantations in Putamayo, the Negroes in Africa with whose bodies the Europeans play a game of catch, are just as near to me . . . I have no special corner in my heart reserved for the ghetto. I am at home wherever in the entire world there are clouds, birds, and human tears.[48]

Why, then, did Disraeli? How can we understand his extraordinary, seemingly self-destructive behaviour?

The answer, first suggested by Hannah Arendt and later elaborated by Isaiah Berlin, is that Disraeli's racial chauvinism was a compensatory counter-myth, forged to combat his feelings of social inferiority through assertions of an ancient racial lineage nobler than that of the English aristocracy.[49] He countered the caste pride of the great landowners, whose acceptance he craved and whose leader he wanted to be, with his own imagined racial pride. He inflated his Jewish birth into a claim of noble birth, Berlin wrote, 'in order to feel that he was dealing on equal terms with the leaders of his family's adopted country, which he so profoundly venerated'.[50] In Disraeli's racial construction of history, the English aristocracy came from less noble stock than his own. They were, he wrote in *Tancred*, 'sprung from a horde of Baltic pirates, who were never heard of during the greater annals of the world'.[51] His people, the Jews, on the other hand, were God's chosen, with whom alone he communicated, the creators of an advanced civilization 'at a time when the inhabitants of England were going half-naked and eating acorns in the forest' and its bishops were 'tatooed savages'.[52]

Arendt suggested that Disraeli's embrace of these ideas represented a calculated strategic move. In her eyes, he was 'the potent wizard' who 'never took himself quite seriously and always played a role to win society and find popularity', a playful charlatan who manipulated his Jewishness to his social and political advantage.[53] What her interpretation ignores, however, is that Disraeli took these ideas seriously, however theatrically he expressed them. These ideas spoke to his deepest feelings; their adoption represented a profound psychological response to his status as an outsider, an alien in both Jewish and Christian society. He came to them through unconscious as

[48] Rosa Luxemburg to Mathilde Wurm, 16 Feb. 1917, in Luxemburg, *Letters*, 7–8.
[49] Arendt, *The Origins of Totalitarianism*, pt. 1, *Antisemitism*, 72–5; Berlin, 'Benjamin Disraeli, Karl Marx and the Search for Identity'.
[50] Berlin, 'Benjamin Disraeli, Karl Marx and the Search for Identity', 268.
[51] Disraeli, *Tancred*, bk. 1, ch. 11.
[52] Quoted in Blake, *Disraeli's Grand Tour*, 126. According to Blake, it comes from *Contarini Fleming*, but he does not indicate where in the novel it appears, and neither I nor Nadia Valman, a student of Disraeli's novels, has been able to locate it.
[53] Arendt, *The Origins of Totalitarianism*, pt. 1, *Antisemitism*, 75.

much as conscious calculations, and in the end he could not leave them alone. When he wrote about Jews, he always went too far, harping on their power, exaggerating their importance, introducing them into contexts in which they did not otherwise belong (witness the chapter on Jews and Judaism in his biography of Lord George Bentinck[54]), 'trying to force his Jewish jackasseries on the world', as Thomas Carlyle saw it.[55] In this sense he was obsessed with Jews and, as is the case with obsessions, unable to take up and put down the subject at will. The emergence of his Jewishness was a psychological transformation, the coalescing of a new self-understanding, what Berlin called 'an inner image of himself with which he could establish for himself a place in the world, and play a part in history and society'.[56]

Expressions of racial pride also allowed Disraeli to assert his independence at a time when, in fact, his advancement was becoming more tied to aristocratic patronage. In 1848 Lord George Bentinck's two brothers lent Disraeli £25,000 to purchase Hughenden Manor, the estate that he needed to occupy a county seat in Parliament and that was a social prerequisite for leading the Tory party. Although the Bentincks had no intention of calling in their loan, viewing it as an investment in the political future of the Tories rather than a business venture, as 'a contribution from one of the great landowning families of England to enable their class to be represented by one of the most brilliant men of the day',[57] Disraeli was in their debt nonetheless. He also remained subordinate to Edward Stanley (earl of Derby from 1851), one of the grand seigneurs of landed England, who headed the Tory protectionists in the 1850s and 1860s. Not until 1868, when Derby became too ill to continue and resigned his post, was the way clear for Disraeli to become undisputed leader of the Tories and prime minister.

The outrageous racial ideas that Disraeli embraced in the 1840s constituted the core of his Jewishness. Aside from them it had little or no content. In Sidonia's pithy formula in *Tancred*, 'All is race; there is no other truth.'[58] He and the other Jewish characters in Disraeli's novels, for example, do not lead identifiably Jewish lives—that is, they do not observe Jewish customs, read or expound Jewish texts, take a role in Jewish communal organizations, socialize in the main with other Jews, or act in ways recognizably different from other characters, other than venting their racial pride. Sidonia is unwilling to marry a non-Jew, Disraeli tells us in *Coningsby*, because he is as devoted to his race as other persons are to their religion: 'No earthly consideration would ever induce him to impair that purity of race on

---

54 Disraeli, *Lord George Bentinck*, ch. 24.
55 Quoted in Reid, *The Life, Letters and Friendships of Richard Monckton Milnes*, i. 436.
56 Berlin, 'Benjamin Disraeli, Karl Marx and the Search for Identity', 270.
57 Blake, *Disraeli*, 253.   58 Disraeli, *Tancred*, bk. 2, ch. 14.

which he prides himself'.[59] Judaism as a body of beliefs, customs, and ethics is usually absent in his fiction and other writings. Like his father, it seems, he believed that the Jewish religion had ceased to be a vital source of inspiration and meaning for modern societies.

Although ethnicity rather than religion was the core of Disraeli's Jewishness, he was not insensitive in middle age to the attractions of religious rituals. In *Alroy*, written when he was in his twenties in his father's house at the same time that Isaac was writing *The Genius of Judaism*, he had mocked rabbinic tradition. But fourteen years later, in *Tancred*, he was more sympathetic. In an extended passage describing the celebration of Sukkot in northern Europe, Disraeli remarked that there was 'something profoundly interesting in this devoted observance of Oriental customs in the heart of our Saxon and Sclavonian cities'.[60] He went on to describe how celebration of the holiday transformed the downtrodden Houndsditch Jew.

The season arrives, and the mind and heart of that being are filled with images and passions that have been ranked in all ages among the most beautiful and the most genial of human experience; filled with a subject the most vivid, the most graceful, the most joyous, and the most exuberant; a subject which has inspired poets, and which has made gods; the harvest of the grape in the native regions of the Vine.[61]

With genuine warmth, Disraeli then described how this humble Jew built his sukkah and how, after returning from the synagogue, 'he sups late with his wife and his children in the open air, as if he were in the pleasant villages of Galilee, beneath its sweet and starry sky'.[62]

In his tribute to Sukkot and its ancient customs, however, Disraeli ignored the historical, redemptive dimension of the holiday, its commemoration of the period after the Exodus from Egypt during which the Israelites dwelled in temporary booths, and instead concentrated on its agricultural aspect, especially the harvesting of grapes and making of wine, a theme that is absent from Jewish tradition. What attracted him were not the religious ideas associated with the holiday but its potential for being given a national or racial twist. Eva, daughter of a wealthy Jewish merchant in Jerusalem, refers to Sukkot as 'one of our great national festivals'. Even though the vineyards of Israel had ceased to exist, and the Jews had no fruits to gather, Disraeli observed, they still persisted in 'celebrating their vintage'. Such a race would 'regain their vineyards', he prophesied. 'What sublime inexorability in the law! But what indomitable spirit in the people.' To reinforce the racial lesson he drew from Jewish ritual perseverance, Disraeli contrasted the

[59] Disraeli, *Coningsby*, bk. 7, ch. 1.   [60] Disraeli, *Tancred*, bk. 5, ch. 6.
[61] Ibid.   [62] Ibid.

'noble' behaviour of his Houndsditch Jew with the boorish, drunken behaviour of a passing party of 'Anglo-Saxons', who sneer at the 'horrible feasts' of the 'cursed Jews'.[63]

Disraeli's frequent references in *Alroy, Tancred*, and elsewhere to the return to Zion suggest that his sense of Jewishness included a nationalist as well as an ethnic dimension. His most unambiguous declaration of interest in the restoration of the Jews came in a conversation with Lord Stanley in January 1851. While walking in the country, Disraeli talked to him 'with great earnestness on the subject of restoring the Jews to their own land'. (Was Disraeli to be the messianic figure who would lead them?) Ignoring the cold, to which he was usually sensitive, and speaking with 'great apparent earnestness', Disraeli set forth a detailed plan. Rothschild and other Jewish bankers would purchase land from the Turks, whose empire was in ruins and who would do anything for money. Agricultural colonies would be established, with their security guaranteed (Disraeli did not say how). The 'question of nationality'—the eventual political status of the reclaimed Jewish homeland—would be postponed until the colonies had taken firm root.[64]

If in the 1840s and 1850s Disraeli entertained fantasies about the territorial restoration of the Jews, he did nothing to advance their realization. Even his purchase of the Khedive's Suez Canal shares much later in 1875 seems to have been unconnected to these earlier fantasies. But as we are concerned more with his state of mind—his feelings, sentiments, and desires— than with his policies, his failure to take action is irrelevant. That he dreamt such dreams and then spoke of them is what is critical. In my view, these fantasies reflected his need to possess a heroic, noble heritage and to see this heritage restored to its former glory. In this sense, he was a Jewish nationalist. However, his thoughts on the future of the Jewish people defy neat categorization. He was no proto-Zionist pure and simple, for when he thought about the restoration of the Jews he tended to associate it with Christian myths and motifs. In the same passage in *Tancred* in which he described Sukkot in nationalist terms, he also referred to the kiddush (the blessing over wine recited at the start of sabbath and festival meals) as 'the very ceremony which the Divine Prince of Israel, nearly two thousand years ago, adopted at the most memorable of all repasts [the Last Supper], and eternally invested with eucharistic grace'.[65] In the same diary entry in which Stanley recorded the conversation mentioned earlier, he also noted that Disraeli once said to him 'with earnestness' that 'if he retired from politics in time enough, he should resume literature, and write the *Life of Christ* from a

---

[63] Ibid.   [64] Stanley, *Disraeli, Derby and the Conservative Party*, 32–3.
[65] Disraeli, *Tancred*, bk. 5, ch. 6.

national point of view, intending it for a posthumous work'. And during the
Commons debate on Jewish emancipation in 1847 he identified his own
views with those of the evangelical Lord Ashley (earl of Shaftesbury from
1851), a millenarian who looked forward to the restoration of the Jews to the
Holy Land and their subsequent conversion.[66]

To assert then that Disraeli was a proud Jewish nationalist, while true, is
not the whole truth. He also remained a believing if somewhat unorthodox
Protestant. In some fundamental religious matters, to be sure, his thinking was quite conventional. He believed (or said he believed) that Jesus
was the Christ, 'blending in his inexplicable nature the divine essence with
the human elements, a sacrificial mediator', whose 'atoning blood' purified
'the myriads that had preceded and the myriads that will follow him'.[67]
In order to be completed, Judaism had to assimilate Christianity. It was
deplorable that 'several millions of the Jewish race should persist in believing in only a part of their religion', but understandable, since it had been
made known to them largely in a debased form (Roman Catholicism) by
peoples who persecuted and tormented them. Now, however, with the Christian nations having grown more humane and tolerant and with the Jews
having better opportunities to know pure, reformed Christianity, different
results could be expected.[68]

While Disraeli's belief that Christianity completed or superseded Judaism was conventional, his other views about the relationship between
Judaism and Christianity were not. (Froude aptly characterized his Christianity as 'something of his own', which 'would scarcely find acceptance in any
Christian community'.[69]) In the late 1840s and early 1850s, as Paul Smith
points out, Disraeli was working to reconcile his Jewish background and his
Christian religion. He was then becoming leader of the party that championed the Established Church and needed to develop a balance (however awkward) between Judaism and Christianity—to explain how a Jew could head
both a Christian party and a Christian state. Although his pronouncements
on this matter will not stand up to rigorous theological scrutiny, there is a
consistent theme or impulse that runs through them: the overwhelming
urge to blur distinctions, bridge gaps, and break down barriers between the

[66] Gilam, 'Benjamin Disraeli and the Emancipation of the Jews', 32.
[67] Disraeli, *Lord George Bentinck*, 498–9.
[68] Ibid. 505–7. Despite his hope for the eventual conversion of the Jews, Disraeli could be
scornful about Jews who tried to mute their Jewishness and 'pass through society without
being discovered, or at least noticed'. See his witty demolition of the fictional social-climbing
Laurella sisters in *Tancred*, who were 'ashamed of their race, and not fanatically devoted to their
religion, which might be true but certainly was not fashionable' (bk. 5, ch. 5).
[69] Froude, *The Earl of Beaconsfield*, 108.

two religious traditions. For example, in the Commons debate on Jewish
emancipation in 1847, he argued for the removal of Jewish disabilities on the
basis of the affinity between Judaism and Christianity and the latter's spiritual and ethical indebtedness to the former. 'Where is your Christianity,'
he asked his fellow legislators, 'if you do not believe in their Judaism?'[70]
In *Tancred* this blurring of theological and historical differences was even
more pronounced. In one passage, Tancred asks Eva whether she worships
Jesus. She replies, 'It sometimes seems to me that I ought, for I am of his
race, and you should sympathise with your race.' He then asks her whether
she has read the Gospels, which, of course, she has, the Anglican bishop
of Jerusalem having given her a copy. And she has found it a good book,
'written . . . entirely by Jews'. 'I find in it many things with which I agree; and
if there be some from which I dissent, it may be that I do not comprehend
them.' Excitedly Tancred tells her that she is already 'half a Christian!'[71] Later
in the novel, in explaining revelation to a Muslim emir, Tancred tells him
that through Jesus, the last and greatest of Israel's princes, the Hebrew mind
came to mould and govern the world. He concludes his explanation with the
arresting but simple-minded formula 'Christianity is Judaism for the multitude, but it is still Judaism'.[72] Disraeli was able to collapse distinctions between Judaism and Christianity in this way because his sense of being
Jewish was rooted in race rather than religion and thus lacked a distinctive
theology, ethics, or ritual. If 'all is race', the Jewish racial background of
Christianity was more significant than the daughter religion's later theological and institutional development.

Disraeli's Christianity was as muddled as his Judaism and for much the
same reason: neither the doctrinal nor experiential side of religion was
important to him. He himself did not find spiritual meaning or consolation
in religion. Indeed, in his diary Stanley noted that Disraeli mocked all religions in private. Some of this irreverence comes through in his correspondence. For example, in a letter to his sister in 1851, he related how the duke of
Portland had sent him half a buck as a present and how he had sent it on to
the Lionel de Rothschilds 'as we [he and his wife] have dined there so often, &
they never with us'. Afterwards, realizing that the meat was not kosher (the
Rothschilds observed the dietary laws), he joked that 'as I mentioned the
donor [Portland], & they love Lords, notwith[standin]g that they throw out
their [emancipation] bill, I think they will swallow it'.[73] When defining his

[70] Quoted in Blake, *Disraeli*, 258.
[71] Disraeli, *Tancred*, bk. 3, ch. 4.   [72] Ibid., bk. 6, ch. 4.
[73] Stanley, *Disraeli, Derby and the Conservative Party*, 179; Benjamin Disraeli to Sarah Disraeli, 1 Aug. 1851, in Disraeli, *Letters*, v. 459.

personal connection to the Church of England, he did so in racial terms. He wrote that he looked upon the Anglican Church as 'the only Jewish institution that remains', and thus 'irrespective of its being the depository of divine truth', he 'must ever cling to it as the visible means which embalms the memory of my race, their deeds and thoughts, and connects their blood with the origin of things'.[74] Hardly a stirring confession of faith! Even on his deathbed, he remained religiously indifferent, refusing clerical ministration or any talk of religion.[75]

In public, of course, Disraeli was a faithful communicant of the Church of England, or at least as faithful as other Tory notables.[76] But then, to have absented himself from church would have been unthinkable. He went because that was what was done, and equally because he saw the Anglican Church as a bastion of tradition and a pillar of the established order. Before he became leader of the Tories, in fact, he had found Catholicism attractive for similar reasons: its antiquity, traditionalism, changelessness, pageantry —and the fact that it stood for everything opposed to Whiggery. In his early novels and his Young England trilogy (*Coningsby*, *Sybil*, and *Tancred*), he invariably treated Catholic characters with great sympathy. Witness the model well-born landowner, the old Catholic Eustace Lyle in *Coningsby*.[77] However, if his opposition to Whiggish and Radical views made him a High Church enthusiast in his Young England phase, he did not remain one afterward. He became increasingly Protestant with time and in 1874, as prime minister, supported a bill to suppress High Church ritualistic practices— without much enthusiasm. He would have preferred to leave the issue alone and took it up largely to please Queen Victoria. In general, he showed little interest in religious issues when he was in office, despite what he had written in *Tancred* and elsewhere. When he had to make Church appointments, for example, he was ignorant of the names and qualifications of candidates for promotion. The dean of Windsor remarked in November 1868 that he 'showed an ignorance about all Church matters, men, opinions, that was astonishing'.[78]

Once Disraeli succeeded in climbing to the top, he ceased to harp on Jewish themes in the way he had in the first two decades of his political career. This was due, in part, to his having less time (or need) to write fiction. From the late 1840s politics absorbed most of his creative energies. But this was

---

[74] Quoted in Monypenny and Buckle, *The Life of Benjamin Disraeli*, iv. 350.

[75] Weintraub, *Disraeli*, 658.

[76] Ridley, *Young Disraeli*, 268, claims that 'Disraeli rarely set foot in a church', but her evidence for the claim is not clear. Perhaps she is referring to the period before he aspired to political leadership.   [77] Disraeli, *Coningsby*, bk. 3, ch. 3–5.

[78] Quoted in Monypenny and Buckle, *The Life of Benjamin Disraeli*, v. 57–8.

also due to a change in his personal fortunes: having gained the Tory leadership, he no longer needed to restate his claims to noble origins with the urgency that drove him earlier. Having made it to the top and won the reluctant admiration of the Tory magnates, who could not produce a leader of equal calibre from their own ranks, he no longer experienced the same pressure to counter their myth with one of his own. He did not, to be sure, abandon or repudiate his earlier views. Rather, he was less insistent in airing them. Having served their purpose, they took a back seat to more immediate political concerns. Tellingly, when once again his Jewishness was used as a club with which to beat him—during the Eastern Crisis of 1876–78—he did not respond, as before, with assertions of Jewish racial pride. In fact, he did not respond at all to the blatant Jew-baiting of his Liberal and Radical critics, who targeted both him personally and English Jews generally. Instead, he took the high road of defending Britain's geopolitical interests as he saw them. As prime minister and from August 1876 a hereditary lord, his ambition had been satisfied; his credentials as an Englishman and a patriot were secure.

A NOTE ON THE JUDAICA IN THE DISRAELI LIBRARY

No catalogue of Isaac D'Israeli's extensive library exists. However, it is possible to reconstruct the Judaica in it—or at least a portion of the Judaica in it—on the basis of a handwritten list that has survived in the Rothschild Archive (DFam/E/1/9A). Nathaniel de Rothschild, later the first Lord Rothschild, was co-executor of Benjamin Disraeli's estate. In October 1881 the estate sold fifty-four books from his library, all but two or three on Jewish subjects, a list of which remained in Lord Rothschild's keeping. Presumably, Disraeli's sole heir, his nephew Coningsby Disraeli, had no interest in them. While at least one of the books had to have been acquired by Benjamin, given its publication date, the bulk, it would seem, belonged to Isaac. On his father's death in January 1848, Benjamin inherited his 25,000-volume library; in serious debt, he sold most of it at Sotheby's, after having culled a number of works for his own library at Hughenden. It seems doubtful that Benjamin would have purchased Judaica published in the eighteenth century or even before the late 1830s, when he first began to take an interest in his Jewish background. Thus I believe it is reasonable to use this list as a guide, however imperfect, to the Judaica to which Isaac and later Benjamin turned for their knowledge of Jewish history and literature. It is, of course, likely that Isaac's collection of Judaica was more extensive and that Benjamin sold some of the Judaica volumes at Sotheby's after his father's death.

I have corrected spelling and other errors and listed the books in a manner consistent with current bibliographical practice. I am grateful to Melanie Aspey of the Rothschild Archive for making the list available to me.

Annunciação Justiniano, Diogo da, *Sermãs do Auto da Fé* (Lisbon, 1705).

—— *The Inquisition and Judaism: A Sermon Addressed to Jewish Martyrs on the Occasion of an Auto da fe at Lisbon, 1705 . . . Also a Reply to the Sermon by David Nieto*, trans. Moses Mocatta (London, 1845).

Bail, Charles Joseph, *État des juifs en France, en Espagne, et en Italie depuis le commencement du cinquième siècle de l'ère vulgaire jusqu'á la fin du seizième* (Paris, 1823).

—— *Des juifs au dix-neuvième siècle* (Paris, 1816).

Barbequière, J. B., *La maçonnerie mesmérienne* (Amsterdam, 1784).

Bauer, Georg Lorenz, *The Theology of the Old Testament, or A Biblical Sketch of the Religious Opinions of the Ancient Hebrews* (London, 1838).

Benjamin of Tudela, *Travels of Rabbi Benjamin*, ed. R. Gerrons (London, 1783).

Beugnot, Auguste Arthur, *Les juifs d'occident, ou recherches sur l'état civil, le commerce, et la littérature des juifs en France, en Espagne, et en Italie pendant la durée du moyen age* (Paris, 1824).

Bible: *The Song of Songs* (1867).

Castro y Rossi, Adolfo, *The History of the Jews in Spain*, trans. Edward D. G. M. Kirwan (Cambridge and London, 1851).

D'Israeli, Isaac, *The Genius of Judaism* (London, 1833).

—— *Narrative Poems* (London, 1803).

—— *Romances*, 3rd rev. edn (London, 1807).

Dulaure, Jacques Antoine, *Des cultes qui ont précédé et amené l'idolatrie, ou l'adoration des figures humaines* (Paris, 1805).

Fleury, Claude, *Essais historiques et critiques sur les juifs anciens et moderns, ou supplément aux moeurs des Israélites* (Lyons, 1771).

—— *Les moeurs des israélites et des chrétiens* (Paris, 1720).

Ganz, David, *Chronologia sacra-profana* (Leiden, 1644).

Gaulmin, Gilbert, *De vita et morte Mosis* (Hamburg, 1714).

Gawler, George, *Observations and Practical Suggestions in Furtherance of Jewish Colonies in Palestine* (London, 1845).

Grégoire, Henri, *An Essay on the Physical, Moral, and Political Reformation of the Jews* (London, 1791).

Le Clerc, Jean, *Twelve Dissertations out of Monsieur Le Clerk's Genesis*, trans. Mr. Brown (London, 1696).

Lettres juives du célèbre Mendelssohn, philosophe de Berlin, avec les remarques et réponses de monsieur le docteur Kölble et autres savants hommes (n.p., 1771).

Leon Templo, Jacob Judah Aryeh, *Tratado de los cherubim* (Amsterdam, 1654).

Levi, David, *A Defense of the Old Testament, in a Series of Letters Addressed to Thomas Paine* (London, 1797).

—— *Letters to Dr. Priestly in Answer to Those He Addressed to the Jews* (London, 1787).

—— *A Succinct Account of the Rites and Ceremonies of the Jews* (London, 1783).

Lewis, Thomas, *Origines Hebraeae: The Antiquities of the Hebrew Republick*, 4 vols. (London, 1724–5).

Lopes, Isaac, *Sermão pregado no K.K. de T.T. em Sabath Emor* (Amsterdam, 1719).

Margoliouth, Moses, *The Jews in Great Britain* (London, 1846).

Meier, Johannes, *Tractatus de temporibus s. et festis diebus Hebraeorum* (Amsterdam, 1724).

Menasseh Ben-Israel, *The Conciliator*, trans. Elias Haim Lindo (London, 1842).

—— *Of the Term of Life*, trans. Thomas Pocock (London, 1699).

—— *Del Conciliador*, pts. 3, 4 (Amsterdam, 1650–1).

—— *De resurrectione mortuorum* (Amsterdam, 1636).

—— *Thesouro dos dinim* (Amsterdam, 1710).

Modena, Leon, *The History of the Present Jews throughout the World*, trans. John Gwen (London, 1707).

—— *The History of the Rites, Customes and Manner of Life of the Present Jews throughout the World*, trans. Edmund Chilmead (London, 1650).

Nieto, David, *Esh dat* (London, 1715).

Pimentel, Abraham Cohen, *Questoes e discursos academicos* (Hamburg, 1688).

Priaulx, Osmond de Beauvoir, *Quaestiones Mosaicae, or The Book of Genesis Compared with the Remains of Ancient Religions* (London, 1842).

Proteus, *A Dissertation on the Celestial Sign of the Rainbow, in Connection with the Sacred 'Oath of the Seventh'* (Dublin, 1879).

Rittangel, Johann Stephan (trans. and ed.), *Liber Iezirah* (Amsterdam, 1642).

Rossi, Giovanni Bernardo de, *Bibliotheca judaica antichristiana* (Parma, 1800).

Rowley, Adam Clarke (trans.), *Joel: A Translation in Metrical Parallelisms according to the Hebrew Method of Punctuation* (London, 1867).

Sabatier de Castres, Antoine, *Apologie de Spinosa et du Spinosisme* (Paris, 1810).

Samuel, Moses, *Memoirs of Moses Mendelssohn*, 2nd edn. (London, 1827).

Stehelin, John Peter, *The Traditions of the Jews, or The Doctrines and Expositions Contain'd in the Talmud and Other Rabbinical Writings*, 2 vols. (London, 1742–3).

Tama, Diogene, *Transactions of the Parisian Sanhedrim*, trans. F. D. Kirwan (London, 1807).

Taylor, Francis (trans.), *Targum prius et posterius in Esteram* (London, 1655).

Yossipon, *A Compendious and Most Marvellous Historie of the Latter Times of the Iewes Common Weale*, trans. Peter Merwyn (London, 1596).

In addition, the list includes one Hebrew book, whose title is not indicated since the clerk who recorded the books was presumably unable to read Hebrew, and two volumes of miscellaneous tracts on Jewish matters, the first covering the period 1747–53, the second, 1753–94. There is also one book whose author and title I have been unable to decipher.

Benjamin Disraeli and the Myth of Sephardi Superiority

O N   T H E   D A Y following Benjamin Disraeli's death Lady Battersea (1843–1931), daughter of Sir Anthony de Rothschild (1810–76), wrote to her husband that their late friend had been 'not only loyal to his Queen and country, but also to the race from which he sprung', adding that 'his racial instincts were his religion and he was true to that religion until he drew his last breath'.[1] Lady Battersea's observation—that Disraeli's ideas about race were central to his self-definition—was consistent with contemporary interpretations of his character and beliefs. Friend and foe alike routinely linked his political behaviour and thinking to his ethnic background, to what Lady Battersea called 'his racial instincts'. In the century following his death, however, his biographers, as well as historians and political scientists, hesitated to view his racial concerns as central to his identity and career, preferring to ignore or at least minimize them. For example, in his biographical triptych *Burke, Disraeli, and Churchill* (1961), Stephen Graubard, though prepared to acknowledge Disraeli's interest in race, confessed to not knowing what to make of it. 'It is difficult to understand', he admitted, 'why Disraeli charged Sidonia with another teaching mission—to instruct Coningsby in the greatness of the Jewish race.'[2] With less hesitation, his biographer Robert Blake dismissed Disraeli's Jewishness in favour of the Italian 'streak' in his character. If national or racial stereotypes were to be introduced at all, Blake believed, then the traits associated with the Mediterranean character were more dominant: pride, vanity, flamboyance, generosity, emotionalism, quarrelsomeness, extravagance, theatricality, an addiction to conspiracy, and a fondness for intrigue. Indeed, in Blake's view, Disraeli's financial ineptitude demonstrated the relative unimportance of the Jewish element in his make-up.[3]

The first historian or political scientist in the twentieth century to accord Disraeli's racial ideas their due was Hannah Arendt, who in *The Origins of*

---

[1] Lady Battersea to Lord Battersea, 20 Apr. 1881, Battersea Papers, Add MSS 47910/5.
[2] Graubard, *Burke, Disraeli, and Churchill*, 123.   [3] Blake, *Disraeli*, 49–50.

Totalitarianism (1951) suggested that Disraeli's declaration of Jewish racial chosenness was a strategy to combat his own sense of social inferiority. In her view, he was acutely sensitive to his status as an outsider in upper-class Tory circles, and to compensate invented a myth of Jewish racial superiority.[4]

It was not Hannah Arendt, however, but Isaiah Berlin who re-established for historical scholarship the central place of racial thinking in Disraeli's sense of self. In his presidential address to the Jewish Historical Society of England in 1967, in which he compared the links between ideology and identity in Disraeli and Marx, Berlin offered what is still the most elegant and authoritative exposition of this interpretation.[5] Published in at least three different forums in English, and translated into several other languages as well, his lecture described how Disraeli overcame a serious obstacle to his career—his Jewish background—by inflating it into a claim to noble birth. As a result in part of the diffusion of this interpretation, there is now a consensus that Disraeli's racial ideas cannot be dismissed as irrelevant. Paul Smith's lecture to the Royal Historical Society on Disraeli's politics (1986), John Vincent's short account of Disraeli's thought in the Oxford Past Masters series (1990), Stanley Weintraub's long biography (1993), and Adam Kirsch's brief biography in the Jewish Encounters series (2008) are testimony to the reintegration of Disraeli's Jewish chauvinism into evaluations of his life and work.[6]

In these and other accounts of Disraeli's Jewishness, one curious current remains unexplored—his use of the long-lived myth of Sephardi superiority, a myth that originated in medieval Spain and later migrated to western and northern Europe with the expansion of the Sephardi diaspora. The core of the myth, which remained more or less constant over the centuries despite changes in its external details, was the belief that Jews from the Iberian peninsula were different in kind from other Jews, that they were superior by virtue of their culture, learning, wealth, descent, manners, or indeed even blood. Illuminating this theme in Disraeli's racial thought, and viewing it in a broad historical context, brings his construction of Jewishness into clearer focus. It also makes his chauvinism seem much less curious. It suggests that what can be viewed—and dismissed—as personal and aberrant was instead a reworking of a well-established Sephardi tradition.

As is well known, Disraeli was not in a strict sense a Spanish or Portuguese Jew. His four grandparents or their parents were born in Italy.

[4] Arendt, *The Origins of Totalitarianism*, pt. 1, *Antisemitism*, 72–5.
[5] Berlin, 'Benjamin Disraeli, Karl Marx and the Search for Identity'.
[6] P. Smith, 'Disraeli's Politics'; Vincent, *Disraeli*; Weintraub, *Disraeli*; Kirsch, *Benjamin Disraeli*.

However, his grandmothers, Sarah Shiprut de Gabay Villa Real D'Israeli (1743–1825) and Rebecca Rieti Basevi (d. 1798), came from Iberian families that had settled in Italy in the late fifteenth century or thereafter. Thus, of his eight great-grandparents, three had Spanish or Portuguese antecedents; the other five were from native Italian stock or from Ashkenazi families that migrated there in the late medieval period.[7] But since there were too few Italian Jews in London to sustain an Italian congregation, his relations who settled there associated with the well-established Spanish and Portuguese synagogue in Bevis Marks. This, rather than knowledge about his grandmothers' families, facilitated his romantic identification with Iberian Jewry.

In Disraeli's telling of his family history, as recorded in a memoir of his father for a new edition of *The Curiosities of Literature* (1849), his ancestors fled from Spain at the end of the fifteenth century and settled in Venice. There they flourished as merchants for two centuries, before his great-grandfather, impressed by the commercial dynamism and religious tolerance of Hanoverian England, sent his youngest son to London in the mid-eighteenth century. In this construction of his family background, which was as much fiction as fact, Disraeli enhanced both the grandeur and demographic strength of the London Sephardim at the time. According to his account, the Jewish families settled there were 'all of them Sephardim' who had been driven 'from their pleasant residences and rich estates in Arragon, and Andalusia, and Portugal'. Ashkenazim, who in fact outnumbered Sephardim by the 1720s, were in Disraeli's account 'then only occasionally stealing into England'. Coming from 'an inferior caste', they were kept at arm's length by the wealthy Sephardim.[8]

In conversation and correspondence as well, Disraeli identified himself with Spanish and Portuguese Jews and emphasized their superiority. Walking at Lord Carrington's park one cold day in January 1851 with Edward Stanley, eldest son of the earl of Derby, he remarked that the one obstacle to the return of the Jews to the Land of Israel was 'the existence of two races among the Hebrews, of whom one, those who settled along the shores of the Mediterranean, look down on the other, refusing even to associate with them'. He called 'the superior race', Stanley noted in his diary, 'Sephardim'.[9] In his letters to Sarah Brydges Willyams, he wrote often of their shared background, of their common descent from the aristocratic Laras, of 'the mysterious sympathy' that bound them together.[10] And in 1844 he wrote to his

---

[7] The most reliable account of Disraeli's ancestry is Roth, *Benjamin Disraeli*, ch. 1. See also Seltzer, 'Benjamin Disraeli's Knowledge of his Ancestry'.

[8] Disraeli, 'On the Life and Writings of Mr. Disraeli', vol. i, pp. viii–ix.

[9] Stanley, *Disraeli, Derby and the Conservative Party*, 32.

[10] Quoted in Weintraub, *Disraeli*, 377.

fellow Tory MP Richard Monckton Milnes, then visiting Berlin, that although German Jews were 'now the most intelligent of the tribes' they did not 'rank high in blood', not being Sephardim.[11]

That Disraeli bestowed Sephardi origins on the international banker Sidonia in his Young England novels *Coningsby* (1844) and *Tancred* (1847) was no accident. 'Descended from a very ancient and noble family of Arragon, that, in the course of ages, had given to the state many distinguished citizens',[12] the multi-talented Sidonia acts as spokesman for Disraeli's racial and Jewish fantasies and as representative of those traits—worldliness, intellect, natural grace, social knowledge, wealth—with which Disraeli longed to be identified. When Sidonia makes an entrance at Lord Monmouth's country home for dinner in *Coningsby*, with but ten minutes to spare, 'there was a stir in the chamber . . . a general pause in the room'. Even the magnificent, haughty Marquess of Beaumanoir 'seemed a little moved' in the presence of this 'gentleman of distinguished air'.[13] Would it be far-fetched to suggest that Disraeli himself would have liked to make such an entrance? Furthermore, Disraeli's choice of an Iberian background for Sidonia meant that he had to ignore what would have been obvious to a keen social observer like himself: a well-connected, cosmopolitan Sephardi banker was a socio-economic anachronism in Victorian Britain. The heyday of Sephardi influence and opulence was long past. In the 1840s, when Disraeli was writing *Coningsby* and *Tancred*, Spanish and Portuguese Jews were absent from the front ranks of City firms engaged in international finance. Sidonia was a ghost from the previous century, brought back to life to meet Disraeli's own needs. Most of the important Jewish banking houses—the Rothschilds chief among them—traced their origins to the Frankfurt ghetto, not the courts and estates of Castile and Aragon. Moreover, in its broad outlines, Sidonia's rise to financial pre-eminence after his arrival in England parallels that of the outstanding Ashkenazi banker of the period, Nathan Rothschild (1777–1836). In fact, Disraeli attributed Sidonia's success to having, like Rothschild, 'a brother, or near relative, in whom he could confide, in most of the principal capitals' of Europe.[14]

In invoking the myth of Sephardi superiority, Disraeli tended to avoid explicit comparisons between Spanish and Portuguese Jews on the one hand and Polish and German Jews on the other.[15] The mere evocation of Sephardi grandeur was sufficient to indicate that an implicit and invidious comparison was being made, given the oft-remarked ties of London's Ashkenazim to

---

[11] Benjamin Disraeli to Richard Monckton Milnes, 29 Dec. 1844, in Disraeli, *Letters*, iv. 153.
[12] Disraeli, *Coningsby*, bk. 4, ch. 10.   [13] Ibid., ch. 9.   [14] Ibid.
[15] John Vincent notes that as a rule 'Disraeli said little about the lower races; his object was to praise, not disparage' (*Disraeli*, 27).

low-status street trades. However, on at least two occasions, Disraeli went further. One was in the memoir of his father mentioned above. The other was a longer passage in *Tancred* in which he contrasted the Sephardim of the sunny Mediterranean with the Ashkenazim of the bleak north, in Hounds-ditch and the Minories in London and the *Judengassen* of Hamburg and Frankfurt. Here he noted how the Sephardim, 'in their beautiful Asian cities or in their Moorish and Arabian gardens', more easily celebrated and iden-tified with the agricultural festivals of Judaism and their nature-based rites, like the building of sukkahs, than the Ashkenazim in their squalid quarters in the icy climes of northern towns. Although he expressed admiration for the latter's steadfast devotion to 'Oriental customs in the heart of our Saxon and Sclavonian cities', he described the typical Ashkenazi Jew as 'an object . . . of prejudice, dislike, disgust, perhaps hatred'. Imagine, he asked his readers:

A being . . . born to hereditary insult, without any education, apparently without a circumstance that can develop the slightest taste, or cherish the least sentiment for the beautiful, living amid fogs and filth, never treated with kindness, seldom with justice, occupied with the meanest, if not the vilest, toil, bargaining for frippery, speculating in usury, existing for ever under the concurrent influence of degrading causes.[16]

In addition, Disraeli knew and used, in private at least, an epithet to refer to Ashkenazim. In a letter to his father in December 1835 he wrote that the merchant banker Isaac Lyon Goldsmid (1778–1859), whom he had just met, was 'not an ass in business, but a sharp Tedesco'.[17] This is, however, the sole occasion in his voluminous correspondence on which he used this pejora-tive term (which is not to say, of course, that he did not use it more often in conversation with family members). But for the most part Disraeli tended to praise Sephardim rather than disparage their northern counterparts, an understandable strategy in that he staked his claim to aristocratic status on the basis of the nobility of the Jewish race in general rather than one small part of it. In fact, at the end of the passage from *Tancred* quoted above con-trasting Sephardim and Ashkenazim, he praised the spiritual nobility of the latter in their attachment to ancient customs.

[16] Disraeli, *Tancred*, bk. 5, ch. 6.
[17] Benjamin Disraeli to Isaac D'Israeli, 15 Dec. 1835, in Disraeli, *Letters*, ii. 109. The word *tudesco* (to use the more common Sephardi orthography) is an Iberianized form of the Italian word *tedesco* ('German'), used by Western Sephardim to refer to Jews from Germany and Poland. Although at first non-pejorative, it became, by the eighteenth century at the latest, a term of contempt, expressing disdain for persons considered to be of low, even disreputable, rank.

Although blessed with a fertile imagination, Disraeli neither created nor even much embellished the myth of Sephardi noble lineage. Rather, he made use of a well-established tradition, whose history has yet to receive the attention it merits. The oldest expression of the myth can be traced back to Muslim Spain, centuries before the Expulsion, when it took the benign form of the genealogical claim that the Jews of Spain were *galut yerushalayim asher bisfarad* (exiles from Jerusalem living in Spain), descendants of the royal tribe of Judah, of the inhabitants of Jerusalem whom Nebuchadnezzar carried off to Babylonia at the end of the sixth century BCE. The emergence of a Jewish courtier elite, who served Spain's monarchs as tax-farmers, physicians, diplomats, astronomers, and political advisers, was seen as confirmation of their own noble origins.[18] Although the theme of Judaean descent was later incorporated into versions of the myth, full-blown claims of superiority arose only in the last century of open Jewish life on the peninsula, in response to Iberian racial antisemitism. The mass conversions sparked by the pogroms of 1391 and the Disputation of Tortosa in 1413–14 created the basis for the entry of thousands of New Christians into offices of the church, the military, the universities, the royal courts, and the municipalities. Their rapid upward mobility provoked a backlash in Old Christian society, which at mid-century exploded in racial polemics against the New Christians. As religion no longer defined what was different about former Jews and their offspring, Old Christians came to believe that it was their racial descent, their blood, their unalterable, baptism-proof essence, that constituted the source of their menace, and explained as well their social and economic success. The introduction of the statutes of *limpieza de sangre*, beginning in 1449 and continuing through the mid-sixteenth century, represented the institutionalization of the spreading belief that there were profound differences between the noble blood of Old Christians and the tainted blood of New Christians.[19]

One response was to counter Hispanic claims of descent with Jewish claims. On the principle that nobility derives from antiquity, Spanish Jews, including some converts, claimed that they were the noblest of all peoples, since they were able to trace their ancestry to Judaea and Jerusalem. The family of Pablo de Santa Maria (né Solomon Halevi), bishop of Burgos, who had converted in 1391, claimed descent from the family of Mary, mother of Jesus, while a Converso family that had settled in Brazil claimed to possess a deed of nobility proving its descent from the Maccabees.[20] Jews who went into exile in 1492 and never donned a New Christian mask celebrated their

[18] Ben Sasson, 'The Generation of Spanish Exiles on its Fate' (Heb.), 23.
[19] Yerushalmi, *Assimilation and Racial Anti-Semitism*.
[20] Bodian, ' "Men of the Nation" ', 62.

descent as well. They also tended to idealize their own immediate past, a natural response to dislocation, recounting with pride (and exaggeration) the learning, wealth, wisdom, and influence of their ancestors, especially the courtier class. In this idealization of their former life, the Jewish communities of Spain, it was claimed, surpassed all other diaspora communities whatever the criteria.[21] The rapid rise of the exiles to dominance in the Jewish communities of northern Africa and the Balkans where they found refuge confirmed their sense of superiority—as did the subsequent 'Sephardization' of these communities, that is, their adoption of the Sephardi *nusah*.

Conversos who returned to Judaism in northern and western Europe in the seventeenth and eighteenth centuries brought with them the Iberian discourse of noble lineage and racial separateness, as did to a lesser extent those few Sephardim from Italy and northern Africa whose ancestors had fled in 1492 and who now migrated northwards.[22] As former New Christians worked to create new Jewish identities for themselves, they used these notions to help establish boundaries, to mark off who they were in relation to Christians in general, the Spanish and Portuguese in particular, and Jews from other lands as well. Their sense of ethnic separateness was nourished even more by their face-to-face encounter, beginning in the seventeenth century, with Polish and German Jews, especially in Hamburg, London, and Amsterdam. Most Ashkenazim who reached these cities were poor and unskilled, with little prior exposure to Western education, culture, and manners. A large number were *Betteljuden*—vagabonds and *shnorrers*, the flotsam and jetsam of the Ashkenazi world, persons without resources or fixed residence who wandered from community to community, begging, stealing, and in general living by their wits.

This encounter between two groups of Jews whose historical experiences differed profoundly bred contempt among Iberian Jews for their northern brethren, and at the same time strengthened their obsession with lineage, descent, and blood, and their desire to hold themselves aloof. In Amsterdam, the centre of the Western Sephardi diaspora, social ties between the two groups failed to develop; with a few exceptions, contacts remained at the instrumental level, between givers and receivers of relief or between masters and mistresses and their servants.[23] The caste pride of the Amsterdam Sephardim manifested itself in discriminatory measures against Jews of

[21] Ben Sasson, 'The Generation of Spanish Exiles on its Fate' (Heb.), 23–9.

[22] On the Iberian legacy of caste pride in the Western Sephardi diaspora, see Y. Kaplan, *From Christianity to Judaism* (Heb.), 269–74; id., 'Political Concepts in the World of the Portuguese Jews of Amsterdam'.

[23] Y. Kaplan, 'The Relationship of Spanish and Portugese Jews to Ashkenazi Jews' (Heb.), 399.

non-Iberian origin from the mid-seventeenth century on. In 1654, for example, the Amsterdam *mahamad* forbade Ashkenazi women (in effect, servants) from attending services in the Sephardi synagogue; in 1657 it banned non-Sephardim from studying in its communal school; in 1671 it prohibited Ashkenazim who married Sephardi women, as well as their offspring, from becoming *yehidim* (members) or being buried in the Sephardi cemetery; in 1697 it revoked the membership of Sephardim who took non-Sephardi wives. Moreover, in 1632, in the hope of discouraging penniless Ashkenazim from settling in Amsterdam, the Spanish and Portuguese leadership prohibited its members from giving charity to beggars at their doors or the gate of the synagogue. In the mid-1630s it also began repatriating German and Polish Jews.[24] (The practice of sending the poorest members of the community to distant lands was first used against indigent Sephardim.) Not surprisingly, few mixed Ashkenazi–Sephardi marriages took place in Amsterdam, even as late as the mid-nineteenth century.[25]

In London, where contact between the two groups was greater, the Bevis Marks authorities imposed humiliating conditions on the celebration of Ashkenazi–Sephardi unions to express their displeasure. In 1745, when the *gabai* (synagogue beadle) Jacob Israel Bernal (d. 1766?) asked permission to marry an Ashkenazi woman, the elders consented but stipulated that no member of the Beth Din (rabbinic court) or *hazan* (cantor) was to officiate, that the groom was not to be called up to the Torah, that no *mi sheberakh* blessings (recited for the person who has been called up to the Torah) were to be made in his honour, and that no celebration of any kind was to be held in the synagogue. In other cases, permission to marry was denied or, when it was given, the name of the bride was omitted from the marriage register, where she was listed as simply *tudesca*. The revised *ascamot* (community regulations) of 1784 prohibited the *hakham*, the chief rabbi of the Spanish and Portuguese community, from officiating at mixed marriages and barred Sephardim who married non-Sephardim or even the Sephardi widows of non-Sephardim from receiving communal relief.[26]

In the seventeenth century Sephardi motives for distinguishing and segregating themselves from other Jews were internal: the emotional need to forge a new, non-Converso, group identity and the practical need to reduce the burden of caring for destitute newcomers from central and eastern Europe. In the eighteenth century, external motives as well came into play.

---

[24] Y. Kaplan, 'The Relationship of Spanish and Portugese Jews to Ashkenazi Jews' (Heb.), 403–6; id., The Portuguese Community in 17th-Century Amsterdam', 33–4, 43–4.

[25] Michman, 'Between Sephardim and Ashkenazim' (Heb.), 136–7.

[26] Hyamson, *The Sephardim of England*, 170–1, 190, 228.

Eager to advance their social integration and improve their legal status, Sephardi polemicists and apologists displayed a lively concern with their public image. In particular, they tried to dissociate themselves from destitute German and Polish Jews then migrating westwards in increasing numbers, whom they believed blackened the name of all Jews. The most famous example of this strategy is found in the reply of the political economist Isaac de Pinto (1717–87) to Voltaire's vulgar remarks about Jews in his *Dictionnaire philosophique*.[27] Pinto charged Voltaire with failing to distinguish between Spanish and Portuguese Jews and 'la foule des autres enfans de Jacob' (the mass of other Jews).[28] The former, he told Voltaire, were descendants of the tribe of Judah who migrated to Spain at the time of the Babylonian captivity. They scrupulously avoided mixing with and marrying other Jews, and though they shared the same religion observed it differently, maintaining separate synagogues. Moreover, the manners and habits of the Portuguese were different. They did not have beards or distinctive dress, while the rich among them cultivated learning, elegance, and pomp to the same extent as other European nations. The gap between the Sephardim and other Jews was so great, he reported, that, if a Portuguese Jew in Holland or England were to wed a German Jewess, he would lose his communal privileges: he would lose his membership in the synagogue, he would be denied all religious honours, he would be cut off from the body of the nation, and he would be refused burial among his Portuguese brethren. German and Polish Jews, on the other hand were degraded, having been deprived of the advantages of social contact, treated with contempt, persecuted, humiliated, and insulted through the ages. A Portuguese Jew from Bordeaux and a German Jew from Metz were 'deux êtres absolument differens' (two absolutely different beings).[29]

When Jewish status was debated in France in the last years of the *ancien régime* and during the revolutionary and Napoleonic period, spokesmen for the Sephardi communities in south-western France invoked this distinction repeatedly. For example, in a memoir to the government in June 1788, Abraham Furtado (1756–1817) and Solomon Lopes-Dubec (1743–1837) emphasized, as Pinto had earlier, the ease with which Sephardim assimilated to their adopted homes in northern and western Europe:

A Portuguese Jew is English in England and French in France, but a German Jew is German everywhere because of his customs from which he deviates rarely; thus one can look at the English and the Germans as brothers who, although sharing the same mother, have nevertheless developed characteristics which are absolutely different, nay even incompatible.[30]

[27] I. de Pinto, *Apologie pour la nation juive*.   [28] Ibid. 15.   [29] Ibid. 10.
[30] Quoted in Malino, *The Sephardic Jews of Bordeaux*, 32.

In August 1806, when the so-called Parisian or Napoleonic Sanhedrin composed its replies to twelve questions about Judaism's relationship to French citizenship, the first draft of its answer to Question 4—did Jews consider Frenchmen as brothers or strangers?—established a difference between Portuguese and German Jews.[31] This strategy of differentiation bore fruit in the end: when Napoleon, disappointed by the failure of French Jews to 'regenerate' themselves following emancipation, imposed new restrictions on Jewish commerce, conscription, and residence, he exempted the Sephardim.

There is both indirect and direct evidence that Isaac D'Israeli (1766–1848) was not only familiar with but embraced the myth of Sephardi superiority. Even if an infrequent visitor to the synagogue in Bevis Marks, he was not a stranger to Sephardi society. His own father was an immigrant to England, like others in his family circle, and was in touch with social and cultural currents that flowed strongly in Sephardi communities abroad. As a teenager, he was sent to live in Amsterdam with his father's agent there. It can also be inferred that he used the term *tudesco*—with all its negative associations, which I discussed earlier; where else would Benjamin have learned the term? In addition, a public debate about Jewish poverty and criminality took place in London in 1802, during which the Sephardi community dissociated itself from the rest of London's Jews. Following publication of a work critical of the Jewish poor, influential Ashkenazim proposed to Parliament the establishment of a Jewish relief board with the authority to tax Jewish ratepayers, centralize the distribution of charity, and jail or deport undesirable aliens. The Spanish and Portuguese community fought inclusion in the scheme, instructing their attorney to see that their name was not connected with it.[32] In a document prepared for an MP who was assisting them, they emphasized that the Portuguese and the Germans formed 'two distinct (not religious, but) political bodies' and that they 'always considered each other (as they actually are) separate and distinct bodies'.[33] It is reasonable to assume that Isaac D'Israeli, who had written about the reform of Jewish culture in a biographical sketch of Moses Mendelssohn in the *Monthly Magazine* in 1798, knew of this debate.[34] A few years later, when the Parisian Sanhedrin convened, he followed its proceedings, publishing two articles about the assembly, again in the *Monthly Magazine*.[35]

---

[31] Tama (ed.), *Transactions of the Parisian Sanhedrim*, 19.

[32] Endelman, *The Jews of Georgian England*, 231–6.

[33] Emanuel (ed.), *A Century and a Half of Jewish History*, 10–12.

[34] D'Israeli, 'A Biographical Sketch of the Jewish Socrates'.

[35] D'Israeli, 'On the Late Installation of a Great Sanhedrim'; id., 'Acts of the Great Sanhedrim'.

The most compelling evidence that Isaac was the conduit through which the Sephardi myth reached Benjamin is in Isaac's anonymous treatise *The Genius of Judaism* (1833). Using similes, rhetorical devices, and illustrations lifted without attribution from Isaac de Pinto's *Apologie pour la nation juive*,[36] D'Israeli restated the claim that the Jews were not one but several nations, each, like the chameleon, reflecting the colour of the spot on which they rested (the simile was Pinto's). Thus: 'After a few generations, the Hebrews assimilate with the character, and are actuated by the feelings, of the nation where they become natives.'[37] The first Jews to settle in England, he told his readers, were Spanish and Portuguese Jews—'noblemen, officers, learned physicians, and opulent merchants'—who brought with them 'their national characteristic . . . their haughtiness, their high sense of honour, and their stately manners'. Subsequent Jewish immigrants from Germany and Poland were 'a race in every respect of an inferior rank'.[38]

The Portuguese Grandees shrunk from their contact; they looked on those lees of the people in bitter scorn, and through a long century the contumely was never forgiven. In every respect these differing races moved in contrast. The one opulent and high-minded; the other humiliated by indigence, and pursuing the meanest, and not seldom the most disreputable, crafts. The one indolent, polished, and luxurious; the other, with offensive habits, active and penurious, hardy in frame, and shrewd in intellect. The one splendid in dress and equipage, while the abject Polander still retained the beard commanded by Moses with the gabardine.[39]

Between the two groups, mutual hatred flourished. D'Israeli even claimed that 'the haughty Lusitanian Jew would have returned to the fires of Lisbon, ere he condescended to an intermarriage with the Jew of Alsace or Warsaw'.[40] If, as is widely acknowledged, Isaac's Tory and royalist sympathies influenced his son's interpretation of English history, it is also probable that his Jewish prejudices left their mark as well. It is no coincidence that Benjamin Disraeli used images and terms similar to those his father used in describing the cultural and social gulf between the two communities.

In tracing this tradition from late medieval Spain to Victorian England, I do not intend to suggest that it, rather than some other influence, is the hitherto unknown key to Disraeli's racial thinking. Multiple cultural and intellectual currents, especially those of a Romantic hue, came together in its

---

[36] I. de Pinto's *Apologie pour la nation juive* does not appear in the list of Judaica from the Disraeli Library sold in October 1881. This does not mean, however, that Isaac did not own a copy, since it was a pamphlet, and the pamphlets from the years 1747 to 1794 were bound together into two volumes and identified only by the terms 'various authors' and 'various publishers' (see appendix to Chapter 9).   [37] D'Israeli, *The Genius of Judaism*, 238.
[38] Ibid. 244–5, 246.   [39] Ibid. 247.   [40] Ibid. 248.

genesis. Disraeli's ideas were part of a broad stream of conservative, organic thought in Britain that targeted Benthamite utilitarianism, free market economics, and liberal doctrines of progress. His ideological bedfellows included Walter Scott, Robert Southey, A. W. N. Pugin, Thomas Carlyle, and to a lesser extent collectors of old armour; builders of picturesque, asymmetrical, battlemented castles; and enthusiasts of the chivalric revival. Moreover, while full-blown deterministic racial theories were rare when Disraeli's outlook was taking shape, inchoate notions of racial hierarchy were not. The discourse of Anglo-Saxonism was widely diffused in the first half of the nineteenth century.[41] The author of *The English and their Origin*, writing in 1866, noted that there were few educated Englishmen who had not been taught as children that 'the English nation is a nation of almost pure Teutonic blood', that its constitution, customs, wealth, and empire were the necessary result of 'the arrival, in three vessels, of certain German warriors' centuries earlier.[42] Isaac D'Israeli's close friend Sharon Turner, who convinced him to make his children Christians and afterwards took them to St Andrew's, Holborn, to be baptized, was the author of a bestselling multi-volume *History of the Anglo-Saxons* (1799–1805) that was shot through with a racial reading of English history.[43]

If racial ideas were 'in the air', it must also be recalled that Disraeli's own needs prepared him to absorb them. Driven by ambition but unable to shake off his Jewish origins (like the Conversos before him), he discovered that the idea of race, when given a novel, 'Jewish' twist, allowed him to counter the hereditary claims of the great English landed families. His ancestral community's obsession with descent helped to determine his novel response, while infusing it at the same time with an Iberian flavour. Without reference to this myth and its history the Sephardi component of his Jewish chauvinism is inexplicable.

Disraeli's reaction to the prejudice that he continued to encounter after his baptism was unusual to say the least. No other Victorian Jew, baptized or otherwise, opted to trumpet these kinds of claims. Jews in Britain (and elsewhere, as well) who desired entry into Christian circles hid, minimized, or at least did not call attention to their Jewishness, even when it was thrown in their faces. To paraphrase Heine, Jewish chauvinism was not their ticket of admission into European society. Their hopes for inclusion rested instead on non-biological, liberal theories of social behaviour and historical development that stressed nurture over nature, the malleability of manners, traits,

---

[41] MacDougall, *Racial Myth in English History*, ch. 5; Poliakov, *The Aryan Myth*, 50–2.

[42] Pike, *The English and their Origin*, 15.

[43] MacDougall, *Racial Myth in English History*, 94.

and character, and in particular the similarity of Jews to other persons in all spheres of human activity other than religion.

Given the eccentricity of Disraeli's response, what is its historical significance and what is its connection to writing the history of 'everyday' Jews? Perhaps it is no more than an entertaining footnote to the main text of modern Jewish history. After all, if his use of the idea of race was unrepresentative—which indeed it was—its links to the concerns of Jews who were not in the limelight are not obvious. Of course, one could argue that Disraeli's solution, however peculiar, is one more telling example of how difficult it was for even well-acculturated Jews to avoid obstacles on the road to integration. And this is fair enough. But there is another, more important historiographical dimension to Disraeli's Jewish chauvinism that comes into focus when his use of the myth of Sephardi superiority is emphasized. For while his racial ideas were untypical, his invocation of the Sephardi myth was not.

From the late eighteenth century, throughout western Europe, both Sephardim and Ashkenazim employed the myth to promote their own cultural, political, and social agendas. As we have seen, Sephardi spokesmen used it repeatedly to dissociate themselves from Jews who, in their view, threatened their own status. In the German states the pioneers of Wissenschaft des Judentums and the leaders of the Reform movement constructed an image of Sephardi Judaism that stressed its cultural openness, philosophical rationalism, and aesthetic sensibilities in order to criticize what they disliked in their own tradition: its backwardness, insularity, and aversion to secular studies. In France, Austria, Germany, Hungary, and the United States communal and congregational boards erected imposing synagogues of so-called Moorish design, assertive symbols of their break with the 'unenlightened' Ashkenazi past. Jewish poets and novelists who were Disraeli's contemporaries—Heinrich Heine (1797–1856), the brothers Phöbus (1807–70) and Ludwig Philippson (1811—89), Berthold Auerbach (1812–82), and Grace Aguilar (1816–47)—were fascinated with the Iberian experience and drew on it for themes and subjects, with the result that their work further augmented its mystique.[44]

Before the end of the century the myth of Sephardi superiority was widely disseminated and available for appropriation by Jews and their enemies alike. In his attack on the historian Heinrich Graetz (1817–91) in 1881, Heinrich von Treitschke (1834–96) maintained that the Spanish and Portuguese Jews were closer to the German people than were the Jews of Poland and Germany because their history was prouder and more distinguished than

---

[44] Schorsch, 'The Myth of Sephardi Supremacy'; Marcus, 'Beyond the Sephardi Mystique'.

that of the latter, who had been scarred by centuries of Christian tyranny.[45] In their battle against racial myths about Jewish deformities, Jewish anthropologists drew on the Sephardi mystique to create a counter-myth of their own—that of the well-bred, aesthetically attractive, physically graceful Sephardi, a model of racial nobility and virility. In their work, John Efron notes, 'the Sephardi served as the equivalent of the Jewish "Aryan" . . . the physical counterpart to the ignoble Jew of Central and Eastern Europe'.[46] For some acculturated Ashkenazim who wished to distance themselves from impoverished east European Jews and their alleged defects, fantasies of Sephardi descent became a strategy for enhancing their own self-image. Theodor Herzl (1860–1904), whose attitudes towards Jews vacillated between pride and disdain, claimed Iberian roots for his family. He told the early English Zionist Jacob de Haas (1872–1937) that his paternal grandfather was a Spanish Jew who had been forced to convert to Christianity and had later fled to Constantinople, where he re-embraced Judaism. In a different version, told to the Hebrew and Yiddish writer Reuben Brainin (1862–1939) in 1904, he traced his descent from a high-ranking Converso monk who returned to Judaism while abroad on a mission.[47]

In a structural sense as well, Disraeli's use of the Iberian Jewish mystique resembled other integrationist strategies in the age of emancipation. Westernized, upper-middle-class Jews unsure of their social status routinely made public declarations that Jews fell into two categories, 'good' Jews and 'bad' Jews. In England, native-born Jews in the period of mass migration struggled to distance themselves from impoverished, Yiddish-speaking, foreign-born newcomers, while Bayswater and Mayfair Jews poured scorn on their less cultured co-religionists in Maida Vale. These distinctions, conveyed in novels, tracts, newspapers, lectures, and other public forums, were intended to convince the non-Jewish world that their authors, 'good' Jews, were nothing like 'bad' Jews and thus merited political rights, social acceptance, exemption from contempt, or whatever else was being denied them. In this sense, the Disraelian strategy was all too representative.

---

[45] Treitschke, 'Noch einige Bemerkungen zur Judenfrage', *Preussische Jahrbücher*, Jan. 1880, in Boehlich (ed.), *Der Berliner Antisemitismusstreit*, 37–8.
[46] Efron, 'Scientific Racism', 76–7.   [47] Kornberg, *Theodor Herzl*, 76–7.

CHAPTER ELEVEN

The Impact of the Converso Experience on English Sephardim

IN JANUARY 1880, as immigration from eastern Europe mounted, the London *Jewish Chronicle* noted that the number of Sephardim in England had scarcely, if at all, increased in the previous 100 years. The newspaper went on to list three reasons for this: conversions to Christianity; defections to the Reform congregation, where Sephardi distinctiveness was diluted or lost, often through marriage to central European Jews; and the disappearance of 'recruiting grounds' for Sephardi immigration to England, there no longer being native Jews in Spain and Portugal.[1] The demographic stagnation to which the *Jewish Chronicle* drew its readers' attention was not confined to England, in fact. After the Napoleonic era, the number of Sephardim in all western European states failed to increase and in some cases even fell. This fundamental demographic fact had far-reaching consequences for the history of the Western Sephardim. It relegated them to the margins of history, where, few in number and without political, economic or cultural influence, they more or less 'disappeared'.

The demographic decline of the Sephardim in England was the outcome of the same currents of radical assimilation that depleted the ranks of acculturated Jews throughout Europe in the modern period. However, in their case there was also the impact of their ancestors' historical experience as Conversos, an experience that the Ashkenazi majority did not share. The train of events set in motion in late medieval Spain and Portugal, I wish to argue, prepared the way for the demographic decline noted by the *Jewish Chronicle*. That none of the descendants of Isaac D'Israeli and 'Jew' King remained members of the Spanish and Portuguese synagogue in London reflects both sets of circumstances: the early modern Converso experience and late Georgian assimilatory currents. While this account will be confined to the Sephardim who settled in England, the line of enquiry pursued here and the conclusions reached are relevant, I believe, to the fate of other West-

[1] *Jewish Chronicle*, 30 Jan. 1880.

ern Sephardi communities—in Holland, France, North America, and the Caribbean—as well.

First, a brief look at the basic demographic features of the history of the Sephardim in England or, to be more precise, London, since few Sephardim settled in the provinces until the second half of the nineteenth century when merchants from the Ottoman empire came to Manchester. As is well known, a Jewish community emerged in England only after Menasseh ben Israel's mission to Oliver Cromwell (1655–6). At the time of his visit, there were about twenty households of New Christian origin in London; at the end of the decade, about thirty-five.[2] In 1684, according to a list prepared by Abraham Israel Zagache for the *mahamad*, there were 414 Sephardim;[3] in 1695, according to the demographic historian Robert Cohen, there were 499.[4] The former New Christians who settled in London during this period came from Holland, Dutch and English colonies in the Caribbean, the Canary Islands, the Iberian peninsula, and France.

For the eighteenth and early nineteenth centuries, precise population figures are not available. Immigration both from Spain and Portugal and from Sephardi communities in western Europe and the Mediterranean continued. Indeed, the number of New Christians who arrived directly from the Iberian peninsula, mainly in response to renewed inquisitorial activity in the 1720s, is now known to be much larger than once believed. On the basis of the number of former New Christian couples who remarried according to Jewish rites at Bevis Marks and the number of former New Christian males who underwent circumcision, Richard Barnett estimated that about 3,000 people came directly from the peninsula in the eighteenth century.[5] Yet, despite this influx—as well as a trickle of arrivals from North Africa, Italy, and Holland that continued into the first decades of the following century— the Sephardi community failed to grow after 1750. At mid-century there were about 2,000 Sephardim in England according to estimates made by Vivian Lipman on the basis of burial and marriage registers; at the end of the century, the number was the same.[6] In 1830, on the basis of estimates made by Francis Henry Goldsmid, it was only marginally higher—2,150 individuals.[7]

[2] Samuel, 'The First Fifty Years', 41. [3] *Bevis Marks Records*, i. 16–20.
[4] Robert Cohen, ' "To Come with their Families and Dwell Here" ' (Heb.), 150.
[5] R. D. Barnett, 'Dr. Samuel Nunes Ribiero', 78–81, appendix 1; *Bevis Marks Records*, iv. 3–5.
[6] Lipman, 'Sephardi and Other Jewish Immigrants', 40–1.
[7] Goldsmid calculated the Jewish population of London on the basis of burial returns for the London synagogues and the ratio between deaths and the population figures for London as a whole. Using this method, he estimated that the Jewish population was 17,986. As burials of Sephardim were 12 per cent of the total, Goldsmid's figures would mean the Sephardi community numbered about 2,150 persons (*Remarks on the Civil Disabilities of British Jews*, 69–70).

In other words, the Sephardi community experienced little growth in the eight decades between 1750 and 1830.

What can explain the striking failure of the Sephardi population to grow? (This was at a time when the English population was growing rapidly, from slightly over 5 million in 1700 to 8.5 million in 1800.[8]) The *Jewish Chronicle* was certainly correct in pointing to social rather than biological causes (such as a decline in births or a rise in infant deaths). However, the second and third causes it adduced are irrelevant. With regard to the second, the Reform congregation was not established until 1840. While those Sephardim who became members usually withdrew from the Spanish and Portuguese synagogue—and thus ceased to be counted as Sephardim—and while their children often married into Ashkenazi families, this contributed little to the demographic decline of the Sephardim, which was already well advanced before 1840. Similarly, with regard to the third cause, the cessation of immigration in the second half of the nineteenth century does not explain the absence of growth earlier, when there was Sephardi immigration. Moreover, even in the absence of immigration, there should have been a surplus of births over deaths within the established community, given the demographic pattern common to Western societies at the time.

What, then, caused the Sephardi population to stagnate? First, and least important, small numbers of Sephardi women married German and Dutch Jews and were absorbed into the larger, Ashkenazi community. As we saw in the previous chapter, the leaders of the Spanish and Portuguese synagogue condemned these unions and treated men who married *tudescas* as second-class members, denying them synagogal honours and refusing to list the names of their brides in the congregational register. The revised *ascamot* of 1784 barred the *ḥakham* from officiating at these 'mixed' marriages. In the case of women who married out, the Sephardi authorities were powerless, of course, to impose sanctions on their husbands but were able to bar the women, should they fall on hard times, from receiving congregational relief. Yet despite these measures, Sephardi–Ashkenazi intermarriages occurred at all social levels. Communal discipline was weak while the Sephardi marriage pool was small. However, it is unlikely that they were common enough to contribute measurably to the demographic decline of the community. If the absence of evidence is a guide, contemporaries did not view such marriages as a threat.

A second, more weighty, cause was Sephardi migration from London to the New World, primarily to the Caribbean but also to North America. Again, there is no firm quantitative evidence. We know that almost forty London

---

[8] R. Porter, *English Society in the Eighteenth Century*, 202, 207.

Sephardim were among the earliest settlers of Savannah, Georgia, in the 1730s, for example, their passage having been paid by the congregation.[9] But the total number of Jews in the United States at the time of the first census in 1790—1,500 at the maximum, of whom only about 250 were Sephardim —does not suggest that the emigration of London Sephardim to North America was substantial.[10] Emigration to the West Indies was undoubtedly greater, but how much so remains elusive. In one case, Surinam, only five of fifty-eight Sephardim who married in the period 1788 to 1818 were from London.[11]

Those who settled in the New World included destitute persons who were shipped there at communal expense. This was a well-established practice in the Sephardi diaspora, dating back at least to the early seventeenth century, when the three Sephardi congregations in Amsterdam united to send their poor, who were seen as both a financial burden and a social embarrassment, to distant Mediterranean lands—Italy, Turkey, Tunisia, and the Land of Israel.[12] In London, in addition to fiscal and social motives, there was the further concern that the poor swelled the ranks of Jewish criminals, whose activities were believed to endanger the entire community.[13] The sums that the London community spent in sending away its poor were considerable: £2,691 in the ten years from 1725 to 1734.[14] However, at the same time that the London community was dispatching its socially marginal members to the New World, other communities in Europe were shipping theirs to London, their passage being paid on the condition that they promise never to return. Amsterdam, for example, sent fifty-six paupers to London between 1759 and 1814.[15] Reluctant to become a dumping ground for the cast-offs of the Old World, the Spanish and Portuguese congregations in the New World retaliated. At great expense, the New York community returned poor Sephardim to London, while also carrying on a lively interchange of

[9] R. D. Barnett, 'Dr. Samuel Nunes Ribiero', 82–8.

[10] The population estimate for 1790 is from Robert Cohen, 'The Demography of Jews in Early America', 145. If we assume that the percentage of Sephardi seat-holders in New York's only synagogue, Shearith Israel, in 1788—15.1 per cent—and in 1795—16.7 per cent—corresponds roughly to the percentage of Sephardim in the total Jewish population, then there were 226 to 251 Sephardim around 1790. The seat-holder figures are from De Sola Pool and De Sola Pool, *An Old Faith in the New World*, 464.

[11] Robert Cohen, 'Patterns of Marriage and Remarriage', 99.

[12] Bartal and Kaplan, 'The Migration of Poor Jews' (Heb.). Persons who refused to emigrate were stricken from the list of those receiving charity.

[13] Endelman, *The Jews of Georgian England*, 196–8, 200–3, 213–15, 227.

[14] Diamond, 'Problems of the London Sephardi Community', 60–1.

[15] Robert Cohen, *Jews in Another Environment*, 22. For more examples, see Szajkowski, 'Population Problems of Marranos and Sephardim', 14.

paupers with Surinam, Curacao, Barbados, Jamaica, and St Eustatius.[16] In the end it is impossible to determine whether London won or lost, although, given its greater financial resources, it likely dispatched more than it received. (In truth, the problem of counting outward-bound and inward-bound migrants is more complex than this, for there was also a slow but constant trickle of successful West Indian Sephardim, who having made their fortunes in the colonies settled in England.)

If the impact of 'mixed' marriages and outward migration is difficult to measure and was in all likelihood limited, there can be no doubt about the demographic impact of radical assimilation. As the *Jewish Chronicle* recognized in 1880, 'conversions to Christianity [and intermarriages without conversion] deprived the Portuguese of many of their best families'.[17] Once again, the data are anecdotal rather than statistical, but their abundance, along with the testimony of contemporaries, leaves no doubt that drift and defection took a heavy toll.[18] By the second decade of the nineteenth century at the latest it was clear to contemporaries that leakage was sapping the strength of the community. In 1813, when Isaac D'Israeli first clashed with the authorities at Bevis Marks, he reminded them that 'the larger part of your society' had become 'partly Jew and partly Gentile'. 'Many of your members are already lost; many you are losing! Even those whose tempers and feelings would still cling to you, are gradually seceding.'[19] In 1841 the families who resigned from Bevis Marks in the previous year to establish the first Reform synagogue in Britain (all wealthy and long resident in the country) told the elders that their motive in updating Jewish worship was 'to arrest and prevent secession from Judaism—an overwhelming evil, which has at various times so widely spread among many of the most respected families of our communities'.[20] Radical assimilation, moreover, was not limited to wealthy families alone. The converted and intermarried included notaries, clerks, small tradesmen, and artisans: persons whose exodus from the communal fold, in the nature of things, attracted less attention.[21]

What can be established with statistical certainty is that the number of persons marrying at Bevis Marks declined from the mid-eighteenth to the early nineteenth century. Omitting the 1720s and 1730s, when the number of marriages was abnormally high due to the remarriage of recently arrived

---

[16] 'The Earliest Extant Minute Books of the Spanish and Portuguese Congregation', 32, 91, 117, 121, 127, 128, 131.   [17] *Jewish Chronicle*, 30 Jan. 1880.

[18] Endelman, *Radical Assimilation in English Jewish History*, ch. 2.

[19] Quoted in Picciotto, *Sketches of Anglo-Jewish History*, 289–90.

[20] The seceding members of the Spanish and Portuguese Synagogue to the Elders, 24 Aug. 1841, quoted in Roth (ed.), *Anglo-Jewish Letters*, 285.

[21] Endelman, *Radical Assimilation in English Jewish History*, 31–2.

ex-Christians from Spain and Portugal, the average annual number of marriages in the 1740s was fourteen. The average then dropped to eleven or twelve per year until the end of the century when it increased slightly to thirteen. In the ten-year period 1812–21, it fell again to twelve per year.[22]

It is possible that further research will reveal in more detail the extent to which each of these currents—intermarriage with Ashkenazim, migration to the New World, and radical assimilation—contributed to the demographic stagnation of the London Sephardi community. It is unlikely, however, that it will reverse the conclusion that leaving the communal fold was chief among them. This being so, we need to look into the connection between the circumstances of Converso life and the dissolution of Jewish loyalties among their ancestors in the age of emancipation.

Since the 1970s historians of the Sephardi diaspora have stressed the fragmentary, ambiguous, unsettled nature of New Christian 'Jewishness'.[23] The Iberian refugees who reached London in the seventeenth and eighteenth centuries were strangers to the rabbinic, law-oriented Judaism of early modern Europe. Up until the time they left the Iberian peninsula or France, they had lived as Catholics among Catholics; their education, reading (with a few exceptions), and cultural orbit were Catholic. Their knowledge of non-biblical Judaism was minimal, haphazard, and often distorted in the absence of synagogues, academies, study houses, texts, schools, rabbis, and other religious functionaries. By the eighteenth century, the period of heaviest New Christian settlement in London, persons of Jewish origin in Spain and Portugal had been cut off from normative Judaism for more than two centuries. Their crypto-Judaism was more a state of mind than a religious discipline or a body of practices. New Christians fleeing the peninsula in the seventeenth century brought with them, in Yosef Yerushalmi's words, 'a pastiche of fragments inherited from parents, gleaned haphazardly from books, disorganized, with significant gaps, sometimes distorted'.[24] Those leaving a century later, it stands to reason, brought with them even less.

Lack of familiarity with a lived Judaism was not the only obstacle to the integration of Conversos into communal life. The Converso experience itself—that is, the very structure of living as a Catholic outwardly and as a Jew inwardly—worked against a smooth, trouble-free incorporation. In some cases persons who had been raised as Christians and then returned to Judaism experienced difficulty in belonging simply and unambiguously to either

[22] Lipman, 'Sephardi and Other Jewish Immigrants', 41.

[23] Yerushalmi, *From Spanish Court to Italian Ghetto*; Y. Kaplan, *From Christianity to Judaism* (Heb.); Pullan, *The Jews of Europe and the Inquisition of Venice*; Yovel, *Spinoza and Other Heretics*, i; Bodian, *Hebrews of the Portuguese Nation*; id., *Dying in the Law of Moses*; Graizbord, *Souls in Dispute*.   [24] Yerushalmi, *The Re-education of Marranos*, 7.

religion. The duality of their religious experience often left them confused, with doubts about both religions and even about revealed religion in general. Scepticism, deism, and secularism were the result. Having lived a crypto-Judaism that was first and foremost a denial of Christian doctrine (rather than the active observance of the *mitsvot*), many Conversos were also inclined to make a distinction, foreign to rabbinic Judaism, between authentic, heart-felt spirituality and external observance. This led them, when faced with the challenge of accepting rabbinic Judaism, to devalue practices that were foreign to them or difficult to observe. In addition, the interiority of their religious life in Iberia, especially their personal encounter with and interpretation of texts, tended to privilege the religious authority of the self, empowering it with the wherewithal to set priorities and make judgements. There were also among the Conversos who found refuge in London some who had never been active Judaizers but who had fled because they were at risk simply by virtue of their New Christian descent.

Most early New Christians in England were strangers to Jewish life.[25] Once safe in London, far from the reach of the Inquisition, some of them remained apart from the synagogue, suspended between Judaism and Christianity or even at times between belief and varieties of disbelief (scepticism, atheism, agnosticism, deism). Others assimilated into the Church of England, either because it was convenient or because its doctrines seemed sensible or even true. In all, only one-third of those who were living in London before 1659 were buried in the Sephardi cemetery at Mile End; two-thirds, it would seem, remained outside the Jewish community.[26] In several well-to-do merchant clans that arrived soon after the readmission (the Mendes da Costas, for example),[27] family members were divided in their religious loyalties, some opting for the Established Church, others for the synagogue. To counter resistance to joining the Jewish community the *mahamad* decided in 1727, as the flow from the Iberian peninsula continued unabated, to refuse assistance to destitute New Christians unable to pay their fares to the captains who had brought them to London unless they were circumcised within fifteen days of their arrival.[28]

As for those former New Christians who joined the community, the way back to Judaism was often troubled and at times impossible. In London, as in Amsterdam, some experienced difficulty in adopting a regimen they had known only incompletely and at second hand. Jacob Sasportas, who served

[25] Y. Kaplan, 'The Jewish Profile of the Spanish-Portuguese Community', 232.
[26] R. D. Barnett, 'The Burial Register of the Spanish and Portuguese Jews'.
[27] Endelman, *Radical Assimilation in English Jewish History*, 12–17.
[28] R. D. Barnett, 'Dr. Samuel Nunes Ribiero', 92.

as the community's rabbi briefly from summer 1664 to summer 1665, clashed repeatedly with the lay leaders of the community on questions of religious discipline. He attacked wealthy members who refused to have their sons circumcised or submit to circumcision themselves, and on one occasion in 1665 expelled uncircumcised men from the synagogue. In the debate that followed, one of the Francia brothers, who were themselves circumcised but had not circumcised their sons, stood up and announced, 'Gentlemen, all this is suited either to very great fools or very wise men', and then proceeded to remove his *talit* (prayer shawl), throw down his *sidur* (prayer book) and walk out.[29] Significantly, after Sasportas fled to Hamburg during the great plague of 1665, the *mahamad* urged the brothers to return to the synagogue, without, however, requiring them to renounce their heterodox views. They both rejoined and in time served as *parnasim* (synagogue wardens).[30] This suggests that what bound the community together was less an allegiance to practice and doctrine than kinship and memory, a shared past and origins, a common language and cultural outlook.[31] In this light, the behaviour of those men who kept a foot in both the Jewish and Christian camps (to use Yosef Kaplan's phrase), marrying and socializing within the community yet remaining Christians in outward appearance, is comprehensible. For them, Judaism was a question of inner identity, not external observances; it was 'no more than a matter of identity of interest with an ethnic group'.[32]

Even former New Christians who re-entered Judaism with apparent ease were primed, by virtue of their historical experience before arriving in London, to drift—or to allow their children to drift—from Jewish tradition. Having lived as Christians, they were strangers to Jewish communal life. Accustomed to satisfying their cultural and social needs in Christian company, they encountered in London a complex, seductive, urban society in which social relations were not rigid and unbendingly hierarchical, but rather, within certain bounds, surprisingly fluid. Without question there were fewer social and legal barriers to integration in London than in any other European city before the French Revolution, as the careers of Isaac D'Israeli and 'Jew' King demonstrate. (Let me add parenthetically that in the Italian states and the Ottoman empire, where political and social lines between Jews and non-Jews remained undisturbed and more or less impermeable, integration into Jewish life was less problematic. In those lands it was also made easier by the presence of Sephardi communities that had

[29] Wolf (ed.), *Jews in the Canary Islands*, 205,
[30] Tishby, 'New Information on the Converso Community in London' (Heb.) 468.
[31] For a similar approach, see Bodian, *Hebrews of the Portuguese Nation*.
[32] Y. Kaplan, 'The Jewish Profile of the Spanish-Portuguese Community', 236.

been established in the wake of the expulsion of 1492, most of whose residents had never lived as Christians.)

In London the problem of integration was compounded by the community's position on the periphery of the Sephardi diaspora. It was a frontier community, small and culturally undistinguished, known for neither its piety nor its learning, lacking both social cohesion and legal autonomy. Its religious leaders were ineffectual in imposing their authority on new arrivals, while its lay leaders were eager to maintain ties to all former Conversos, whatever their religious outlook. Those who were active in communal life often engaged in commercial ventures with those who remained on its periphery and were unlikely to antagonize them. In Hamburg and Amsterdam, by contrast, communal leaders drew clear distinctions between those who accepted the discipline of Judaism and those who did not, frequently excommunicating transgressors and deviants.[33] In short, circumstances in London were not conducive to the integration of former New Christians into traditional Judaism.

In the first generation or two after immigration from the peninsula, ethnic attachments tended to counteract or mute the full impact of that part of the Converso historical experience that encouraged heterodoxy, drift, and defection. Most Sephardim continued to socialize and do business with, as well as marry, other Sephardim, whatever their religious views and ritual commitments. Most of them also remained members of the community, even if Judaism as a body of doctrines and practices was unimportant to them. Recall that Isaac D'Israeli withdrew from the Spanish and Portuguese congregation only when ordered to serve as a warden or pay a fine, which was the expectation in the case of non-observant members like him. However, in time toleration and opportunities for social integration weakened these ethnic ties. Then the full force of the centrifugal, disintegrative features of the Converso experience kicked in. By the first decades of the nineteenth century it was clear even to contemporaries, often the last to see the direction in which history is heading, that there was little that could be done to slow or halt it. The establishment of a Reform synagogue in the 1840s was an attempt in this direction, but its influence was limited. In the end, the Converso past and the openness of English society (relative, of course, to other Western societies at the time) operated in tandem to sap the vitality of the Sephardi community. Only further immigration in the twentieth century—from India, the Middle East, North Africa, and the Balkans—allowed it to survive, and often the newcomers who kept it alive lacked roots in the Iberian peninsula.

[33] Ibid. 238–9.

CHAPTER TWELVE

The Frankaus of London

I

THE RADICAL ASSIMILATION of entire Jewish families was not an uncommon occurrence in western and central Europe between the Enlightenment and the Second World War. Drift and defection removed the names of thousands of families from communal rosters, although immigration often masked the demographic consequences of their departure. Mapping the scope and character of this social process is a challenge because of the nature of the evidence that survives. As I explained in Chapter 5, in the case of liberal states like England and France, where no government or church agency gathered data on conversion and intermarriage, historians must reconstruct the course of radical assimilation on the basis of so-called anecdotal evidence. Consequently the precise contours of the phenomenon remain unknowable. Yet even when statistical evidence is available, as in the case of central European Jewish communities, there are limits to what it can reveal. Conversion data, for example, cannot be made to disclose the subjective experience of conversion, that is, how Jews understood and represented their transformation into Christians and how they regarded their Jewish background in later years. Nor, of course, can they illuminate how former Jews fared as Christians. In addition, statistical data do not reveal changes in attitude and behaviour in the generations that preceded the act of conversion, that is, changes among parents and grandparents whose cumulative impact later enabled a definitive break with the community. This is critical because radical assimilation was in most cases the outcome of changes over several generations rather than a sudden, sharp break with traditional beliefs and affiliations.

One strategy to overcome the limitations of quantitative data is to follow the transformation of Jewish practice, affiliation, and self-reflection in a single family over three or more generations. This method, of course, cannot disclose the extent of radical assimilation in a community, but it can provide a wealth of detail about the road to conversion, the concrete circumstances in which it occurred, and the success of former Jews and their descendants in shaking off the taint of Jewish antecedents. A number of studies in German Jewish history—David Landes's 'Bleichröders and Rothschilds' (1975), Fritz Stern's *Gold and Iron* (1977), Werner Mosse's *The German-Jewish Economic Elite* (1989), and Steven Lowenstein's *The Berlin Jewish Community* (1994)— suggest the fruitfulness of a multigenerational perspective on radical assimilation, even if that was not their authors' primary goal.

The chief obstacle to employing this research strategy is a paucity of evidence regarding Jewish consciousness and observance in successive generations of one family. For historians of Anglo-Jewry, the problem is even more acute, for English Jews in comparison to their German counterparts were reticent about recording their experiences and emotional states. Anglo-Jewish memoirs, journals, and correspondence from the nineteenth and twentieth centuries are not plentiful. I was thus fortunate to come upon the Frankau family of London, which, over the course of four generations stretching from the 1830s to the 1960s, produced a remarkable succession of writers who addressed questions of Jewish identity in their work. Moreover, because several of the Frankaus and their relations were minor public figures, other often equally minor public figures recorded what they did and said, thus leaving an additional source from which to reconstruct the Frankaus' departure from Jewish history.

2

The first member of the Frankau family to settle in England was Joseph Frankau (1813–57), a native of Diespeck, a village in Middle Franconia, near Neustadt an der Aisch.[1] Like many young village Jews whose opportunities were limited by occupational and residence restrictions, Joseph migrated: first to Frankfurt am Main and then in 1837 to London.[2] In 1841, when the first British census was conducted, he was living in Great Prescot Street, in the home of Frankfurt-born Joseph Geiger (d. 1870), a cigar merchant, and his sister Amelia (1813–63), first cousins of the Reform rabbi Abraham Geiger and his brother Solomon, a prominent figure in Frankfurt Orthodoxy.[3] Great Prescot Street was in the heart of the Jewish quarter of London, just to the east of the City boundary. Its residents were almost entirely Jews of modest but respectable means—small merchants, cigar manufacturers,

[1] In 1837, the year in which Joseph Frankau migrated to London, there were 270 Jews in Diespeck, about one-third of the village population. In 1867 there were only 117, migration having taken its toll in the intervening thirty years (Ophir (ed.), *Encylopedia of Jewish Communities* (Heb.), 319). [2] Jacobi, 'The Geiger Family'.
[3] 1841 Census, HO107 716/8; Dietz, *Stammbuch der Frankfurter Juden*, 101.

jewellers, opticians, pencil makers, glass dealers, umbrella makers.[4] Perhaps the Frankau and Geiger families were already acquainted in Frankfurt before Joseph moved to London. In any case, it is not surprising that he lodged with the Geigers during his first years in London, given their common background.

Joseph Geiger was already doing business as a manufacturer and importer of cigars when Joseph Frankau settled in London. This was a new and rapidly expanding area of trade at the time and one in which Jews, especially recent immigrants from Germany, quickly made their mark. In the eighteenth century, cigars were practically unknown in England. Their use was introduced after the Peninsular War (1807–14), when British officers who had served in Spain and Portugal returned home with a taste for smoking tobacco in what was then a novel form. The new habit did not become popular at once, however, since the duty on cigars was prohibitive. In 1823, for example, only 26 pounds of manufactured cigars were imported into Britain. The duty was then reduced and cigar consumption began to rise almost immediately: in 1824, 15,380 pounds were imported. In 1829 the rate was slashed in half, and the following year 253,882 pounds were imported. In the 1830s cigar-smoking replaced snuff-taking in the world of fashion, and by the 1850s what had been an aristocratic luxury had become an integral part of the social ritual of the male middle class—half of the tobacco smoked in English cities in the 1850s was in the form of cigars.[5]

Jews, both English- and German-born, entered the London cigar trade in its infancy and prospered as the habit of cigar-smoking grew in popularity. As was frequently the case in Europe and America, their previous experience in the marketplace—as pedlars, shopkeepers, wholesalers, and importers — made them sensitive to shifting tastes and developing markets. The migration of Geiger and Frankau to London was part of a larger movement of German Jewish traders to what was then the richest consumer market in the world. In the middle decades of the century, hundreds of German Jewish merchants established businesses in London (and the provinces to a much lesser extent) to supply its middle-class residents with pianos, cigars, antiques, picture frames, jewellery, stationery, leather goods, furniture, and various other 'fancy goods'. In the case of cigars, Jews in Germany were already prominent in the importation and distribution of tobacco, and this may have encouraged their entry into the cigar trade in London.

[4] *Post Office London Directory for 1844*, 257–8; Lipman, 'Jewish Settlement in the East End of London', 27.

[5] Fairholt, *Tobacco*, 213; Apperson, *The Social History of Smoking*, 137, 139, 166; E. H. Pinto, *Wooden Bygones of Smoking*, 48–9, 56, 59.

It is not clear whether Frankau worked for his future brother-in-law when he first arrived. If so, he did not remain in a dependent position with him for long, for by 1840 at the latest he was in partnership with Lesser Friedlander, in Haydon Square, the Minories, importing leeches and cigars.[6] This arrangement lasted for only a few years, and by 1844 he was doing business as Joseph Frankau & Co., importer of leeches and cigars, in 33 Great Alie Street, in the same neighbourhood.[7] His decision to set out on his own was undoubtedly connected to his marriage, in March 1843, to Joseph Geiger's sister Amelia (or Emilie, as she appears in some sources). The wedding ceremony took place at the Western Synagogue in St Alban's Place, Haymarket, and was performed by H. A. Henry (1800–79), minister of the congregation.[8]

That the couple were married in the Western Synagogue, which was a mile west of the City and whose members lived primarily in the Strand, Covent Garden, Soho, and Pall Mall, and not in one of the city synagogues, which were an easy walk from their home, is peculiar. It is impossible to know whether Geiger and Frankau belonged to the congregation or worshipped there regularly, since most of the congregational records for the period have disappeared. One possibility—and it is only that and nothing more—is that they were attracted to the Western Synagogue because it was viewed as more liberal than other congregations and more sympathetic to the newly established West London Synagogue of British Jews, the first Reform congregation in Britain. In 1842, a few days before the consecration of the West London Synagogue, Chief Rabbi Solomon Hirschell issued what was in effect a *ḥerem* (excommunication) against the secessionist group and ordered that it be read in all the synagogues of Britain. The Western Synagogue alone among London congregations refused to do so. Moreover, it also undertook a programme of cosmetic reforms designed to improve congregational decorum and correct other abuses.[9] Its minister was also sympathetic to moderate reforms. He preached regular sabbath sermons in English—a novelty at the time—and after he left the congregation in 1849 to settle in the United States served congregations in Cincinnati and San Francisco that

---

[6] *Post Office London Directory for 1840*, 98. In the directories for 1838 and 1839, Frankau does not appear as a partner of Friedlander. In 1837 Friedlander was doing business as Friedlander & Beyfus, importers of cigars and leeches, at the same address as in 1840 (*Post Office London Directory for 1837*, 210). In his autobiography, Gilbert Frankau errs when he writes that the firm J. Frankau & Co. was founded by his grandfather in 1837 to import leeches from France. Joseph Frankau did not go into business by himself initially, and when he did he apparently imported both cigars and leeches from the start (G. Frankau, *Self-Portrait*, 16).

[7] *Post Office London Directory for 1840*, 98.

[8] Register of marriages 1837–63, entry for 19 Mar. 1843, Western Synagogue, London.

[9] A. Barnett, *The Western Synagogue*, 181–8.

also introduced moderate reforms.[10] (Membership of the Reform congregation would have been out of the question—its members were almost exclusively from the wealthier strata of London Jewry.)

It is impossible to say much about the religious outlook and behaviour of Joseph and Amelia Frankau. We know for certain that they lived in a Jewish neighbourhood early in their married life. But some time between 1847 and 1851, they moved their residence from the Goodman's Fields area just east of the City to a substantial terraced house in Duncan Terrace, Islington (not far from the present-day Angel Underground station), a clear sign of their increasing prosperity.[11] Although middle-class Jews began settling in Islington in the 1840s, the Jewish ambience there and in other north London neighbourhoods to which Jews were migrating was much less pronounced than in the old areas of settlement in the City and the streets immediately to the east. In 1853 there were only two other Jewish families (at most) living in Duncan Terrace.[12] Moreover, at the time of the Frankaus' move there were no synagogues or other Jewish institutions in the immediate area. A congregation was established in Upper Street, Islington, only in 1860—by which time the Frankaus had departed for a more exclusive area north of Regent's Park.[13] In 1854 or 1855 the family moved to Benario Villas in Upper Avenue Road (now Avenue Road), where there were even fewer Jews than in Islington.[14] Yet it would be incorrect to infer from Joseph's and Amelia's desire to live in choice neighbourhoods that they were eager to escape all contact with other Jews. Their son Arthur (1848(?)–1904) received part of his education at the Realschule der israelitischen Gemeinde in Frankfurt, and the four of their five children who married all took Jewish spouses.[15]

Word of Joseph Frankau's business success apparently encouraged others in his family to try their luck in London as well. His unmarried brother Henry, then aged 21, was living with him at the time of the 1851 census and was then employed as his clerk. In the early 1850s a Sidney Frankau, who

[10] *The Jewish Encyclopedia*, s.v. 'Henry, Henry A.'.

[11] 1851 census, HO107 1501/62. Joseph's and Amelia's daughter Ida was born in 1847 (Jacobi, 'The Geiger Family') in Whitechapel (according to the 1851 census, which gives incorrect ages for the three Frankau children alive at the time). Thus, the family must have moved to Islington after her birth but before the census enumerator called in 1851.

[12] *Watkins's Commercial and General London Directory and Court Guide for 1853*, 602. The other residents in the street who might have been Jewish were D. N. Henriques and George Wulff.   [13] *Jewish Chronicle*, 18 Dec. 1863.

[14] *Post Office London Directory for 1854*, 1895; *Watkins's Commercial and General London Directory and Court Guide for 1855*, 1762. Joseph died in 1857 and by 1859 his widow had moved from Upper Avenue Road (*Post Office London Directory for 1859*, 722). I have been unable to trace Amelia's movements between 1859 and her death in 1863.

[15] G. Frankau, *Self-Portrait*, 24; Jacobi, 'The Geiger Family'.

almost certainly was also a brother, lived in Claremont Square, Islington, a few minutes walk from Duncan Terrace, where Joseph was living. Sidney moved to a house in Upper Avenue Road at the same time that Joseph did. He was in business initially with a third brother, Adolph (1823(?)–56), but later set up on his own as an importer of fancy goods and meerschaum pipes with an office in Bishopsgate Street in the City.[16] Nothing more is known about Sidney and Henry Frankau or their descendants (if there were any); it is possible that they returned to Germany.

Adolph, on the other hand, remained in England, where he, like his brother Joseph, prospered, thus providing the material basis for his descendants' integration into the English middle class. Initially Adolph, along with a Nathan Frankau (another brother in all likelihood), had migrated to the United States, settling in the early 1840s in New Haven, Connecticut, where a small community of Bavarian Jews had formed at the beginning of the decade. Like thousands of other Jewish immigrants at this time from southern and south-western German states, Adolph and Nathan started their business careers as pedlars, but they did not remain itinerant traders for long. In city directories for 1844–5 and 1845–6, Nathan appears as a pedlar, but in the directory for 1846–7 he, Adolph, and Henry (d. 1895) and Louis Feldman (1814–93) are listed as partners in a dry-goods business. (In 1856 Henry Feldman, then a merchant living in New London, Connecticut, married Bavarian-born Frederica Frankau, a resident of New Haven and in all likelihood a sister of Nathan and Adolph.) Nathan remained in New Haven and became a successful retailer. He also became an active member of Congregation Mishkan Yisra'el, which he joined soon after his arrival, unlike his brother Adolph, who remained distant from Judaism. During the American Civil War, Nathan served briefly as a captain in the Twelfth Regiment Connecticut Volunteers, but was dishonourably discharged in New Orleans in November 1862 for taking bribes to issue passes to disloyal persons.[17]

Adolph undoubtedly intended to remain in the United States and make his fortune there, for he became a naturalized citizen in New Haven in 1844. But for some reason he changed his mind and in 1847 recrossed the Atlantic,

[16] 1851 census, HO107 1501/62; *Post Office London Directory for 1854*, 876, 1895; *Watkins's Commercial and General London Directory and Court Guide for 1855*, 198; *Post Office London Directory for 1856*, 2162B; *Post Office London Directory for 1866*, 1039.

[17] Werner Hirsch of New Haven kindly provided me with information about the Frankaus in New Haven from his own research on early New Haven Jewry in city directories, synagogue archives, army records, newspapers, and other local sources. See also Osterweis, *Three Centuries of New Haven*, 213, 217. Let me note that there is no conclusive evidence that Adolph, Nathan, and Frederica were siblings. However, given the rarity of the family name, their common roots in Bavaria, and the close business ties among Adolph, Nathan, and Frederica's future husband, it is difficult to believe that they were not linked in this way.

settling permanently in London.[18] He carried on a successful business in the city as an importer of meerschaum pipes and smoking accessories. In 1853, about the time that his brothers Joseph and Sidney moved to Upper Avenue Road, he married and moved into a newly built semi-detached house in nearby Adelaide Road, just north of Primrose Hill. His wife, Rosetta Neuberg (1816(?)–80), was a native of Würzberg who had lived previously in Nottingham with her brother Joseph (1806–67), a successful merchant. Adolph died in 1856, aged 36, leaving her with two infant children.[19]

Rosetta Frankau was an ambitious woman, as distant from Jewish practice as her deceased husband had been, and eager to see her children rise in the world. In Nottingham, where she had spent much of her adult life before marriage, there were no synagogues and few practising Jews. Most of the German Jewish lace and hosiery merchants there were either Jews in name only or members of the Unitarian Chapel.[20] In London she was a member of the Rosslyn Hill Unitarian Chapel in Hampstead. Her son Frederick Joseph (1854–1933) was sent to Rugby School in the 1860s, when professing Jews would not have been welcome there. He did not enter the family business, which continued to prosper after Adolph's death under the management of Louis Blumfeld, a native of Württemberg who had been Adolph's clerk and was still boarding with the family at the time of the 1861 census. Instead, Frederick chose (or was encouraged to choose) a path that took him far from the German Jewish merchant milieu into which he had been born. After Rugby he went on to Gonville and Caius College, Cambridge, became a barrister, and married an Englishwoman. Neither he nor his two children, both of whom were educated at Rugby, had links to Jewish life. The elder, George Neuberg Frankau (1881–1969), became a mechanical engineer; the younger, Sir Claude Howard Stanley Frankau (1883–1967), was a distinguished surgeon—whose wife, Isabella, a psychiatrist, was notorious for prescribing heroin and cocaine from her elegant Wimpole Street consulting rooms in the 1960s for a Bohemian circle of poets, writers, artists, and musicians. His sister, Gertrude (1856–1913), never married, continued to live in

---

[18] Adolph was naturalized on 1 Apr. 1844 at the city court in New Haven. The naturalization document records his age as 21 and lists his surname as *Frankan* (Connecticut Naturalization Index, National Archives, New England Region, Waltham, Mass.). Interestingly his brother Joseph appears as Joseph *Frankan* in the 1841 census but as Joseph *Frankau* in the 1843 Western Synagogue marriage register. It would appear that the family name became standardized only from the late 1840s.

[19] Adolf Frankau & Co., *100 Years in the Service of Smokers*; Frankau family tree and biographical notes, in possession of John Howard Frankau, Cobham, Surrey; Register of Death of Adolph Frankau, 5 Nov. 1856, Hampstead Registration District, General Registry Office, London; 1861 census, RG9 91/44; *Post Office London Directory for 1855*.

[20] Aronsfeld, 'German Jews in Nottingham', 8; Wylie, *Old and New Nottingham*, 141.

Hampstead, and like her mother and Louis Blumfeld was a member of the Rosslyn Hill Unitarian Chapel.[21] According to Colonel J. H. Frankau, a son of George Neuberg Frankau, his father's generation 'hid the fact of their Jewish ancestry'.[22]

Rosetta's brother, Joseph Neuberg, was equally committed to a course of radical assimilation. A native of Würzburg, he served a commercial apprenticeship in Frankfurt and then Hamburg. In the late 1820s he was sent by an uncle in Hamburg to Nottingham.[23] This was a common practice at the time among German firms that distributed English goods on the Continent. With agents and warehouses in the major textile manufacturing towns of England—Manchester, Leeds, Bradford, and Nottingham—they hoped to gain greater control over the quality and cost of the goods they handled. Shortly after settling in Nottingham, Neuberg was a made a partner in the firm, which prospered and made him a wealthy man. But material success alone failed to satisfy him. As he later remarked, a businessman who satisfies only his 'meaner half' and fails to provide for his 'spiritual life' must of necessity become 'blinded, dwarfed, stupefied'.[24] To quench his thirst for the 'spiritual life', Neuberg, though a recent immigrant, took a keen interest in current political and cultural affairs and played a leading role in middle-class philanthropic efforts in Nottingham to enlighten and uplift the working class. In particular, he actively supported the Nottingham Mechanics' Institution, serving for some years as head of its literature section. He secured the appearance of guest lecturers and frequently spoke himself on literary themes, including, on one occasion, the work of Thomas Carlyle, whom he especially admired.[25]

In December 1839 Neuberg wrote an enthusiastic letter of appreciation to Carlyle, thanking him for the way he interpreted 'German thoughts to our English brethren'.[26] Carlyle responded warmly and at length. There matters rested until in December 1847 Ralph Waldo Emerson, who was a guest in Neuberg's home while on a lecture tour of England, offered to arrange a personal meeting between the two men when he became aware of Neuberg's

[21] Frankau family tree and biographical notes; Adolph Frankau & Co., *100 Years in the Service of Smokers*; 1861 census, RG9 91/44; Rosslyn Hill Chapel, list of members, 1 Jan. 1875, Rosslyn Hill Chapel Records, RNC, 38.189; minute book, 1907–22, Rosslyn Hill Chapel Records, RNC 38.132. Blumfeld was eventually made a partner in the firm, a position he held until 1899, when the business was converted into a limited company. He then became director and chairman. For Lady Frankau's notoriety, see Pizzichini, *Dead Men's Wages*, 181–3.
[22] Col. J. H. Frankau to Todd M. Endelman, 16 Sept. 1995, in possession of author.
[23] J. W. Carlyle, *Letters*, p. v; Aronsfeld, 'German Jews in Nottingham', 8.
[24] Quoted in Aronsfeld, 'German Jews in Nottingham', 8.
[25] Ibid.; 'Carlyle and Neuberg', 280.
[26] Joseph Neuberg to Thomas Carlyle, 5 Dec. 1839, in T. Carlyle, *Collected Letters*, xi. 231–2.

esteem for Carlyle. Rosetta Neuberg (as she was then) apparently told Emerson that Neuberg 'would give his little finger to know Carlyle'.[27] When Emerson was in London the following spring he brought the two men together.[28] They met for the first time at Carlyle's home in Chelsea and thereafter a friendship developed. In a letter to Emerson in December 1848, Carlyle described his visitor as 'a welcome, wise kind of man'.[29]

The following summer Neuberg decided to retire from business and devote himself wholly to literature and in particular to Carlyle. He was sufficiently prosperous to be able to live on the income of his investments —he described his occupation in the 1861 census as 'fundholder'[30]— and there was nothing to keep him in Nottingham. (His wife Mary Ann Stirland, a Scotswoman, had died several years before after only six years of marriage.[31]) He moved to London and, until his death in 1867, volunteered as Carlyle's research assistant, secretary, and translator. He did research for him at the British Museum and the Public Record Office, performed secretarial work at his Chelsea home, and served as his companion on long walks in London. He handled the practical arrangements for and accompanied him on trips to Germany in 1852, when Carlyle was gathering material and impressions for his biography of Frederick the Great, and in 1858, when he wanted to visit the scenes of Frederick's great battles. He also translated into German *Past and Present*, *Heroes and Hero-Worship*, and the bulk of *Frederick the Great*.[32]

Neuberg was devoted to Carlyle. He idolized him and treasured his utterances and pronouncements. In letters to his sister Rosetta, he quoted at length from his conversation and offered details about meals and other mundane domestic matters in the Carlyle home. Neuberg thought of Carlyle as a warm, sympathetic, and generous 'employer', who valued his companionship and services, and in one sense this was true. At Neuberg's death, Carlyle wrote to Rosetta, 'No kinder friend had I in this world; no man of any day, I believe, had so faithful, loyal, and willing a helper as he generously was to me for the last twenty or more years.'[33] In an unpublished sketch, written

---

[27] 'Carlyle and Neuberg', 280.   [28] J. W. Carlyle, *Letters*, p. vi.

[29] Thomas Carlyle to Ralph Waldo Emerson, 6 Dec. 1848, in T. Carlyle, *Correspondence*, 446.

[30] 1861 census, RG9 91/44.

[31] J. W. Carlyle, *Letters*, p. vi. Neuberg never remarried; he unsuccessfully courted Barbara Leigh Smith, later a leader of the Victorian women's movement, in summer 1855. They met at the home of the radical publisher John Chapman, where Neuberg boarded for long periods. Leigh Smith had turned down an offer of marriage from the Jewish mathematician James Joseph Sylvester a year earlier (Hirsch, *Barbara Leigh Smith Bodichon*, 101–2, 105).

[32] F. Kaplan, *Thomas Carlyle*, 388, 389, 396, 416, 418; 'Carlyle and Neuberg'; Fielding (ed.), 'Carlyle's Sketch of Joseph Neuberg', 6. In 1856, when Neuberg began supporting his recently widowed sister and her two children, he returned part-time to business, this time in London.

[33] Quoted in 'Carlyle and Neuberg', 297.

about a week after Neuberg's funeral, he referred to him in similar terms: 'For the last twenty or twenty-five years, he had been my most attached adherent, ever-loyal, ever-patient, ardent, ever-willing to do me service in every kind.' He was, he also noted, a 'Jew of the *better* type or almost of the best'.[34]

Neuberg's attachment to Carlyle was remarkable in several respects. First, it was unusual at the time for Jews in England to take an active interest in cultural matters outside their own community. Most were not well educated; few had received an advanced secondary education; even fewer had attended university. They contributed little—either as patrons or producers —to the literary or artistic life of the nation, in marked contrast to their counterparts in German-speaking lands, who believed (wrongly, as it turned out) that their cultural achievements would accelerate their political and social acceptance. In this sense, Neuberg's enthusiasm for literature reflected the influence of his German upbringing rather than his English surroundings.

Second, Carlyle was capable of expressing great hostility to Jews in his work.[35] He was not an obsessive or systematic antisemite, blaming Jews for the social ills and political upheavals of the day. Nor was he a proponent of governmental measures to restrict Jewish participation in public life. But he did share the prejudices of his time and gave vent to them in his work, frequently identifying Jews with those things he especially disliked, such as capitalism and materialism. In *Past and Present* (1843), for example, in which he compared the contemporary world with that of a twelfth-century monastic community, he equated Jews with insatiable greed. He described how Abbot Hugo, in need of funds to repair the fabric of St Edmundsbury abbey, was forced to turn to 'usurious, insatiable Jews, every fresh Jew sticking on him like a fresh horseleech, sucking his and our life out'.[36] Similarly, in *Sartor Resartus* (1833), a fantasy about an imaginary German transcendentalist philosopher and his treatise on the 'philosophy of clothes', he associated the Jewish old-clothes dealers of Monmouth Street, London, with materialism and superficiality. He wrote:

We too have walked through Monmouth Street, but with little feeling of 'Devotion', probably in part because the contemplative process is so fatally broken in upon by the brood of money-changers who nestle in that Church and importune the worshipper with merely secular proposals.[37]

His illiberalism and hostility to Jews led him to oppose, though not publicly, legislation to permit Jews to enter political life. He wrote in 1847 to his friend

---

[34] Fielding (ed.), 'Carlyle's Sketch of Joseph Neuberg', 4, 5.
[35] Park, 'Thomas Carlyle and the Jews'.
[36] T. Carlyle, *Past and Present*, bk. 2, ch. 4.   [37] T. Carlyle, *Sartor Resartus*, bk. 3, ch. 6.

Richard Monckton Milnes, a keen supporter of Jewish emancipation, that 'a real Jew' could be neither a citizen nor a legislator of any country 'except his own wretched Palestine, whither all his thoughts and steps and efforts tend—where, in the Devil's name, let him arrive as soon as possible, and make us quit of him!'[38]

As we saw in Chapter 6, some Jews who dissociated themselves from the Jewish community voiced non-Jewish prejudices about Jews, hoping thereby to prove the authenticity of their own transformation. One variation of this was to associate with antisemites and pay homage to Jew-baiting geniuses. The conductor Hermann Levi (1839–1900) worshipped Richard Wagner and thus endured his and his entourage's taunts, while Leonard Woolf (1880–1969) patiently suffered his wife's and Bloomsbury's snide remarks. How did Neuberg cope with Carlyle's hostility to Jews? Perhaps he convinced himself that he was exempt from his comments since he had broken with Judaism and the Jewish community. Moreover, he had abandoned the pursuit of material gain to devote himself heart and soul to the cultivation of spiritual matters. Indeed, it is possible that he drew comfort from Carlyle's anti-Jewish remarks, for they offered a benchmark against which he could confidently measure his own distance from what was commonly believed to be 'Jewish'.

But even if we put to one side Carlyle's anti-Jewish remarks, Neuberg's uncritical admiration for him is remarkable in another respect. Like other middle-class European Jews, Neuberg owed his wealth and social advancement to the decline of *ancien régime* ideas and institutions. Without their demise, Jewish emancipation and *embourgeoisement* would have been impossible. Most middle-class Jews understood this and rallied to the banner of liberalism. Neuberg, on the other hand, devoted himself to an illiberal, antirationalist, Romantic visionary who scorned democracy and laissez-faire capitalism. He idealized the organic, feudal society of the Middle Ages—a society, it should be remembered, in which Jews were marginalized and persecuted. Perhaps Neuberg found in Carlyle's attacks on contemporary materialism and superficiality another way in which he could distance himself from what in truth he really was—a successful Jewish capitalist. If so, there was in his undiscriminating embrace of Carlyle and his views a strong element of self-contempt.

Interestingly, Neuberg was not alone among Jews outside the Jewish community who found such views attractive. Recall that Disraeli, in his three political novels of the 1840s, *Coningsby*, *Sybil*, and *Tancred*, expressed politi-

---

[38] Thomas Carlyle to Richard Monckton Milnes, 30 Dec. 1847, quoted in F. Kaplan, *Thomas Carlyle*, 527.

cal and social views that were similar to those of Carlyle: reverence for great men who can change the course of history, nostalgia for organic communities of an earlier period, disenchantment with liberalism, urbanization, and industrialization. Like Neuberg's, Disraeli's enthusiasm for illiberal ideas reflected his distance from mainstream Anglo-Jewry, which was then campaigning for the removal of all civil disabilities and had pinned its hopes for success on the triumph of liberalism. Unlike Neuberg, however, Disraeli confronted head on the stigma of Jewishness, turning it upside down and revelling in its nobility.

3

The connection between the family of Adolph Frankau and Anglo-Jewry was severed within one generation. The descendants of Adolph and Rosetta blended successfully and, to all appearances, painlessly into the professional middle class, and their subsequent history need not detain us. Joseph's offspring, on the other hand, maintained a connection to the community for one more generation, and even after formally abandoning Judaism discovered that their Jewishness was not so easily left behind.

Like his brother Adolph, Joseph Frankau died early, at 45, leaving five young children. The business he had founded continued to operate under the management of clerks, one of whom, German-born Joseph Grünbaum (1835–1908), married Della Frankau (1845–98), Joseph's and Amelia's eldest daughter, in 1868. Eventually, Grünbaum and his brothers-in-law, Arthur and Edwin Frankau (1854–1903), became partners in the firm.[39] Arthur, the elder son, whose descendants will be the focus of the remainder of this chapter, was very much the model of the self-denying, hard-working, family-oriented, successful Jewish businessman of legend. According to his son Gilbert (1884–1952), he was personally abstemious, saving his money or spending it on his family rather than on himself. He never owned a horse, abhorred personal debt—the one occasion on which Gilbert saw him lose his temper was when he discovered that Gilbert had not paid an overdue bootmaker's bill—and after moving the family to Mayfair, with money he had inherited from his unmarried brother, Edwin, failed to derive pleasure from the upmarket surroundings.[40] In Gilbert's words, he 'had no zest for the Mayfair game'.[41] Appropriately, he was a Liberal in politics (unlike his Tory wife and son, about whom more later).[42]

Although educated for a time at a Jewish school in Frankfurt, Arthur Frankau was not sympathetic to the Jewish religion. He was, according to

[39] Jacobi, 'The Geiger Family'. [40] G. Frankau, *Self-Portrait*, 16, 38.
[41] Ibid. 77. [42] Ibid. 33.

Gilbert, an agnostic whose only fault was 'a slight bias against certain members of the faith which his conscience had rejected'.[43] When he married Julia Davis (1859–1916) in 1883, the ceremony took place at the Reform synagogue, of which his mother-in-law, Isabella Davis (1824(?)–1900), was a member. He himself joined the congregation the month before his wedding, but his own extreme religious views soon brought him into conflict with its leaders. When his son Gilbert was born in 1884, he refused to have him circumcised, even after being ordered to do so by the wardens of the synagogue. Circumcision, in his view, was an unenlightened practice, while the bylaw requiring male circumcision was 'an interference with matters which should be beyond the prescription of any congregation'. Realizing that the wardens would not yield, he resigned his membership in 1885 (without, however, failing to enclose a six guinea cheque to settle his account).[44]

Arthur Frankau's aversion to circumcision was not idiosyncratic. In the second half of the century, circumcision was viewed as the defining mark on the body of the male Jew throughout Europe. In medical discourse, the Jewish male was represented as not quite whole because of his severed foreskin: he was not only different, but deformed, damaged, and incomplete. Currents in medical literature saw in his circumcised penis the marker of his allegedly diseased character and associated it with syphilis and masturbation.[45] At the same time, historians, anthropologists, social theorists, and other writers who drew on developmental, evolutionary thought linked circumcision to earlier, more primitive periods in the history of civilization. Writing in the *Westminster Review* in 1863, the liberal essayist Bernard Cracroft noted that Jews continued to practise 'the barbaric rite of circumcision' while 'the great bulk of intelligent men throughout Europe' had abandoned it.[46] For the historian Goldwin Smith, writing in the *Nineteenth Century* in 1878, 'the primaeval rite' of circumcision was the mark of the Jews' tribal separation, the sign of Judaism's failure to evolve beyond the state of tribalism to religious universalism.[47]

Frankau's refusal placed him outside the pale of institutional Judaism, even the liberal wing of Reform Judaism. Although some radical reformers in Germany condemned the practice as a crude cultic holdover from Judaism's youth—for Abraham Geiger, it was 'a barbaric bloody act which

[43] G. Frankau, *Self-Portrait*, 24.

[44] Register of marriages, 1842–89, entry no. 248, 28 Mar. 1883; members accounts, 1870–80, entry for 11 Sept. 1870; minute book of the council, 1875–88, entries for 25 Feb. 1883 and 29 Nov. 1885; minute book of the wardens, 1882–93, entries for 22 July and 12 Aug. 1884; Arthur Frankau to Isidore Harris, 23, 25, and 29 July 1884, AJA/59/9/16; resignations of membership, AJA/59/10/12; West London Synagogue of British Jews.

[45] Gilman, *The Jew's Body*, 91–6, 155.   [46] Quoted in Feldman, *Englishmen and Jews*, 88–9.

[47] Ibid. 90. On attacks on circumcision in Germany, see Judd, *Contested Rituals*.

fills the father with fear'[48]—its deep emotional hold mitigated against its elimination. No Reform synagogue, synod, or congregational association in Europe or America ever claimed that it was not religiously binding. Arthur Frankau's repudiation of Jewish practice went further, however, than failing to initiate his son into the covenant. Having broken with the synagogue, he and his wife took steps to bolster the future integration of Gilbert and his siblings into upper-middle-class English society. They raised their children in the Church of England and sent them to elite private schools, although they did not have Gilbert baptized until he was 13 and thus 'old enough to understand things for himself'.[49] Remarkably, they did not tell Gilbert that he was of Jewish ancestry until he was 'more than sixteen'.[50] To cement his own break with Judaism, Arthur left instructions that when he died his body was not to be buried in a Jewish cemetery.[51] (He was buried, along with his wife, in the non-denominational Hampstead Cemetery in west Hampstead. In 1997 thieves stole the quarter-ton bronze urn that was the centrepiece of the art nouveau family monument.)[52]

Arthur Frankau's wife Julia shared his outlook on Jewish matters, despite her own religious upbringing. Her father, Hyman Davis (1824–75), came from a well-established Anglo-Jewish family, some branches of which were wealthy. He had hoped to make a career as a painter, but the demands of supporting a family forced him to abandon this idea. He practised dentistry in Dublin from 1849 to 1863 and then, after returning to London, worked as a portrait photographer, with a studio in his home, first in Bruton Street in the West End and then from about 1870 in Warrington Crescent, Maida Vale. The family belonged to the West London Synagogue of British Jews, but it would be wrong to infer from this that they were therefore indifferent to religious tradition. The London Reform congregation was more conservative in both theology and practice than Reform congregations in Germany and the United States, and the native Jewish middle class in general in the Victorian period was more observant than its counterparts elsewhere. In the Davis home, the children recited early morning prayers daily and faithfully attended synagogue on the sabbath. Julia and her young sister Eliza (1866–1931) were educated at the strictly Orthodox Belisario school. Miss Belisario, 'a Jewess of the most rigid kind', Eliza recalled, would enter the classroom during a thunderstorm and upbraid her charges for failing to pronounce the traditional Hebrew benediction on hearing thunder.[53]

[48] Quoted in Meyer, *Response to Modernity*, 96.   [49] G. Frankau, *Self-Portrait*, 24.
[50] Ibid.   [51] *Jewish Chronicle*, 24 Mar. 1916.
[52] *Hampstead and Highgate Express*, 20 June 1997.
[53] L. Hyman, *The Jews of Ireland*, 134–5; Aria, *My Sentimental Self*, 3–4, 9; 1871 census, RG10 11/45. The school, which attracted children from the Sephardi community in particular, was

Julia Davis received little formal education after leaving the Belisario school. For a while she was tutored at home by a Mr Gilmour and by Laura Lafargue, the daughter of Karl Marx, but this ended around the time of her father's death, when she was about 16.[54] Energetic, imaginative, and talented (she began writing stories as a child), she found the largely Jewish social milieu in which she was growing up narrow and conventional, but as a woman there were few avenues of escape available to her except marriage. However, through her elder brother James (1853–1907) she managed to glimpse an exciting world outside her own. James (Jimmy) Davis was a well-known man-about-town and popular figure in bohemian circles. Educated at University College, London, he practised as a solicitor from 1874 to 1886 and then turned full-time to journalism and the theatre. He owned and edited a number of society journals, including *Pan*, *The Bat*, *The Cuckoo*, and *The Phoenix*, and served as drama critic for *The Sporting Times*. Beginning in 1893, he became a successful librettist, writing some of the most popular West End musicals of the 1890s and 1900s. Although successful, he was unable to control his addiction to horse-racing, high living, and writing libellous portraits of statesmen and celebrities (he was successfully sued five times). He lost most of the money he earned from his writing in gambling at the race track and in buying and selling racehorses. He went bankrupt several times, and when he died left only £200. Some said that his pseudonym, 'Owen Hall', derived from his usual predicament of 'owing all'.[55]

Although James Davis married within the fold (his wife, Esther Andrade (1854–1946), was from a Sephardi family), as an adult he had no connection to Jewish institutions and moved largely in non-Jewish circles. Through him, Julia, then in her late teens and early twenties, was introduced to a broader social world. While James was still living at home he brought to the house literary and theatrical figures, including Oscar and Willie Wilde, who would play tennis in a nearby public garden with Julia and Eliza. After James married, the sisters were allowed to attend the remarkable parties he hosted at his house in Curzon Street, Mayfair. These evenings attracted an unconventional mix of persons—journalists, dramatists, novelists, actors, music-hall comics and singers, aristocrats, sportsmen, 'pretty ladies of high

kept by the four daughters of Abraham Belsario, a Jamaica merchant (M. Brown, 'The Jews of Hackney', 84). One of the sisters, Miriam Mendes Belisario (1820(?)–85), compiled a Hebrew and English vocabulary for the daily prayers and wrote *Sabbath Evenings at Home*, a collection of conversations on Judaism for children. (*Jewish Encyclopedia*, s.v. 'Belisario, Miriam Mendes').

[54] Aria, *My Sentimental Self*, 10–11.
[55] L. Hyman, *The Jews of Ireland*, 134–5; *Jewish Chronicle*, 12 Apr. 1907; Gänzl, *Encyclopedia of the Musical Theatre*, ii. 851–2; Aria, *My Sentimental Self*, 7, 15–20; Frazier, *George Moore*, 121, 492 n. 62.

and low degree' (Eliza's phrase), and assorted hangers-on. The novelist George Moore remembered them fondly for their champagne, late hours, evening clothes, passionate discussions of literature and art, and 'fabulous bohemianism'.[56]

In 1887, about two years after the Frankaus quit the Reform synagogue, Julia, using the pen name Frank Danby, published her first novel, *Dr. Phillips: A Maida Vale Idyll*, an unflattering portrait of the social milieu in which she had been raised.[57] The central figure in the novel, the charming Jewish physician Benjamin Phillips, 'the pet of Maida Vale drawing rooms', has built up an extensive, almost exclusively Jewish, practice. He is greedy and sensual. Repulsed by his unattractive, overweight, infertile, German-born wife, whom he married for her money, he finds an outlet for his sensuality in his slim, fair, beautiful, non-Jewish mistress, who bears him a child. He finds himself hopelessly in love with her but cannot continue to support two households in the wake of some ruinous investments. In order to marry his mistress and at the same time save himself from financial disaster, he murders his wife with an overdose of morphine as she is recovering from surgery for an ovarian tumour. His mistress, who has meanwhile grown to loathe him, rejects him for a young, athletic, handsome, Eton-educated man who is heir to his uncle's estate. When the Jews of Maida Vale learn of his extramarital affair, they too abandon Dr Phillips.

The Jews in the novel are repugnant. They are almost without exception uneducated, narrow, clannish, vulgar, materialistic, and tasteless. They live in large over-furnished houses filled with 'floating suggestions of a Bond Street showroom'—in marked contrast to the comfortable, tastefully arranged, Liberty-decorated rooms inhabited by Phillips's non-Jewish mistress. They gesticulate and talk at the top of their voices, especially in public places, dance ungracefully—'Judaea, when it dances, is an ungainly spectacle'— and, in the case of women, tend to obesity and prefer bright colours and blazing diamonds. They are ignorant of politics, literature, and art; indeed, they take no interest in the world beyond their families and friends, businesses and homes. They stick together, preferring their own company, and invite few non-Jews into their homes.[58]

The root cause of Maida Vale's degeneration, according to Frankau, is its inordinate love of money. In a passage reminiscent of Karl Marx's identification of Judaism with self-interest, huckstering, and money in *Zur Judenfrage* (1844), she writes:

[56] Aria, *My Sentimental Self*, 17–18; Moore, *Confessions of a Young Man*, 184–7; Rossmore, *Things I Can Tell*, 125–8.
[57] The novel was completed by summer 1886 (*Jewish Chronicle*, 30 June 1916).
[58] J. Frankau, *Dr. Phillips*, 5, 55, 82, 168.

The great single Deity, the 'I am the Lord thy God, and thou shalt have no other,' that binds Judaism together, is as invincible now as it was when Moses had to destroy the Golden Calf on Mount Horeb. And that Deity is Gain.

And that deity is never more ardently worshipped than at the card table.

The red light played on the money, on the cards, on the diamonds, on eager faces and grasping fingers. The play went on almost in silence; no light jest or merry quip, no sacrilegious sound of laughter disturbed the devotion of Judaism to its living God.[59]

Indeed, Frankau's Jews take little interest in amusements at which no money changes hands. At a tennis tournament at Eastbourne, a seaside vacation spot popular with London Jews, the men immediately begin placing bets with each other on the competitors in the final round; one of them even offers odds to bystanders who are otherwise strangers, provoking a few 'audible observations about Jews'.[60]

The Jewish religion, as distinct from the Jewish people, also fares poorly in *Dr. Phillips*. It is identified with Dr Phillips's heavy, foreign-born, unintelligent wife, whose kindling of sabbath candles prompts her husband to berate her for 'devoting your very limited intellect to keeping up all the exploded traditions invented by fools for fools'.[61] Phillips himself has 'drifted away from many of the forms that bound him to his race' and has discovered that he manages just as well without them.[62] This, in fact, seems to be true for most of Frankau's Jews. They do, however, worry about their children marrying outside the fold, a concern that is for Frankau the very essence of their narrow-minded tribalism. Thus, she mocks Mrs Collings, who 'would rather see one of her children dead than married to a Christian', and Mrs Detmar, who 'would not go quite so far as that, only she would, certainly, rather see hers married to the poorest Jew that ever walked, even to an absolute pauper'.[63] Those who oppose intermarriage are 'entirely unemancipated', that is, shut off from the world beyond 'their people', while those who break with the tribe attain new levels of understanding.[64] When young Florie Collings experiences romantic rapture in the company of her non-Jewish suitor, Alec Murphy, she is transformed. Her passion melts the accumulation of centuries of tribal loyalty and prejudice.[65] The suggestion here is that Jewish–Christian unions, by lifting Jews from their clannish isolation, can cure them of their defects.

As a novelist, Julia Frankau was much influenced by French naturalism, to which she was introduced by George Moore, a friend of her brother Jimmy

[59] J. Frankau, *Dr. Phillips*, 15. [60] Ibid. 148–9. [61] Ibid. 27.
[62] Ibid. 29. [63] Ibid. 165. [64] Ibid. 192. [65] Ibid. 112.

since the early 1880s.[66] Moore went so far as to claim that he had a hand in the writing of the book, that is, that he 'invented the story' and oversaw its writing. Whatever the case, he did arrange for its publication with his publisher, Henry Vizetelly.[67] The influence of French naturalism, as mediated by Moore, can be seen in her harsh delineation of character and frank treatment of sexual themes. No sentimental 'lady novelist', she believed that 'the realistic representation of life was the only desideratum of novel-writing, the only consideration that would make it worthwhile', as Malcolm Salaman wrote in a tribute at her death.[68] These convictions no doubt contributed to the unflattering way in which Jews are represented in *Dr Phillips*. (Frankau's non-Jewish characters are also morally, but not physically, unattractive: Phillips's mistress is a vicious schemer and a terrible mother while Alec Murphy is vapid and naive.) And, in all fairness, there is a kernel of truth in what she wrote. Maida Vale Jewry was *nouveau riche* in the literal sense of the term. Most middle-class Jews at this time were not well educated or inclined to take an interest in art, literature, politics, or science. Nor was Frankau alone in attributing to Anglo-Jewry an unhealthy devotion to card-playing. Among others, the Reverend Simeon Singer of the Bayswater Synagogue, hardly a self-hating Jew, thought the community was 'far too much addicted to card playing as the one unfailing resource to kill the demon of ennui'.[69]

And yet it is also clear that this is no measured ethnographic account of middle-class Anglo-Jewish life. Frankau's hostility to the milieu of her upbringing is ferocious, crude, and unrelenting. What seems to be driving her is a strong desire to escape identification with the common run of Jews by distancing herself from them. The Jews in *Dr. Phillips* embody all the negative qualities that contemporaries associated with Jews and that Frankau feared could be attributed to her by virtue of her background. By assigning these flaws and failings to other Jews, she was both reassuring herself and announcing to the world at large that she was different, that she had escaped the tribal compound. Indeed, she made it quite clear in *Dr. Phillips* that exceptional Jews could transcend the narrowness of their origins if they exerted themselves: 'Sections [of middle-class Jewry] are trying very hard to struggle against this race-barrier, and with a modicum of success. But they have much to contend against.'[70]

Julia Frankau's novel was a milestone in representations of Jewishness in Britain. With the notable exception of Benjamin Disraeli, English Jews were

[66] Cheyette, 'The Other Self', 103. Moore was a major proponent of French naturalism in England in the 1880s.   [67] Frazier, *George Moore*, 142–3, 504 n. 131.
[68] *Jewish Chronicle*, 24 Mar. 1916.   [69] Singer, *Literary Remains*, i. 107.
[70] J. Frankau, *Dr. Phillips*, 61.

not in the habit of airing their feelings about being Jewish in public. If they experienced ambivalence, they did so in private, without giving literary expression to their struggle to resolve it. Becoming English, it seems, was a more private affair than becoming German, and probably a less fraught, tension-filled task as well. It is difficult to locate English Jews in the first half of the nineteenth century who struggled with or expressed alienation from their Jewishness in the public way that Rahel Varnhagen (1771–1833), Heinrich Heine (1797–1856), Ludwig Börne (1786–1837), and Karl Marx (1818–83) did. As I argued in Chapter 6, English Jews were less prone to self-loathing than their German counterparts. The only significant literary expression of Jewish self-hatred before the 1880s with which I am familiar is Samuel Phillips's *Caleb Stukeley* (1841), in which dirt-encrusted, dark-complexioned, grasping Jewish tradesmen play minor roles. Phillips (1814–54), the son of a London Jewish tradesman, joined the Church of England while a young man and after a chequered career eventually became a literary critic for *The Times*.[71] He was unusual, however: few converts in England were moved to express hostility to their former co-religionists in order to demonstrate their Christian bona fides. In any case, it failed to obscure his Jewish origins. His critical reviews of several works of William Makepeace Thackeray in the 1850s, for example, led the novelist to harp on the converted critic's origins in correspondence with friends.[72]

Dr. Phillips was the first of several novels by Jewish (and half-Jewish) authors in the late Victorian period that incorporated negative representations of Jews and Judaism.[73] It was followed by Amy Levy's *Reuben Sachs* (1888), Cecily Ullmann Sidgwick's *Isaac Eller's Money* (1889) and *Lesser's Daughter* (1894), and Leonard Merrick's *Violet Moses* (1891). This body of work registers the shift that occurred in the attitude towards Jews in the last decades of the century, when antisemitism was more overt and focused. The arrival of tens of thousands of east European immigrants and the penetration of Jewish financiers and Randlords (businessmen who dominated the South African diamond- and gold-mining industries in their pioneering phase) into high society, especially the Prince of Wales's circle, along with the spread of racial thinking and the crisis of liberalism, combined to focus public attention on Jews to an unprecedented degree. Jews like Julia Frankau, Amy Levy, and Leonard Merrick, eager to distance themselves from the community of their birth, were sensitive to this shift. One response was

---

[71] Endelman, *Radical Assimilation in English Jewish History*, 103.

[72] Prawer, *Israel at Vanity Fair*, 342–3.

[73] Cheyette, 'From Apology to Revolt'; Beckman, *Amy Levy*; Valman, *The Jewess in Nineteenth-Century British Literary Culture*, ch. 6.

to assert their difference from ordinary Jews—in the case of these novelists, by offering for public consumption critical views of the group to which they were linked by birth.

The publication of *Dr. Phillips* brought Julia Frankau notoriety rather than fame. The reviews were mostly hostile. The *Athenaeum*, for example, deplored the 'unsavory topics', 'repulsive personages', and 'dreary crudities of Mr. Danby's pages' and detected in the author's animus towards Jews 'a personal grievance' rather than 'a conscientious effort after impartiality'.[74] *Punch* dismissed her work summarily: 'It should never have been written. Having been written, it should never have been published. Having been published, it should not be read.'[75] Within the Jewish community it created a storm. According to Frankau's sister, Eliza Aria, its publication 'fluttered the dovecotes of Maida Vale' and 'rattled the skeletons in the cupboards and the stout ladies at the card-tables'.[76] To many Jews Frankau was a traitor and turncoat, feeding the fires of Jew-hatred with her lurid descriptions of Jewish clannishness, materialism, and lust. When several London dailies 'swallowed' her portraits as 'true representations of Jewish life', and a decade later the anti-alien publicist Arnold White thrice cited *Dr. Phillips* as evidence of the 'aloofness of Israel' in his strident tract *The Modern Jew*, their worst fears came true.[77]

The scandal of *Dr. Phillips* was compounded by publication the following year of Amy Levy's *Reuben Sachs*. Levy was almost as harsh as Frankau in her delineation of Jewish manners and morals, and the two works became linked in public discussion, the notoriety of each reinforcing that of the other. In his column in the *Jewish Standard*, Israel Zangwill, himself a communal gadfly, denounced Frankau and Levy in tandem for their propensity to view the community in either black or white terms. In his view, they had been 'goaded into undiscriminating hostility by the cramping materialism around them' and had 'painted Jews as if they were as destitute of any redeeming quality as a two-year-old pawnticket'.[78] The outcry was such that Frankau felt compelled to deny she hated Jews in a preface to a second edition that appeared the same year. She claimed that the book was not 'an attack upon a body of people whom I both respect and esteem'. Rather, it was

---

[74] *Athenaeum*, 19 Mar. 1887, 376.

[75] Quoted in G. Frankau, *Self-Portrait*, 23. [76] Aria, *My Sentimental Self*, 22.

[77] *Jewish Standard*, 8 Mar. 1889; White, *The Modern Jew*, 60, 165, 168. Three years after the novel's publication, *Jewish Society* (14 Feb. 1890) noted that the initial fuss had 'quite died out' but that 'everyone' had 'a surreptitious, much-thumbed copy, which they read and abuse at intervals'.

[78] *Jewish Standard*, 1 Mar. 1889. For more on Zangwill's response to Frankau and Levy, see Rochelson, *A Jew in the Public Arena*, 59–61, 66.

'a picture of a small and little known section of society before it yields to the influences of advanced civilization and education'.[79]

Adding to the sensation the novel created were rumours that Frankau had based the character of Dr Phillips on Ernest Abraham Hart (1837–98), an eminent physician, medical journalist, and public health campaigner. In her memoirs Eliza Aria denied that the novel ever 'merited the popular suspicion that the hero was taken from life', although she conceded in another context that her sister Julia preferred living models for her characters and 'took them unconscionably'.[80] Julia's son Gilbert, on the other hand, often stated that his mother had used Hart as a model and claimed that she had known him intimately.[81] Her close friend Marie Belloc Lowndes also thought that Phillips was based on a well-known doctor and that he 'must have felt the cap fitted his head, for he bought up and destroyed every copy he was able to procure'—which would explain the scarcity of copies today.[82] Furthermore, when the manuscript first came to Vizetelly, it bore the title *Dr. Abrams*, which he insisted be changed since it was too close to Hart's middle name. When the fictional physician and his alleged inspiration are compared, the similarities are striking. Both took scores of prizes as students, served as editors of medical journals, won fame as diagnosticians, and loved luxurious surroundings. More significantly, Hart's first wife, Rosetta Levy, died suspiciously in 1861 from accidental poisoning, and rumours circulated in medical circles for years afterwards that Hart had murdered her. His second wife, like the fictional physician's mistress, was a Christian. Still, Frank Vizetelly, son of Julia Frankau's publisher, claimed that she had never met Hart and knew nothing about the circumstances of his wife's death.[83] In the end, whether true or not, the rumours enhanced the novel's notoriety.

The unpleasantness created by *Dr. Phillips* convinced Frankau to abandon, at least for the time, Jewish themes. She continued to write—reviews, novels, and three studies of eighteenth-century engravings (which she collected)—but she did not produce another 'Jewish' novel until 1903, when *Pigs in Clover* appeared. A response in part to the 'rich-Jew' antisemitism ignited by the Boer War (1899–1902), this novel offered more differentiated constructions of the Jew. The central figure, Karl Althaus, son of a Wardour Street bric-a-brac dealer, has made his fortune in South African diamond mines. Although willing to use dishonest methods in making his millions, he is at heart a generous if uncultured fellow who learns in the course of the

---

[79] J. Frankau, *Dr. Phillips*, 2nd edn., 3.   [80] Aria, *My Sentimental Self*, 22, 56.
[81] *Jewish Chronicle*, 30 June 1916.   [82] Lowndes, *The Merry Wives of Westminster*, 57.
[83] For Hart, see the obituaries in the *Jewish Chronicle* (14 Jan. 1898) and *The Lancet* (15 Jan. 1898); Lock, Introduction to J. Frankau, *Dr. Phillips*; Bartrip, *Mirror of Medicine*, 63–7, 76–80; genealogical material, Sir Thomas Colyer-Fergusson Collection.

novel that promoting British imperial interests is nobler than making money. As an English woman with whom he is in love realizes, 'there pulsed beneath these sordid, grasping, greedy Jews . . . a wealth and warmth of goodness, generosity, of which the colder, slower, Northern men were scarcely capable'.[84] Frankau indicates that Karl is not a practising Jew. Indeed, he repudiates Judaism, viewing it less as a religion than, in words reflecting his creator's outlook, 'a thing of forms and goods, a race habit', 'a tradition, an obstinacy', 'an empty thing of ceremonies'.[85] He wishes he could believe in Christianity and dreams of bringing the story of Jesus to London's immigrant Jews so they can attain the belief for which he longs. To achieve this end, he considers establishing a theatre in Houndsditch to stage passion and miracle plays, as in Oberammergau. Though this scheme brings him 'much *undeserved obloquy*', the author adds that there is in his idea 'a germ that may some day bear fruit'.[86] This seems like a conversionist blueprint or fantasy for the radical assimilation of the English Jewish masses.

In *Pigs in Clover*—in contrast to *Dr. Phillips*—there are both 'good' and 'bad' Jews, the latter represented by Karl's charming, well-mannered half-brother, Louis. Unlike Karl, who wishes to serve both British imperialism and Christianity, Louis resists redemption to the end. Unscrupulous and manipulative, completely without morals, he bears responsibility for the suicide of Karl's Christian wife, the most sympathetic character in the novel. In words echoing accepted communal wisdom, a well-born MP and victim of Louis notes: 'It is the misfortune of the Jews that one of their community cannot misbehave without earning opprobrium for their whole body.'[87] If so, are 'good' Jews to be blamed for separating themselves from their 'bad' brethren, especially as their religion is dead?

Julia and Gilbert Frankau came from the Anglo-Jewish bourgeoisie but were not content to remain within its borders. Julia was an energetic hostess, particularly after the death of her husband in 1904. Her guests were drawn from the largely non-Jewish worlds of journalism, publishing, literature, theatre, and the arts. Her friends included the novelists George Moore and Ada Leverson, the editor Frank Harris, the actor Henry Irving (her sister Eliza's lover for many years), the publisher Sidney Pawling, the humorist Max Beerbohm, the essayist and journalist A. B. Walkley, Marie Belloc Lowndes, and the dramatist and critic Malcolm Salaman, one of the few Jews in her circle, aside from her siblings. Her work on eighteenth-century engravings brought her into contact with well-born and often titled collec-

---

[84] J. Frankau, *Pigs in Clover*, 114.   [85] Ibid. 95–6.
[86] Ibid. 343–4 (my emphasis).   [87] Ibid. 278.

tors, and in the preface to her study of the engraver John Raphael Smith she emphasized that her chosen field of collecting put her in an elite group of cultivated persons. Her subject, she wrote, appealed only to a small 'cultured, perceptive public'.[88] In central Europe Jews who moved in these worlds could not escape the company of other Jews, but in Britain Jews were much less prominent in artistic, literary, and intellectual life, whether as creators, patrons, or interpreters. Thus, even if she had not been in flight from her Jewishness, she would have found herself in overwhelmingly non-Jewish precincts, simply by virtue of her cultural interests.

In conversation, as in her fiction, Julia Frankau distanced herself and her husband from their origins. She boasted to Marie Belloc Lowndes that her husband's fine qualities were due to the German Lutheran stock from which he came and the absence of any Jewish blood (Lowndes was convinced that she was being absolutely truthful). She also enjoyed gossiping to Lowndes about 'unpleasing traits' in the characters of well-known Jews of the day, as if to demonstrate by her willingness to betray the flaws of the Jews that she was not really one of them.[89] In politics as well, she detached herself from the mass of Jews. While most middle-class Jews at this time, including her husband, supported the Liberal Party, she was a strident Conservative and an ardent imperialist. During the coal miners' strike of 1912, she told Arnold Bennett: 'Of course, I'm feudal. I'd batten them down. I'd make them work. They *should* work. I'd force them down.'[90]

Julia's sister Eliza also became a writer—but in her case out of need. At the age of 18, in the wake of Julia's marriage and departure from home, she rushed into an ill-fated marriage with David Bonito Aria (1860(?)–1913), handsome, charming, and slender alike in waist, intellect, and integrity, as she later wrote. They were married in the Reform synagogue in March 1884, he having become a member one month earlier. From the start the marriage was a disaster. Aria was a poor businessman and an inveterate racetrack gambler like his brother-in-law. When he lost, he pawned their wedding gifts and her jewellery and borrowed money from her family. Their love for each other cooled, and after five years they separated, her family paying his way to South Africa and taking care of his creditors.[91] With a young daughter to support, Eliza responded positively to a suggestion from a family friend in the newspaper business that she try writing. She started with weekly con-

[88] J. Frankau, *An Eighteenth-Century Artist & Engraver*, p. v.
[89] Lowndes, *The Merry Wives of Westminster*, 58–60.   [90] Bennett, *Journals*, ii. 45.
[91] Aria, *My Sentimental Self*, 27–30; ead., *Woman and the Motor Car*, 18–22; register of marriages, 1842–89, entry no. 261, 26 Mar. 1884; members accounts A–J, Oct. 1880–Aug. 1891, West London Synagogue of British Jews. Some details in the account of her marriage in *Woman and the Motor Car* are fictionalized.

tributions on fashion and shopping to *Jewish Society*, a short-lived icono-
clastic rival to the *Jewish Chronicle*.[92] After its demise in November 1890, her
fashion articles began appearing in *The Gentlewoman*, a journal for which
Julia was already writing. She then went on to edit the fashion pages of
Hearth and Home. Finally, with financial backing from Harry H. Marks
(1855–1916), proprietor of the *Financial News* and son of the Reform minister
D. W. Marks, she launched her own fashion monthly, *The World of Dress*,
which featured fashion news from Paris, Vienna, and New York and inter-
views about dress with famous people. She also contributed a gossip column
('Mrs. A.'s Diary') for many years to Henry Labouchere's bi-weekly *Truth*,
which was known for its exposés of frauds, including Jewish moneylending
schemes, and worked freelance for half a dozen newspapers.[93]

Described by the *Jewish Chronicle* in 1900 as 'perhaps the most successful
lady journalist of the day', Eliza Aria was a 'personality' (her term) on the
London social scene. Her 'great capacity for friendship . . . coupled with her
social gifts both as guest and hostess, made her welcome in any circles she
cared to penetrate'.[94] For more than thirty years, she presided over a salon
where the worlds of literature, art, and theatre mixed. Her regular guests
included the dramatists Alfred Sutro, Cecil Raleigh, and John Van Druten,
the actors Henry Irving, Herbert Beerbohm Tree, and Sybil Thorndyke, the
poet and critic Humbert Wolfe, and the novelists Harold Begbie, Michael
Arlen, G. B. Stern, Ford Madox Ford, and H. G. Wells. Her obituary in *Truth*
noted that 'she knew most of the leading writers, actors, and actresses of the
last four decades'. She never remarried but eventually succeeded Ellen Terry
as Henry Irving's mistress, remaining with him until his death.[95]

Like her sister, Eliza Aria removed herself from the Maida Vale milieu of
Dr. Phillips, but unlike her she was not driven to distance herself from that

---

[92] It was rumoured at the time that Julia Frankau was connected with *Jewish Society*, even
that she was its nominal editor or proprietor. Hermann Adler told contemporaries that he
believed that she was a front for an unknown person or persons who were opposed to his election as chief rabbi. (See the correspondence columns in the *Jewish Chronicle*, 8, 15, and 22 Dec.
1916). It was even claimed that the paper ceased publication once Adler was elected (in May
1890), although, in fact, it continued to appear for another six months (forty-four issues were
published between 31 Jan. and 26 Nov. 1890). Cecil Roth repeated this rumour, as fact, in the
Jewish Chronicle, 1841–1941, 161. In light of the views she expressed in *Dr. Phillips* and her own
lack of involvement in communal affairs, I find it difficult to believe she would have become
associated with a Jewish periodical, however critical of the communal establishment it was.
Still, there may have been some basis to the rumour.

[93] Aria, *My Sentimental Self*, 32, 33, 35, 37.   [94] *Jewish Chronicle*, 27 Apr. 1900.

[95] Aria, *My Sentimental Self*, 7; Lowndes, *Diaries and Letters*, 25–6; York, Introduction to P.
Frankau, *The Willow Cabin*, p. v; G. Frankau, *Self-Portrait*, 187, 400; interview, Diana Raymond,
1 Sept. 1989, Hampstead. The obituary from *Truth* was reprinted in the *Jewish Chronicle*, 18
Sept. 1931.

world in her writing or in other public forums. In her memoirs, for example, which appeared in 1922, she recounted her Jewish upbringing straightforwardly, expressing neither mockery nor contempt. She continued to identify herself as a Jew throughout her life and became a member of the Liberal (radical Reform) synagogue established in 1911, in whose cemetery she was buried. Her only child, Nita (d. 1923), however, married a non-Jewish imperial officer who served in Burma for many years, and had no connection to Anglo-Jewry.[96]

4

Julia and Arthur Frankau had four children. One son, Paul Ewart (1890–1917), known as Jack, was an unsuccessful farmer in Rhodesia and died in Allenby's attack on Gaza during the First World War—and thus, ironically, was buried in the Land of Israel. The other three, it seems, inherited the drive of their Jewish forebears and achieved prominence in their chosen fields—in entertainment, academia, and literature. Ronald (1894–1951), who was sent to Eton and then studied for a short time at the Guildhall School of Music, became a comedian and singer performing in night clubs, hotel lounges, and musical revues, and then, beginning in the late 1920s, on radio, and from 1931 in films. A master of the double entendre, he was known for his risqué songs and skits delivered in an upper-class, Eton-educated accent. According to his son Simon Frankau, Ronald, who *was* circumcised, was in no way troubled by his Jewish background, of which he spoke positively with his children. Even though married to a Christian, he did not have Simon baptized, believing that he should make the decision for himself when he was old enough to know what he wanted. Aline (1896–1986), known as Joan, was educated at Wycombe Abbey, in Hamburg and Paris, and then at Girton College, Cambridge, where she obtained a first in English. In 1920 she married Stanley Bennett, a fellow of Emmanuel College, and herself became a fellow of Girton and a lecturer in English. In a period in which few women were prominent in the academy, she won acclaim for her work on the metaphysical poets, George Eliot, and Virginia Woolf. A student at Cambridge in the 1940s recalled that for Bennett Jewishness was 'not even a memory, but simply a genealogical fact, a documentation that she had been born of Jewish parents'. She made no effort to hide her antecedents; in fact, she took some pride in them, but she was totally ignorant of all things Jewish, having been raised outside Jewish society.[97]

[96] *Jewish Chronicle*, 18 Sept. 1931; *Observer*, 11 Feb. 1923.
[97] *The Times*, 12 Sept. 1951; Bradbrook, 'Queenie Leavis', 56–7; Aryeh Newman, 'Jewish Identity', 176; Simon R. Frankau to Aryeh Newman, 10 June 1996; Simon R. Frankau to Todd M. Endelman, 23 Sept. 1996, both in possession of author.

For Gilbert, the firstborn, however, awareness of his Jewish background was a source of discomfort for much of his life. He was educated at Eton, like Ronald, where he would have been exposed to a certain amount of abuse because of his Jewishness, but he was silent on this score in his memoirs. Despite a strong record at school, he left in 1901, before reaching the sixth form. He entered the family cigar business, then flourishing but soon to suffer a serious reversal when it ceased to be the exclusive agent for Upmann cigars in Great Britain. The loss of sole agency was a great blow, which according to Gilbert hastened his father's death in 1904. Since the only surviving partner, Gilbert's uncle Joseph Grünbaum, was then almost 70, Julia bought him out and a new company was formed, with Gilbert, just 21, as managing director.[98] Gilbert worked hard and sales remained solid, but he lacked his father's commercial judgement. He made an incautious investment in a cigarette-manufacturing firm in Brixton and lavished money unnecessarily on refurbishing the Frankau warehouse and office in Gracechurch Street. In the end the profits earned from selling cigars were not sufficient to cover the losses sustained from manufacturing cigarettes. Following Julia's death in 1916, both the cigarette factory and the family cigar business were sold.

While not successful in business, Gilbert Frankau was a commercial success as a novelist and journalist, selling over 2 million copies of his novels during his lifetime.[99] He began writing before the war, but after the sale of the firm and his discharge from the army he turned to writing full-time, winning almost immediate recognition. His second novel, *Peter Jackson, Cigar Merchant* (1919), sold over 100,000 copies. In 1926 the critic Patrick Bray-brooke described him as 'one of the most widely read novelists of the present day', attributing his appeal to his perfect knowledge of 'what the ordinary man and woman want to read'.[100] In 1932 Q. D. Leavis bracketed him with Rudyard Kipling and Arnold Bennett as three of the most successful, best-selling novelists of the time. In her view, of course, this was not praise, since

[98] The fortunes of J. Frankau & Co. and Gilbert's conduct of the firm are thinly fictionalized in his first two novels, *The Woman of the Horizon* (1917) and *Peter Jackson, Cigar Merchant* (1919). The initials of the protagonist in the former novel, Francis Gordon, when reversed, are those of Gilbert Frankau. Details on the demise of the firm can be found in Gilbert's memoir, *Self-Portrait*. Grünbaum's two sons were not interested in business and became distinguished physicians. Albert Sidney (b. 1869), a pathologist, died before the First World War. Otto Fritz (1875–1936), an authority on diabetes (the disease that killed his aunt Julia), married a Christian, changed his name from Grünbaum to Leyton in 1915, and was buried as an Anglican (*The Times*, 24 Jan. 1938). Their sister, Ida Florence (b. 1879), who changed her name to Greenwood, spent two years at Newnham College, Cambridge, and then taught at Notting Hill High School (*Newnham College Register*, i. 166).

[99] H. Cecil, *The Flower of Battle*, 208.   [100] Braybrooke, *Novelists*, 60, 72.

she thought that popular novelists like Frankau threatened cultural standards by pandering to herd prejudice and debasing 'emotional currency by
touching grossly on fine issues'.[101] But this kind of criticism failed to dis-
comfit Frankau, who was contemptuous of what he called 'highbrow' intellectuals and saw himself, in the words of his daughter Pamela (1908–67), as
'a paid entertainer, who must never for a minute lose sight of his public'.
Unlike her 'highbrow' friends, he did not regard himself as 'a hothouse-
blooming genius'.[102] For him, writing was a commercial venture, like selling
cigars, at which he toiled in a methodical, disciplined way. *Punch*'s judgement that he was 'perhaps as good a storyteller as we have in England at the
moment' was high praise in his eyes.[103]

Frankau's fiction reveals how his Jewishness continued to haunt him.
Like Disraeli, he was unable to set aside his biological background, that is,
his awareness that he was a descendant of Jews, and to merge effortlessly
into Christian society. In the novels he wrote in the late 1910s and 1920s,
he introduced minor Jewish characters, with exaggerated and often crude
stereotypical features, whose presence, as Jews, was incidental or irrelevant
to the stories he was telling. In his first novel, *The Woman of the Horizon*
(1917), the cigar merchant Peter Jackson, who is calling on potential cus-
tomers abroad, meets a young English Jew working as a shop assistant in
Port Said, whom Frankau describes as 'lacking in personal reticence as any
other of his race'.[104] The Jewish cigarette manufacturer Marcus Bramson in
his best-selling *Peter Jackson* is stout, voluble, wheedling, and gesticulating,
wears shabby, greasy clothes, and, although worth a quarter of a million
pounds, spends nothing and is content to live 'in an eighty-pound villa at
Maida Vale'. His cousin Sam 'Pretty' Bramson, who panics at the outbreak of
war, fearing conscription, and is later discharged from the army for health
reasons, is associated with cowardice and effeminacy.[105] Roddy Marks, a
swarthy, olive-skinned, dark-haired entertainment mogul in *Life—and Erica*
(1925), is linked to sexual danger and corruption. The innocent Erica is hor-
rified and nauseated when she discovers her old school chum Doffy has
become Roddy's mistress. She admits that his face is handsome and that
most women find this kind of face attractive. Yet, for her, it is 'a trifle too
swarthy, perhaps; a trifle too eager-eyed, too red-lipped, too—she hesitated
over the description—oriental'.[106]

Frankau's recourse to stereotypical language like this may have been a
half-conscious strategy to emphasize his own Englishness and at the same

---

[101] Leavis, *Fiction and the Reading Public*, 67, 197–8.   [102] P. Frankau, *Pen to Paper*, 185–8.
[103] *Punch*, 17 Jan. 1940, 82.   [104] G. Frankau, *The Woman of the Horizon*, 23.
[105] G. Frankau, *Peter Jackson*, 103–6.   [106] G. Frankau, *Life—and Erica*, 87.

time to demonstrate his independence from Jews. Alternatively it may have been a consequence of his immersion in English circles in which such representations were commonplace and deployed unthinkingly. Whatever the case, he continued to use crude stereotypes throughout his writing career. In addition, he incorporated elements of racial thinking into his fiction, insisting, contrary to what one might expect, on the persistence of Jewish racial traits in the descendants of former Jews. For example, he described the cousins Peter Jackson and Francis Gordon in his first novel as almost like brothers in appearance. 'In each, a trace of the same Hebrew strain—legacy of a mutual grandmother on the distaff side—was apparent.'[107] More than physical appearance is at stake, however. Jewish blood, no matter how diluted, continues to influence behaviour generation after generation in Frankau's fiction. In Hong Kong, Francis is about to offer financial help to an expensive whore with whom he has fallen in love, but then decides otherwise. 'His own money sense—despised legacy of the Hebrew strain which had saved him so many of the youth-follies of his kind—woke to rare consciousness in his brain.'[108] Later, when he learns that the family firm is failing and that he will have to live more modestly, he wonders how he will manage. 'The blood of his Hebrew grandparent' asks, 'Could one get five per cent with safety?'[109] Similarly, at the end of *Peter Jackson*, when the eponymous hero, who has been wounded in battle and is unfit to resume military duty, must decide what to do with his life—the family cigar firm has been sold—'the Jew in him' urges him to exploit the commercial possibilities of the country property he has acquired.[110]

It is curious that Frankau gave credence to racial notions that challenged the efficacy of social and cultural self-transformation. One would have thought that a convert from a background such as his would have taken the opposite view, arguing that the leopard could indeed change its spots. One explanation is that racial thinking was a ubiquitous part of the mental landscape of the period and few writers, including Jews, were spared its influence. While true, there is more to Frankau's 'racism' than this. In his case, his repeated insistence on the indestructibility of racial traits and their power to assert themselves even in the most deracinated representatives of Jewry reads like an autobiographical confession, a statement of his own psychological inability to set aside his Jewish past. Unlike his sister Joan, to whom Jewishness was 'a genealogical fact' and nothing more, his Jewish antecedents were a burden, a source of discomfort and unease. Racial thinking helped him to understand his powerlessness to be free of his Jewish past.

---

[107] G. Frankau, *The Woman of the Horizon*, 9,
[108] Ibid. 119.   [109] Ibid. 227.   [110] G. Frankau, *Peter Jackson*, 380.

From the mid-1920s on, Frankau used a further strategy to protect himself from being associated with so-called Jewish traits. In his fiction he began to distinguish between 'good' and 'bad' Jews, a strategy I described earlier in Chapter 6 and one that his mother had employed two decades earlier in *Pigs in Clover*. In *Masterton* (1925), a political novel inspired in part by Italian fascism, one of the central characters, Adrian Rose, is a model of the right kind of Jew. He is an Eton-educated successful playwright, a decorated war hero who would have been awarded the Victoria Cross if he had not been a Jew. Physically, he is 'a forceful rock of a man', with 'only slightly Hebraic nostrils' and 'an even less Hebraic mouth', who looks 'more like an old-time prize-fighter than a modern playwright'.[111] What makes Rose a 'good' Jew is his politics. Like Masterton, he is a right-wing patriot—anti-union, anti-communist, anti-socialist, pro-imperial. He is convinced that the Labour Party has been captured by 'a heterogeneous mass of arid intellectuals, sterile agitators, sentimental old women, disgruntled office-holders, renegade Irishmen, renegade Jews and renegade Parsees', 'backed, bolstered and Bolshevized by the infamous I.L.P. [Independent Labour Party]'.[112] To save Britain and the empire, Rose founds and directs the right-wing Fellowship of Loyal Citizens. 'Bad' Jews, of course, are left-wing Jews, which, in interwar Britain, meant a great many Jews of east European background—as well as Gilbert's brother Ronald, who was a communist. Rose explains to Masterton that 'these Bolshevik Jews are the dregs of my race' and that they are 'just as much anti-Gentile as the dregs of yours are anti-Semite'.[113] Given the prominence of the Bolshevik theme in the political antisemitism in the 1920s,[114] Frankau's willingness to exploit the association indicates how divorced he was from the mass of Jews, as well as how desperate he was to distinguish between patriotic and disloyal Jews. And yet at the same time he also re-affirmed the racial character of Jews, even 'good' Jews like Rose and presumably himself. Masterton, who admires Rose and considers him an intimate friend, cannot forget that he is a Jew, 'a creature altogether unlike himself', although he reprimands himself for thinking this way—'damned unfair of me, of course'.[115] Still, Frankau concludes, between Masterton and Rose 'there yawned that deep gulf which separates, and will always separate, the soul of the Christian from the soul of the Jew'.[116]

In the 1930s, Nazism in Germany, violence in Palestine, and Blackshirt campaigns in the East End focused unprecedented attention on Jews. As E. M. Forster noted at the end of the decade, 'Jew-consciousness' was in the

---

[111] G. Frankau, *Masterton*, 85.   [112] Ibid. 201.   [113] Ibid. 202.
[114] Kadish, *Bolsheviks and British Jews*, ch. 1.   [115] G. Frankau, *Masterton*, 99.
[116] Ibid. 102.

air.[117] It was increasingly difficult for public figures with Jewish 'blood' to ignore their origins. Some who had been indifferent to Jewish matters in the past were now roused to embrace Zionism, campaign against antisemitism, or aid refugees. But Gilbert Frankau experienced no such transformation. He kept his distance and continued to draw invidious comparisons between acceptable and unacceptable Jews. The most notorious instance was an article he wrote for the *Daily Express* in May 1933 with the provocative title 'As a Jew I Am Not against Hitler'. In it he argued that the outcry in Britain against Hitler was overdone and that his attempts to rid Germany of Jews who were not 'good' Germans were justified. Writing as an Englishman 'of Jewish blood, though not of the Jewish faith', he maintained that there was 'a substratum of truth' to the Nazi charge that Jews were not Germans. 'Many German Jews are entirely out of sympathy with the aspirations of the Nordic tribes among whom they have made their homes.' As evidence, he cited the communist movement, which was largely fomented by Jews in his view. Such Jews imperilled every country they inhabited, and Hitler was certainly justified in kicking them out. Fortunately, he added, British Jews were patriotic, proud of their country, loyal to its flag, and free of the 'ghetto-spirit' still found in their co-religionists in Germany.[118]

In two works of fiction from this period, Frankau also addressed the absorption of Jews into English society. In both, the central Jewish male figures are strikingly 'un-Jewish', which is undoubtedly how Frankau himself wished to be seen. Harold Ingram in the short story 'An Outlier from his Tribe' (1927) is 'even less of a Jew than the name implies'. He is over six feet tall and his hair, 'though there's a trace of curl in it, is very nearly Viking-colour'. His eyes are also 'Viking-colour'—'blue, with the far-away-sea-look'. His nose, a critical marker, 'except for a queer dilation about the nostrils, is almost pure Greek'. Having done 'three pretty good years at the Front', he still 'carries himself like a soldier'.[119] David Lewis, the protagonist of the novel *Farewell Romance* (1936), moves like an athlete; his black but straight hair, prominent nose, and vocal inflections do not betray his 'racial origins'.[120]

In social and religious terms, Ingram and Lewis have broken their Jewish ties. Most of Harold Ingram's friends are non-Jews, and 'like most people nowadays' he is an agnostic. Thus, 'one wouldn't go far wrong in describing him as an outlier from the main tribe'. And like all outliers, 'his bias . . . was primarily against rather than for his own tribe', although Frankau hastens to

---

[117] Forster, *Two Cheers for Democracy*, 25.
[118] *Daily Express*, 9 May 1933.
[119] G. Frankau, 'An Outlier from his Tribe', 121.
[120] G. Frankau, *Farewell Romance*, 8.

add that he was not 'one of your Jew-hating Jews'.[121] Yet when he finds himself in a pub that is *'the* Mecca of [his] tribe at Christmas time', surrounded by Jews 'just a bit more flamboyant about their clothes, just a little less restrained of voice, than the other people', radiating their own particular 'clan atmosphere', he resents their presence. ' "These aren't *my* people," his eyes seem to say. "These are the people I've broken loose from. And I'm glad I broke loose from them. They're not my kind." '[122] David Lewis, a successful wholesale draper, has severed his communal ties as well. His wife and close friends are not Jewish and, like his father, he is a scoffer, for whom religion is 'just superstition, bred by fear out of ignorance'.[123] When asked to contribute to a fund for German Jewish refugees, he wonders about his relationship to them—'were those people his?' 'The question puzzled, irritated, confused him. Admittedly he was sorry for these "poor wretches" . . . But could he feel any kinship with them? "Definitely, no," he decides, "because I neither worship their god nor speak their language." '[124]

Nonetheless, despite their distance from other Jews, both Ingram and Lewis are unable to completely sever their ties to 'the clan-folk'. For Jewishness, Frankau explains in 'An Outlier from his Tribe', is reducible to neither blood nor religion, rather 'it's a mental attitude; a soul-tie, a bond of psychological and atavistic kinship'. It is inescapable and in the end resistant to even the most strenuous efforts to banish it. Ingram, 'for all his outlying habits', is 'very nearly as much of the tribe as your latest immigrants into Whitechapel or Jaffa'.[125] Engaged to marry the well-bred granddaughter of the former owner of what is now his country home, Ingram rejects her at the last moment for the strawberry-blonde, 'un-Hebraic looking' Doris Mendelson. When push comes to shove, he is unable to resist 'the tribal deities'.[126] Similarly, David Lewis finds himself drawn, almost against his will, into rescue work on behalf of German Jews. Although he continues to protest that he is an Englishman first and a Jew second, he increasingly reacts to events, personal and political, in 'Jewish' ways. When his wife dies, his emotional self-control—in Frankau's mental economy, a marker of authentic Englishness—dissolves and he weeps unashamedly. Later he wonders: 'Queer, how he had given way like that. So Jewish of him. Well, why not? He had never been ashamed of being a Jew.'[127] But there are limits to his reclaimed Jewishness. While supportive of Palestine as a refuge from persecution, he balks at becoming a Zionist. 'Too emotional. Too fanatical.' Fearful of being seen as

[121] G. Frankau, 'An Outlier from his Tribe', 121–2.   [122] Ibid. 134–5.
[123] G. Frankau, *Farewell Romance*, 222.   [124] Ibid. 302.
[125] G. Frankau, 'An Outlier from his Tribe', 122.   [126] Ibid. 135–7.
[127] G. Frankau, *Farewell Romance*, 476.

too much the Jewish partisan, he attributes the economic development of Palestine to British rather than Jewish efforts and, in a final attempt to distance himself from full identification with Jews, declares that 'we' English must see that 'fair play' is done to both sides, Jews and Arabs, in Palestine.[128]

These emotionally reserved, faultlessly groomed, 'un-Hebraic-looking', strong Jewish men mirror the persona that Frankau presented to the real world. 'Well into his middle age, assisted by Savile Row tailoring, he kept his Edwardian matinee-idol looks.' His 'dark, curly hair' was 'impeccably barbered'. He wore handmade shoes from Peel's, 'platinum and gold glinted in his flawless cuffs', and in his wardrobe were forty white ties so that in the course of a long evening he would never be seen without a clean one. 'His demeanour was suave and controlled'; he wanted to be seen as 'a sophisticated, insouciant man-about-town, fashionable writer, and *homme d'affaires*'.[129] His work habits were bourgeois, but he lived beyond his means and was in constant debt, despite the large sums he earned from his writing. He married three times—none of his wives was Jewish—which was itself an extravagance. His second wife, Aimée de Burgh, for example, spent £1,000 a year on clothing and landed him in court in 1931 when her dressmaker's bills went unpaid.[130] Energetic, arrogant, dashing, and tough, like the protagonists in his novels, Frankau fished, hunted, fenced, and motored, as if he were a born aristocrat. In a promotional pamphlet he wrote for the cigar trade in 1925, he associated cigar-smoking (and himself) with 'the born leaders of mankind', those of reliable judgement who accepted responsibility, 'the dominant type which is more than ever needed in the higher branches of our present-day existence' to prevent the planet from sinking into 'mere food-hunting barbarism'.[131] Is it surprising that he was 'much read by the governing class', according to Q. D. Leavis?[132] But much of this was a pose, overcompensation for fears and doubts about who he really was. As a result of shell shock, he suffered a nervous breakdown while serving in the First World War and was invalided out of the army in 1918. He confessed to his closest friends that he was terrified of riding and was haunted by the fear that at bottom he was really a coward.[133] And if his fiction is a guide, he was also tormented by the knowledge that he was descended from Jews.

Frankau's politics in the interwar years complemented his tales of strong men of action. Impressed by Benito Mussolini and Italian fascism on a visit to San Remo in early 1923, he publicly championed right-wing causes. He introduced fascist ideas into his novels *Gerald Cranston's Lady* (1923) and

[128] Ibid. 496.
[129] H. Cecil, *The Flower of Battle*, 185.
[130] *The Times*, 21 Nov. 1931.
[131] G. Frankau, *The Dominant Type of Man*, 6–8.
[132] Leavis, *Fiction and the Reading Public*, 282 n. 26.
[133] *Dictionary of National Biography, 1951–1960*, s.v. 'Frankau, Gilbert'.

Masterson (1925), a weekly political column in the Tory *Sunday Pictorial,* and the short-lived illustrated weekly *Britannia,* which he edited from November 1928 to April 1929. He made a speaking tour of the United States in 1926, 'thinly disguised as an emissary of the English-Speaking Union' (in the words of *Time* magazine), proclaiming his 'resolute hatred of socialism'. (*Time* described him as 'a small Semite, suavely overlaid with English polish'—he really was unable to escape his origins.[134]) His political programme was standard fascist fare, minus the antisemitism: party politics were weakening national resolve, trade unions were too powerful, capital and labour needed to cooperate, free trade was harmful to workers, strong imperial ties were Britain's last hope against its enemies abroad.[135] Frankau remained a man of the right until his death, but once he understood what the Hitler regime was about he came to see fascism as a threat to liberty and had no further truck with it. In his memoirs, which he finished in 1939, he referred to it as a 'virus' and admitted he had been 'too intolerant, too intransigent, too much the diehard' fifteen years earlier.[136]

Pamela Frankau, the younger of Gilbert's two daughters by his first wife, Dolly Drummond-Black, echoed her father's uneasiness about Jews in her earliest works of fiction, where she represents them as exotic and materialistic. In the 1930s, however, she moved in the opposite direction, largely as a result of her nine-year affair with the poet Humbert Wolfe, who was then rethinking the meaning of his own Jewishness.[137] From then on, she went out of her way to defend and identify with Jews, although she had been raised an Anglican and was baptized a Catholic in 1942. She once remarked, in explaining her enlistment in the Auxiliary Territorial Service during the Second World War, that she loved her country 'with the peculiarly ardent love of England that is felt by some English Jews'.[138] In 1935 she wrote: 'If I were capable of cataloguing my preference among people I should head the list with writers and Jews.'[139] A few years later she became active in relief work for German Jewish refugees, which annoyed her father, with whom her relations were often testy. At a party she gave in support of Tythrop House (a farm in Oxfordshire where young German refugees received agricultural training before emigrating to Palestine), Gilbert told her that he was 'bored' by her rush to identify herself with 'the Jewish race', particularly, he added, when he had taken the trouble to provide her with a Christian mother. Reflecting on his remark, she summed up the difference in attitude between them in this way: 'Gilbert took his Jewish blood more light-heartedly than I

[134] *Time,* 31 May 1926.   [135] See, for example, *Britannia,* 26 Oct. 1928, 386–7.
[136] G. Frankau, *Self-Portrait,* 262.
[137] Gonda, ' "A Roller Coaster of a Life with Everything in It" ', 183–4.
[138] *The Times,* 9 June 1967.   [139] P. Frankau, *I Find Four People,* 277.

took my half-share.' She then recounted a story he had told her. When an English admiral in Malta had said to him, 'You'll agree with me, Frankau, about these damned Jews', he had responded with a loud laugh. She asked her father whether he had told the admiral that he was a Jew. He replied that he certainly had not, that it was none of the bastard's business, to which she responded by saying that she would always 'weigh in' and that it was cowardly not to.[140]

Pamela Frankau erred when she wrote that her father took his Jewishness more light-heartedly than she. If his background had been truly a matter of indifference to him, he would have responded differently to the admiral in Malta and then forgotten the incident altogether. Nor would he have been upset that his daughter devoted time to Jewish refugee work. Indeed, the truth is the opposite of what Pamela suggested: it was Gilbert, not she, whose attitude towards Jewishness was obsessive. Not that she was indifferent of course. In her fiction she defended Jews from the casual antisemitism that was endemic in middle-class English society. In *A Wreath for the Enemy* (1954), when the conventional, unimaginative Mr Bradley makes snide remarks about a Jew being made master of the local hunt, his son replies that he is a great horseman, knows the country backwards and forwards, and has done more for the hunt than anyone else. Mr Bradley retorts that that is the way parvenu Jews always get in, to which his son responds: 'The racialist would do well to remind himself once a day that Our Lord was a Jew.'[141] And in *The Winged Horse* (1953) the sculptor Anthony Carey recalls a regimental dinner when a half-Jewish officer stood up to protest some anti-Jewish remarks and talked for half an hour, becoming angrier and angrier and making his fellow officers increasingly uncomfortable. When someone suggested that it was bad manners and that he should have kept quiet (as Gilbert had in Malta), Carey answered that 'he would have felt like a coward, sitting there, letting some chucklehead talk about "kikes" and pretending it didn't touch or concern him'.[142]

Pamela Frankau could also wax rhapsodic about Jews, which would have been impossible for her father. For example, in *The Devil We Know* (1939) the part-Jewish Sally Fisher muses about the fate of the Jews and her relationship to them: 'She thought with affection of the race of whose blood there was a little in her; loving them for their kindness, for their easy slant into melodrama, for the gentle, elusive quality that the best of them had, for their childish defiance of the world that was their imposition.' Their purpose is now clear to her. They are 'the leaven of the human race, the secret of its live-

[140] P. Frankau, *Pen to Paper*, 202–3.   [141] P. Frankau, *A Wreath for the Enemy*, 108–9.
[142] P. Frankau, *The Winged Horse*, 381–2.

liness'.[143] This way of thinking about Jews is, of course, as essentialist as her father's, for it assumes that Jews possess innate ('racial') characteristics, manifestations of an essential Jewishness. What separated Pamela from Gilbert—and this is critical—was that for her these traits, at least from the 1930s, were admirable rather than unfortunate and embarrassing. She could also write with sensitivity and insight about emotionally tortured, self-hating Jews. The scriptwriter Philip Meyer in *The Devil We Know*, the nephew of deracinated German Jewish textile merchants in Bradford and the object of anti-Jewish barbs since grammar school, describes himself as a 'hateful, ill-mannered little Jew'. He goes mad, so consumed is he with self-loathing, but he regains his sanity eventually, as he is reconciled with his Jewishness.[144] (The great love of Pamela's life, Humbert Wolfe, came from a background similar to that of the fictional Meyer and probably inspired his character.[145])

Pamela Frankau was able to feel more comfortable about her Jewish antecedents than her father probably because she had been raised in unambiguously Christian surroundings. (Her parents divorced when she was a young child and she saw little of Gilbert and his relatives until she was an adult.) Her 'ethnic' identity was fixed from birth and not open to question. Her connection with her Jewish background was thus a matter of choice, not an obsession from which there was no escape. As a child and adolescent, she was too distant, in every sense, from Jewish or once Jewish circles to suffer from assimilationist anxieties. Her father, on the other hand, was raised in a home that was neither Jewish nor Christian. His younger siblings were able to emerge from this social and religious indeterminacy without apparent difficulty. But for Gilbert, less resilient perhaps and put together differently, the ambiguous character of his upbringing continued to exert its influence throughout his entire life. His Jewishness was not something he took lightheartedly, whatever he told himself or others. Perhaps if public interest in Jews had been weaker in interwar Britain, if 'Jew-consciousness' had not been in the air, he would have been able to do so. But, then, we cannot choose the times in which we live.

5

The story of the Frankaus and their relatives lends itself to two broad interpretations. On one level, it can be read as a success story, testimony to the openness of English society and its toleration of ambitious newcomers. The children, in-laws, and grandchildren of the economically successful

---

[143] P. Frankau, *The Devil We Know*, 487–8.
[144] Ibid. 92.   [145] Interview, Diana Raymond, 1 Sept. 1989, Hampstead.

immigrants Adolph and Joseph Frankau entered non-commercial, upper-middle-class society, where they made their mark in a diverse group of fields: law, medicine, engineering, literature, scholarship, journalism, and entertainment. Their ascent was rapid and, it seems, unencumbered by their Jewish and German backgrounds. Whatever the level of hostility to Jews in English cultural and political discourse—and it was considerable—it had little impact on the rise of the Frankaus, although it influenced, to be sure, their own self-image and attitudes towards other Jews. Even Carlyle, who represented Jews in his work as materialistic and unspiritual, tolerated, indeed embraced, Joseph Neuberg as friend and soulmate. In this sense, the representation of Jews in cultural and political discourse is not a reliable guide to how flesh-and-blood Jews fared in concrete social terms.

But there is a less celebratory interpretation of this story as well. The Frankaus did not enter upper-middle-class English society as observant Jews but rather as disaffiliated Jews, converted Jews, and children of converted Jews. This raises the question of whether their success was predicated on their renunciation of Judaism, their radical assimilation. Was there a quid pro quo at work in their successful integration? Were they expected to disavow Judaism and Jewish attachments in exchange for acceptance? In a formal sense, no. With the completion of political emancipation in the mid-nineteenth century, no statutory barriers to Jewish integration remained. Nor, in practice, were occupational and social advancement closed to Jews because of informal or bureaucratic discrimination. To be sure, Frederick Joseph Frankau would not have been able to attend a public school like Rugby in the 1860s if he had remained Jewish, but there were other avenues to the Bar that were open to professing Jews. In fact, for every successful Frankau, it would be possible to cite numerous parallel cases of entry into the non-commercial middle class in which Jewish affiliation remained intact.[146] Heine's oft-cited aphorism—'the baptismal certificate is the ticket of admission to European culture'—does not ring true in the British case.

However, in this context it should be remembered that the Frankau brothers, their wives, and Joseph Neuberg were immigrants from Germany. In the period of reaction following Waterloo and the Congress of Vienna, German Jews remained an actively persecuted minority, the despised, harassed targets of legal discrimination and social contempt. As we saw in Chapter 7, some Jews who were raised in these circumstances, especially those without firm religious commitments, experienced their Jewishness as a burden or misfortune. Those who emigrated to Victorian Britain often brought with them attitudes like these and behaved as if they were still living

---

[146] See the many examples in Tropp, *Jews in the Professions*; Cooper, *Pride versus Prejudice*.

in Germany, where radical assimilation was a common response to discrimination and denigration. The behaviour of the Frankaus fits this pattern, with an exception or two, of course, like Nathan Frankau, who settled in New Haven, Connecticut, and became a pillar of the local Jewish community.

But this does not explain the behaviour of Julia and Gilbert Frankau or the English-educated children of the immigrant generation, although in the latter case it can be assumed that parental attitudes were important. In the absence of barriers to Jewish integration, why did Julia and then Gilbert, who was, after all, a member of the Church of England, find their Jewishness so troublesome? The answer is linked to the reading of the Frankau story that emphasizes their loss of Jewishness rather than their social and occupational attainments. Although few obstacles blocked Jewish integration into the non-commercial middle class, English culture in the broadest sense was hostile to expressions of cultural diversity. Jews and Judaism continued to be represented in negative terms in literature, drama, sermons, political debate, and other public forums. Circles and institutions willing to tolerate Jews as intimate associates were familiar with, tolerated, and disseminated these representations. Convinced, moreover, of their own superiority to other peoples and nations, indeed, incapable of cultural relativism in any sense, English men and women up and down the social ladder were unwilling to endorse the perpetuation of a separate Jewish culture or to see any value in the customs or beliefs of the Jewish religion. As Jews came to figure more prominently in public discourse from the 1870s on, these attitudes hardened and were expressed more sharply and frequently. As a consequence, it became more common for Jews in the throes of full absorption to express publicly their contempt for and distance from the group they had left behind. Gilbert Frankau's contemporaries Leonard Woolf and Edwin Montagu, as we saw earlier, were just as eager to resist association with the mass of Jews. Woolf, in fact, was so embarrassed by his background that he refused to invite his own mother to his wedding.[147]

In this light, the Frankau saga cannot be accounted a success story. It exposes the narrowness of English cultural horizons, including contempt for Jewish particularism, and the pressure this exerted on individuals wishing to participate in social and cultural spheres outside the Jewish community. Even if this pressure to conform was muted and subtle in comparison to other states, it took its toll nonetheless. In the case of people like Julia and Gilbert Frankau, the road to integration was unpleasant and troubled, at least psychologically. Reminded of their Jewishness by the increasing attention paid to Jews in public discourse, they felt compelled to return to it repeatedly,

---

[147] Woolf, *Letters*, 157–8.

if only to stress how little they resembled other Jews. There is then a tragic or sombre dimension to the Frankau story. What can be said in mitigation is that in its extreme outcome it was not typical of the course of Anglo-Jewish integration before the Second World War, if only because most Jews, their feet firmly planted in the world of business, were content to enjoy each other's company and remain largely within the social boundaries of Anglo-Jewry.

CHAPTER THIRTEEN

Jewish Converts in
Nineteenth-Century Warsaw

I

AMONG THE 445,000 Jews crowded into the Warsaw ghetto at its peak were 2,000 Christians of Jewish origin.[1] In the hastily constructed world of the ghetto, they occupied an unusual niche. By the racial standards of the German occupation of course, they were Jews like the ghetto's other inhabitants and in the end shared their fate. However, before the mass deportations of summer 1942 ended the 'normal' life of the ghetto, they enjoyed de facto a privileged social position. Many were wealthier and better educated than most Warsaw Jews, and they moved rapidly into high-ranking positions in the ghetto administration. The most prominent was Józef Szeryński (né Sheinkman), a colonel in the Polish police before the war, whom Adam Czerniaków appointed as the first commander of the ghetto police force. Szeryński, in turn, surrounded himself with other converts. Baptized Jews were also conspicuous as hospital administrators and as heads of clinics and other public health units. In his journal, Emmanuel Ringelblum wrote that 100 baptized Jews served in prominent positions in the police force, and recorded a current saying: 'You want a job in the Judenrat? Convert!'[2]

Converts also benefited from the assistance of the Catholic charity Caritas, which operated from the two parish churches in the ghetto, All Saints on Gryzbowski Square and Most Holy Virgin on Leszno Street. It operated soup

[1] There are several estimates of the number of converts in the Warsaw ghetto. In one of the earliest studies of the ghetto community, first published in 1954, Philip Friedman estimated that there were 6,000 ('Social Conflicts in the Ghetto', 144). The more conservative estimate of Yisrael Gutman, which I prefer given Gutman's intimate knowledge of the sources, is that there were about 2,000 (*The Jews of Warsaw*, 59). Charles G. Roland claims that there were no more than 1,600 converts (*Courage under Siege*, 31). Gunnar S. Paulsson, citing statistics from the *Judenrat*, believes that there were at least 1,700 (*Secret City*, 32–3).
[2] Ringelblum, *Notes from the Warsaw Ghetto*, 138, 226. On the role of converts in the ghetto administration, see Adler, *In the Warsaw Ghetto*, 23–5, 169–72; Blady-Szwajger, *I Remember Nothing More*, 40, 218; Roland, *Courage under Siege*, 31; Hirszfeld, *Historia jednego życia*, 228; Trunk, *Judenrat*, 355.

kitchens, made loans, distributed financial aid, and let apartments on church premises. The children of converts were also allowed to play in the gardens of the two churches, a privilege denied to other ghetto children.[3] Understandably, the relative good fortune of the converts—indeed, their very presence in the ghetto—aroused curiosity, resentment, and envy. They were both familiar and alien, and crowds used to gather in front of the ghetto's churches on Sundays to watch the spectacle of well-dressed, well-fed former Jews attending mass. At Easter services in 1942, the crowds were so large that the ghetto police stationed a special detachment to maintain order.[4]

While converts in the Warsaw ghetto suffered less material deprivation than other residents, at least at the start, their emotional distress was probably more acute. To be thrown back into a milieu that they had fled—decades earlier in some cases—was an unending trauma. In their view, there was little in common between themselves and the mass of Jews, whom they viewed through the spectacles of Polish antisemitism as uncultured, devious, and immoral. The wife of a high-ranking bank officer, who with her husband had been a Lutheran for thirty years, told an interviewer for the Oneg Shabat group that they had had no contact with Jews 'and here, all of a sudden, they pushed us right into the black Jewish masses'. This couple, according to the interviewer, 'had no compassion for Jews, not even in the confines of the ghetto'. On the contrary, they had begun 'loathing them, having learned all their defects and ugly traits'.[5] The Hebrew diarist Chaim Kaplan also noted the converts' dislike of other Jews. In his entry for 7 March 1941 he wrote: 'I don't know what their end will be, but one thing I know for a certainty. Their enmity to Israel will never cease.'[6]

Some converts were first-generation Christians; others were second-generation, the children of converts and thus born into Christianity, people without 'the slightest feeling for Judaism, either religiously or racially', according to Kaplan.[7] But others were freshly baptized, having become Christians between the start of the war in September 1939 and the sealing of the ghetto in November 1940. A report in the Oneg Shabat archive observed that in this period 'baptism went on daily', even after the Germans introduced racial restrictions.[8] Some new Christians counted on incomplete files of birth registrations to hide their Jewish origins; others bribed priests, Kaplan noted, to certify on a birth certificate that 'So-and-so is an Aryan from

---

[3] Ringelblum, *Notes from the Warsaw Ghetto*, 214; Adler, *In the Warsaw Ghetto*, 171; Kermish (ed.), *To Live with Honor and Die with Honor!*, 626.   [4] Roland, *Courage under Siege*, 32.

[5] Kermish (ed.), *To Live with Honor and Die with Honor!*, 628–9.

[6] C. Kaplan, *The Warsaw Diary*, 250.   [7] Ibid.

[8] Kermish (ed.), *To Live with Honor and Die with Honor!*, 622.

a long line of Aryans'.[9] Still others, not knowing what the future held, reasoned that converts would be treated more leniently.

Contrary to what one might assume, the converts included both acculturated, Polish-speaking Jews and more humble, Yiddish-speaking Jews. The Oneg Shabat report, referring to a list of baptized Jews, noted that it included persons with names like Moszek and Szaja, 'clear proof of their origins in families who did not assimilate, since those who did gave for almost the last 75 years Polish names to their sons'.[10] Moreover, even after ghettoization there were Jews desperate to gain some advantage who took this step. Some did so in order to be fed and cared for by Caritas. Ringelblum heard of a newly baptized Jew who when asked why he had converted replied, 'To get a bigger loaf of bread.'[11] Others believed that conversion, while not exempting them from persecution, would nonetheless offer them some protection or benefit. Rumours circulated, for example, that converts would be allowed to leave the ghetto or that a separate ghetto would be established for them in Żoliborz, one of the nicer Warsaw neighbourhoods.[12] A few became Christians from conviction. The bacteriologist Ludwik Hirszfeld, who had converted before the war, recalled Jewish students of his who asked him to serve as godfather at their ghetto baptisms. He asked himself what motivated them, since changing their religion did not change their legal position in any way. His answer, whether correct or not, was that the charm of the religion of love, the religion of the nation to which they felt they belonged, was pulling them. In the case of Tadeusz Endelman, a young lawyer and friend of Hirszfeld who was baptized in July 1942 knowing that deportation awaited him, it is clear that religious consolation was his only object.[13] (Soon after this the Germans closed the two ghetto churches.)

2

This brief account of the convert community in the Warsaw ghetto is an arresting reminder that radical assimilation in the modern period was not limited to status-conscious circles in London, Paris, Berlin, and Vienna. In nineteenth-century Europe, both East and West, wherever the old order began to give way to the new, however uneven and erratic the transforma-

[9] C. Kaplan, *The Warsaw Diary*, 249.

[10] Kermish (ed.), *To Live with Honor and Die with Honor!*, 622. Jerzy Kłoczowski notes that hundreds, possibly thousands, of Jews throughout Poland asked to be baptized from autumn 1939 ('The Religious Orders and the Jews in Nazi-Occupied Poland', 240).

[11] Ringelblum, *Notes from the Warsaw Ghetto*, 214.

[12] Ibid. 225–6. See also Czarnecki, 'All Saints Parish', 208–10.

[13] Hirszfeld, *Historia jednego życia*, 255–6, 271.

tion, some Jews chose to seek their fortune as Christians rather than Jews. Although Russian control in the nineteenth century arrested the development of a modern political system in Poland, the Polish capital became, nonetheless, a dynamic commercial and industrial centre. This, along with the relaxation of restrictions on Jewish residence, encouraged Jewish migration to a city that earlier was of little importance in Polish Jewish life. Its Jewish population grew from 16,000 in 1816 to 41,000 in 1856 and then skyrocketed to 337,000 on the eve of the First World War.[14] Even by the middle of the nineteenth century, Warsaw Jewry was the largest in the world. Stratified in both economic and religio-cultural terms, it was subject to a range of secularizing, assimilatory pressures similar to but not identical with those that influenced communities further to the west, and as was the case in those communities a number of its members responded to these pressures by embracing Christianity, hoping thereby to escape the collective fate of the Jewish people. (That they often failed to achieve this end is a matter that will be discussed below.) Those who formally cut their links to Judaism were a small minority—and in Warsaw an even smaller minority than in other European capitals. Yet, however unrepresentative, their complete rejection of Judaism and Jewishness reflected historical currents to which much larger numbers of Jews were subject. Conversion in Warsaw, as elsewhere, stood at one end of a spectrum of Jewish responses to new conditions and pressures rather than outside it, the aberrant behaviour of a breed of marginal misfits.

Conversion in Poland and Russia is not unexplored territory. In the early twentieth century, journalists and historians published biographical sketches of famous—and often infamous—converts.[15] More anecdotal than analytic, these melodramatic, moralistic accounts emphasize the curious, the tragic, and even the amusing. They do not seek to view conversion as part of a broader process of social and cultural adaptation, a process whose incidence and make-up were linked to other historical currents. Since the 1980s there have been efforts to correct this and view conversion in eastern Europe in a broader context.[16] Historians and sociologists of Polish Jewry have also written about the Polish-speaking, upper-middle-class, integrationist[17] elite

[14] Garncarska-Kadary, *The Role of the Jews in the Development of the Economy of Warsaw* (Heb.), 25.

[15] Tsitron, *Behind the Curtain* (Heb.); Frenk, *Apostates in Poland* (Yid.); Ginsburg, *Apostates in Tsarist Russia* (Yid.); Mieses, *Z rodu żydowskiego*.

[16] Stanislawski, 'Jewish Apostasy in Russia'; Agursky, 'Ukrainian–Jewish Intermarriages'; id., 'Conversions of Jews to Christianity in Russia'; Freeze, 'When Chava Left Home'; Manekin, 'The Lost Generation'; Avrutin, 'Returning to Judaism'.

[17] Historians of Polish Jewry usually describe the Warsaw *haute bourgeoisie* as 'assimilationist', but I prefer the less ambiguous, less pejorative term 'integrationist'. In defence of this

of Warsaw Jewry, from whose ranks a disproportionate number of converts came.[18] Their work has one unintended drawback, however: it can leave the false impression that the flight from Jewishness was confined to the well-to-do and the well educated. As I will show, Warsaw Jews from all social ranks—the rich, the poor, and those in between—became Christians in the nineteenth century.

A more comprehensive view of conversion in Warsaw emerges from a quantitative analysis of data in a volume of anti-Jewish historical research, Teodor Jeske-Choiński's *Neofici polscy: Materiały historyczne*. A prolific writer (of criticism, fiction, drama, history, and journalism) Jeske-Choiński (1854–1920) was well known for his virulent, anti-modern, conspiratorial anti-semitism.[19] In 1904 he published *Neofici polscy*, a volume listing Jews who converted to Christianity in Warsaw between 1800 and 1903. His motives for undertaking this curious project were at once ideological and mercenary. Exposing the Jewish origins of Poles who were former Jews or the descendants of former Jews was a well-honed, time-honoured weapon in the arsenal of Polish antisemitism, connected originally, no doubt, to the mass absorption of Frankists in the previous century.[20] At the same time, Jeske-Choiński profited from the book's publication, although not in the usual fashion of those who write for a living. Not wishing to see their Jewish roots exposed in public, some rich converts paid the author hush money to omit their names, while others hastened to buy up and destroy copies of the book after its publication.[21] (One result is that the book is now a rarity; the copy that I used in the Harlan Hatcher Graduate Library at the University of Michigan came from the library of the Berlin Jewish community.)

Jeske-Choiński's book records more than the names of converts: it also includes the year of their baptism, their age at baptism, their sex, the church to which they were converted (Roman Catholic, Lutheran, Calvinist), and in the case of adult males their occupation. It is thus a unique source for reconstructing the social history of conversion in Warsaw. (Jeske-Choiński

term, Ezra Mendelsohn, who pioneered its usage, notes that most Westernized Jews in Poland wanted to be integrated into the Polish nation without being swallowed up and disappearing altogether (*On Modern Jewish Politics*, 16).

[18] Heller, *On the Edge of Destruction*, ch. 6; Joseph Lichten, 'Notes on the Assimilation and Acculturation of Jews in Poland'; Cała, 'The Question of the Assimilation of Jews in the Polish Kingdom'; A. Hertz, *The Jews in Polish Culture*; Guterman, 'Attitudes of Warsaw Assimilationists towards Conversion' (Heb.); id., 'The Origins of the Great Synagogue'; Kieniewicz, 'Assimilated Jews in Nineteenth-Century Warsaw'.

[19] Weeks, 'The "International Jewish Conspiracy" Reaches Poland'.

[20] The Frankists were descendants of the followers of the false messiah Jacob Frank who converted to Catholicism in the mid-eighteenth century.

[21] Shatzky, 'Alexander Kraushar', 170; A. Hertz, *The Jews in Polish Culture*, 111.

recorded a small number of conversions that took place outside the capital, but I have not included them in this account.) There is, of course, the question of how accurate and comprehensive the author was, given his motives. His reputation and the distorted view of Polish Jewish history with which he introduces the book do not inspire confidence; some scholars dismiss its utility out of hand.[22] Still, even with its inaccuracies and omissions, whether due to the bribes the author accepted or defects in the church registers he consulted, the book is not irredeemable as a historical source. (Its lengthy introduction is another matter altogether.) There is no evidence that Jeske-Choiński's antisemitism significantly distorted how he collected and recorded baptismal data. No critic has ever suggested that he fabricated cases of conversion or their details. In fact, the problem is the opposite: the number of conversions in Warsaw was greater than the number he recorded. In addition to those he omitted inadvertently due to defective records or his own carelessness and those he was paid to omit, it seems that he did not include those whom Anglican missionaries, agents of the London Society for the Promotion of Christianity among the Jews, baptized, probably because he did not have access to their records. The London Society's mission was the oldest, the most active, and the best funded in nineteenth-century Poland.[23] Between 1821, when the London Society established a station in Warsaw, and 1854, when the government closed it and expelled its agents, it baptized 361 Jews. Later, following its re-establishment, it baptized another 354 Jews between 1874 and 1898.[24] In all, from its establishment to 1907, the London Society's agents in Warsaw converted 949 Jews. Its influence, however, was greater than these numbers suggest, since an unknown number of Jews whom it succoured and instructed chose to be baptized in Lutheran or Calvinist churches.[25] If the Jews whom the London Society converted in Warsaw were similar to those whom it converted at its other foreign and domestic missions, most were poor and desperate with few emotional and material resources to fall back on in their hour of need. It should be borne in mind that the Jeske-Choiński register of baptisms omits these converts, as well as a smaller but unknown number from prominent, well-to-do families. Neither omission, however, nor for that matter Jeske-Choiński's own jaundiced view of Jews, constitutes an

---

[22] e. g. A. Hertz, *The Jews in Polish Culture*, 87.

[23] Mahler, 'Policy towards Missionaries in Congress Poland' (Heb.).

[24] Frederick Smith to W. T. Gidney, 27 Jan. 1909, Church Mission to the Jews Collection, Dep CMJ d. 51/2; Alexander Murray to the Bishop of London, 4 Mar. 1899, Church Mission to the Jews Collection, Dep CMJ d. 51/5.

[25] Gidney, *The History of the London Society*, 163, 541, 601.

insurmountable obstacle to using his data as an *approximate* guide to the contours of conversion in nineteenth-century Warsaw.

3

Before the modern period conversions in the Polish–Lithuanian Commonwealth were rare. It is impossible to know, in even the most approximate terms, how many took place, but clearly the number was small—with the one exception of the collective Frankist apostasy of 1759–60.[26] For the few who took this step, no simple formula explains either their background or motives. Their ranks included criminals who ran afoul of the law and converted to save themselves from a death sentence or prison term; deserted wives who were unable to remarry and converted to start a new life; dissidents and troublemakers who converted to escape the penalties of *ḥerem*; the wealthy who converted to improve their social position (until 1764, converts were able to join the *szlachta* (nobility)) or gain membership in the burgher estate; and the poor, the destitute, and the marginal who converted to save themselves from starvation and material distress. In the eighteenth century women and girls were especially prominent in the ranks of the converted. In Lithuania the mission-minded priest S. Turczynowicz targeted women and girls from the lowest strata of Jewish society because of their vulnerability (lack of education and poverty), and in 1737 founded an order of Catholic sisters, Mariae Vitae, whose abbeys housed recent female converts and converts-to-be who were taking instruction. In its first thirty years the order was responsible for the baptism of about 400 girls.[27] Noticeable by their absence among Polish converts were second-rank religious functionaries—slaughterers, cantors, teachers, tutors, itinerant preachers, collectors for charities—who were so prominent among converts in the German states from the sixteenth to the eighteenth centuries.[28] In addition to voluntary conversions, an unknown number of children were removed from their families and forced to become Christians. Turczynowicz and the Mariae Vitae in particular were known for their zeal in kidnapping and forcibly baptizing children, and after Turczynowicz's death the bishop of Vilna, who opposed blatant coercion, was able to obtain the temporary suppression of the order.[29]

[26] Goldberg, *Converts in the Polish–Lithuanian Commonwealth* (Heb.), 11–12; Katz, *Exclusiveness and Tolerance*, 67; Fram, 'Perception and Reception of Repentant Apostates', 319–20; Teter, 'Jewish Conversions to Catholicism'.

[27] Goldberg, *Converts in the Polish–Lithuanian Commonwealth* (Heb.), 37–8; Klausner, *Vilna in the Age of the Gaon* (Heb.), 226.   [28] Carlebach, *Divided Souls*.

[29] Goldberg, *Converts in the Polish–Lithuanian Commonwealth* (Heb.), 34–9.

Spiritual concerns—revelations, yearnings, visions, and the like—were absent or inconspicuous in the conversion experiences of pre-modern Polish Jews. The circumstances of Jewish life—in particular, its cultural and social self-sufficiency—provided few opportunities for Jews to become familiar with Christian doctrine. Potential converts learned about Christian beliefs only when non-spiritual causes disturbed their relations with their fellow Jews, motivating them to look outside their own community for aid or consolation. Their new faith, to which they testified at the time of their baptism, was the outcome of a prior process of social disaffection. Their knowledge of Christian doctrine came to them while they were being prepared to enter the church and rarely beforehand.[30] In this sense, they differed from their counterparts in the nineteenth and twentieth centuries, for whom conversion was often the result of a gradual, long-term process of acculturation and integration that led in the end to complete absorption.

Whatever the motives, conversion in the Polish–Lithuanian Commonwealth resulted in total separation from Jewish society. Those who chose baptism changed not only their religion, but their social standing, legal status, nationality, and surroundings as well. Integration into one of the three estates in Polish society was often strewn with obstacles, but however rocky the path there was no middle, religiously neutral ground where converts could find shelter, as there was to some extent later on. Both learned and popular opinion viewed those who left with disgust—and some apprehension, since they often wreaked havoc on their former co-religionists by slandering and libelling them before the authorities. The Polish rabbinate was cool, even hostile, to receiving repentant converts back into the fold, unlike their counterparts in the Sephardi diaspora or in medieval Ashkenaz.[31] Indeed, the enmity between Jews and converted Jews was so great that there were instances of converts being murdered by members of their own families.[32]

The thousand or so Frankists who embraced Catholicism in Lvov, Warsaw, and Kamienec in 1759 and 1760 were an exception.[33] Although historians disagree about the exact mix of circumstances and considerations that led to their decision to leave Judaism, some of which were clearly worldly, none deny the role of Jacob Frank's radical antinomian reworking of the

[30] Ibid. 19–20, 26.   [31] Fram, 'Perception and Reception of Repentant Apostates'.
[32] Goldberg, *Converts in the Polish–Lithuanian Commonwealth* (Heb.), 40.
[33] There is no consensus about the number of Frankists who converted. The estimate of 1,000 is that of Gershom Scholem ('The Sabbatian Movement in Poland' (Heb.), 133). Bernard D. Weinryb estimates that there were about 600 (*The Jews of Poland*, 254). Abraham Duker puts the figure at several thousand ('Polish Frankism's Duration', 301–2 and n. 90). Mieses' estimate of 12,000 is untenable (*Z rodu żydowskiego*, 13).

mystical messianism of Sabbatai Zevi (1626–76).[34] Moreover, at the start Frank and his lieutenants hoped to maintain a distinctive collective religious profile after baptism, combining elements of Christianity, Judaism (such as the ban on eating pork), and their own messianic mysticism. And, in fact, they did so for one or two generations. Instead of being absorbed as individuals into Polish society, they lived a sectarian existence, marrying chiefly among themselves, much like the New Christians of Spain and Portugal, whose group identity outlived their conversion by several centuries. In the case of the Frankists, however, belief in Frank's doctrines, along with endogamous marriage, declined within a matter of decades. Gradually, the Frankists merged with their neighbours—without, however, managing to obliterate Polish awareness of their origins, which antisemites cited as evidence of the insincerity of Jewish converts in general through much of the nineteenth century. But this is to anticipate later developments.

4

The history of conversion in Warsaw is linked to the history of Jewish residential status there. From 1527 Warsaw enjoyed the crown-bestowed privilege of *de non tolerandis Judaeis*. Although Jews continued to visit the city to do business, no permanent community was authorized until the nineteenth century. The ban on Jewish settlement, however, did not extend to noble estates on the outskirts of old Warsaw, where magnates exercised their own authority, and here, on lands that eventually were incorporated into the city, Jews continued to reside throughout the early modern period. Moreover, the ban on Jewish settlement within the city was not absolute. Exceptional individuals received special privileges; lesser merchants and traders infiltrated and did business until discovered and expelled in periodic crackdowns. Thus, in 1792, 515 Jews lived within Warsaw proper, while 6,150 lived in Praga, a suburb outside the city's borders. During the Prussian occupation (1795–1807), the ban on Jewish settlement was not enforced. The number of Jews increased to about 12,000 in 1805 and continued to grow from decade to decade. Successive governments introduced measures to halt or slow the increase—burdensome taxes, temporary residential permits, bans on registering new Jewish residents, roundups of Jews without proper documents—but in the end they were unable to keep the Jewish population in check, however difficult they made life for the mass of Jews without money or influence. Under the Prussians Jewish status was regularized

---

[34] See e.g. Scholem, 'The Sabbatian Movement in Poland' (Heb.), 122–8; Weinryb, *The Jews of Poland*, 244–61.

(but restricted) and Jewish communal institutions established. In 1809 the authorities banned Jews from living in the town centre, thus encouraging the formation of a Jewish quarter in the western districts of the city, and in 1824 forced Jews living elsewhere in the city to move there. This 'ghetto without walls' existed until 1862, when tsarist officials removed all restrictions on Jewish residence along with many other disabilities.[35]

Most Jews who settled in Warsaw in the first half of the century were artisans, small-scale traders, carters, innkeepers, and unskilled labourers. They were part of a broad movement to the cities that swept Polish Jewry in the nineteenth century, set in motion in part by expulsions from villages and border regions. Like Jewish newcomers in Western capitals, they struggled to make a living—the streets of Warsaw were no more paved with gold than those of New York—but in their case they faced an additional hardship: circumventing rules intended to prevent their permanent settlement in the city. A small number of the new arrivals, on the other hand, were welcomed with open arms. From the late eighteenth century to the withdrawal of the French in 1814, in the absence of a native *haute bourgeoisie*, successive regimes courted Western financiers and entrepreneurs to settle in Warsaw. Among the Germans, Austrians, Dutch, and English who came to the city was a handful of Jews, largely but not exclusively from Prussia, Silesia, and Moravia. They brought with them capital and experience, and grew rich, first in banking, army contracting (a million soldiers passed through Warsaw between 1790 and 1815), wholesale commerce, and leasing taxes and other state monopolies, and then later in industry and railways. The founders of most of the great nineteenth-century Warsaw Jewish fortunes arrived in this wave of migration: Kronenbergs, Rosens, Epsteins, Frankels, Natansons, Rotwands, Bersohns. Because of their wealth, they were exempt from the residence laws that burdened other Jews. In 1815, 48 families enjoyed the privilege of living outside the Jewish quarter; in 1836, 124 families; and in 1842, 131 families, or 1.7 per cent of the Jews in Warsaw.[36]

Data drawn from Jeske-Choiński mirror the hardships that ordinary Jews faced in this period (see Table 13.1). Of the approximately 1,800 conversions in Warsaw between 1800 and 1903 that Jeske-Choiński recorded, 48 per cent occurred in the first half of the century and 52 per cent in the second, despite the four- or fivefold growth of Warsaw's Jewish population in the second half (from less than 50,000 to over 200,000). Indeed, almost as many Jews became Christians in the 1830s and 1840s (536), when residence and other restrictions were in effect, as in the 1880s and 1890s (562), when they were

---

[35] The history of Jewish settlement and population growth in Warsaw is covered at length in Garncarska-Kadary, *The Role of the Jews in the Development of the Economy of Warsaw* (Heb.), ch. 1.

[36] Eisenbach, *The Emancipation of the Jews in Poland*, 225.

Table 13.1. Number of converts per decade, 1800–1903

Decade	No. of converts	% of total
1800s	27	1.5
1810s	53	3.0
1820s	243	13.5
1830s	200	11.1
1840s	336	18.7
1850s	164	9.1
1860s	60	3.3
1870s	48	2.7
1880s	232	12.9
1890s	330	18.4
1900–3	103	5.7
Total	**1,796**	**100.0**

not but the Jewish population was far greater. In other words, relative to the number of Jews in Warsaw, there was a dramatic drop in the number of conversions in the second half of the century. This suggests a strong connection between the disabilities that burdened Jews before 1862 and the this-worldly benefits of conversion. The decline in the absolute number of conversions in the two decades following the removal of disabilities supports this suggestion. In the 1850s, 164 Jews converted, but in the 1860s the number dropped to 60 and in the 1870s even further to 48.

If we consider the social background of those who left Judaism,[37] the case for linking conversion motives to residential and economic restrictions becomes even stronger (see Table 13.2). Most converts came from ordinary rather than privileged backgrounds, from strata whose economic survival was most threatened by government efforts to control the Jewish population. In the 1830s, 67 per cent of all converts[38] came from the two lowest socio-

[37] For this study, I divided the Warsaw Jewish population into the following six social/occupational categories: (1) *haute bourgeoisie* (bankers, industrialists, manufacturers, entrepreneurs, landowners); (2) professionals (lawyers, physicians, engineers, professors); (3) commercial middle class (wholesale and retail merchants); (4) non-commercial middle class (artists, musicians, bookkeepers, managers, agents, stewards); (5) lower middle class (artisans, shopkeepers, clerks, tavern keepers); (6) lower class (unskilled labourers, pedlars, servants).

[38] Jeske-Choiński did not provide occupational information for most female converts (either their own or that of their husbands or fathers). Thus, conclusions about the social makeup of Warsaw converts refer, strictly speaking, to men not women. However, were information regarding women available, I do not believe that it would significantly change the picture.

Table 13.2. Social background of male converts per decade, 1800–1903 (% of total of all decades)

Decade	Haute bourgeoisie	Professionals	Commercial middle class	Non-commercial middle class	Lower middle class	Lower class
1800s	0.30	0.00	0.00	0.00	0.15	0.00
1810s	0.15	0.15	0.00	0.00	0.15	0.15
1820s	0.15	0.90	0.30	1.20	3.16	0.30
1830s	0.15	1.81	1.66	0.75	6.63	2.26
1840s	1.20	2.41	1.36	1.66	17.02	3.31
1850s	0.75	0.75	0.60	1.66	4.67	1.36
1860s	0.75	0.15	0.30	0.30	1.05	0.15
1870s	0.00	0.45	0.75	0.15	0.60	0.00
1880s	1.20	1.96	4.82	2.11	1.05	0.15
1890s	0.60	5.72	5.42	3.77	3.92	0.45
1900–3	0.15	2.71	1.66	1.66	0.90	0.00
Total	5.42	17.02	16.87	13.25	39.31	8.13

economic strata in the Warsaw community—the lower middle class and the lower class; in the 1840s, 75 per cent. To underscore the material basis of Jewish conversions, Jeske-Choiński noted that in their baptismal applications many poor Jews included pleas for material aid.[39] What is striking about the background of these converts is how representative they were of characteristic Jewish trades in Warsaw and indeed throughout Poland: bookbinders, bookkeepers, clerks, day labourers, printers, salesmen, servants, shoemakers, tailors, tavern keepers, and weavers far outnumber bankers, industrialists, lawyers, and physicians, occupational groups who figure so prominently in the historiography of radical assimilation in western and central Europe. By the end of the century, the number of lower- and lower-middle-class converts (relative to the four higher strata) had plummeted. In the 1880s, 11 per cent were from the two lowest groups; in the 1890s, 22 per cent. To make the same point from a different perspective: 60 per cent of all lower-middle-class conversions between 1800 and 1903 occurred in the 1830s and 1840s; 69 per cent of all lower-class conversions. These were decades of economic reversal and stagnation, due in the main to restoration of the tariff barrier between Poland and Russia from 1831 to 1851 as punishment for the insurrection of 1830–1. The Warsaw textile industry, 80 per cent

[39] Jeske-Choiński, *Neofici polscy*, 116.

of which was in Jewish hands, suffered in particular from loss of the Russian market and went into rapid decline after 1831.

While well-to-do Jews in Warsaw were able to circumvent the residential and occupational restrictions that burdened the lives of the poor, they were subject nonetheless to influences and pressures that weakened their attachment to Judaism. Those who came from German lands (a majority in the early nineteenth century) had been exposed to efforts to modernize Jewish life before their settlement in Warsaw, even if they themselves cannot be described as maskilim or patrons of the Haskalah. Through their contacts with foreign banking and merchant houses, they remained in touch with the transformations in Jewish life taking place in the West. They wore European dress (the men were clean-shaven), gave their children a secular education, often educating their sons in Germany, and discarded or attenuated old customs. In their petitions to obtain municipal citizenship and civil rights (for themselves and their families, not for the community as a whole), they dissociated themselves from the mass of traditional Jews in Poland, emphasizing their own sartorial and linguistic acculturation, enlightenment, and services to the state.[40] The ambitious among them established salons—they were not welcome in aristocratic homes in the early nineteenth century— and with the permission of the tsar bought landed estates.[41] Some became active members of Masonic lodges, starting in the first decade of the nineteenth century and continuing until 1821, when the government closed them.[42] Undergirding this assimilatory behaviour was the need to feel comfortable when mixing in offices, salons, and drawing rooms with government officials, the dispensers of civil privileges and economic monopolies.

In the end, however, there were limits to what wealth alone was able to procure, and when ambitious Jews found their social or economic progress blocked some chose to convert. One of the first was Samuel Fraenkel, who came to Warsaw as the representative of a Berlin Jewish banking house after the third partition of Poland in 1795. His marriage in 1798 to a daughter of the army contractor and leather merchant Samuel Zbytkower raised him to the front rank of Jewish factors and financiers. But in 1806, when France defeated Prussia, he converted to Catholicism (along with his wife and two daughters) rather than be forced to leave the city as a Prussian subject.[43] In 1822, when the army contractor Ignacy Neumark failed to obtain civil rights for his family and the right to purchase land freehold, they were baptized; the

---

[40] Eisenbach, *The Emancipation of the Jews in Poland*, 219—23.   [41] Ibid. 227, 259–61.
[42] Hass, 'Żydzi i "kwestia żydowska" w dawnym wolnomularstwie polskim'; id., *Sekta farmazonii warszawskiej*, 335, 391–3, 401, 439, 548–51, 564–5.
[43] Mieses, *Z rodu żydowskiego*, 86–7.

same day he acquired an estate in the Sandomierz region.[44] Leopold Kronenberg's path to the baptismal font was equally straightforward. Youngest son of a banker and court factor who had come to Warsaw from Prussia in the late eighteenth century, Kronenberg received a broad secular education in a Catholic school and some Jewish instruction at home. His conversion occurred in 1845, just as the lucrative tobacco monopoly came open, which he was then awarded. In general, in the first half of the century, the only Jews to become officials in the tobacco monopoly were those who had been baptized.[45]

In the second and third generations conversion was more common. The four sons of Posen-born Natan Glücksberg, bookseller, publisher, and Freemason, were baptized in the 1820s; all of them became prominent publishers and booksellers.[46] The daughters from the second and third marriages of Samuel Zbytkower, founder of the first Jewish cemetery and synagogue in Warsaw since 1527, became Christians. The youngest of the five sons of Jacob Epstein, who headed the Warsaw *kehilah* (Jewish community) several times, converted in 1830 to marry a German Christian. Three other sons remained active in Jewish affairs, especially in the defence of Jewish rights (the eldest son was killed in the uprising of 1863), but they and their sisters ceased to maintain Jewish traditions in their homes and all of their children, the third generation, became Christians.[47] Over the decades leakage in these circles continued until entire families—Bergsons, Bersohns, Blochs, Flataus, Glücksbergs, Heryngs, Januschs, Kronenbergs, Laskis, Natansons, Orgelbrands, Toeplitzes—disappeared from the communal rolls. By the end of the century, the Christian heirs of the Jewish notables who had founded the imposing Great Synagogue in the 1870s were placing advertisements in the Polish-language integrationist newspaper *Izraelita* offering to sell their front-row seats.[48] By the interwar period, not one great wealthy family remained Jewish.[49]

---

[44] Eisenbach, *The Emancipation of the Jews in Poland*, 227.

[45] Jeske-Choiński, *Neofici polscy*, 114, 135; Garncarska-Kadary, *The Role of the Jews in the Development of the Economy of Warsaw* (Heb.), 56.

[46] Kieniewicz, 'Assimilated Jews in Nineteenth-Century Warsaw', 179.

[47] Guterman, 'Attitudes of Warsaw Assimilationists towards Conversion' (Heb.), 63–4.

[48] Guterman, *From Assimilation to Nationalism* (Heb.), 104.

[49] Ciechanowiecki, 'Remarks on, and a Supplement to, the "Genealogical Sketches" of Kazimierz Reychman', 377; Guterman, 'Attitudes of Warsaw Assimilationists towards Conversion' (Heb.), 65.

5

In the 1860s Jewish legal status in Congress Poland underwent a sea change. The contradiction between the economic role of Jews and the anachronistic restrictions that limited their activities, the quest of Polish nationalists for allies in their struggle against Russia, and the participation of Jews in the wave of patriotic demonstrations that swept Warsaw in 1861 created conditions favourable to an improvement in Jewish status. In response to requests from officials in Poland, who wished to deprive the nationalists of Jewish support, Alexander II granted partial emancipation in 1862 to the Jews of Congress Poland. (While most restrictions were abolished, Polish Jews were still barred, for example, from the production and sale of liquor in villages. Nonetheless, their legal position became at once better than that of Jews in Russia proper.) The active support of the Jewish middle class for the insurrection of 1863 created a more positive attitude towards Jewish integration, as did the ascendancy of Warsaw positivism among the intelligentsia of Russian Poland during the 1860s and 1870s.[50] Secular, anti-clerical liberals, the positivists hoped to enlist Poland's Jews in their campaign to eradicate backwardness and modernize economic and social life. Believing, as the novelist Bolesław Prus wrote in 1876, that 'Jews have been, are, and will be what their surroundings make them',[51] they affirmed that Jews could become Poles (through acculturation), and declared their willingness to embrace those who did. Although the Warsaw positivists were intolerant of Jewish cultural distinctiveness and never divested themselves of old anti-Jewish attitudes, they nonetheless championed integration (on their terms, of course) into the Polish nation, thus holding out to Polonized Jews the expectation of a better future.

One result of these legal and attitudinal changes was a dramatic drop in the number of conversions. No longer burdened with residential and occupational restrictions, and at the same time more hopeful about the future, Warsaw Jews turned to conversion much less often to improve their circumstances. Whereas 336 Jews converted in the 1840s and 164 in the 1850s, only 60 left Judaism in the 1860s and 48 in the 1870s. Given the rapid growth in Warsaw's Jewish population at this time—from 73,000 in 1864 to 128,000 in 1882[52]—the decline was in fact even more dramatic. Viewed from a

[50] Brian Porter notes that 'the vocabulary of liberalism [the vocabulary of the Warsaw positivists] enjoyed an almost hegemonic ascendancy among the intelligentsia of Russian Poland in the late-1860s and 1870s' and that 'positivism set the parameters of public life in the Russian partition of Poland' during this period ('The Social Nation and its Futures', 1475, 1490).

[51] Quoted in Segel (ed.), *Stranger in Our Midst*, 217.

[52] Corrsin, 'Aspects of Population Change and of Acculturation in Jewish Warsaw', 124.

different perspective, about 6 per cent of the conversions that took place in nineteenth-century Warsaw occurred in these two decades of optimism and reform. Moreover, with the abolition of residential and occupational restrictions, those who most suffered from them ceased to make up the bulk of those leaving the Jewish fold. In the 1860s converts from the two lowest socio-economic strata were 44 per cent of the total; in the 1870s, 31 per cent; in the 1880s, 11 per cent; and in the 1890s, 22 per cent.

Beginning in the late 1870s the climate towards Jewish integration again shifted, this time for the worse. Two events in 1881 symbolize this reversal. First, on Christmas Day a pogrom erupted in Warsaw. For three days, with little interference from the authorities, rioters assaulted Jewish passers-by and attacked Jewish shops, taverns, residences, and prayer houses. Although no Jews died, almost 2,000 families suffered personal injuries or property losses, the latter amounting to almost 2 million rubles.[53] Second, in the wake of the pogrom, Jan Jeleński, the first Polish writer to call himself an antisemite and the first to discuss Polish–Jewish relations in terms of an irreconcilable struggle for survival, purchased a struggling magazine, and, renaming it *Rola* (Field), converted it into the first Polish periodical devoted to the propagation of virulent antisemitism. Gradually, in the 1880s and 1890s, antisemitism became a respectable and integral ingredient of Polish nationalism. Positivist support for the enlightenment and integration of the Jews, now marked as irrevocably alien, faded and disappeared. The elderly Polish clerk Rzecki in Bolesław Prus's novel *Lalka* (*The Doll*, 1890) set in late 1870s Warsaw, registered this shift with these words: 'In general, I have noticed over the last year or two that dislike of the Hebrews is increasing; even people who, a few years ago, called them Poles of the Mosaic persuasion, now call them Jews. And those who recently admired their hard work, their persistence and their talents, today see only their exploitation and deceit.'[54] Indicative of the Polish loss of faith in Jewish assimilation was the re-emergence of doubts about the Polish and Christian feelings of the descendants of Frankists, who had left Judaism more than a hundred years earlier. The radical assimilationist Aleksander Kraushar, who converted in 1895, wrote his Polish-language history of the Frankists (1895) in part to answer such questions. In the introduction, he stated unequivocally that in the second generation the descendants of the original followers of Frank had already cut their ties to his teachings and that they and their offspring had become 'genuine, believing Christians and citizens of their country'.[55]

---

[53] Gelber, 'The Warsaw Pogroms of 1881' (Heb.), 116. [54] Prus, *The Doll*, 145.
[55] Kraushar, *Frank and his Sect* (Heb.), i. 38.

With the start of what Artur Eisenbach called the 'counter-emancipation' period,[56] the absolute number of conversions shot upwards—from 48 in the 1870s to 232 in the 1880s, 330 in the 1890s, and 103 in the years 1900–3 (1903 being the last year in Jeske-Choiński's list of baptisms). Those who left Judaism in response to the worsening social and political climate tended to come from the upper rather than the lower rungs of the social ladder. In the 1880s, 71 per cent were drawn from the ranks of financial, industrial, large-scale commercial, and professional families (who, it should be recalled, were a small segment of the total Jewish population); in the 1890s, 59 per cent; and in the period 1900–3, 64 per cent.

This shift reflected an increase in the number of Warsaw Jews who were middle-class, Polish-speaking, and Western in their habits and attitudes. Before 1862 the most serious problem confronting Warsaw Jews was residential and occupational discrimination, restrictions that made day-to-day living an unrelenting struggle. Aside from the very wealthiest families, whose roots were in Germany rather than Poland, few Jews at this time were interested in or prepared for integration into social circles outside their own community. Acculturation to Western, bourgeois norms of dress, education, worship, and social conduct was slow, while Polonization—adoption of the Polish language as a common means of communication and immersion in Polish culture—was even slower. Few Jews, for example, were educated in Polish secondary schools or universities. In the school year 1839–40 only thirty-five Jewish pupils were enrolled in Warsaw's two secondary schools. (Well-to-do, Western-oriented Jewish parents preferred to send their sons to the inaptly named Rabbinic School, a modern secondary school established in 1820, in which non-Jewish subjects were taught in Polish.) On the religious front, Western-style, ideological reforms were absent altogether. The two synagogues that served middle-class Westernized Jews—*di daytshe shul* (the German synagogue), established by the Berlin banker and merchant Isaac Flatau in 1802, and the Polish-oriented synagogue attached to the Rabbinic School, which closed in the 1840s but was replaced in 1850 by a similar synagogue supported by graduates of the school—shunned radical reforms, limiting themselves to cosmetic issues (decorum, sermons, trained cantors, and so on).[57]

In the second half of the century, especially after 1862, the Jewish middle class in Warsaw expanded, and at the same time became more Polish in its outlook and habits. Symptomatic of its growth was the emergence of a self-

[56] Eisenbach, *The Emancipation of the Jews in Poland*, 520.
[57] Kieniewicz, 'Assimilated Jews in Nineteenth-Century Warsaw', 174–6; Guterman, 'The Origins of the Great Synagogue', 183–95.

conscious, modernizing integrationist movement whose ideal Jew was the 'Pole of the Mosaic religion'. Like their counterparts in the West, its adherents believed in integration into the Polish nation on the basis of acculturation and productivization—but not at the price of religious apostasy. In the 1860s its supporters founded two Polish-language Jewish periodicals, the short-lived *Jutrzenka* (*Dawn*, 1861–3) and the more successful *Izraelita* (1863–1913). They embodied their vision of Polish–Jewish synthesis in the Great Synagogue in Tłomackie Street, which opened in 1878, a monumental, 2,000-seat, architect-designed structure, in which Western-style decorum and dress and trained cantorial voices set the tone. (The liturgy itself, however, remained unreformed.) The decision to erect the synagogue, made a decade or more earlier, reflected the inability of the two existing 'modern' synagogues, which together seated only 500 worshippers, to accommodate the hundreds of Polonized families who wanted membership.

Embourgeoisement and Polonization in turn prepared the way for an increase in the number of Jewish professionals—physicians, lawyers, engineers, academics, writers, and so on. One estimate is that in 1897 4,000 Jews in Warsaw were members, or the dependents of members, of the liberal professions.[58] Polonization, moreover, filtered down the social scale to include representatives of the middling ranks of Warsaw Jews, such as the clerk Henry Szlangbaum in Prus's novel *The Doll*, who, before the tide turned against integration, called himself Szlangowski, celebrated Easter and Christmas, and ate as much sausage (but without garlic, for he could not abide garlic!) as pious Catholics.[59] In 1856 Polonized clerks and sales agents in Warsaw established the Mutual Aid Society of Salesmen of the Mosaic Confession. In addition to providing the usual welfare benefits, it also organized lecture series for the self-improvement of its members, and in 1866 established its own 'modern' synagogue, featuring Polish-language sermons.[60]

Polonized, middle-class Jews were not sheltered from antisemitism, but experienced it differently from poor Jews. While it did not condemn them to living in poverty, it did erect roadblocks to their occupational and social mobility, depriving them of opportunities commensurate to their education, talents, and expectations. Unconverted Jews, for example, were barred from careers in government service and the courts—which explains, to a large extent, why lawyers, physicians, and students were so prominent among

[58] Kieniewicz, 'Assimilated Jews in Nineteenth-Century Warsaw', 177.

[59] Prus, *The Doll*, 146.

[60] Lichten, 'Notes on the Assimilation and Acculturation of Jews in Poland', 114; Bolesław Prus, *Kroniki*, excerpt in Segel (ed.), *Stranger in Our Midst*, 210; Guterman, 'The Origins of the Great Synagogue', 195.

Warsaw converts—13.5 per cent of the total number. Barriers like these became more widespread from the 1880s on, at the very moment that the number of Polonized Jews (and potential candidates for such posts) multiplied. Close social ties between middle-class, Polonized Jews and Poles, while not impossible, were not common either. Ambitious Jewish plutocrats, for example, even converted ones, had no access to aristocratic salons. Rich integrationists worked to make a place for themselves by generously contributing to Polish charities; turning their homes into private museums of old Polish furniture, paintings, and books; becoming patrons of literature, art, music, and the theatre; and subsidizing Polish-language journals and scientific publications. Aleksander Kraushar's father Herman, a successful stockbroker, collected Polish antiques to underscore his Polish patriotism, supported Polish writers, and contributed more to Polish than to Jewish charities.[61] But efforts like his were never repaid with full, unqualified acceptance. Just as painful as being denied access to desirable social circles was the uncomfortable knowledge that wealth and Polish manners had not removed the taint of Jewishness, the realization that the stigma of belonging to a despised group remained as strong as ever. In a letter to the novelist Józef I. Kraszewski, Aleksander Kraushar bitterly contrasted the camaraderie of the early 1860s, when Poles and Jews linked arms against a common Russian foe, with the antisemitism of the late 1880s. He complained that Jews who considered themselves Poles faced the 'truly unbearable pain' of being 'barely tolerated if not rejected by those who now lead the orchestra of racial hatred'. And he went on to express despair about what would happen to his 11-year-old son: 'What future awaits my poor boy? He was born a Pole, the Muscovites want him to become a Muscovite, Jelenski denies him the right to be a Pole, while he does not wish to become a German and cannot be a Jew any longer.'[62] In fact, the only Polish circles that welcomed unconverted Polonized Jews were the small, socialist underground movements, such as Proletariat, the Polish Socialist Party, and the Social Democracy of the Kingdom of Poland and Lithuania, whose revolutionary world-view stressed class rather than ethnic and religious divisions. Ironically, in these circles, which existed in a clandestine netherworld on the margins of respectable society, a small number of sons and daughters of wealthy families achieved social integration, mixing daily on an intimate basis with non-Jewish Poles. Some —Rosa Luxemburg, Stanisław Mendelson, Feliks Perl, Adolf Warszawski— became prominent activists. (Few Jews from Yiddish-speaking, working-

---

[61] Shatzky, 'Warsaw Jews in Polish Cultural Life'; id., 'Alexander Kraushar', 150.
[62] Quoted in Opalski and Bartal, *Poles and Jews*, 135.

class backgrounds were attracted to revolutionary socialism before the end of the century.[63])

The rise in conversions in Polonized, middle-class circles received a boost as well from increasing secularization. Although integrationists affirmed Judaism's importance, most were, in fact, indifferent to its rituals and rites. As a rule, they absented themselves from the synagogue, attending only on the High Holidays. The German synagogue, for example, was almost empty on normal sabbaths. (The demand for seats reflected the social status that membership conferred, not religious enthusiasm.) Raising funds for the building of the Great Synagogue went more slowly than its backers expected because indifference to religion within Polonized circles extended even to decorous, Westernized ritual.[64] After opening in 1878 it failed to attract the next generation, which according to the historian of the Great Synagogue was 'educated in the atmosphere of Polish nationalist Romanticism and, in some cases, socialism' and 'knew nothing of religion and was completely indifferent to matters of religion and faith'.[65] Their alienation —and propensity to convert—was so marked that in the 1880s a small circle of progressive members, led by S. H. Peltyn, editor of *Izraelita*, agitated to introduce German-style radical reforms in the belief they would reclaim the younger generation and stem the tide of defection. Unable to convince the congregation's board to act, the group then talked of establishing an independent Reform synagogue, in which they would be free to introduce whatever changes they wished.[66]

For the younger generation, conversion was not a dramatic transformative experience. It did not mark a wholesale or decisive break with past practices and beliefs, but was rather the final step in a lengthy and gradual process of disengagement from Judaism—in contrast to what had been the case in earlier centuries. In Aleksander Hertz's words: 'Secularization created an atmosphere in which changing religion ceased to be a matter of such profound inner conflict as it formerly had been . . . Religion was becoming a social convention; the acceptance of another convention could make possible a fundamental change in one's social standing.'[67] Like their counterparts in Berlin and Vienna, Warsaw Jews converted for this-worldly rather than other-worldly reasons, for convenience rather than from conviction. They changed their religion because they did not want to be Jews, not because they hoped to find salvation in Christianity.

---

[63] Cała, 'Jewish Socialists in the Kingdom of Poland'.
[64] Guterman, 'The Origins of the Great Synagogue', 196, 199.
[65] Guterman, *From Assimilation to Nationalism* (Heb.), 67.   [66] Ibid. 54–66.
[67] A. Hertz, *The Jews in Polish Culture*, 109.

Table 13.3. Gender of converts per decade, 1800–1903 (%)

Decade	Male	Female
1800s	55.56	44.44
1810s	39.62	60.38
1820s	58.44	41.56
1830s	67.00	33.00
1840s	72.32	27.68
1850s	70.12	29.88
1860s	46.67	53.33
1870s	56.25	43.75
1880s	60.78	39.22
1890s	54.24	45.76
1900–3	67.96	32.04
Overall	**61.90**	**38.10**

Evidence from Jeske-Choiński's list of baptisms reinforces the claim that most conversions in nineteenth-century Warsaw were strategic rather than spiritual in character. First, men converted more frequently than women, accounting for 62 per cent of all conversions between 1800 and 1903 (see Table 13.3). This suggests a link between the decision to convert and career choice, exposure to antisemitism, and frequent contact with Poles. Polonized men were able to pursue professional and commercial careers outside the social borders of the Jewish community and thus ran head-on into discrimination and exclusion, while their female counterparts, especially those in the middle class, were not expected to have careers or contribute to the household's economic well-being. They remained enclosed in a private network of family and close friends, more cut off from the social and occupational temptations that encouraged conversion than men. Interestingly, the difference between male and female conversions lessened or was even reversed in those decades when the overall rate of conversion was at its lowest—in the 1800s, the 1810s, the 1860s, and the 1870s—that is, at those moments when external pressures to convert were weakest. (The relatively small gap between male and female conversions in the 1890s, however, seems to be an exception to the pattern.) If religious concerns had been paramount or even more prominent, one would expect the difference between male and female rates to have been less pronounced.

Second, age at baptism also suggests that there was a strategic dimension

Table 13.4. Christian affiliation of converts per decade, 1800–1903 (%)

Decade	Calvinist	Lutheran	Roman Catholic
1800s	0.00	0.00	100.00
1810s	5.66	0.00	94.34
1820s	13.99	6.58	79.42
1830s	34.00	19.00	47.00
1840s	42.26	26.79	30.95
1850s	39.63	21.95	38.41
1860s	35.00	36.67	28.33
1870s	29.17	64.58	6.25
1880s	60.78	22.84	16.38
1890s	50.00	25.76	24.24
1900–3	51.46	24.27	24.27
Overall	**39.31**	**22.05**	**38.64**

to the decision to become a Christian. Among all converts, both male and female, 15 per cent were 12 or under, 59 per cent were in their teens or twenties, and 16 per cent were in their thirties. That is, 90 per cent converted towards the start of their adult lives, at a time when career and marriage decisions were made. The three ages at which conversion most frequently occurred were 18, 22, and 20 (in that order), which together accounted for 16.9 per cent of all conversions. Again, if there had been a significant religious dimension to conversions in Warsaw, one would expect the age distribution to have been broader—unless one assumes that religious awakening is a monopoly of the young.

Third, denominational choice also underscores the pragmatic nature of conversions in nineteenth-century Warsaw. Contrary to expectation, most Jews who became Christians did not become Roman Catholics (see Table 13.4). In fact, only 39 per cent did so, the same percentage as became Calvinists. The remaining 22 per cent were baptized as Lutherans. In the last decades of the century, converting Jews were even less likely to become Catholics. In the 1820s, 79 per cent of converts chose Catholicism; in the next decade the Catholic share fell to 47 per cent. But the fall towards the end of the century was even more dramatic: only 16 per cent of converts chose Catholicism in the 1880s, 24 per cent in the 1890s, and 24 per cent as well in the years 1900 to 1903. On the face of it this seems inexplicable. Common sense would seem to dictate that Jews who took the trouble to convert would embrace the majority faith. Why exchange membership of one minority group for membership of another? The claim that Polishness and Catholicism had become impossible to separate and that conversion was 'a final step toward unity with the Polish people', a positive, symbolic act of identification, rather than a pragmatic, opportunistic act, is at odds with the evidence, at least for the nineteenth century.[68] Even converts from the two highest socio-economic strata, those who were most eager to become exemplary Poles, chose Protestantism more often than Catholicism: among converts from the wealthiest stratum, only 38 per cent became Catholics; among those from the next stratum down, only 20 per cent. After the turn of the century, however, Polishness and Catholicism did become identified with each other, and as a result some Protestant families of Jewish origin converted once again, this time to Catholicism, hoping thus to cement their ties to the Polish nation.[69]

The paradox of Jews becoming Protestants in an overwhelmingly Catholic milieu becomes less paradoxical if their change of religion is viewed more as a decision to flee membership of the Jewish community and the disabilities and disadvantages it imposed and less as a decision to embrace Christianity and Polonism. Jews who became Christians chose Protestantism more often than Catholicism because it was less offensive to them as secularists and victims of religious intolerance. Roman Catholicism seemed idolatrous and ritualistic, while Protestantism appeared enlightened and rational.[70] An English official in Warsaw who asked converts why they did not join the Russian Orthodox Church was commonly told, 'It is against my principles.'[71] In other words, no form of Christianity was attractive in its own right. Rather, Protestantism was the least offensive alternative to being Jewish. In this respect, the behaviour of Warsaw Jewish converts was similar to that of converts in Vienna, St Petersburg, and Moscow, who often preferred (but not to the same extent) to become Christians under Protestant rather than Catholic or Orthodox auspices. In Vienna, for example, about one-quarter of all Jews quitting the *Gemeinde* between 1867 and 1914 became Protestants.[72]

[68] Lichten, 'Notes on the Assimilation and Acculturation of the Jews in Poland', 112; Shatzky, 'Alexander Kraushar', 165; A. Hertz, *The Jews in Polish Culture*, 109.

[69] Ciechanowiecki, 'Remarks on, and a Supplement to, the "Genealogical Sketches" of Kazimierz Reychman', 375–6. Jeske-Choiński did not record these conversions, of course, since those converting were not, at least in religious terms, Jews but Lutherans and Calvinists who had been Jews or whose parents had been Jews.

[70] A. Hertz, *The Jews in Polish Culture*, 109; Jeske-Choiński, *Neofici polscy*, 176.

[71] Bishop Wilkinson, speech, Anglican Church Conference, Zurich, 1–2 June 1904, Church Mission to the Jews Collection, Dep CMJ d. 51/8. Wilkinson was quoting a Mr Macleod in regard to Jews converted by the Revd Ellis in Warsaw.   [72] Rozenblit, *The Jews of Vienna*, 136.

There was an additional, perhaps more important, reason as well for pre-ferring Protestantism: the conversion process itself was less bothersome. Catholic priests required longer and more rigorous preparation than their Protestant counterparts before they would baptize Jews. Jeske-Choiński remarked that when a Jew needed a baptismal certificate at short notice, in order to obtain a government contract or post, he went to a Protestant min-ister, not a Catholic priest, who required several weeks of preparation.[73] Indeed, throughout the Russian empire, Protestant clergymen were reputed to be less scrupulous, more eager to win Jewish souls (and augment their own minority ranks) than their Catholic and Orthodox counterparts. As *The Jewish World* noted in 1911, 'it is well known in Russia that any Jew who does not feel equal to the task of professing Christianity by regular baptism obtains the necessary certificate of having been duly baptized from some obliging Protestant clergyman or missionary.'[74] When young Russian Jews wishing to circumvent university quotas turned up in large numbers asking to be baptized, Orthodox priests rejected them, causing them to seek bap-tism from other Christian groups. The newspaper *Ha'olam* reported that a group of students in Elizavetgrad were even willing to consider conversion to Islam.[75] (It should be recalled that over 900 conversions in nineteenth-century Warsaw were due to the missionary work of the militantly Protestant London Society for Promoting Christianity among the Jews.)

6

As in Berlin and Vienna, conversion in nineteenth-century Warsaw was both a success and a failure in this-worldly terms. Before 1862 it provided relief from legal disabilities, and after emancipation it eased access to professional and bureaucratic positions. However, it failed miserably on other fronts. It neither established the Polishness of converts nor erased the stigma of their Jewishness, and thus it failed to reward them with social acceptance and peace of mind.

In pre-partition Poland before the Frankist debacle, converts did not experience insurmountable obstacles to finding a place for themselves in Polish society. Conversion caused a decisive, unambiguous break with the

---

[73] Jeske-Choiński, *Neofici polscy*, 177; see also Cała, *Asymilacja Żydów w Królestwie Polskim*, 90.   [74] Judaeus, 'Baptismal Disease in Russia'.
[75] Quoted in Knaani, *The Second Workers' Aliyah* (Heb.), 73. Vladimir Medem noted in his memoirs that his parents, most of their siblings, and most converted Jews whom he knew in his youth became Protestants because the process involved fewer ceremonial and external difficulties (*The Life and Soul of a Legendary Jewish Socialist*, 5).

Jewish community—in economic and social as well as religious terms, since in the Polish Commonwealth, as everywhere in *ancien régime* Europe, there was no neutral or ambiguous space between the two communities—that is, there was no alternative to some measure of integration. Moreover, the crown, the church, and the nobility facilitated the social absorption of neophytes. Wealthy merchants, heads of monasteries, nobles, even great magnates and the monarch served as godparents for Jewish converts, thus obligating themselves to help them economically and, in the case of unmarried women, to provide them with dowries. The clergy also took an active role in arranging marriages for converts—preferably to Poles of 'Old Christian' stock, since they believed 'intermarriages' would strengthen the faith of the recently converted. Baptized Jews with property were able to acquire noble status, and in the eighteenth century some contracted marriages with the daughters of old noble families. Of course, there were Poles who harboured reservations about converts and others who viewed them with little respect and much condescension, but these feelings tended to fade with time rather than harden and become an impermeable barrier.[76]

After the Frankist baptisms, however, Poles viewed converts less favourably. In 1764 the Sejm revoked the statute allowing converts to be admitted into the *szlachta*, largely because of the rise in the number of Jews, both Frankists and non-Frankists, who had been changing their religion. As in Spain and Portugal in the fifteenth century, mass conversion, however desirable in theory, was viewed as problematic when it became a reality. Polish Catholics doubted the sincerity of the Frankist neophytes and their descendants, believing that they observed Jewish rites in secret, shunned Christian observances, nourished messianic hopes, refused to intermarry, and continued to eat *kugel* and *gefilte* fish. Despite the lack of abundant, unambiguous evidence, it seems that these suspicions were more or less justified. For at least two or three generations Polish Frankists cultivated a separatist, collective existence, mixing fully into the Polish majority only in the fourth and fifth generations.[77] But whether justified or not, what is critical is that doubts about Jewish converts and their motives were widespread before Warsaw Jews began to convert for their own pragmatic reasons in the nineteenth century. These doubts mingled with and reinforced the growing sense that baptism failed to erase the essential Jewishness of the Jew. As in central Europe, this perception was linked to the increase in the number of conversions, especially in prominent families. From at least the 1860s, if not earlier, con-

---

[76] A. Hertz, *The Jews in Polish Culture*, 64, 87, 88, 91; Goldberg, *Converts in the Polish–Lithuanian Commonwealth* (Heb.), chs. 3–4.

[77] Duker, 'Polish Frankism's Duration'.

verts were viewed as Jews, opportunistic Jews whose baptism was insincere and thus unable to change their character or outlook. The financier and railroad contractor Jan Bloch, who converted in 1851, while in his teens, acknowledged this widespread perception: 'Can you find one person in Warsaw, from the most malicious [aristocrat] . . . to the servant in my house, who does not know that I am a Jew? Whether Yoineh or Ignacy is written on the sign . . . the public knows very well that it is a Jewish business.'[78] However wealthy, talented or educated, Jews like Bloch faced growing resistance to their acceptance. Leopold Kronenberg, for example, found it difficult to secure Polish husbands for his daughters.[79] In most cases, neither converts nor their children were absorbed fully into the majority society. As a result, their social milieu was neither Christian nor Jewish; it was rather a heterogeneous mix of converted and unconverted (but indifferent) Jews, with a sprinkling of unconventional Poles (liberals, artists, intellectuals, freethinkers, radicals, bohemians). Even observant Jews, unlike their ancestors, maintained contact with converts in business and public life and took pride in their achievements.[80] The persistence of social and economic ties between the converted and the unconverted reinforced, in turn, the popular perception that the former were insincere in their new faith or at best ambivalent. In particular, Poles took offence at the willingness of wealthy, well-connected converts like Bloch to defend the Jewish community and intervene on its behalf.[81] Again, this development was not unique to Warsaw. In Vienna, Budapest, Berlin, and St Petersburg, converts were as likely to socialize with each other—and with *religionslos* Jews, intermarried Jews, and indifferent Jews—as they were with 'old' Christians.

The perception that a baptized Jew remained a Jew, while not causing the absolute number of conversions to fall, took a heavy emotional toll on those who fled Judaism to escape the stigma of belonging to the Jewish group. 'The shadow of the caste forever dogs their heels', Aleksander Hertz wrote about socially ambitious neophytes.[82] Fearing identification with Jews, they lived in constant uncertainty, worrying about how others saw them. To quiet their

[78] Quoted in Garncarska-Kadary, *The Role of the Jews in the Development of the Economy of Warsaw* (Heb.), 108. Opalska and Bartal discuss the widespread mistrust of converts in Polish literature from the 1860s (*Poles and Jews*, 64–5).

[79] Cała, 'The Question of the Assimilation of Jews in the Polish Kingdom', 135; Kieniewicz, 'Assimilated Jews in Nineteenth-Century Warsaw', 179.

[80] Garncarska-Kadary, *The Role of the Jews in the Development of the Economy of Warsaw* (Heb.), 108.

[81] Ibid. 270. Bloch outraged Polish nationalists when he returned to Radom, the city of his birth, and spoke in Yiddish to the Jews who had gathered at the railroad station to greet him.

[82] A. Hertz, *The Jews in Polish Culture*, 70.

doubts and anxieties, converts often took extraordinary measures to demonstrate that they no longer behaved or thought like Jews. Some embraced and propagated antisemitism, assuming that this, along with their prior baptism, would demonstrate how alien Jewishness was to them. In his account of Warsaw society in the late 1880s, Antoni Zaleski noted: 'It often happens that the main matadors of anti-Semitism are those *meches*[83] who pretend not to know that they too are called "Jews" by the world and with their anti-Semitism naively seek to obliterate their own semitic blood.'[84] While not embracing full-blown antisemitism, others accepted the premise that Jews deserved the misfortunes that befell them by virtue of their unsocial, disreputable traits. When the English Zionist Israel Cohen visited the Cambridge-trained physicist Władisław Natanson in Warsaw in 1919, the professor, who had converted in 1910, told him that Jews were as responsible as Poles for the post-war pogroms. In his view, Poles who attacked Jews were only taking revenge for Jewish dishonesty and chicanery.[85] Still others took more benign measures, most commonly cultivating an exaggerated, compensatory enthusiasm for traditions and symbols of Polishness. In the case of Aleksander Kraushar, this meant identification with the most reactionary model of Polonism—the Catholic aristocracy of feudal, pre-partition Poland. When his wife Jadwiga died in 1912, for example, he ordered one of the most elaborate Catholic funerals ever seen in Warsaw, with more than a hundred priests, a bishop at their head, participating in the funeral procession.[86] For others this meant 'an exaggerated care in using perfect language, a pedantic observation of customs considered specifically Polish, a cult of Polish literature and art'.[87]

7

Relative to the size of its Jewish population, the number of converts in nineteenth-century Warsaw was not great. Much smaller communities in the

[83] In the late nineteenth century, the term *meches* began to be used in Polish to describe converts from Judaism. The term, which came, it seems, from the Hebrew word *mekhes* (customs, tax, levy) and referred to the metaphorical levy (baptism) that Jews had to pay to enter non-Jewish society, was used by both Jews and Poles as a term of opprobrium. For more fanciful etymologies of *meches*, see Duker, 'Polish Frankism's Duration', 299 n. 49, and Garncarska-Kadary, *The Role of the Jews in the Development of the Economy of Warsaw* (Heb.), 261. The novelist and journalist Antoni Zaleski used the term in his survey of Warsaw society in the late 1880s, adding that he did not know its origins (*Towarzystwo warszawskie*, i. 270). Marian Gawalewicz published a two-volume novel, *Mechesi*, in 1894 about converts in *fin-de-siècle* Warsaw in which the main plot concerns the efforts of a convert to marry into a financially strapped aristocratic family (A. Hertz, *The Jews in Polish Culture*, 215).

[84] Zaleski, *Towarzystwo warszawskie*, i. 271.   [85] I. Cohen, *Travels in Jewry*, 61.
[86] Shatzky, 'Alexander Kraushar', 172–3.   [87] A. Hertz, *The Jews in Polish Culture*, 129.

West, like Berlin and Vienna, produced much larger numbers, in both absolute and relative terms. This is not remarkable, given the greater acculturation, secularization, and wealth of these communities and the failure of integration in Germany and Austria to keep pace with these developments. (In communities where secularization and acculturation were just as advanced, like Paris, London, Amsterdam, and New York, but integration into state and society was less obstructed, conversion was not common.) What is remarkable is the diversity of social backgrounds from which nineteenth-century Warsaw converts came. Before 1862 workers, craftsmen, small shopkeepers, and salesmen—typical rather than exceptional Jews—were more numerous than financiers, industrialists, and professionals; even after the removal of onerous residential and occupational disabilities they constituted 20–30 per cent of the total in any decade. In most Western Jewish communities, aside from the flotsam and jetsam whom missionaries rescued from the depths of material need and emotional confusion, conversion was more a strategy of the wealthy, the ambitious, and the well educated, those whose Judaism blocked their integration into elite non-Jewish circles or who had absorbed non-Jewish standards and judged themselves by them. Jews from modest backgrounds (except those from the very lowest stratum, who were in truly desperate straits) were less likely to convert. (Towards the end of the century, lower-middle-class women who lacked a dowry sufficient to attract a Jewish husband were also converting in larger numbers.) This too is not difficult to understand. Jewish craftsmen, traders, and shopkeepers in Western states gained little in turning Christian. Doing so did nothing to improve their economic circumstances or raise their social standing. They were content to find, or look for, companionship, love, affection, and recognition among other Jews. Their own sense of worth rested on what other Jews, their friends and family—not non-Jews—thought of them. In Warsaw, on the other hand, conversion was a rational choice for even humble Jews: it had concrete advantages, especially before emancipation, when the humble and the poor outnumbered the comfortable and the prosperous among those who left the community.

Yet, despite these broad differences, there was one critical respect in which the Warsaw experience differed little from the Western pattern of conversion. There, as in the West, the rate of conversion was at all times sensitive to shifts in Jewish status, in popular attitudes towards Jews, and in the political climate in general. In the two decades of relative improvement in Jewish status in Poland between the emancipation decree of 1862 and the pogrom of 1881, the number of converts plummeted—only to climb once again after the pogrom. Indeed, one would be hard pressed to name a more sensitive indicator of how Jews (certainly acculturated Jews) assessed the state of antisemitism and their chances for social and material success and even survival, whether in Warsaw or in other European capitals. In the nineteenth and twentieth centuries, whenever pessimism replaced optimism, Jews who had loosened their ties to the world of tradition turned to radical solutions: emigration, socialism, nationalism, suicide—and conversion. It is no coincidence that conversion rates soared in Berlin and Vienna in the late nineteenth and twentieth centuries, as we saw in Chapter 5, nor, to cite an even more specific instance, that more than 7,000 Jews were baptized in Budapest in the last five months of 1919, that is, during the White Terror that followed the collapse of Béla Kun's short-lived communist regime. Unlike historians' assessments of the relative strength or weakness of antisemitism in this or that European state, which often consider no more than the fortunes of right-wing antisemitism in the national political arena, the decision to leave Judaism reveals the impact of antisemitism at the level of life as it is actually lived. Patterns of apostasy uncover depths of desperation and despair, the loss of hope in a better future, along with the spread of indifference to and alienation from traditional loyalties and customs. They also indicate those within the community on whom discrimination and exclusion weighed most heavily, thus reminding us that antisemitism, however much the rhetorical plaything of politicians and pamphleteers, embittered the lives of flesh-and-blood Jews in concrete ways specific to their social status.

CHAPTER FOURTEEN

Memories of Jewishness

IN MARCEL PROUST'S EPIC, multi-volume novel *In Search of Lost Time*, Charles Swann—'one of the most distinguished members of the Jockey Club, a particular friend of the Comte de Paris and of the Prince of Wales, and one of the men most sought after in the aristocratic world of the Faubourg Saint-Germain'[1]—is both Jewish and not-Jewish simultaneously. The narrator (Marcel) regards Swann as a Jew, as do other characters, even before the Dreyfus affair erupts and heightens their 'Jew-consciousness'. In addition to referring to him as a Jew, they attribute his politics, appearance (red hair and large nose), and ailments (eczema and constipation) to his Jewish extraction.[2] Even Swann begins to identify himself as a Jew towards the end of his life. Mortally ill and under attack for his Dreyfusard views, he tells Marcel that 'at heart all these people [the *salonnards* of the Faubourg Saint-Germain] are anti-Semites'[3] and that 'when all's said and done these people belong to a different race' than the Jews, among whom he now counts himself.[4] As Marcel observes, Swann had returned 'to the paths which his forebears had trodden and from which he had been deflected by his aristocratic associations'.[5]

What is curious about these attributions of Jewishness to Swann is that he is not a Jew in any conventional sense of the term. He does not observe the Jewish (or any other) religion nor participate even marginally in Jewish communal, social, or philanthropic activities. In fact, he moves in circles to which Jews as a rule are not admitted. A man of fashion, he leads 'a brilliant social life', frequenting aristocratic Parisian salons 'on whose like no stockbroker or associate of stockbrokers had ever set eyes'.[6] He is not a Jew according to Jewish law, both his parents having been Christians from birth. Indeed, to find unconverted Jews in the Swann family tree, one must return to the generation of his grandparents (one of whom was a French Protestant, in any case), in which the decision to abandon Judaism was made.[7] Charles

---

[1] Proust, *In Search of Lost Time*, i. 19.
[2] Swann 'suffered from ethnic eczema and from the constipation of the prophets' (ibid. 571).　　　　[3] Ibid. iii. 796.　　　　[4] Ibid. 797–8.
[5] Ibid. 798.　　　　[6] Ibid. i. 21.　　　　[7] Ibid. i. 476, iv. 92.

himself, like his father before him, was ostensibly born and raised in the Catholic faith. Viewed objectively, his Jewishness is no more than a matter of background, descent, extraction, several generations removed.

Why then do Marcel and others in the aristocratic world of the Faubourg Saint-Germain regard Swann as a Jew? Indeed, why does Swann see himself in a similar light, at least towards the end of his life? These questions transcend the fictional text that generates them and point to crucial shifts in the ways in which Jewishness was perceived, in France and elsewhere in Europe, in the two centuries following the French Revolution. In broad terms they ask why the lines demarcating Jews from Christians became blurred between the French Revolution and the Second World War and how this blurring affected Jews who had converted to Christianity and whose fate depended on the maintenance of clear distinctions between adherents of the two religions.

With the important exception of the Iberian Conversos, Jews in medieval and early modern Europe were not troubled by issues of collective identity. The lines between Jew and Christian were firm and well marked. The half-Jewish Proust (his mother was an unbaptized, non-observant Jew) was as a type quintessentially modern with few if any medieval or early modern analogues. Before the second half of the eighteenth century, Jews were Jews and Christians were Christians. Religious identity and social and political status were coextensive. When Jews rejected Judaism and became Christians, for whatever reason, they exchanged one well-defined legal and cultural status for another, moving juridically from one corporate community to another. This was true whether their motives were spiritual and intellectual, as was the case with noted medieval converts such as Peter Alfonsi and Pablo Christiani, or whether they were rooted in material and emotional distress, as was the case with otherwise unknown deserted wives (*agunot*) in early modern Poland.[8] To be sure, their transformation into Christians was not always effortless and trouble-free. Some learned converts in early modern Germany, for example, felt that they remained Jewish in some way and emphasized their Jewish upbringing and learning in order to advance their careers as teachers and scholars. But these converts, however strong their own sense that spiritually they were neither fully Jewish nor fully Christian, in fact ceased to move in a Jewish environment.[9] Churchmen might question their motives, but they did not blur the distinction, as Proust's narrator did, between unconverted Jews and converted Jews and their descendants,

[8] J. Cohen, 'The Mentality of the Medieval Jewish Apostate'; Goldberg, *Converts in the Polish–Lithuanian Commonwealth* (Heb.), 22.   [9] Carlebach, *Divided Souls*.

indiscriminately lumping them together. In the eyes of the state and the church, they remained two distinct communities.

In the modern period several hundred thousand Jews in Europe and North America (it is impossible to be more precise) left their ancestral community and became, at least in name, Christians. With a few notable exceptions, their motives were pragmatic rather than spiritual. They became Christians because religion (theology, worship, ritual) had ceased to matter to them and because they hoped that baptism would improve their chances in life and allow them to escape the stigma of Jewishness. In the Russian and Austro-Hungarian empires, an additional factor was at work: in the absence of civil marriage, Jews who wished to marry Christians had first to become Christians. At the same time, however opportunistic their aims, most converts also identified with the societies whose religion they embraced. In this sense, their change of faith was driven by conviction as well, that is, conviction that Judaism had become fossilized and irrelevant and that the future belonged to the Christian societies that had emancipated them. For them, conversion meant not so much a change of religion as cultural and social identification with the dominant society.

On the face of it, the transaction was simple and straightforward, one that Christians appeared to desire and encourage. But as is often the case theory and practice diverged. Conversion signalled neither full withdrawal from Jewish circles nor full integration into non-Jewish ones. Moreover, as we saw in the case of Charles Swann, it did not prevent new Christians and their offspring from being labelled as Jews. A gap between what conversion promised and what it delivered opened because baptism was an inappropriate or unsuitable response to the Jewish predicament. It failed to address the Jewish problem, as non-Jews defined it in the age of emancipation. Put simply, conversion, a religious response to a religious problem, was anachronistic in an age in which material and racial concerns increasingly took precedence over spiritual and theological ones. It was an appropriate strategy for integration in those centuries in which the Jew's difference was defined in religious terms, but in the nineteenth and twentieth centuries, non-religious criteria became as important, if not more so, in defining Jews. From the viewpoint of the non-Jewish world, the problem with Jews was not their Judaism, which in the West was becoming weak and nominal in any case, but their Jewishness, that is, their race, ethnicity, nationality. There was, then, a mismatch between the traditional solution for the integration of the Jews—their conversion—and the problem—their essential Jewishness, which was seen as rooted in their flesh and blood and in the innermost recesses of their mind and was, thus, impervious to baptism.

People on both sides of the Jewish–Christian divide were aware of this tension (although this did little to stem the tide of conversion). In humorous stories and witticisms poking fun at converts and mocking Christian pieties, Jews voiced their belief that baptism was a superficial, meaningless gesture. In Alter Druyanov's classic three-volume collection of Jewish humour, which first appeared in 1922 but included material that circulated in eastern and western Europe at the turn of the century (and undoubtedly earlier), conversion is seen to change nothing. For example, Druyanov tells the story of a Catholic priest who converted a Jew and the next day, a Friday, when Catholics are forbidden to eat meat, found him eating a roast goose. The convert looked at the priest, and seeing how furious he was told him not to worry, that he was eating fish. This angered the priest even more, causing him to accuse the convert of being both a transgressor and a liar. The convert then explained: 'God forbid, dear priest, I am neither a transgressor nor a liar. I have simply done as you have done. You threw pure water on me and said, "Until now, you were a Jew; from now on, you are a Catholic." I threw pure water on the goose and said to it, "Until now, you were a goose; from now on, you are a fish." '[10] The same point is made in a story about the banker Otto Kahn that the Viennese-born psychoanalyst Theodor Reik included in his study *Jewish Wit*. Kahn, the story goes, was strolling along Fifth Avenue with the humorist Marshall Wilder, who was a hunchback. Pointing to a church, Kahn said, 'Marshall, that's the church I belong to. Did you know that I once was a Jew?' Wilder answered, 'Yes, Otto, and once I was a hunchback.'[11] Or, in the words of one pithy saying, 'In three places water is useless—in the ocean, in wine, and in the baptism of Jews.'[12]

Gentile critics and observers expressed the same sentiments, but seriously, not humorously. Racial thinkers, of course, believed that Jewish social habits and mental structures persisted after baptism since for them Jewishness was linked to blood not belief. Theorists of racial antisemitism in imperial Germany—Eugen Dühring, Wilhelm Marr, Otto Glagau, for example—made no distinction between baptized and unbaptized Jews. 'From the baptized minister to the last Polish *shnorrer*', Glagau wrote in 1874, 'they constitute a united chain.'[13] But belief in the failure of baptism to change the Jew's essence pre-dated this systematization of racial thinking by several decades. In the first half of the century, nationalist and Romantic opponents of emancipation were questioning the ability of conversion to change the Jew's character. In attacking Ludwig Börne in 1831, for example,

[10] Druyanov, *The Book of Jokes and Wit* (Heb.), ii. 138. [11] Reik, *Jewish Wit*, 90.
[12] Landmann, *Der jüdische Witz*, 439.
[13] Quoted in Katz, *From Prejudice to Destruction*, 269.

the *Gymnasium* master Eduard Meyer remarked that 'the many hateful characteristics of these Asiatics . . . cannot be laid aside so easily through baptism—the impudence and arrogance so frequent among them, the immorality and wantonness, their forward nature, and their often mean disposition'.[14] In the heat of the 1848 revolution in Vienna, a journalist warned readers to beware 'above all of any *baptised* Jews unto the tenth generation'. Another explained: 'That is how the Jews *were*, and that is how they *will be*, and neither will baptismal water cleanse them.'[15] By the 1860s views such as these were widespread enough that Moses Hess noted that baptism had ceased to protect Jews from 'the nightmare of German Jew-hatred'. As he wrote in his early nationalist tract *Rome and Jerusalem* (1862), 'Jewish noses cannot be reformed and the black frizzy hair of Jews cannot be made blond through baptism or smooth through combing'.[16] His fellow exile in Paris, Heinrich Heine, came to the same conclusion: Jewishness, the worst of the three evil maladies that afflicted poor, sick Jews, 'the thousand-year-old family affliction', was an 'incurable deep-seated hurt', impervious to treatment 'by vapor bath or douche [baptism]'.[17]

This belief—that there was little difference between converted and unconverted Jews—eventually became a stumbling block to the successful integration of former Jews and their children into non-Jewish circles, especially in central and eastern Europe. Before the last quarter of the nineteenth century, when conversion and other forms of radical assimilation began to increase dramatically, baptized Jews did not find their access to Christian circles and institutions barred. Racial thinking was weak in comparison to what it would become, and the number of converts seeking admission was small, again relative to the number later on. However, from the last decades of the century it became increasingly difficult for converted Jews to shake the taint of their origins, even when they were able to achieve limited integration such as civil service and university appointments. For example, in Germany, while converts were able to change their names with relative ease before 1900, from that date on it became almost impossible. The ministry of the interior denied most applications, tending to approve only those of applicants who were able to prove that they were Christians of long standing, that their friends and family members were also long-standing Christians, and that they had severed all social ties to Jews who remained unconverted.[18] In Russia the state forbade converts to change their names a half-century

---

[14] Quoted in Katz, *The Darker Side of Genius*, 16–17.
[15] Quoted in Rürup, 'The European Revolutions of 1848 and Jewish Emancipation', 47.
[16] M. Hess, *Rom und Jerusalem*, 14.
[17] Heine, 'The New Israelite Hospital in Hamburg', in id., *Complete Poems*, 399.
[18] Bering, *The Stigma of Names*.

earlier, in 1850. In the first decade of the twentieth century, when *racial* anti-semitism gained a following for the first time, extreme nationalists began to call on the government to ban converts from voting, purchasing and leasing land, and holding positions in the civil service, the judiciary, and the armed forces. While tsarist officials refused to accede to these demands, they main-tained the glass ceiling that prevented converted Jews in the civil service and army from rising.[19] In central Europe, where conversion was a *de facto* (but not *de jure*) requirement for appointment to and advancement in the civil service, the academy, the military, the judiciary, and other elite enclaves, Jews who had taken this step, along with children of theirs who were Christian from birth, could still find their origins an impediment to promotion or a source of innuendo and intrigue. Paul Kayser, tutor to the children of Otto von Bismarck, came under vicious attack from antisemites. Karl Julius von Bitter, *Regierungspräsident* in Silesia, was rejected as Minister of the Interior in 1895 because of 'his still somewhat Semitic tendencies'; a year later Chan-cellor Hohenlohe prevented his appointment as Minister of Trade because he was 'ein jüdischer Streber' (a pushy Jew).[20] The most notorious case of this sort occurred in the last year of the Weimar Republic, when the Nazis exposed the 'Jewish origins' of Theodor Düsterberg, co-founder and vice-president of the Stahlhelm and candidate of the German National Party in the March 1932 presidential election, thus destroying his chances and for-cing him to withdraw from the run-off election in April. (One grandparent was a baptized Jew.)[21]

On the social front, Jewish origins weighed more heavily. Whereas con-version was often an effective stratagem for career advancement, it was much less successful in gaining entry to fashionable or upper-class circles, that is, spheres in which birth took precedence over merit as a matter of prin-ciple. In imperial Germany converted Jews from even the wealthiest families often faced difficulties in finding marriage partners of 'old Christian' upper-middle-class birth, let alone aristocratic birth. The fruitless search of the second-generation banker Paul Wallich, described so poignantly by Werner Mosse, was not unusual. Baptized at birth in 1882, Wallich devoted himself

[19] Rogger, *Jewish Policies and Right-Wing Politics*, 35–6; Beizer, *The Jews of St. Petersburg*, 15; Weinerman, 'Racism, Racial Prejudice, and Jews in Late Imperial Russia'; Verner, 'What's in a Name?', 1058–9. Stanislawski observes: 'In Russia alone in Christendom, the state required that the descendants of Jews bear their Jewish surnames as a mark of their tainted origin forever' (*Tsar Nicholas I and the Jews*, 148). As Bering's work on name-changing in Germany shows, this is not entirely true (*The Stigma of Names*). On the other hand, while the ban in Rus-sia was in theory absolute, it was not enforced rigorously, as was true with much Russian legis-lation regarding Jews.   [20] Röhl, 'Higher Civil Servants in Germany', 111–12.
[21] Eyck, *A History of the Weimar Republic*, ii. 356; Leschnitzer, *The Magic Background of Mod-ern Anti-Semitism*, 217–18.

to raising his social standing. In his youth, this led him to pursue three goals: membership in a nationalist student corps at university, at which he failed; appointment as a reserve officer following military service, at which he succeeded; and marriage to a woman *von Familie*. As the converted son of a Jewish banker, the majority of the eligible young women whom he knew, women who were part of the Wallich family circle, were themselves Jewish or of Jewish extraction. His overtures to non-Jewish women from his own stratum met with rejection. Some former Jews in his position solved their marriage problem by taking wives from abroad, but Wallich was too uncosmopolitan to take such a step. In the end out of necessity he married down, taking as his wife a woman whose father was an academic instructor in a military school.[22] For women from Wallich's milieu, the prospects for successful integration were marginally better. Female converts who succeeded in finding husbands from 'old Christian' families—and thus shed their Jewish names at marriage—were in some cases able to see their children move freely in non-Jewish circles. Most converts and their children, however, remained in circles that were ethnically if not religiously Jewish, there being hardly any social relations between the Jewish *haute bourgeoisie* (in the ethnic sense) and the German *haute bourgeoisie* and aristocracy.[23]

In Warsaw, where few wealthy Jewish families remained Jewish for more than two or three generations, complete absorption also became difficult in the late nineteenth century. As we saw in the previous chapter, aristocrats rarely admitted converted Jews to their salons or, in turn, frequented Jewish salons, whose visitors were drawn from the worlds of government administration, commerce, science, and industry. The dynamic industrial and financial magnate Leopold Kronenberg, who became a Roman Catholic in 1846 but was always referred to as a Jew, was hard pressed to secure Polish husbands for his daughters, who were viewed as 'too Jewish'.[24] As we saw in the previous chapter, nationalists like Teodor Jeske-Choiński took steps to 'unmask' families of Jewish origin, inaugurating what has become a tradition in Polish politics to this day. Recall also the new epithet for convert—*meches*—that entered the Polish language in the late nineteenth century.

Throughout Europe, in both liberal and illiberal societies, converts and the children of converts who attracted public attention, for whatever reason, risked having their origin thrown in their face by critics and enemies. When

---

[22] W. E. Mosse, 'Problems and Limits of Assimilation'.

[23] All this is set out in admirable detail and clarity in W. E. Mosse, *The German-Jewish Economic Elite*.

[24] Guterman, 'Attitudes of Warsaw Assimilationists towards Conversion' (Heb.), 68; Cała, 'The Question of the Assimilation of Jews', 135; Levinson, *History of the Jews of Warsaw* (Heb.), 139.

Benjamin Disraeli first stood for election to Parliament in the 1830s, as I noted in Chapter 9, he encountered what was for him an unprecedented level of anti-Jewish hostility. The taunts were mild, to be sure, compared with the abuse he suffered as prime minister between 1874 and 1880, but by that time he had become a full-blown racial chauvinist and had provided his enemies with rich material from which to select their barbs.[25] But even converts who were less ambitious and less in the limelight found that their descent was a source of potential reproach. After Samuel Phillips, literature critic for *The Times* at mid-century and like Disraeli a Christian since his youth, reviewed William Makepeace Thackeray's work unfavourably, the latter referred continually to the converted critic's origins in correspondence with friends.[26]

If converts in Britain who were public figures risked being attacked for their Jewishness, how much more so their counterparts in Germany and the Habsburg lands, where racial antisemitism was a regular feature of politics and culture after 1880. It would be difficult, if not impossible, to name a well-known ex-Jewish, central European politician, artist, musician, writer, intellectual, or academic who escaped being reminded that he or she used to be a Jew, and having his or her activities and work attributed to that fact. The examples are endless. Bewilderment, frustration, and amazement were the reactions of two of the earliest German Jewish intellectuals to experience this. Six months after his baptism, Heinrich Heine wrote to his close friend Moses Moser, like him a one-time member of the Verein für Kultur und Wissenschaft der Juden, that Christian and Jew alike now detested him and that he regretted his conversion. 'I do not see that things have gone any the better with me since: on the contrary, I have had nothing but misfortune. Is it not ridiculous? I am no sooner baptized than I am upbraided as a Jew.'[27] Ludwig Börne, writing from exile in Paris in the 1830s, was equally dumbfounded; despite his baptism in 1818, no one ever forgot he was a Jew. Those who reproached him for being a Jew, as well as those who forgave him or praised him for it, were all hopelessly trapped in a way of thinking that did not allow them to forget it.[28] To their amazement and chagrin, Heine and Börne discovered, as did countless other German Jews in the decades that followed, that the rules of the game had changed without their being told.

It would seem that at some stage most converts, at least in central and eastern Europe, realized that their Jewish past was not irrelevant to their future and that it could continue to haunt them—and possibly their children

[25] Wohl, ' "Dizzi-Ben-Dizzi" '.   [26] Prawer, *Israel at Vanity Fair*, 342–3.
[27] Heinrich Heine to Moses Moser, 9 Jan. 1826, in Heine, *Memoirs*, i. 172.
[28] Börne, *Briefe aus Paris*, 449–50.

as well. Of course, given the nature of the evidence that survives and the fact that most persons do not record or reveal their most intimate feelings, we can do no more than speculate here. Most baptized Jews, after all, left no account of how they fared as Christians, preferring to draw as little attention to themselves as possible. Thus what we know comes from the more articulate and ambitious converts who, their hopes deflated or crushed, vented their feelings about being unable to escape their Jewish descent.[29] At first, this would seem to be an unrepresentative group. The Heines, Börnes, Disraelis, and Prousts of this world are an exceptional lot. But, it should be remembered, however exceptional their creative achievements, their emotional experiences were not unusual, but were shared by other former Jews. Where Heine and the others differed was in their articulation of those feelings (this was in part how they engaged with them). Less accomplished converts also ran into obstacles and insults and were no less disappointed, embarrassed, confused, frustrated, and angered. At times their voices can be heard, but in the nature of things their reactions, especially their inner turmoil and confusion, are less accessible than those of their better-known, more articulate fellow converts.

No simple formula can capture the complex of behavioural patterns and emotional states that the failure of integration generated. Nonetheless, one generalization is possible. Most converts who met with disappointment undertook, one way or another, to increase the distance between themselves and the group with which they remained identified. Baptism having failed to secure their escape from Jewishness, they undertook to convince doubters and detractors (and perhaps themselves as well) that indeed their loyalties, thoughts, and feelings were no longer Jewish. Their strategies for accomplishing this ranged from the subtle to the crude; at times they were the outcome of foresight and planning, while at other times they were the result of more or less unconscious thought processes, arrived at without careful reflection.

At its most extreme, distancing took the form of defaming Jews. In these instances, which were a minority, converts and the children of converts embraced and disseminated anti-Jewish critiques of Jews and Judaism. The logic underlying their behaviour, even if unconscious, was that this, along with their prior baptism, would demonstrate how far they had travelled.

[29] Less ambitious converts did not face slights and exclusions to the same extent since they were content with a lower level of integration and social acceptance. Frequently, their motives for becoming Christians in the first place were tied to immediate, short-term occupational goals rather than burning emotional and social needs. That is, they were not fleeing their Jewishness as much as advancing their careers. Converts like these continued to mix socially with Jews—converted, *Konfessionslos*, non-observant, intermarried, and the like.

What better way, in other words, to dispel doubts about their own allegiances than to damn the Jews, harping on their alienness, malevolence, and corruption? As we saw in Chapter 6, this form of self-hatred was more common where converts faced the most obstacles to integration and social acceptance. In late nineteenth- and early twentieth-century Warsaw, for example, converts were notorious for their Jew-baiting. Recall the comments of Antoni Zaleski: 'It often happens that the main matadors of anti-Semitism are those *meches* who pretend not to know that they too are called "Jews" by the world and with their anti-Semitism naively seek to obliterate their own Semitic blood.'[30] In the interwar period, persons of Jewish descent were found among antisemitic nationalist agitators. When publicly reminded of their background they naturally suffered acute distress, as they did later when the Nazis forced them into the Warsaw ghetto. Among them was Susanna Rabska, a writer and agitator for the National Democratic Party (Endecja), whose father was the historian of Frankism, Aleksander Kraushar.[31]

Most converts, however, in responding to baptism's failure to solve their Jewish problem, employed less extreme measures to distance themselves from their background. A more common response was an exaggerated, compensatory enthusiasm for traditions and symbols of the dominant group, a strategy often termed being 'more Catholic than the pope'. This assumed diverse, often remarkable, forms. For the interwar English novelist Gilbert Frankau, as we saw in Chapter 12, it meant acting like a country-bred aristocrat—fishing, fencing, and hunting (despite being terrified of riding)—cultivating a suave, insouciant demeanour and espousing right-wing, labour-bashing imperialist politics. For Aleksander Kraushar, it meant identifying with the most reactionary model of Polonism—the Catholic aristocracy of pre-partition Poland. For Charles Swann, it meant connoisseurship, exquisite aristocratic manners, and research into the coinage of the Order of St John of Jerusalem (the Knights Hospitaller). As the Duc de Guermantes remarks, without a trace of irony, 'it's astonishing the passion people of one religion have for studying others'.[32] A story that circulated at the turn of the century captures this link between exaggerated devotion to art and antiquities and uneasiness about being a convert, with Jewish family skeletons lurking in the closet. As told by Druyanov, a group of visitors came to see the newly built house of a rich Berlin convert. He ushered them into his salon and said, 'Here, gentlemen, everything is done in the style of the eighteenth century.' He then took them into his study and said, 'Here is the style of the

---

[30] Zaleski, *Towarzystwo warszawskie*, i. 271.
[31] Heller, *On the Edge of Destruction*, 200, 206, 320 n. 35; A. Hertz, *The Jews in Polish Culture*, 128; Roland, *Courage under Siege*, 31. [32] Proust, *In Search of Lost Time*, iii. 787.

German renaissance of the sixteenth century.' Finally they reached a room at the far end of the house, but he did not take them in. One of them asked, 'What style is this room done in?' The owner answered offhandedly, 'Oh, just some old things of my father's', prompting the banker Carl Fürstenberg to quip: 'Ah, the pre-Christian period.'[33]

The Lithuanian-born art critic and connoisseur Bernard Berenson, who became an Episcopalian at Harvard in 1885 and then a Roman Catholic near Siena in 1891, carried this kind of role-playing to an extreme. Having absorbed the likes and dislikes of Boston's fashionable Back Bay as a young man, he forged for himself an elegant, impeccably mannered persona, seeking to make his life itself a polished work of art. At his exquisite villa, I Tatti, in the Tuscan hills, he surrounded himself with Italian Renaissance paintings, old furniture and hangings, and a magnificent art library. There, from 1900 to his death in 1959, in the role of aesthete and arbiter of taste, he hosted streams of art-collecting socialites, writers, intellectuals, celebrities, and hangers-on, preaching the *fin-de-siècle* Romantic doctrine of aesthetic experience as sacred reality and pretending to have no contact with the world of commerce. Until the Second World War forced him into hiding and induced a radical inner upheaval, he distanced himself from his impoverished, east European immigrant background. In non-Jewish company he never talked about his early years or his origins, dropping his mask (his own metaphor) only when in the company of Jewish visitors like Israel Zangwill and Leo and Gertrude Stein. After the war he recalled what an effort it had been, even if he had been unaware of it at the time, 'to act as if one were a mere Englishman or Frenchman or American'.[34] When he did mention Jews in conversation or correspondence with non-Jews, he tried to dissociate himself from them. For example, after visiting a large Reform synagogue in Berlin on an early trip to Europe, he wrote to his Boston patron Isabella Gardner about the beauty of the building, choir, and service but then added, in a characteristic gesture, that despite the attempt to create elegance the worshippers 'seemed to be selling old clothes'.[35]

Yet however much Berenson expressed his disdain for commerce and nouveau riche Jews and preference for well-born 'thoroughbreds', he could not escape the knowledge that his own wealth (as well as the art it allowed him to purchase) derived from his long-standing but unpublicized art dealings, especially his thirty-year secret partnership with the London Jewish art dealer Joseph Duveen, who paid him a percentage on the sale of Old Master

[33] Druyanov, *The Book of Jokes and Wit* (Heb.), ii. 145.
[34] Berenson, *Sunset and Twilight*, 323.
[35] Quoted in Fixler, 'Bernard Berenson of Butremanz', 138.

paintings for which he did attributions.[36] The Paris art dealer Armand Lowengard commented on Berenson's hypocrisy to his fellow dealer René Gimpel (who was Duveen's brother-in-law): 'You've seen how the snob plays at being disinterested in the eyes of the world; well, you ought to see his letters asking for money, the baldness of it.'[37] Berenson was not blind to his own hypocrisy. His dealings, by linking him to the world of Jewish trade, caused him much anguish and eventually led him to renounce dealing after the war and to make amends by leaving his villa and its collections to Harvard, his alma mater.

In the West converts like Berenson who tried (unsuccessfully) to remake themselves tended to express ambivalence rather than undiluted scorn for Jews and things Jewish. To be sure, this ambivalence was in no sense balanced between affirmation and negation, with attraction and repulsion experienced in equal measure. The positive side of the equation often was no more than an acknowledgement of Jewish suffering and steadfastness, with an occasional nod to Jewish wit, cooking, family life, or genius. Proust's treatment of Jews in *In Search of Lost Time* demonstrates how such ambivalence worked. On the one hand, Proust reproduced common antisemitic clichés about Jews, especially upwardly mobile, well-acculturated Jews—like himself and his Jewish relatives and friends. Bloch is a hook-nosed, ill-bred, tactless social climber; his female relatives are clannish, overdressed, and oversexed; his father and great-uncle are alternately fawning and boastful in the presence of Christians. (In contrast, the ideal non-Jew, the young aristocrat Robert de Saint-Loup, is tall, slim, erect, elegant, and graceful, 'a young man with penetrating eyes whose skin was as fair and his hair as golden as if they had absorbed all the rays of the sun'.[38]) Jews, both men and women, are also linked to uninhibited, brazen sexuality. Bloch introduces the narrator Marcel to brothels, where the first girl he is offered is Rachel, whom the madam considers 'a special treat' because she is Jewish.[39] The young Jewish women vacationing at Balbec are 'a horde of ill-bred sluts who carried their zeal for "seaside fashions" so far as to be always apparently on their way home from shrimping or out to dance the tango', while Bloch's sisters in particular are 'at once overdressed and half naked, with their languid, brazen, ostentatious, slatternly air'.[40] But above all, Proust equates Jewishness with homosexuality, about which he, himself a homosexual, was decidedly ambivalent. In a much-quoted passage in the 'Sodom and Gomorrah' volume, he makes this explicit. Homosexuals, like Jews, constitute a cursed race afflicted with 'an incurable disease'; their social position is unstable,

---

[36] Simpson, *The Partnership.*   [37] Gimpel, *Diary of an Art Dealer,* 248.
[38] Proust, *In Search of Lost Time,* ii. 421.   [39] Ibid. 205.   [40] Ibid. 435, 660.

forcing them, like Jews once again, to shun one another and seek out 'those who are most directly their opposite', but 'who do not want their company', and thus treat them with contempt and condescension. Like Jews, 'they form in every land an oriental colony, cultured, musical, malicious, which has charming qualities and intolerable defects'.[41] So close is this identification in Proust that he asks facetiously whether a Sodomist movement, similar to the Zionist movement, will arise to rebuild the biblical Sodom.[42]

Yet, as Proust's comments about homosexuals suggest, he thought that Jews too had 'their charming qualities'. Bloch senior is an affectionate father. Bloch junior has a pleasing face—even Albertine agrees that he is not bad looking, though as a rule she does not like 'Yids' and 'their creepy ways', and Bloch makes her feel 'quite sick'.[43] The 'unassimilated' Jewish intellectuals and bohemians in a cafe at which Marcel and Saint-Loup dine repel Marcel: 'their hair was too long, their noses and eyes were too big, their gestures abrupt and theatrical'. Nonetheless, 'they had plenty of wit and goodheartedness, and were men to whom, in the long run, one could become closely attached'. Indeed, in one respect, they outshine Marcel's new aristocratic friends: 'there were few whose parents and kinsfolk had not a warmth of heart, a breadth of mind, a sincerity, in comparison with which Saint-Loup's mother and the Duc de Guermantes cut the poorest of moral figures by their aridity, their skin-deep religiosity'.[44] More importantly, Proust endowed Jews with the capacity to change. Despite believing in racial inheritances and atavisms, in deep, ineluctable forces that erupted 'from a nature anterior to the individual himself',[45] he also affirmed his belief in the transformative power of French culture and manners. Accordingly, his Jews represent various points on the spectrum of assimilationist behaviour, with the refined, almost aristocratic Swann at one extreme and Bloch, in his worst moments, at the other. And even Bloch, who possesses all the faults that Marcel most dislikes, exhibits the capacity to grow over the course of the novel, at the end of which he has become a successful writer and *salonnard*. In fact, Swann himself, in the years before the novel's start, was more Bloch-like in character and behaviour. In the course of his life, he 'contrived to illustrate in turn all the successive stages through which those of his race had passed, from the most naive snobbery and the crudest caddishness to the most exquisite good manners'.[46]

Emblematic of Proust's ambivalence is the fate of his Jews at the novel's end. While Swann is dead, his daughter, Gilberte, has become successively the wife of Robert de Saint-Loup and the Duc de Guermantes; Bloch, his

---

[41] Ibid. iv. 19–22. [42] Ibid. 43. [43] Ibid. ii. 629.
[44] Ibid. iii. 559–60. [45] Ibid. ii. 644. [46] Ibid. 2.

name changed to Jacques du Rozier (an allusion to the rue des Rosiers in the heart of Paris's immigrant Jewish quarter), has become a successful, salon-going dramatist; Rachel, the former whore and mistress of Saint-Loup, has become a famous actress; and Madame Verdurin, in whom Marcel's Jew-sniffing grandfather detects Jewish ancestors, has established an exclusive salon and become Princesse de Guermantes. Their social ascent, however, has come at a price—and here we see Proust's ambivalence—the eradication of their Jewishness. They have ceased to be Jews in every sense of the term; their immersion in French society is radical and complete (with the exception of Bloch's ineptly chosen new name).

In the West ambivalence was the hallmark of most converts unable to escape their Jewish past. There were a few exceptions, of course: a handful became Jew-baiters,[47] but none, to my knowledge, moved in the opposite direction, 'returning' to their people as champions of Jewish causes, like Zionism, or defenders of Jewish rights. In Russia and Poland, however, where the Jewish question was more acute (Russians Jews, for example, remained un-emancipated until 1917), converts exhibited more extreme, highly charged attitudes to their Jewish past. As we have seen, there were ex-Jews in Poland who strove to authenticate their Polishness by embracing radical nationalist antisemitism. In Russia converts were prominent in the articulation and diffusion of contempt for Jews. The most notorious were Jacob Brafman, missionary, censor of Jewish books, and author of the infamous work *The Book of the Kahal* (1869), which launched the canard that clandestine communal bodies exercised absolute control over Russia's Jews, and became the most successful antisemitic text in Russian history, and Ippolit Lyutostansky, author of several pseudo-scholarly books publicizing the blood libel and attacking the Talmud as a font of anti-Christian hatred.[48] Others included Aleksandr Alekseev (Wolf Nakhlas), a one-time missionary to Jewish cantonists and crude agitor, whose hatred of Jews was said to be so fanatical that later in life he never looked a Jew in the face or permitted one to enter his house; Semen Efron-Litvinov, a writer for the right-wing St Petersburg daily *Novoe vremya*, whose speciality was discovering skulduggery in rabbinic literature; and Anatoly Grigoryevich Gassmann, a high-ranking official in

[47] In his memoirs, Arthur Schnitzler described one who did. When he was a medical student at the University of Vienna from 1879 to 1885, there was an organization that lent money to needy medical students. Antisemites agitated to bar Jews from receiving this aid. Among those who spoke in favour of the ban was a baptized Jew who had become a German nationalist. According to Schnitzler, 'he became the butt of a slogan that was popular at the time: "Anti-Semitism did not succeed until the Jews began to sponsor it" ' (*My Youth in Vienna*, 130).

[48] The most recent account of Brafman and Lyutostansky is in Klier, *Imperial Russia's Jewish Question*, 263–83, 423–7.

St Petersburg who repeatedly turned a deaf ear to Jewish requests for assistance.[49]

The undiluted hatred that these and other Russian converts felt for their former people reflected in part the harsh nature of the tsarist regime and its treatment of Jews. That is, having cast their lot with the dominant society, they embraced its views heart and soul, including its views of Jews. But it also reflected a feature in Russian conversions that was absent from or less prominent in the West. When Jews in Berlin or Paris or London left the communal fold, their departure marked the end of a process of disengagement from Jewish life that usually stretched over several generations. Most came from homes in which Jewish knowledge, observance, and attachments were already weak and vestigial, in which markers of Jewish distinctiveness (however defined) were disappearing. In contrast, converts in Russia tended to come from far more traditional backgrounds. Most had grown up in Yiddish-speaking, religiously observant homes in the Pale of Settlement, had attended *ḥeder* and, in some cases, yeshiva and had spent their formative years living entirely in the company of other traditional Jews. For them, to move from being a Jew to being a Christian was an enormous leap. The distance between their present and past lives was almost as great as it had been in the case of medieval and early modern conversions. Because they were so close to the world of Jewish tradition, because they had known and absorbed its habits and outlook from their earliest days, it remained 'alive' within them even after conversion. Their need to purge themselves of this past, to demonstrate that it had been left behind, was greater than that of most Western converts, whose memories of Jewish ritual, language, learning, worship, and social distinctiveness were, by comparison, fragmented and weak. Their need to distance themselves from their Jewish past was acute—and what better way to meet this need than by attacking, in public and with gusto, those still living in that past?[50]

This explanation also illuminates one other curious feature of the history of conversion in eastern Europe. In Russia and Poland, there were converts whose outlook on Jewish matters swung to the opposite, or 'philosemitic', end of the spectrum. Instead of abusing Jews, they became their advocates— in print, before government authorities, and in courtrooms—using the influence or wealth which their conversion had made possible to ease the

---

[49] For biographical details and anecdotes about these figures, see Tsitron, *Behind the Curtain* (Heb.).

[50] For some, there was one other, overlapping, motive as well. Having suffered at the hands of the communal authorities when they began to stray from the Jewish fold, their attacks on Judaism became an outlet for the bitterness they felt about the way they had been treated and a means of getting back at their former persecutors.

impact of harsh decrees and popular prejudices. The archetype of this sort of ex-Jew was the semiticist Daniel Khvolson, who converted in 1855 to obtain an academic post in St Petersburg. Khvolson became a legend in Russian Jewry for defending Judaism against the libel that its ritual required Christian blood. He also helped to found the Society for the Diffusion of Enlightenment among the Jews in 1863 and served on its executive committee for a decade, although he eventually broke with its maskilic backers. Rabbis and other traditional Jews spoke warmly of him and at his death eulogized him as a great Jew.[51]

Khvolson was not the only prominent convert to campaign against the blood libel. In 1883 the St Petersburg contractor Iosif Nikolaevich Sorkin translated Isaac Baer Levinsohn's *Efes damim* (1837), a Hebrew refutation of the blood libel, into Russian and wrote a bitter, no-holds-barred introduction to it, in which he did not spare even the government for its support of anti-semitism. He then used his own money to distribute the translation widely among provincial officials and St Petersburg ministers and bureaucrats. The following year he published a Russian translation of a German-language anthology of anti-blood-libel testimonies from prominent Europeans; this too he distributed freely in Russian officialdom. Eventually he withdrew completely from business and devoted all his time and energy to Jewish matters.[52] Other converts also supported the work of the Society for the Diffusion of Enlightenment, whose progressive, integrationist goals dovetailed with their own personal aspirations. The baptized physician Joseph Bartenson, who spent most of his life in government service in the field of public health, rising to the post of court physician, served alongside Khvolson on the society's executive committee.[53] The St Petersburg censor of Jewish books Nikander Vasilevich Susman, who had been, in succession, a yeshiva student, a maskil, and a freethinker before his conversion to the Orthodox Church in the mid-1870s, used his position and friendship with the Minister of Education, Count Delyanov, to improve conditions for Jews. He wrote reports defending Jewish legal literature, helped Jewish students gain admission to the university in St Petersburg, and passed information about impending anti-Jewish measures to the capital's Jewish notables. All the time, in order to remain in favour with high bureaucratic figures, he kept up Russian Orthodox observances, attending church daily, and celebrating its holy days.[54]

[51] Tsitron, *Behind the Curtain* (Heb.), vol. i, ch. 1.   [52] Ibid. i. 58–61.
[53] Greenberg, *The Jews in Russia*, i. 176–7; Berk, *Year of Crisis, Year of Hope*, 31.
[54] Tsitron, *Behind the Curtain* (Heb.), i. 77–9. See also the remarkable story of the St Petersburg photographer Constantine Shapira, which the Zionist activist Meir Jacob Fine recounted in his memoirs, *Days and Years* (Heb.), ii. 206–19.

In Warsaw as well there were influential ex-Jews who came from traditional homes and continued to feel the pull of Jewish attachments long after becoming Christians. The two best-known nineteenth-century figures were the brothers-in-law Leopold Kronenberg and Jan Bloch. The former intervened on behalf of the Jewish community with government officials, with whom he was in close contact because of his economic activities, supported Jewish charities with anonymous contributions, and donated 6,000 roubles towards the erection of the Great Synagogue, Warsaw's first modern, architect-designed, Western-style synagogue, which opened in 1878. Bloch, a financier and railway contractor who converted at 15, was even more active in the Jewish world. He supported the productivization schemes of Baron de Hirsch, including Jewish agricultural settlements in Poland and Argentina; founded a private statistical bureau to conduct research on the economic condition of the Jews in Poland; befriended Theodor Herzl; and like Khvolson and others laboured to counter the blood libel. In his personal life, he surrounded himself with Jewish clerks and assistants (some of whom were baptized), and supported the only one of his brothers who did not convert, asking him specifically to remain Jewish. His will began with the words, 'All my life I have been a Jew and as a Jew I die.'[55]

Despite dissimilar reactions towards their former co-religionists, both kinds of east European converts—those who embittered the lives of Jews and those who tried to relieve their suffering—resembled each other in one critical sense: all were unable to escape their Jewish past. Long after having changed their religion, their origins and upbringing continued to weigh heavily on their consciousness, shaping their feelings and behaviour. Powerful, highly charged memories tied them to a collective identity from which baptism was supposed to have severed them. Remorse, regret, and guilt about having betrayed parents, family, and friends were common. The converts whom Rabbi Max Lilienthal met in Moscow and St Petersburg in 1840 enthused about their freedom from discriminatory laws and their children's prospects for advancement but suffered 'inexpressible pangs and tortures of conscience'. On Rosh Hashanah and Yom Kippur, he noted, 'remorse pursues them like an evil specter, and thus their life is one of uneasiness, repentance, luxury and apprehension'.[56] In Warsaw it was said that Leopold Kronenberg used to visit the Jewish cemetery on the sabbath and festivals, when Jews would not be there, and kneel at the grave of his parents.[57] In St

[55] Levenson, *History of the Jews of Warsaw* (Heb.), 139; Guterman, 'The Origins of the Great Synagogue', 200; id., 'Attitudes of Warsaw Assimilationists towards Conversion' (Heb.), 63.

[56] Lilienthal, *American Rabbi*, 175.

[57] Guterman, 'Attitudes of Warsaw Assimilationists towards Conversion' (Heb.), 63.

Petersburg Russified former Jewish nationalists who had converted after the pogroms of 1881—a group that included the historian of Russian literature Semen Vengerov, the lawyer and publicist Leonid Slonimsky, and the poet and essayist Nikolay Minsky (the latter two were married to sisters of Vengerov) —marked Passover with a Seder and attended synagogue on Yom Kippur to hear Kol Nidrei.[58] One indication of the extent of remorse is that in the five years after the issuance of the decree of 17 April 1905 permitting converts to the Orthodox Church to return to their original faith, 476 Jews returned to Judaism.[59] In 1917, after the fall of the tsarist regime, more than 200 baptized Jews in St Petersburg formally reconverted at the Choral Synagogue.[60]

In western and central Europe it is difficult to find analogues to this kind of behaviour. Disraeli, with his unfettered Jewish chauvinism, might seem at first to fit the bill; after all, he outstripped most converts in touting Jewish genius and character. However, his 'return' to Jewishness, as I argued in Chapter 9, had no content other than an overblown Romantic celebration of racial pride. He remained a church-going Anglican all his adult life, taking no particular interest in the fate and fortunes of flesh-and-blood Jews in Britain or elsewhere. He never acted as *shtadlan*, or intercessor, for Anglo-Jewry, nor did communal leaders, who knew full well how limited his Jewish commitments were, turn to him for aid. In this sense, his Jewishness was similar to that of Charles Swann and other converts in western and central Europe who 'returned' to their Jewish origins when antisemitism erupted. For them, 'returning' was a mental process, an adjustment more in attitude than behaviour, a facing of facts undertaken to satisfy their honour and pride. These converts resembled those religiously indifferent Jews, like the young Theodor Herzl or Walther Rathenau, who refused to convert because it was a dishonourable, craven, opportunistic act, especially in a period of heightened antisemitism, not because they saw any positive value in Judaism or Jewish culture. Thus, for Disraeli, Swann, and other converts, 'returning' did not mean a return to ritual, worship, learning, or involvement in communal affairs. But, then, how could it have been otherwise? Converts like these came from homes in which visible, distinctive marks of Jewishness had more or less disappeared. Their memories of Jewishness were less vivid and compelling than those of their east European counterparts. Often there was no positive content to them at all. If conversion had worked as they had hoped it would, rewarding them with integration, acceptance, honour, and ethnic oblivion, it seems likely that they would have remembered little, if anything, about their Jewish pasts.

[58] Tsitron, *Behind the Curtain* (Heb.), i. 235, ii. 174.
[59] *Jewish Chronicle*, 7 July 1911.   [60] Beizer, *The Jews of St. Petersburg*, 185.

Bibliography

Archives

Archives of the Spanish and Portuguese Synagogue, London

Basil Henriques Papers: Anglo-Jewish Archives, Parkes Library, University of Southampton

Battersea Papers: British Library, London

Census Records: National Archives, Kew

Church Mission to the Jews Collection: Bodleian Library, Oxford

Charles Booth Collection: British Library of Political and Economic Science, London School of Economics

Herbert Bentwich Papers: Central Zionist Archives, Jerusalem

Redcliffe Nathan Salaman Papers: Cambridge University Library

Rosslyn Hill Chapel Records: Dr Williams's Library, London

Rothschild Archive, London

Sir Thomas Colyer-Fergusson Collection: Anglo-Jewish Archives, Parkes Library, University of Southampton

West London Synagogue of British Jews Collection: Anglo-Jewish Archives, Parkes Library, University of Southampton

Western Synagogue, London, Records: London Metropolitan Archives

Published Sources

ABERBACH, DAVID, *Realism, Caricature and Bias: The Fiction of Mendele Mocher Seforim* (London: Littman Library of Jewish Civilization, 1993).

ADLER, STANISLAW, *In the Warsaw Ghetto, 1940–1943, An Account of a Witness: The Memoirs of Stanislaw Adler*, trans. Sara Philip (Jerusalem: Yad Vashem, 1992).

ADOLF FRANKAU & CO., *100 Years in the Service of Smokers: Adolf Frankau of London Celebrate their Centenary* (London, 1947).

AGURSKY, MIKHAIL, 'Conversions of Jews to Christianity in Russia', *Soviet Jewish Affairs*, 20/2–3 (1990), 69–84.

—— 'Ukrainian–Jewish Intermarriages in Rural Areas of the Ukraine in the Nineteenth Century', *Harvard Ukrainian Studies*, 9 (1985), 139–44.

AHAD HA'AM [ASHER GINSBERG], *Collected Writings* [Kol kitvei aḥad ha'am] (Tel Aviv: Devir, n.d.).

ALBERTI, CONRAD, 'Judentum und Antisemitismus: Eine zeitgenössische Studie', *Die Gesellschaft*, 4/12 (Dec. 1889), 1718–33.

ALGER, JOHN GOLDWORTH, *Napoleon's British Visitors and Captives, 1801–1815* (New York: J. Pott, 1904).

ALTMANN, ALEXANDER, *Moses Mendelssohn: A Biographical Study* (Tuscaloosa: University of Alabama Press, 1973).

APPERSON, GEORGE L., *The Social History of Smoking* (London: Martin Secker, 1914).

APPLEBY, JOYCE, LYNN HUNT, and MARGARET JACOB, *Telling the Truth about History* (New York: W. W. Norton, 1994).

ARENDT, HANNAH, *Eichmann in Jerusalem: A Report on the Banality of Evil* (New York: Viking Press, 1963).

—— *The Jewish Writings*, ed. Jerome Kohn and Ron H. Feldman (New York: Schocken, 2007).

—— *The Origins of Totalitarianism* (1951), Harvest Book edn., 3 pts. (New York: Harcourt, Brace & World, 1968).

—— *Rahel Varnhagen: The Life of a Jewish Woman*, rev. edn., trans. Richard Winston and Clara Winston (New York: Harcourt Brace Jovanovich, 1974).

ARIA, ELIZA, *My Sentimental Self* (London: Chapman & Hall, 1922).

—— *Woman and the Motor Car: The Autobiography of an Automobilist* (London: Sidney Appleton, 1906).

ARKUSH, ALLAN, *Moses Mendelssohn and the Enlightenment* (Albany: State University of New York Press, 1994).

ARONSFELD, C. C., 'German Jews in Nottingham', *AJR Information*, 10/12 (Dec. 1955), 8.

—— 'German Jews in Victorian England', *Leo Baeck Institute Year Book*, 7 (1962), 312–29.

ASHTON, ROSEMARY, *Little Germany: Exile and Asylum in Victorian England* (Oxford: Oxford University Press, 1986).

ASQUITH, CYNTHIA, *Diaries, 1915–1918* (London: Hutchinson, 1968).

ASQUITH, H. H., *Letters to Venetia Stanley*, ed. Michael Brock and Elizabeth Brock (Oxford: Oxford University Press, 1982).

ASQUITH, RAYMOND, *Life and Letters*, ed. John Joliffe (London: Collins, 1980).

AUGUSTINE, DOLORES L., *Patricians and Parvenus: Wealth and High Society in Wilhelmine Germany* (Oxford: Berg, 1994).

Authentic Memoirs, Memorandums, and Confessions Taken from the Journal of his Predatorial Majesty, the King of the Swindlers (London [1798?]).

AVIV, CARYN, and DAVID SHNEER, *New Jews: The End of the Jewish Diaspora* (New York: New York University Press, 2005).

AVRUTIN, EUGENE, 'Returning to Judaism after the 1905 Law on Religious Freedom in Tsarist Russia', *Slavic Review*, 65/1 (2006), 90–110.

BAGGULEY, PHILIP, *Harlequin in Whitehall: A Life of Humbert Wolfe, Poet & Civil Servant, 1885–1940* (London: Nyala Publishing, 1997).

BAKER, LEONARD, *Days of Sorrow and Pain: Leo Baeck and the Berlin Jews* (New York: Oxford University Press, 1980).

BARKAI, AVRAHAM, 'German-Jewish Migrations in the Nineteenth Century, 1830–1910', *Leo Baeck Institute Year Book*, 30 (1985), 301–18.

BARNETT, ARTHUR, *The Western Synagogue through Two Centuries (1761–1961)* (London: Vallentine Mitchell, 1961).

BARNETT, RICHARD D., 'The Burial Register of the Spanish and Portuguese Jews, London, 1657–1735', *Miscellanies of the Jewish Historical Society of England*, 6 (1962), 1–72.

—— 'Dr. Samuel Nunes Ribeiro and the Settlement of Georgia', in Aubrey Newman (ed.), *Migration and Settlement: Proceedings of the Anglo-American Jewish Historical Conference... July 1970* (London: Jewish Historical Society of England, 1971).

BARON, LAWRENCE, 'Theodor Lessing: Between Jewish Self-Hatred and Zionism', *Leo Baeck Institute Year Book*, 26 (1981), 323–40.

BARON, SALO W., 'Ghetto and Emancipation: Shall We Revise the Traditional View?', *Menorah Journal*, 14 (June 1928), 515–26.

—— 'The Modern Age', in Leo W. Schwarz (ed.), *Great Ages and Ideas of the Jewish People* (New York: Modern Library, 1956), 313–484.

—— *Social and Religious History of the Jews*, 3 vols. (New York: Columbia University Press, 1937).

BARTAL, YISRAEL, and YOSEF KAPLAN, 'The Migration of Poor Jews from Amsterdam to the Land of Israel at the Beginning of the Seventeenth Century' (Heb.), *Shalem*, 6 (1991/92), 175–93.

BARTRIP, PETER W. J., *Mirror of Medicine: A History of the British Medical Journal* (Oxford: Clarendon Press, 1990).

BAUER, YEHUDA, *They Chose Life: Jewish Resistance in the Holocaust* (New York: American Jewish Committee, 1973).

BECKMAN, LINDA HUNT, *Amy Levy: Her Life and Letters* (Athens: Ohio University Press, 2000).

BEHR, ALEXANDER, 'Isidore Gerstenberg (1821–1876): Founder of the Council of Foreign Bondholders', *Transactions of the Jewish Historical Society of England*, 17 (1953), 207–13.

BEHRENS, JACOB, *Sir Jacob Behrens* (privately published, c.1925).

BEIZER, MIKHAIL, *The Jews of St. Petersburg: Excursions through a Noble Past*, trans. Michael Sherbourne, ed. Martin Gilbert (Philadelphia: Jewish Publication Society, 1989).

BEN SASSON, HAIM HILLEL, 'The Generation of Spanish Exiles on its Fate' (Heb.), *Zion*, 26 (1961), 23–64.

BENDIX, REINHARD, *From Berlin to Berkeley: German–Jewish Identities* (New Brunswick: Transaction Books, 1986).

BENJAMIN, LEWIS S., 'The Passing of the English Jews', *Nineteenth Century*, 72 (1912), 491–504.

BENNETT, ARNOLD, *The Journals of Arnold Bennett*, ed. Newman Flower, 3 vols. (London: Cassell, 1932–3).

BENTHAM, JEREMY, *A Defence of Usury*, 2nd edn. (Philadelphia: Manly, Orr, and Lippincott, 1842).

BENTWICH, NORMAN, 'Humbert Wolfe: Poet and Civil Servant', *Menorah Journal*, 31 (1943), 34–45.

BERENSON, BERNARD, *Sunset and Twilight* (New York: Harcourt, Brace & World, 1963).

BERING, DIETZ, *The Stigma of Names: Anti-Semitism in German Daily Life, 1812–1933*, trans. Neville Plaice (Ann Arbor: University of Michigan Press, 1992).

BERK, STEPHEN M., *Year of Crisis, Year of Hope: Russian Jewry and the Pogroms of 1881–1882* (Westport, Conn.: Greenwood Books, 1985).

BERLIN, ISAIAH, 'Benjamin Disraeli, Karl Marx and the Search for Identity', in Henry Hardy (ed.), *Against the Current: Essays in the History of Ideas* (London: Hogarth Press, 1979), 252–86.

BETTELHEIM, BRUNO, *The Informed Heart: Autonomy in a Mass Age* (Glencoe, Ill.: Free Press, 1960).

Bevis Marks Records: Contributions to the History of the Spanish and Portuguese Congregation of London, vol. i: *The Early History of the Congregation from the Beginning until 1800*, ed. Lionel D. Barnett (Oxford: Oxford University Press, 1940); vol. ii: *Abstracts of the Ketubot or Marriage-Contracts of the Congregation from Earliest Times until 1836*, ed. Lionel D. Barnett (Oxford: Oxford University Press, 1947); vol. iv: *The Circumcision Register of Isaac and Abraham de Paiba (1715–1775)*, ed. Miriam Rodrigues-Pereira and Chloe Loewe (London: Jewish Historical Society of England, 1991); vol. v: *The Birth Register (1767–1881) of the Spanish & Portuguese Jews' Congregation, London, together with the Circumcision Registers*, ed. Richard D. Barnett (London: Spanish and Portuguese Jews' Congregation, 1993).

BIRNBAUM, PIERRE, *Les Fous de la République: Histoire politique des Juifs d'état de Gambetta à Vichy* (Paris: Fayard, 1992).

——and IRA KATZNELSON (eds.), *Paths of Emancipation: Jews, States, and Citizenship* (Princeton: Princeton University Press, 1995).

BLADY-SZWAJGER, ADINA, *I Remember Nothing More: The Warsaw Children's Hospital and the Jewish Resistance*, trans. Tasya Darowska and Danusia Stok (London: Collins Harvill, 1990).

BLAKE, ROBERT, *Disraeli* (New York: St Martin's Press, 1967).

——*Disraeli's Grand Tour: Benjamin Disraeli and the Holy Land, 1830–31* (New York: Oxford University Press, 1982).

BLOM, J. C. H., and J. J. CAHEN, 'Jewish Netherlanders, Netherlands Jews and Jews in the Netherlands, 1870–1940', in J. C. H. Blom, R. G. Fuks-Mansfeld, and I. Schöffer (eds.), *The History of the Jews in the Netherlands*, trans. Arnold J. Pomerans and Erica Pomerans (Oxford: Littman Library of Jewish Civilization, 2002), 230–95.

BLUMENFELD, ERWIN, *Eye to I: The Autobiography of a Photographer*, trans. Mike Mitchell and Brian Murdoch (London: Thames & Hudson, 1999).

BLYTH, HENRY, *Hell and Hazard, or, William Crockford versus the Gentlemen of England* (Chicago: Henry Regnery, 1970).

BODIAN, MIRIAM, *Dying in the Law of Moses: Crypto-Jewish Martyrdom in the Iberian World* (Bloomington: Indiana University Press, 2007).

—— *Hebrews of the Portuguese Nation: Conversos and Community in Early Modern Amsterdam* (Bloomington: Indiana University Press, 1997).

—— '"Men of the Nation": The Shaping of Converso Identity in Early Modern Europe', *Past & Present*, 143 (May 1994), 48–76.

BOEHLICH, WALTHER (ed.), *Der Berliner Antisemitismusstreit* (Frankfurt am Main: Insel Verlag, 1965).

BOEKMAN, E., *Demographie van de Joden in Nederland* (Amsterdam: M. Hertzberger, 1936).

BOLITHO, HECTOR, *Alfred Mond, First Lord Melchett* (London: Martin Secker, 1933).

BOLKOSKY, SIDNEY M., *The Distorted Image: German Jewish Perceptions of Germans and Germany, 1918–1935* (New York: Elsevier, 1975).

BÖRNE, LUDWIG, *Briefe auf Paris*, ed. Alfred Estermann (Frankfurt am Main: Insel Verlag, 1986).

BOUREL, DOMINIQUE, *Moses Mendelssohn: La Naissance du Judaïsme moderne* (Paris: Gallimard, 2004).

BOYARIN, DANIEL, and JONATHAN BOYARIN, 'Diaspora: Generation and the Ground of Jewish Identity', *Critical Inquiry*, 19 (Summer 1993), 693–725.

BRABAZON, JAMES, *Alfred Schweitzer: A Biography* (New York: G. P. Putnam's Sons, 1975).

BRADBROOK, M. D., 'Queenie Leavis: The Dynamics of Rejection', *The Cambridge Review*, 20 Nov. 1981, 56–9.

BRAYBROOKE, PATRICK, *Novelists: We Are Seven* (London: C. W. Daniel, 1926).

BREUER, EDWARD, *The Limits of Enlightenment: Jews, Germans, and the Eighteenth-Century Study of Scripture* (Cambridge, Mass.: Harvard University Center for Jewish Studies, 1996).

BROWN, CALLUM G., 'The Secularisation Decade: What the 1960s Have Done to the Study of Religious History', in Hugh McLeod and Werner Ustorf (eds.), *The Decline of Christendom in Western Europe* (Cambridge: Cambridge University Press, 2003), 29–46.

BROWN, MALCOLM, 'The Jews of Hackney before 1840', *Transactions of the Jewish Historical Society of England*, 30 (1989), 71–89.

BUBER, MARTIN, *Der Jude und sein Judentum: Gesammelte Aufsätze und Reden*, 2nd edn. (Gerlingen: L. Schneider, 1993).

BYRNE, PAULA, *Perdita: The Literary, Theatrical, Scandalous Life of Mary Robinson* (New York: Random House, 2004).

BYRON, GEORGE GORDON, *Letters and Journals*, ed. Leslie Marchand: vol. i: *'In my hot youth', 1798–1810*; vol. ii: *'Famous in my time', 1810–1812* (London: John Murray, 1973).

CAŁA, ALINA, *Asymilacja Żydów w Królestwie Polskim (1864–1897): Postawy, konflikty, stereotypy* (Warsaw: Państwowy Instytut Wydawniczy, 1989).

CAŁA, ALINA, 'Jewish Socialists in the Kingdom of Poland', *Polin*, 9 (1996), 3–13.

—— 'The Question of the Assimilation of Jews in the Polish Kingdom, 1864–1897: An Interpretive Essay', *Polin*, 1 (1986), 130–50.

CALISHER, HORTENSE, 'Old Stock', in ead., *The Collected Stories of Hortense Calisher* (New York: Arbor House, 1975), 263–75.

CANTOR, GEOFFREY, *Quakers, Jews, and Science: Religious Responses to Modernity and the Sciences in Britain, 1650–1900* (Oxford: Oxford University Press, 2005).

CARLEBACH, ELISHEVA, *Divided Souls: Converts from Judaism in Germany, 1500–1750* (New Haven: Yale University Press, 2001).

CARLYLE, JANE WELSH, *Letters of Jane Welsh Carlyle to Joseph Neuberg, 1848–1862*, ed. Townsend Scudder (London: Oxford University Press, 1931).

CARLYLE, THOMAS, *The Collected Letters of Thomas and Jane Welsh Carlyle*, 28 vols. to date, ed. Charles Richard Sanders (Durham: Duke University Press, 1970–).

—— *The Correspondence of Emerson and Carlyle*, ed. Joseph Slater (New York: Columbia University Press, 1964).

'Carlyle and Neuberg', *Macmillan's Magazine*, 50 (Aug. 1894), 280–97.

CASTLE, CHARLES, *Oliver Messel: A Biography* (London: Thames & Hudson, 1986).

CECIL, HUGH, *The Flower of Battle: British Fiction Writers of the First World War* (London: Secker & Warburg, 1995).

CECIL, LAMAR, 'Jew and Junker in Imperial Berlin', *Leo Baeck Institute Year Book*, 20 (1975), 47–58.

CHADWICK, OWEN, *The Secularization of the European Mind in the Nineteenth Century* (Cambridge: Cambridge University Press, 1975).

CHAPMAN, STANLEY, *Merchant Enterprise in Britain from the Industrial Revolution to World War I* (Cambridge: Cambridge University Press, 1992).

—— *The Rise of Merchant Banking* (London: Unwin Hyman, 1984).

'Characteristic Portrait of a Modern Apostate', *The Scourge*, 10 (1815), 218–23.

'Charles King', *The Scourge*, 1 (1811), 457–63.

CHEYETTE, BRYAN, *Constructions of 'The Jew' in English Literature and Society: Racial Representations, 1875–1945* (Cambridge: Cambridge University Press, 1993).

—— 'From Apology to Revolt: Benjamin Farjeon, Amy Levy and the Post-Emancipation Anglo-Jewish Novel, 1880–1900', *Transactions of the Jewish Historical Society of England*, 29 (1988), 253–65.

—— 'The Other Self: Anglo-Jewish Fiction and the Representation of Jews in England, 1875–1905', in David Cesarani (ed.), *The Making of Modern Anglo-Jewry* (Oxford: Basil Blackwell, 1990), 97–111.

CHORLEY, KATHARINE, *Manchester Made Them* (London: Faber & Faber, 1950).

CHURCH, ROY A., *Economic and Social Change in a Midland Town: Victorian Nottingham, 1815–1900* (London: Frank Cass, 1966).

CIECHANOWIECKI, ANDRZEJ S., 'Remarks on, and a Supplement to, the "Genealogical Sketches" of Kazimierz Reychman', *Polin*, 5 (1990), 372–84.

COHEN, GARY B., *The Politics of Ethnic Survival: Germans in Prague, 1861–1914* (Princeton: Princeton University Press, 1981).

COHEN, ISRAEL, *Travels in Jewry* (New York: E. P. Dutton, 1953).

COHEN, J. M., *The Life of Ludwig Mond* (London: Methuen, 1956).

COHEN, JEREMY, 'The Mentality of the Medieval Jewish Apostate: Peter Alfonsi, Hermann of Cologne, and Pablo Christiani', in Todd M. Endelman (ed.), *Jewish Apostasy in the Modern World* (New York: Holmes & Meier, 1987), 20–47.

COHEN, LUCY, *Arthur Cohen: A Memoir by his Daughter for his Descendants* (London: Bickers & Son, 1919).

COHEN, NAOMI, *Encounter with Emancipation: The German Jews in the United States, 1830–1914* (Philadelphia: Jewish Publication Society, 1984).

COHEN, RICHARD, Introduction to David Friedländer, *Sendschreiben an seine hochwürden herrn Oberconsistorialrath und Probst Teller*, trans. Miriam Dinur (Jerusalem: Zalman Shazar Center for Jewish History, 1975), pp. iii–xii.

COHEN, ROBERT, 'The Demography of Jews in Early America', in Paul Ritterband (ed.), *Modern Jewish Fertility* (Leiden: E. J. Brill, 1981), 144–59.

——*Jews in Another Environment: Surinam in the Second Half of the Eighteenth Century* (Leiden: E. J. Brill, 1991).

——'Patterns of Marriage and Remarriage among the Sephardi Jews of Surinam, 1788–1818', in Robert Cohen (ed.), *The Jewish Nation in Surinam: Historical Essays* (Amsterdam: S. Emmering, 1982), 89–100.

——'"To Come with their Families and Dwell Here": London Sephardi Jewry in the Second Half of the Seventeenth Century' (Heb.), in Yosef Kaplan and David S. Katz (eds.), *Exile and Return: Anglo-Jewry through the Ages* [Galut veshivah: yehudei angliyah beḥilufei hazemanim] (Jerusalem: Zalman Shazar Center for Jewish History, 1993), 147–58.

COHEN, STEVEN M., *American Assimilation or Jewish Revival?* (Bloomington: Indiana University Press, 1988).

COHEN, STUART A., *English Zionists and British Jews: The Communal Politics of Anglo-Jewry, 1895–1920* (Princeton: Princeton University Press, 1982).

COKAYNE, GEORGE EDWARD (ed.), *The Complete Peerage of England, Scotland, Ireland, Great Britain, and the United Kingdom, Extant, Extinct, or Dormant*, 13 vols. (London: St Catherine Press, 1910–59).

COOPER, DUFF, *A Durable Fire: The Letters of Duff and Diana Cooper, 1913–1950*, ed. Artemis Cooper (London: Collins, 1983).

COOPER, JOHN, *Pride versus Prejudice: Jewish Doctors and Lawyers in England, 1890–1990* (Oxford: Littman Library of Jewish Civilization, 2003).

CORRSIN, STEPHEN D., 'Aspects of Population Change and of Acculturation in Jewish Warsaw at the End of the Nineteenth Century: The Censuses of 1882 and 1897', *Polin*, 3 (1988), 122–41.

COWEN, ANNE, and ROGER COWEN, *Victorian Jews through British Eyes* (Oxford: Littman Library of Jewish Civilization, 1986).

COX, JEFFREY, 'Master Narratives of Long-Term Religious Change', in Hugh McLeod and Werner Ustorf (eds.), *The Decline of Christendom in Western Europe* (Cambridge: Cambridge University Press, 2003), 201–17.

CZARNECKI, ANTONI, 'All Saints Parish', in Władysław Smólski (ed.), *Za to groziła śmierć: Polacy z pomocą Żydom w czasie okupacji* (Warsaw: Instytut Wydawniczy Pax, 1981).

DARNTON, ROBERT, 'Intellectual and Cultural History', in Michael Kammen (ed.), *The Past Before Us: Contemporary Historical Writing in the United States* (Ithaca, NY: Cornell University Press, 1980), 327–54.

DAVIS, RICHARD, *The English Rothschilds* (Chapel Hill: University of North Carolina Press, 1983).

DE SOLA POOL, DAVID, and TAMAR DE SOLA POOL, *An Old Faith in the New World: Portrait of Shearith Israel, 1654–1954* (New York: Columbia University Press, 1956).

DELLAPERGOLA, SERGIO, and UZIEL O. SCHMELZ, 'Demographic Transformations of American Jewry: Marriage and Mixed Marriage in the 1980s', *Studies in Contemporary Jewry*, 5 (1989), 169–200.

——'A Rejoinder to Calvin Goldscheider', *Studies in Contemporary Jewry*, 5 (1989), 209–14.

DEMAKOVSKY, RONALD M., 'Jewish Anti-Semitism and the Psychopathology of Self-Hatred', Ph.D. diss. (California School of Professional Psychology, 1978).

DIAMOND, A. S., 'Problems of the London Sephardi Community, 1720–1733: Philip Carteret Webb's Notebooks', *Transactions of the Jewish Historical Society of England*, 21 (1968), 39–63.

DIETZ, ALEXANDER, *Stammbuch der Frankfurter Juden: Geschichtliche Mitteilungen über die Frankfurter jüdischen Familien von 1349–1849* (Frankfurt am Main: J. St Goar, 1907).

DISRAELI, BENJAMIN, *Letters*, 8 vols. to date, ed. M. G. Wiebe et al. (Toronto: University of Toronto Press, 1981–).

——*Lord George Bentinck: A Political Biography* (London: Colburn, 1851).

——'On the Life and Writings of Mr. Disraeli', in Isaac Disraeli, *Curiosities of Literature*, new edn., 3 vols. (London: G. Routledge, 1858).

——'Preface to Alroy', in *Alroy. Ixion in Heaven. The Infernal Marriage. Popanilla*, new edn. (London: Longmans, Green, and Co., 1845), pp. v–vii.

D'ISRAELI, ISAAC, 'Acts of the Great Sanhedrim at Paris', *Monthly Magazine*, 24/2 (1807), 134–6, 243–8.

——'A Biographical Sketch of the Jewish Socrates', *Monthly Magazine*, 6/2 (1798), 38–44.

——*The Genius of Judaism* (London: E. Moxon, 1833).

——'On the Late Installation of a Great Sanhedrim of the Jews in Paris', *Monthly Magazine*, 24/2 (1807), 34–8.

DOHM, CHRISTIAN WILHELM VON, *Concerning the Amelioration of the Civil Status of the Jews*, trans. Helen Lederer (Cincinnati: Hebrew Union College–Jewish Institute of Religion, 1957).

DORON, JOACHIM, 'Classic Zionism and Modern Antisemitism: Parallels and Influences (1883–1914)', *Studies in Zionism*, 8 (Fall 1983), 169–204.

DRUYANOV, ABRAHAM ALTER, *The Book of Jokes and Wit* [Sefer habediḥah vehahidud], 3 vols. (Tel Aviv: Devir, 1980).

DUKER, ABRAHAM, 'Polish Frankism's Duration', *Jewish Social Studies*, 25 (1963), 287–333.

'The Earliest Extant Minute Books of the Spanish and Portuguese Congregation Shearith Israel, 1728–1786', *Publications of the American Jewish Historical Society*, 21 (1913), 1–171.

EFRON, JOHN M., *Defenders of the Race: Jewish Doctors and Race Science in Fin-de-Siècle Europe* (New Haven: Yale University Press, 1994).

—— 'Scientific Racism and the Mystique of Sephardi Racial Superiority' *Leo Baeck Institute Year Book*, 38 (1993), 75–96.

EGAN, PIERCE, *Finish to the Adventures of Tom, Jerry, and Logic in their Pursuits through Life in and out of London* (London, 1830).

EINSTEIN, ALBERT, *On Peace*, ed. Otto Nathan and Heinz Norden (New York: Schocken, 1960).

EISENBACH, ARTUR, *The Emancipation of the Jews in Poland, 1780–1870*, ed. Antony Polonsky, trans. Janina Dorosz (Oxford: Basil Blackwell, 1991).

ELEY, GEOFF, *A Crooked Line: From Cultural History to the History of Society* (Ann Arbor: University of Michigan Press, 2005).

—— 'What Are the Contexts for German Antisemitism?', *Studies in Contemporary Jewry*, 13 (1997), 100–32.

ELLENSON, DAVID, *After Emancipation: Jewish Religious Responses to Modernity* (Cincinnati: Hebrew Union College Press, 2004).

EMANUEL, CHARLES H. L. (ed.), *A Century and a Half of Jewish History Extracted from the Minute Books of the London Committee of Deputies of the British Jews* (London: George Routledge & Sons, 1910).

EMDEN, PAUL H., *Jews of Britain: A Series of Biographies* (London: Sampson Low, Marston, 1943).

ENDELMAN, TODD M., 'Communal Solidarity and Family Loyalty among the Jewish Elite of Victorian London', *Victorian Studies*, 28 (1985), 491–526.

—— *England: Good or Bad for the Jews?*, Jubilee Parkes Lecture, May 2002, Parkes Institute Pamphlet 3 (Southampton: Parkes Institute, University of Southampton, 2003).

—— 'Introduction: Comparing Jewish Societies', in id. (ed.), *Comparing Jewish Societies* (Ann Arbor: University of Michigan Press, 1997), 1–22.

—— *The Jews of Georgian England, 1714–1830: Tradition and Change in a Liberal Society*, 2nd edn. (Ann Arbor: University of Michigan Press, 1999).

ENDELMAN, TODD M., *Leaving the Jewish Fold: Conversion and Radical Assimilation in Europe and America from the Enlightenment to the Present* (Princeton: Princeton University Press, forthcoming).

—— *Radical Assimilation in English Jewish History, 1656–1945* (Bloomington: Indiana University Press, 1990).

—— 'Secularization and the Origins of Jewish Modernity: On the Impact of Urbanization and Social Transformation', *Simon-Dubnow-Institut Jahrbuch*, 6 (2007), 155–68.

ENGEL, DAVID, 'Crisis and Lachrymosity: On Salo Baron, Neobaronianism, and the Study of Modern Jewish History', *Jewish History*, 20 (2006), 243–64.

ERSKINE, THOMAS, *Reflections on Gaming, Annuities, and Usurious Contracts*, 3rd edn. (London, 1777).

EYCK, ERICH, *A History of the Weimar Republic*, 2 vols., trans. Harlan P. Hanson and Robert G. L. Waite, (Cambridge, Mass.: Harvard University Press, 1967).

FAIRHOLT, F. W., *Tobacco: Its History and Associations* (London: Chapman & Hall, 1859).

FELDMAN, DAVID, *Englishmen and Jews: Social Relations and Political Culture, 1840–1914* (New Haven: Yale University Press, 1994).

FELIX, DAVID, *Walther Rathenau and the Weimar Republic: The Politics of Reparation* (Baltimore: Johns Hopkins University Press, 1971).

FELSENSTEIN, FRANK, *Anti-Semitic Stereotypes: A Paradigm of Otherness in English Popular Culture, 1660–1830* (Baltimore: Johns Hopkins University Press, 1995).

FERET, CHARLES JAMES, *Fulham Old and New*, 3 vols. (London: Leadenhall Press, 1900).

FIELDING, K. J. (ed.), 'Carlyle's Sketch of Joseph Neuberg', *Carlyle Annual*, 13 (1992–93), 3–9.

FINE, MEIR JACOB, *Days and Years: Memories and Sketches of Fifty Years* [Yamim veshanim: zikhronot vetsiyurim mitkufah shel hamishim shanah], 2 vols., trans. Avraham Zamir (Tel Aviv: Devir, 1938–9).

FINESTEIN, ISRAEL, 'The Lay Leadership of the United Synagogue since 1870', in Salmond S. Levin (ed.), *A Century of Anglo-Jewish Life, 1870–1970: Lectures to Commemorate the Centenary of the United Synagogue* (London: United Synagogue, n.d.), 29–41.

FIXLER, MICHAEL, 'Bernard Berenson of Butremanz', *Commentary* (Aug. 1963), 135–43.

FORSTER, E. M., *Two Cheers for Democracy* (London: Edward Arnold, 1951).

FRAENKEL, ABRAHAM A., *Lebenskreise: Aus der Erinnerungen eines jüdischen Mathematikers* (Stuttgart: Deutsche Verlag-Anstalt, 1967).

FRAM, EDWARD, 'Perception and Reception of Repentant Apostates in Medieval Ashkenaz and Premodern Poland', *AJS Review*, 21 (1996), 299–339.

FRANKAU, GILBERT, *The Dominant Type of Man* (London: n. p., 1925).

—— *Farewell Romance* (London: Hutchinson, 1936).

——*Life—and Erica*, The Definitive Edition of Gilbert Frankau's Novels and Short Stories (London: MacDonald, n.d.).

——*Masterton: A Story of an English Gentleman* (London: Hutchinson [1925]).

——'An Outlier from his Tribe', in id., *Twelve Tales* (London: Hutchinson [1927]), 121–39.

——*Peter Jackson, Cigar Merchant: A Romance of Married Life*, 26th edn. (London: Hutchinson, 1922).

——*Self-Portrait: A Novel of His Own Life* (London: Hutchinson [1940]).

——*The Woman of the Horizon* (New York: Century, 1923).

FRANKAU, JULIA, *Dr. Phillips: A Maida Vale Idyll* (London: Vizetelly, 1887).

——*An Eighteenth-Century Artist & Engraver: John Raphael Smith—His Life and Works* (London: Macmillan, 1902).

——*Pigs in Clover* (London: Heinemann, 1903).

FRANKAU, PAMELA, *The Devil We Know* (New York: E. P. Dutton, 1939).

——*I Find Four People* (London: Ivor Nicholson & Watson, 1935).

——*Pen to Paper: A Novelist's Notebook* (London: Heinemann, 1961).

——*The Willow Cabin* (London: Virago Press, 1988).

——*The Winged Horse* (London: Virago Press, 1989).

——*A Wreath for the Enemy* (London: Virago Press, 1988).

FRANKEL, JONATHAN, and STEVEN J. ZIPPERSTEIN (eds.), *Assimilation and Community: The Jews in Nineteenth-Century Europe* (Cambridge: Cambridge University Press, 1992).

FRASER, JOHN FOSTER, *The Conquering Jew* (London: Cassell, 1915).

FRASER, WILLIAM, *Disraeli and his Day*, 2nd edn. (London: Kegan Paul, Trench & Trubner, 1891).

FRAZIER, ADRIAN, *George Moore, 1852–1933* (New Haven: Yale University Press, 2000).

FREEZE, CHAERAN, 'When Chava Left Home: Gender, Conversion and the Jewish Family in Tsarist Russia', *Polin*, 18 (2005), 153–88.

FRENK, AZRIEL NATHAN, *Apostates in Poland in the Nineteenth Century* [Meshumodim in poyln in nayntsentn yorhundert], 2 vols. (Warsaw: Freyd, 1923–4).

FRIEDMAN, PHILIP, 'Social Conflicts in the Ghetto', in id., *Roads to Extinction: Essays on the Holocaust*, ed. Ada June Friedman (Philadelphia: Jewish Publication Society, 1980), 131–52.

FROUDE, JAMES ANTHONY, *The Life of the Earl of Beaconsfield*, Everyman Library (London: J. M. Dent & Sons, 1914).

GALCHINSKY, MICHAEL, *The Origin of the Modern Jewish Woman Writer: Romance and Reform in Victorian England* (Detroit: Wayne State University Press, 1996).

GÄNZL, KURT, *The Encyclopedia of the Musical Theatre*, 2nd edn., 3 vols. (New York: Schirmer Books, 2001).

GARNCARSKA-KADARY, BINA, *The Role of the Jews in the Development of the Economy of Warsaw, 1816/20–1914* [Ḥelkam shel hayehudim behitpatḥut hata'asiyah shel varshah bashanim 1816/20–1914] (Tel Aviv: Hamakhon Leheker Hatefutsot, 1984).

GARTNER, LLOYD P., *History of the Jews of Cleveland*, 2nd edn. (Cleveland: Western Reserve Historical Society, 1987).

—— *History of the Jews in Modern Times* (Oxford: Oxford University Press, 2001).

GELBER, NATAN M., 'The Warsaw Pogroms of 1881' (Heb.), *He'avar*, 10 (1963), 106–17.

GIDNEY, W. T., *The History of the London Society for Promoting Christianity amongst the Jews from 1809 to 1908* (London: London Society for Promoting Christianity amongst the Jews, 1908).

GILAM, ABRAHAM, 'Benjamin Disraeli and the Emancipation of the Jews', *Disraeli Project Newsletter*, 5/1 (1980), 26–46.

—— *The Emancipation of the Jews in England, 1830–1860* (New York: Garland, 1982).

GILMAN, SANDER, *Jewish Self-Hatred: Anti-Semitism and the Hidden Language of the Jews* (Baltimore: Johns Hopkins University Press, 1986).

—— *The Jew's Body* (London: Routledge, 1991).

GIMPEL, RENÉ, *Diary of an Art Dealer*, trans. John Rosenberg (New York: Farrar, Straus & Giroux, 1966).

GINSBURG, SAUL, *Apostates in Tsarist Russia* [Meshumodim in tsarishn rusland] (New York: Cyco Bicher Farlag, 1946).

GIRARD, PATRICK, *Les Juifs de France de 1789 à 1860* (Paris: Calmann-Lévy, 1976).

GITELMAN, ZVI, 'Jewish Identity and Secularism in Post-Soviet Russia and Ukraine', in Zvi Gitelman (ed.), *Religion or Ethnicity? Jewish Identities in Evolution* (New Brunswick: Rutgers University Press, 2009), 241–66.

GLENDINNING, VICTORIA, *Leonard Woolf: A Biography* (New York: Free Press, 2006).

GLENN, SUSAN A., 'The Vogue of Jewish Self-Hatred in Post-World War II America', *Jewish Social Studies*, NS 12/3 (Spring/Summer 2006), 95–136.

GLUCK, MARY, 'The Budapest Flâneur: Urban Modernity, Popular Culture, and the "Jewish Question" in Fin-de-Siècle Hungary', *Jewish Social Studies*, NS 10/3 (Spring/Summer 2004), 1–22.

GOFFMAN, ERVING, *Stigma: Notes on the Management of Spoiled Identity* (Englewood Cliffs: Prentice-Hall, 1963).

GOLDBERG, JACOB, *Converts in the Polish–Lithuanian Commonwealth* [Hamumarim bemamlekhet polin-lita] (Jerusalem: Zalman Shazar Center for Jewish History, 1985).

GOLDSCHEIDER, CALVIN, 'American Jewish Marriages: Erosion or Transformation?', *Studies in Contemporary Jewry*, 5 (1989), 201–8.

—— *Jewish Continuity and Change: Emerging Patterns in America* (Bloomington: Indiana University Press, 1986).

—— *Studying the Jewish Future* (Seattle: University of Washington Press, 2004).

—— and ALAN S. ZUCKERMAN, *The Transformation of the Jews* (Chicago: University of Chicago Press, 1984).

GOLDSMID, FRANCIS HENRY, *The Arguments Advanced against the Enfranchisement of the Jews* (London: Colburn and Bentley, 1831).

—— *Remarks on the Civil Disabilities of British Jews* (London, 1830).

GOLLANCZ, HERMANN, *Sermons and Addresses*, 1st ser. (London: Unwin Brothers, 1909).

—— *Sermons and Addresses*, 2nd ser. (London: Chapman & Hall, 1916).

GONDA, CAROLINE, '"A Roller-Coaster of a Life with Everything in It": Pamela Frankau (1908–67)', in Frederick Roden (ed.), *Jewish/Christian/Queer: Crossroads and Identities* (Farnham, Surrey: Ashgate, 2009), 181–203.

GOODMAN, JEAN, *The Mond Legacy: A Family Saga* (London: Weidenfeld & Nicolson, 1982).

GRAETZ, HEINRICH, 'The Correspondence of an English Lady on Judaism and Semitism', in *The Structure of Jewish History and Other Essays*, ed. and trans. Ismar Schorsch (New York: Jewish Theological Seminary, 1975), 191–258.

—— *History of the Jews*, 6 vols. (Philadelphia: Jewish Publication Society, 1891–8).

GRAETZ, MICHAEL, *The Periphery Became the Center: Chapters in the History of French Jewry in the Nineteenth Century from Saint Simon to the Founding of the Alliance Israélite Universelle* [Haperiferyah haytah lamerkaz: perakim betoledot yahadut tsarfat bame'ah hatesha esreh misent-simon ad lisud kol yisra'el ḥaverim] (Jerusalem: Mosad Bialik, 1982).

GRAIZBORD, DAVID, *Souls in Dispute: Converso Identities in Iberia and the Jewish Diaspora, 1580–1700* (Philadelphia: University of Pennsylvania Press, 2004).

GRAUBARD, STEPHEN R., *Burke, Disraeli, and Churchill: The Politics of Perseverance* (Cambridge, Mass.: Harvard University Press, 1961).

GREENBERG, LOUIS, *The Jews in Russia: The Struggle for Emancipation*, 2 vols. in 1 (New York: Schocken Books, 1976).

GRONOW, REES HOWELL, *Reminiscences of Captain Gronow*, 2nd rev. edn. (London: Smith, Elder, 1862).

GUROCK, JEFFREY S., *When Harlem Was Jewish, 1870–1930* (New York: Columbia University Press, 1979).

GUTERMAN, ALEXANDER, 'Attitudes of Warsaw Assimilationists towards Conversion' (Heb.), *Gal-Ed*, 12 (1991), 57–77.

—— *From Assimilation to Nationalism: Chapters in the History of the Great Synagogue in Warsaw, 1806–1942* [Mehitbolelut lilumiyut: perakim betoledot beit hakeneset hagadol hasinagogah bevarshah, 1806–1942] (Jerusalem: Karmel [1993]).

—— 'The Origins of the Great Synagogue in Warsaw on Tłomackie Street', in Władysław Bartoszewski and Antony Polonsky (eds.), *The Jews in Warsaw: A History* (Oxford: Basil Blackwell, 1991), 181–211.

GUTMAN, YISRAEL, *The Jews of Warsaw, 1939–1943: Ghetto, Underground, Revolt*, trans. Ina Friedman (Bloomington: Indiana University Press, 1983).

HARRISON, J. F. C., *The Second Coming: Popular Millenarianism, 1780–1850* (London: Routledge & Kegan Paul, 1979).

HART, MITCHELL B., *Social Science and the Politics of Modern Jewish Identity* (Stanford: Stanford University Press, 2000).

HASS, LUDWIK, *Sekta farmazonii warszawskiej: Pierwsze stulecie wolnomularstwa w Warszawie (1721–1821)* (Warsaw: Państwowy Instytut Wydawniczy, 1980).

—— '*Żydzi i "kwestia żydowska" w dawnym wolnomularstwie polskim (do lat dwudziestych XIX w.)*', *Biuletyn Żydowskiego Instytutu Historycznego w Polsce*, 4 (1977), 3–27.

HEBRON, MOSES [pseud.], *The Life and Exploits of Ikey Solomons* (London [1829]).

HEINE, HEINRICH, *A Biographical Anthology*, ed. Hugo Bieber, trans. Moses Hadas (Philadelphia: Jewish Publication Society, 1956).

—— *The Complete Poems of Heinrich Heine: A Modern English Version*, trans. Hal Draper (Boston: Suhrkamp/Insel, 1982).

—— *Memoirs: From his Works, Letters, and Conversations*, ed. Gustave Karpeles, trans. Gilbert Cannan, 2 vols. (New York: John Lane, 1910).

—— '*The Town of Lucca*', in *Heinrich Heine: Selected Prose*, ed. and trans. Ritchie Robertson (London: Penguin Books, 1993), 145–92.

HELLER, CELIA S., *On the Edge of Destruction: Jews of Poland between the Two World Wars* (New York: Columbia University Press, 1977).

HERTZ, ALEKSANDER, *The Jews in Polish Culture*, trans. Richard Lourie (Evanston, Ill.: Northwestern University Press, 1988).

HERTZ, DEBORAH, '*Seductive Conversion in Berlin, 1770–1809*', in Todd M. Endelman (ed.), *Jewish Apostasy in the Modern World* (New York: Holmes & Meier, 1987), 48–82.

HERTZBERG, ARTHUR, *The French Enlightenment and the Jews* (New York: Columbia University Press, 1968).

—— (ed.), *The Zionist Idea: A Historical Analysis and Reader*, Harper Torchbook (New York: Harper & Row, 1966).

HESS, JONATHAN M., '*Fictions of a German-Jewish Public: Ludwig Jacobowski's Werther the Jew and its Readers*', *Jewish Social Studies*, NS 11/2 (Winter 2005), 202–30.

HESS, MOSES, *Rom und Jerusalem, die letze Nationalitätsfrage* (Leipzig: Wengler, 1862).

High Pavement Chapel, *A Biographical Catalogue of Portraits* (Nottingham: n.p., n.d.).

HILBERG, RAUL, *The Destruction of the European Jews* (1961; New York: Harper Colophon, 1979).

HIRSCH, PAM, *Barbara Leigh Smith Bodichon, 1827–1941: Feminist, Artist and Rebel* (London: Chatto & Windus, 1998).

HIRSCHFIELD, CLAIRE, 'The Tenacity of Tradition: *Truth* and the Jews, 1877–1957', *Patterns of Prejudice*, 28/3–4 (1994), 67–85.

HIRSZFELD, LUDWIK, *Historia jednego życia* (Warsaw: Czytelnik, 1946).

HOLCROFT, THOMAS, *The Life of Thomas Holcroft*, 2 vols., ed. Elbridge Colby (London: Constable, 1925).

HOMA, BERNARD, *A Fortress in Anglo-Jewry: The Story of the Machzike Hadath* (London: Shapiro Vallentine, 1951).

HONIGMANN, PETER, *Die Austritte aus der Jüdischen Gemeinde Berlin, 1873–1941: Statistische Auswertung und historische Interpretation* (Frankfurt am Main: Peter Lang, 1988).

——'Jewish Conversions—A Measure of Assimilation? A Discussion of the Berlin Secession Statistics of 1770–1841', *Leo Baeck Institute Year Book*, 34 (1989), 3–45.

HYAMSON, ALBERT M., *The Sephardim of England: A History of the Spanish and Portuguese Jewish Community, 1492–1951* (London: Methuen, 1951).

HYMAN, LOUIS, *The Jews of Ireland from Earliest Times to the Year 1910* (London: Jewish Historical Society of England, 1972).

HYMAN, PAULA E., *The Emancipation of the Jews of Alsace: Acculturation and Tradition in the Nineteenth Century* (New Haven: Yale University Press, 1991).

——*From Dreyfus to Vichy: The Remaking of French Jewry, 1906–1939* (New York: Columbia University Press, 1979).

——'The Ideological Transformation of Modern Jewish Historiography', in Shaye J. D. Cohen and Edward L. Greenstein (eds.), *The State of Jewish Studies* (Detroit: Wayne State University Press, 1990), 143–57.

——'Joseph Salvador: Proto-Zionist or Apologist for Assimilation?', *Jewish Social Studies*, 34/1 (1972), 1–22.

ITZKOWITZ, DAVID C., 'Cultural Pluralism and the Board of Deputies of British Jews', in R. W. Davis and R. J. Helmstadter (eds.), *Religion and Irreligion in Victorian Society: Essays in Honor of R. K. Webb* (London: Routledge, 1992), 85–101.

JACOBI, PAUL J., 'The Geiger Family', mimeograph (Jerusalem, Nov. 1964).

JACOBS, JOSEPH, *Studies in Jewish Statistics: Social, Vital and Anthropometric* (London: D. Nutt, 1891).

JAFFE, BENJAMIN, 'A Reassessment of Benjamin Disraeli's Jewish Aspects', *Transactions of the Jewish Historical Society of England*, 27 (1982), 115–23.

JANIK, ALLAN, 'Viennese Culture and the Jewish Self-Hatred Hypothesis: A Critique', in I. Oxaal, M. Pollak, and G. Botz (eds.), *Jews, Antisemitism and Culture in Vienna* (New York: Routledge & Kegan Paul, 1987), 75–88.

JESKE-CHOIŃSKI, TEODOR, *Neofici polscy: Materiały historyczne* (Warsaw: P. Laskauera, 1904).

'John King', *The Scourge*, I (1811), 1–27.

JOLL, JAMES, *Intellectuals in Politics: Three Biographical Essays* (London: Weidenfeld & Nicolson, 1960).

JONES, ERNEST, *The Life and Work of Sigmund Freud*, 3 vols. (New York: Basic Books, 1953).

JONES, LAWRENCE EVELYN, *An Edwardian Youth* (London: Macmillan, 1956).

JOSEPHS, ZOË, *Birmingham Jewry, 1749–1914* (Birmingham: Birmingham Jewish History Research Group, 1980).

JOST, ISAK MARCUS, *Die Geschichte des Judenthums und seiner Sekten*, 3 vols. (Leipzig: Doerffling & Franke, 1857–9).

JUDD, ROBIN, *Contested Rituals: Circumcision, Kosher Butchering, and Jewish Political Life in Germany, 1843–1933* (Ithaca, NY: Cornell University Press, 2007).

KADISH, SHARMAN, *Bolsheviks and British Jews: The Anglo-Jewish Community, Britain and the Russian Revolution* (London: Frank Cass, 1992).

KAPLAN, CHAIM, *The Warsaw Diary of Chaim A. Kaplan*, rev. edn., ed. and trans. Abraham I. Katsh (New York: Collier Books, 1973).

KAPLAN, FRED, *Thomas Carlyle: A Biography* (Ithaca, NY: Cornell University Press, 1983).

KAPLAN, MARION A., 'Friendship on the Margins: Jewish Social Relations in Imperial Germany', *Central European History*, 34/4 (2001), 471–501.

——*The Making of the Jewish Middle Class: Women, Family, and Identity in Imperial Germany* (New York: Oxford University Press, 1991).

——'Tradition and Transition—The Acculturation, Assimilation, and Integration of Jews in Imperial Germany—A Gender Analysis', *Leo Baeck Institute Year Book*, 27 (1982), 3–35.

KAPLAN, YOSEF, *From Christianity to Judaism: The Life and Work of the Converso Isaac Orobio de Castro* [Minatsrut leyahadut: ḥayav ufe'alo shel ha'anus yitsḥak orobio de kastro] (Jerusalem: Magnes Press, 1982).

——'The Jewish Profile of the Spanish-Portuguese Community of London during the Seventeenth Century', *Judaism*, 41 (1992), 229–40.

——'Political Concepts in the World of the Portuguese Jews of Amsterdam during the Seventeenth Century: The Problem of Exclusion and the Boundaries of Self-Identity', in Yosef Kaplan, Henri Méchoulan, and Richard Popkin (eds.), *Menasseh ben Israel and his World* (Leiden: E. J. Brill, 1989), 45–62.

——'The Portuguese Community in 17th-Century Amsterdam and the Ashkenazi World', in Joseph Michman (ed.), *Dutch Jewish History*, vol. ii (Jerusalem: Institute for Research on Dutch Jewry, Hebrew University of Jerusalem, 1989), 23–45.

——'The Relationship of Spanish and Portuguese Jews to Ashkenazi Jews in Amsterdam in the Seventeenth Century' (Heb.), in Shmuel Almog et al. (eds.), *Transformations in Modern Jewish History: Essays Presented to Shmuel Ettinger* [Temurot hahistoriyah hayehudit haḥadashah: kovets ma'amarim shai lishmu'el etinger] (Jerusalem: Zalman Shazar Center for Jewish History, 1987), 389–412.

KATZ, JACOB, *The Darker Side of Genius: Richard Wagner's Anti-Semitism* (Hanover, NH: University Press of New England, 1986).

——'Emancipation and Jewish Studies', in *Jewish Emancipation and Self-Emancipation* (Philadelphia: Jewish Publication Society, 1986), 75–85.

—— *Exclusiveness and Tolerance: Jewish–Gentile Relations in Medieval and Modern Times* (New York: Schocken, 1962).

—— *From Prejudice to Destruction: Anti-Semitism, 1700–1933* (Cambridge, Mass.: Harvard University Press, 1980).

——'German Culture and the Jews', in Jehudah Reinharz and Walter Schatzberg (eds.), *The Jewish Response to German Culture from the Enlightenment to the Second World War* (Hanover, NH: University Press of New England, 1985), 85–99.

—— *Out of the Ghetto: The Social Background of Jewish Emancipation, 1770–1870* (Cambridge, Mass.: Harvard University Press, 1973).

——(ed.), *Toward Modernity: The European Jewish Model* (New Brunswick: Transaction Books, 1987).

KAUFMAN, DAVID, *Shul with a Pool: The 'Synagogue-Center' in American Jewish History* (Hanover, NH: University Press of New England, 1999).

KAUFMANN, MYRON S., *Remember Me to God* (Philadelphia: Lippincott, 1957).

KAUFMANN, YEHEZKEL, 'The Destruction of the Soul' (Heb.), in id., *The Pangs of the Age* [Beḥevlei hazeman] (Tel Aviv: Devir, 1936), 257–74.

KENA'ANI, DAVID, *The Second Workers' Aliyah and its Relation to Religion and Tradition* [Ha'aliyah hasheniyah ha'ovedet veyaḥasah ladat velamasoret] (Tel Aviv: Sifriyat Po'alim, 1976).

KERMISH, JOSEPH (ed.), *To Live with Honor and Die with Honor! Selected Documents from the Warsaw Ghetto Underground Archives 'O. S.' ('Oneg Shabbath')*, trans. M. Z. Prives et al. (Jerusalem: Yad Vashem, 1986).

KERR, ALFRED, *Walther Rathenau: Erinerungen eines Freundes* (Amsterdam: Querido, 1935).

KERSHEN, ANNE J., and JONATHAN A. ROMAIN, *Tradition and Change: A History of Reform Judaism in Britain, 1840–1995* (London: Vallentine Mitchell, 1995).

KESSLER, HARRY, *Walther Rathenau: His Life and Work*, trans. W. D. Robson-Scott and Lawrence Hyde (London: G. Howe, 1929).

KEY, ELLEN, *Rahel Varnhagen: A Portrait*, trans. Arthur G. Chater (New York: G. P. Putnam's Sons, 1913).

KIENIEWICZ, STEFAN, 'Assimilated Jews in Nineteenth-Century Warsaw', in Władysław Bartoszewski and Antony Polonsky (eds.), *The Jews in Warsaw: A History* (Oxford: Basil Blackwell, 1991), 171–80.

KING, CHARLOTTE [CHARLOTTE DACRE, pseud.], *Zofloya, or The Moor*, World's Classics (Oxford: Oxford University Press, 1997).

KING, JOHN, *Fourth Letter from Mr. King to Mr. Thomas Paine at Paris* (London [1795]).

—— *Mr. King's Apology, or, A Reply to his Calumniators*, 5th edn. (London, 1798).

KING, JOHN, Mr. King's Speech at Egham, with Thomas Paine's Letter to Him on It, and Mr. King's Reply, 10th edn. (Egham, 1793).

—— Oppression Deemed No Injustice towards Some Individuals, Illustrated in the Late Treatment of Mr. John King under a Commission of Bankruptcy (London [1798?]).

—— Third Letter from Mr. King to Mr. Thomas Paine at Paris (Egham [1793]).

—— Thoughts on the Difficulties and Distresses in which the Peace of 1783 Has Involved the People of England, 5th edn. (London, 1783).

KIRSCH, ADAM, Benjamin Disraeli, Jewish Encounters (New York: Schocken, 2008).

KLAUSNER, ISRAEL, Vilna in the Age of the Gaon: Spiritual and Social War in the Vilna Community in the Age of the GRA [Vilna bitkufat haga'on: hamilhamah haruhanit vehahevratit bikhal vilna bitkufat hagera] (Jerusalem: R. Mas, 1942).

KLIER, JOHN DOYLE, Imperial Russia's Jewish Question, 1855–1881 (Cambridge: Cambridge University Press, 1975).

KŁOCZOWSKI, JERZY, 'The Religious Orders and the Jews in Nazi-Occupied Poland', Polin, 3 (1988), 238–43.

KORNBERG, JACQUES, Theodor Herzl: From Assimilation to Zionism (Bloomington: Indiana University Press, 1993).

KOSMIN, BARRY, and SIDNEY GOLDSTEIN, Highlights of the CJF 1990 National Jewish Population Survey (New York: Council of Jewish Federations, 1991).

KRAUSHAR, ALEKSANDER, Frank and his Sect, 1726–1816: Historical Research and Interpretation [Frank ve'adato, 1726–1816: mehkar umidrash bedivrei hayamim], trans. Nahum Sokolow, vol. i (Warsaw: Levinski, 1895).

KURZWEIL, BARUCH, Our New Literature: Continuity or Revolution? [Sifrutenu hahadashah: hemshekh o mahapekhah?], 2nd rev. edn. (Jerusalem: Schocken, 1964).

KWIET, KONRAD, 'The Ultimate Refuge: Suicide in the Jewish Community under the Nazis', Leo Baeck Institute Year Book, 29 (1984), 135–67.

LAMB, CHARLES, 'Imperfect Sympathies', in id., Essays of Elia, 1st ser. (New York, 1845).

LAMBERTI, MARJORIE, Jewish Activism in Imperial Germany: The Struggle for Civil Equality (New Haven: Yale University Press, 1979).

LANDES, DAVID S., 'Bleichröders and Rothschilds: The Problem of Continuity in the Family Firm', in Charles E. Rosenberg (ed.), The Family in History (Philadelphia: University of Pennsylvania Press, 1975), 95–114.

—— 'Two Cheers for Emancipation', in Francis Malino and Bernard Wasserstein (eds.), The Jews in Modern France (Hanover, NH: University Press of New England, 1985), 288–309.

LANDMANN, SALCIA, Der jüdische Witz: Soziologie und Sammlung (Olten and Freiburg im Breisgau: Walter, 1960).

LANDSBERGER, ARTHUR (ed.), Judentaufen (Munich: Georg Müller, 1912).

LAQUEUR, WALTER, The Terrible Secret: Suppression of the Truth about Hitler's 'Final Solution' (Boston: Little, Brown, 1980).

LASK ABRAHAMS, BETH-ZION, 'Emanuel Deutsch of "The Talmud" Fame', *Transactions of the Jewish Historical Society of England*, 23 (1971), 53–63.

LE BRETON, ANNA LETITIA, *Memories of Seventy Years*, ed. Mary Emma Martin (London: Griffith & Farran, 1883).

LE ROI, J. F. A. DE, *Judentaufen im 19. Jahrhundert: Ein statistischer Versuch* (Leipzig: J. C. Hinrichsche Buchhandlung, 1899).

LEAVIS, Q. D., *Fiction and the Reading Public* (London: Chatto & Windus, 1965).

LEBRECHT, NORMAN, *Mahler Remembered* (London: Faber & Faber, 1987).

LEDERHENDLER, ELI, *Jewish Responses to Modernity: New Voices in America and Eastern Europe* (New York: New York University Press, 1994).

LESCHNITZER, ADOLPH, *The Magic Background of Modern Anti-Semitism: An Analysis of the German–Jewish Relationship* (New York: International Universities Press, 1956).

LESSING, THEODOR, *Einmal und nie wieder: Lebenserinnerungen*, 2nd edn. (Gütersloh: Bertelsmann, 1969).

—— *Der jüdische Selbsthass* (Berlin: Jüdischer Verlag, 1930).

LESTSCHINSKY, YAAKOV, 'Apostasy in Different Lands' (Heb.), *Ha'olam*, 5 (1911), no. 1, 14–16; no. 4, 5–6; no. 5, 4–5; no. 6, 6–7; no. 8, 4–6; no. 9, 3–5; no. 10, 5–7; no. 11, 6–8; no. 12, 3–6.

LETOURNEAU, PAUL, 'Rathenau et la question juive', *Revue d'Allemagne*, 13/3 (July–Sept. 1981), 527–34.

Letters from Perdita to a Certain Israelite, and his Answers to Them (London, 1781).

LEVENSON, ALAN, 'The Conversionary Impulse in Fin-de-Siècle Germany', *Leo Baeck Institute Year Book*, 40 (1995), 107–22.

—— 'Jewish Reactions to Intermarriage in Nineteenth-Century Germany', Ph.D. diss. (Ohio State University, 1990).

—— 'Radical Assimilation and Radical Assimilationists in Imperial Germany', in Marc Lee Raphael (ed.), *What is Modern about the Modern Jewish Experience?* (Williamsburg, Va.: Department of Religion, College of William and Mary, 1997), 32–48.

LEVI, DAVID, *Dissertations on the Prophecies of the Old Testament*, 3 vols. (London, 1796–1800); rev. edn., introd. John King, 2 vols. (London, 1817).

LEVINE, NAOMI B., *Politics, Religion and Love: The Story of H. H. Asquith, Venetia Stanley and Edwin Montagu, Based on the Life and Letters of Edwin Samuel Montagu* (New York: New York University Press, 1991).

LEVINSON, ABRAHAM, *History of the Jews of Warsaw* [Toledot yehudei varshah] (Tel Aviv: Am Oved, 1956).

LEVY, AMY, *The Complete Novels and Selected Writings of Amy Levy, 1861–1889*, ed. Melvyn New (Gainesville: University of Florida Press, 1993).

LEWALD, FANNY, *The Education of Fanny Lewald: An Autobiography*, ed. and trans. Hanna Ballin Lewis (Albany: State University of New York Press, 1992).

LIBERLES, ROBERT, 'The Origins of the Jewish Reform Movement in England', *AJS Review*, 1 (1976), 121–50.

LICHTEN, JOSEPH, 'Notes on the Assimilation and Acculturation of Jews in Poland, 1863–1943', in Chimen Abramsky, Maciej Jachimczyk, and Antony Polonsky (eds.), *The Jews in Poland* (Oxford: Basil Blackwell, 1986), 106–29.

LICHTHEIM, RICHARD, *A Remnant Shall Return: Memoirs of a Zionist from Germany* [She'ar yashuv: zikhronot tsiyoni migermanyah] (Jerusalem: Hahistadrut Hatsiyonit, 1953).

LILIENTHAL, MAX, *American Rabbi: Life and Writings*, ed. David Philipson (New York: Bloch, 1915).

LIPMAN, VIVIAN DAVID, 'Jewish Settlement in the East End of London, 1840–1940: The Topographical and Statistical Background', in Aubrey Newman (ed.), *The Jewish East End, 1840–1939* (London: Jewish Historical Society of England, 1981), 17–40.

——'Sephardi and Other Jewish Immigrants in England in the Eighteenth Century', in *Migration and Settlement: Proceedings of the Anglo-American Jewish Historical Conference . . . July 1970* (London: Jewish Historical Society of England, 1971), 37–62.

——*Social History of the Jews in England, 1850–1950* (London: Watts & Co., 1954).

LIPTZIN, SOLOMON, *Germany's Stepchildren* (Philadelphia: Jewish Publication Society, 1944).

LISSAUER, ERNST, 'Bemerkungen über mein Leben', *Bulletin des Leo Baeck Instituts*, 17–20 (1962), 286–301.

LITTMANN, ELLEN, 'David Friedländers Sendschreiben an Probst Teller und sein Echo', *Zeitschrift für Geschichte der Juden in Deutschland*, 6 (1935), 92–112.

LOCK, STEPHEN, Introduction to Julia Frankau, *Dr. Phillips* (London: British Medical Association, 1989).

LOEWE, RAPHAEL, 'Solomon Marcus Schiller-Szinessy, 1820–1890', *Transactions of the Jewish Historical Society of England*, 21 (1968), 148–89.

LOEWENBERG, PETER, 'Antisemitismus und jüdischer Selbsthass', *Geschichte und Gesellschaft*, 5 (1979), 455–75.

——'Walther Rathenau and German Society', Ph.D. diss. (University of California, 1966).

——*Walther Rathenau and Henry Kissinger: The Jew as a Modern Statesman in Two Political Cultures*, Leo Baeck Memorial Lecture 24 (New York: Leo Baeck Institute, 1980).

LOWENSTEIN, STEVEN M., *The Berlin Jewish Community: Enlightenment, Family, and Crisis, 1770–1830* (New York: Columbia University Press, 1994).

——*The Mechanics of Change: Essays in the Social History of German Jewry* (Atlanta: Scholars Press, 1992).

LOWNDES, MARIE BELLOC, *Diaries and Letters*, ed. Susan Lowndes (London: Chatto & Windus, 1971).

—— *The Merry Wives of Westminster* (London: Macmillan, 1946).

LUXEMBURG, ROSA, *The Letters of Rosa Luxemburg*, ed. Stephen Eric Bronner (Boulder: Westview Press, 1978).

McCALMAN, IAIN, 'The Infidel as Prophet: William Reid and Blakean Radicalism', in Steve Clark and David Worrall (eds.), *Historicizing Blake* (New York: St Martin's Press, 1994), 24–42.

—— 'New Jerusalems: Prophecy, Dissent and Radical Culture in England, 1786–1830', in Knud Haakonssen (ed.), *Enlightenment and Religion: Rational Dissent in Eighteenth-Century Britain* (Cambridge: Cambridge University Press, 1996), 312–35.

—— *Radical Underworld: Prophets, Revolutionaries and Pornographers in London, 1795–1845* (Cambridge: Cambridge University Press, 1988).

MACAULAY, THOMAS BABINGTON, *Critical and Historical Essays Contributed to the Edinburgh Review*, 2 vols. (London: Longman, Brown, Green & Longmans, 1854).

MACDOUGALL, HUGH A., *Racial Myth in English History: Trojans, Teutons, and Anglo-Saxons* (Hanover, NH: University Press of New England, 1982).

McGINITY, KEREN R., *Still Jewish: A History of Women and Intermarriage in America* (New York: New York University Press, 2009).

MAHLER, RAPHAEL, 'Policy towards Missionaries in Congress Poland in the Period of the Holy Alliance' (Heb.), in *Sefer shiloh*, ed. Michael Handel (Tel Aviv: Department of Education and Culture, Municipality of Tel Aviv, 1960), 169–81.

MALINO, FRANCIS, *The Sephardic Jews of Bordeaux: Assimilation and Emancipation in Revolutionary and Napoleonic France* (University: University of Alabama Press, 1978).

MANEKIN, RACHEL, 'The Lost Generation: Education and Female Conversion in Fin-de-Siècle Kraków', *Polin*, 18 (2005), 189–219.

MARCUS, IVAN, 'Beyond the Sephardi Mystique', *Orim: A Jewish Journal at Yale*, 1/1 (1985), 35–53.

MARRUS, MICHAEL R., 'European Jewry and the Politics of Assimilation: Assessment and Reassessment', *Journal of Modern History*, 49 (1977), 89–109.

—— *The Politics of Assimilation: A Study of the French Jewish Community at the Time of the Dreyfus Affair* (Oxford: Clarendon Press, 1971).

MARTIN, DAVID, *A General Theory of Secularization* (New York: Harper & Row, 1979).

MARX, KARL, 'Contribution to the Critique of Hegel's Philosophy of Right: Introduction', in T. B. Bottomore (ed.), *Karl Marx: Early Writings* (New York: McGraw-Hill, 1964), 43–59.

—— 'On the Jewish Question', in T. B. Bottomore (ed.), *Karl Marx: Early Writings* (New York: McGraw-Hill, 1964), 1–40.

MAUTHNER, FRITZ, In Landsberger, Arthur A. (ed.), *Judentaufen* (Munich: Georg Müller, 1912), 74–7.

MEDEM, VLADIMIR, *The Life and Soul of a Legendary Jewish Socialist*, ed. and trans. Samuel A. Portnoy (New York: Ktav, 1979).

MEINECKE, FRIEDRICH, *Strassburg, Freiburg, Berlin, 1901–1919* (Stuttgart: K. F. Koehler, 1949).

MENDELSOHN, EZRA, *On Modern Jewish Politics* (New York: Oxford University Press, 1993).

——'Should We Take Notice of Berthe Weill?', *Jewish Social Studies*, NS 1/1 (1994), 22–39.

MENDES-FLOHR, PAUL, 'Martin Buber and the Metaphysicians of Contempt', in Jehuda Reinharz (ed.), *Living with Antisemitism: Modern Jewish Responses* (Hanover, NH: University Press of New England, 1987), 133–64.

MERRICK, LEONARD, *Violet Moses*, 3 vols. (London: Richard Bentley & Son, 1891).

MEYER, MICHAEL A., *Jewish Identity in the Modern World* (Seattle: University of Washington Press, 1990).

——*The Origins of the Modern Jew* (Detroit: Wayne State University Press, 1967).

——'Reflections on Jewish Modernization', in Elisheva Carlebach, John M. Efron, and David N. Myers (eds.), *Jewish History and Jewish Memory: Essays in Honor of Yosef Hayim Yerushalmi* (Hanover, NH: University Press of New England, 1998), 369–77.

——*Response to Modernity: A History of the Reform Movement in Judaism* (New York: Oxford University Press, 1988).

MEYERSTEIN, E. H. W., *Of My Early Life (1889–1915)*, ed. Rowland Watson (London: Neville Spearman, 1957).

——*Some Letters of E. H. W. Meyerstein*, ed. Rowland Watson (London: Neville Spearman, 1959).

MICHMAN, JOSEPH, 'Between Sephardim and Ashkenazim in Amsterdam' (Heb.), in Issachar Ben-Ami (ed.), *The Sephardi and Oriental Jewish Heritage* [Moreshet yehudei sefarad vehamizraḥ], vol. ii (Jerusalem: Magnes Press, 1982), 135–49.

MIESES, MATTHIAS, *Z rodu żydowskiego: Zasłużone rodziny polskie krwi niegdyś żydowskiej* (1938; repr. Warsaw: WEMA, 1991).

MONYPENNY, W. F., and G. E. BUCKLE, *The Life of Benjamin Disraeli, Earl of Beaconsfield*, 6 vols. (London: John Murray, 1910–20).

MOORE, DEBORAH DASH, *At Home in America: Second Generation New York Jews* (New York: Columbia University Press, 1981).

MOORE, GEORGE, *Confessions of a Young Man*, ed. Susan Dick (Montreal: McGill-Queen's University Press, 1972).

MOSSE, GEORGE L., *German Jews beyond Judaism* (Bloomington: Indiana University Press, 1985).

MOSSE, WERNER E., *The German-Jewish Economic Elite, 1820–1935: A Socio-Cultural Profile* (Oxford: Clarendon Press, 1989).

——'Problems and Limits of Assimilation: Hermann and Paul Wallich, 1833–1938', *Leo Baeck Institute Year Book*, 33 (1988), 43–65.

MYERS, DAVID N., Introduction to David N. Myers and David B. Ruderman (eds.), *The Jewish Past Revisted: Reflections on Modern Jewish Historians* (New Haven: Yale University Press, 1998).

NECHELES, RUTH F., *The Abbé Grégoire, 1787–1831: The Odyssey of an Egalitarian* (Westport, Conn.: Greenwood, 1971).

NEHRU, JAWAHARLAL, *An Autobiography* (London: John Lane, Bodley Head, 1936).

NEUMANN, ROBERT, *The Plague House Papers* (London: Hutchinson, 1959).

NEUSNER, JACOB, 'Assimilation and Self-Hatred in Modern Jewish Life', in *Stranger at Home: 'The Holocaust', Zionism, and American Judaism* (Chicago: University of Chicago Press, 1981), 49–57.

NEWMAN, ARYEH, 'Jewish Identity: Cambridge, 1941–44', *The Cambridge Review*, 25 (Oct. 1983), 176–9.

NEWMAN, AUBREY (ed.), *Provincial Jewry in Victorian Britain* (London: Jewish Historical Society of England, 1975).

Newnham College Register, 1871–1950, ed. A. B. White (Cambridge: n.p. [1965?]).

NIETZSCHE, FRIEDRICH WILHELM, *Beyond Good and Evil: Prelude to a Philosophy of the Future*, trans. and ed. Marion Faber (New York: Oxford University Press, 1998).

NIEWYK, DONALD L., *The Jews in Weimar Germany* (Baton Rouge: University of Louisiana Press, 1980).

NORDAU, MAX, 'The Decadence of Judaism in France', *Jewish Chronicle*, 18 Jan. 1907, 10.

OGDEN, JAMES, *Isaac D'Israeli* (Oxford: Clarendon Press, 1969).

OPALSKA, MAGDALENA, and ISRAEL BARTAL, *Poles and Jews: A Failed Brotherhood* (Hanover, NH: University Press of New England, 1992).

OPHIR, BARUCH ZVI (ed.), *Encyclopedia of Jewish Communities from their Foundation until after the Holocaust of World War II—Germany—Bavaria* [Pinkas hakehilot: entsiklopediyah shel hayishuvim hayehudiyim lemin hivasdam ve'ad le'aḥar sho'at milḥemet ha'olam hasheniyah—germaniyah—bavariyah] (Jerusalem: Yad Vashem, 1972).

ORD-MACKENZIE, W., and THOMAS CHAPLIN, *Report of Visit to Continental Missions, August and September 1886* (London: Alexander and Shepheard, n.d.).

OSTERWEIS, ROLLIN G., *Three Centuries of New Haven, 1638–1938* (New Haven: Yale University Press, 1953).

PARK, T. PETER, 'Thomas Carlyle and the Jews', *Journal of European Studies*, 20 (1990), 1–21.

PAUL, CHARLES KEGAN, *William Godwin: His Friends and Contemporaries*, 2 vols. (London: Henry S. King, 1876).

PAULSSON, GUNNAR S., *Secret City: The Hidden Jews of Warsaw, 1940–1945* (New Haven: Yale University Press, 2002).

PENDLEBURY, ALYSON, *Portraying 'the Jew' in First World War Britain* (London: Vallentine Mitchell, 2006).

PERSOFF, MEIR, *Faith against Reason: Religious Reform and the British Chief Rabbinate, 1840–1990* (London: Vallentine Mitchell, 2008).

PETUCHOWSKI, JACOB J., 'Karaite Tendencies in an Early Reform Haggadah: A Study in Comparative Liturgy', *Hebrew Union College Annual*, 31 (1960), 223–49.

PFEFFER, JEREMY I., *'From One End of the Earth to the Other': The London Bet Din, 1805–1855, and the Jewish Convicts Transported to Australia* (Brighton: Sussex Academic Press, 2008).

PICCIOTTO, JAMES, *Sketches of Anglo-Jewish History*, ed. Israel Finestein (London: Soncino Press, 1956).

PIERSON, RUTH LOUISE, 'German Jewish Identity in the Weimar Republic', Ph.D. diss. (Yale University, 1970).

PIKE, LUKE OWEN, *The English and their Origin* (London: Longmans, Green, 1866).

PINTO, EDWARD H., *Wooden Bygones of Smoking and Snuff Taking* (London: Hutchinson, 1961).

PINTO, ISAAC DE, *Apologie pour la nation juive, ou, réflexions critiques sur le premier chapitre du VII tome des œuvres de monsieur de Voltaire au sujet des juifs* (Amsterdam, 1762).

PIZZICHINI, LILIAN, *Dead Men's Wages* (London: Picador, 2003).

PLACE, FRANCIS, *The Autobiography of Francis Place*, ed. Mary Thale (Cambridge: Cambridge University Press, 1972).

POLIAKOV, LEON, *The Aryan Myth: A History of Racist and Nationalist Ideas in Europe*, ed. and trans. Edmund Howard (New York: New American Library, 1977).

POLLINS, HAROLD, *Economic History of the Jews in England* (Rutherford, NJ: Fairleigh Dickinson University Press, 1982).

POPKIN, RICHARD, 'David Levi, Anglo-Jewish Theologian', *Jewish Quarterly Review*, NS 87 (1996), 79–101.

PORTER, BRIAN, 'The Social Nation and its Futures: English Liberalism and Polish Nationalism in Late-Nineteenth Century Warsaw', *American Historical Review*, 101 (1996), 1470–92.

PORTER, ROY, *English Society in the Eighteenth Century*, rev. edn. (Harmondsworth: Penguin Books, 1982).

PRAWER, S. S., *Israel at Vanity Fair: Jews and Judaism in the Writings of W. M. Thackeray* (Leiden: E. J. Brill, 1992).

PRESTON, DAVID L., 'The German Jews in Secular Education, University Teaching and Science: A Preliminary Inquiry', *Jewish Social Studies*, 38 (1976), 99–116.

PRIESTLEY, J. B., *English Journey* (London: William Heinemann, 1934).

PROUST, MARCEL, *In Search of Lost Time*, 6 vols., trans. C. K. Scott Moncrieff and Terence Kilmartin, rev. D. J. Enright (New York: Random House, 1992–3).

PRUS, BOLESŁAW, *The Doll*, trans. David Welsh (New York: Twayne, 1972).

PULLAN, BRIAN, *The Jews of Europe and the Inquisition of Venice, 1550–1670* (Oxford: Basil Blackwell, 1983).

RAHDEN, TILL VAN, *Juden und andere Breslauer: Die Beziehungen zwischen Juden, Protestanten und Katholiken in einer deutschen Grossstadt von 1860 bis 1925* (Göttingen: Vandenhoeck & Ruprecht, 2000).

RAPHAEL, MARC LEE, *Jews and Judaism in a Midwestern Community: Columbus, Ohio, 1840–1975* (Columbus: Ohio Historical Society, 1979).

RATCLIFFE, BARRIE M., 'Some Jewish Problems in the Early Careers of Emile and Isaac Pereire', *Jewish Social Studies*, 34 (1972), 189–206.

RATHENAU, WALTHER, *Briefe*, new edn., 2 vols. (Dresden: C. Reissner, 1927).

——'Höre, Israel!', *Die Zukunft*, 18 (1897), 454–62.

——'Staat und Judentum: Eine Polemik', in *Gesammelte Schriften*, 5 vols. (Berlin: S. Fischer, 1925), i. 183–207.

REID, T. WEMYSS, *The Life, Letters, and Friendships of Richard Monckton Milnes*, 2 vols. (London: Cassell, 1890).

REIK, THEODOR, *Jewish Wit* (New York: Gamut Press, 1962).

REINHARZ, JEHUDA, *Fatherland or Promised Land? The Dilemma of the German Jew, 1893–1914* (Ann Arbor: University of Michigan Press, 1975).

——(ed.), *Living with Antisemitism: Modern Jewish Responses* (Hanover, NH: University of New England Press, 1987).

REITTER, PAUL, *The Anti-Journalist: Karl Kraus and Jewish Self-Fashioning in Fin-de-Siècle Vienna* (Chicago: University of Chicago Press, 2008).

REMBA, ISAAC, *The Children Have Eaten Sour Grapes* [Banim akhlu boser] ([Tel Aviv?]: Public Committee for the Publication of the Writings of Isaac Remba, 1973).

RÉMOND, RENÉ, *Religion and Society in Modern Europe*, trans. Antonia Nevell (Oxford: Blackwell, 1999).

RICHARZ, MONIKA, 'Demographic Developments', in Michael Meyer (ed.), *German-Jewish History in Modern Times*, vol. iii: *Integration in Dispute, 1871–1918* (New York: Columbia University Press, 1997), 7–44.

——(ed.), *Jüdisches Leben in Deutschland: Selbstzeugnisse zur Sozialgeschichte im Kaiserreich* (Stuttgart: Deutsche Verlags-Anstalt, 1979).

RICHMOND, CHARLES, 'Disraeli's Education', in Charles Richmond and Paul Smith (eds.), *The Self-Fashioning of Disraeli, 1818–1851* (Cambridge: Cambridge University Press, 1998), 16–41.

RIDLEY, JANE, *Young Disraeli, 1804–1846* (New York: Crown Publishers, 1995).

RIFF, MICHAEL ANTHONY, 'Assimilation and Conversion in Bohemia—Secession from the Jewish Community in Prague, 1868–1917', *Leo Baeck Institute Year Book*, 26 (1981), 73–88.

RINGELBLUM, EMANUEL, *Notes from the Warsaw Ghetto: The Journal of Emanuel Ringelblum*, ed. and trans. Jacob Sloan (New York: McGraw-Hill, 1958).

RITTERBAND, PAUL, and HAROLD S. WECHSLER, *Jewish Learning in American Universities: The First Century* (Bloomington: Indiana University Press, 1994).

ROBERTSON, RITCHIE, 'From the Ghetto to Modern Culture: The Autobiographies of Salomon Maimon and Jakob Fromer', *Polin*, 7 (1992), 12–30.

——*The 'Jewish Question' in German Literature, 1749–1939: Emancipation and its Discontents* (Oxford: Oxford University Press, 1999).

ROBINSON, MARY, *Perdita: The Memoirs of Mary Robinson*, ed. M. J. Levy (London: Peter Owen, 1994).

ROCHELSON, MERI-JANE, *A Jew in the Public Arena: The Career of Israel Zangwill* (Detroit: Wayne State University Press, 2008).

——'Jews, Gender and Genre in Late-Victorian England: Amy Levy's *Reuben Sachs*', *Women's Studies*, 25 (1996), 311–28.

ROGGER, HANS, *Jewish Policies and Right-Wing Politics in Imperial Russia* (Berkeley: University of California Press, 1986).

ROHL, J. C. G., 'Higher Civil Servants in Germany, 1890–1900', in Walter Laqueur and George L. Mosse (eds.), *Education and Social Structure in the Twentieth Century*, Harper Torchbook (New York: Harper & Row, 1967), 101–21.

ROLAND, CHARLES G., *Courage under Siege: Starvation, Disease, and Death in the Warsaw Ghetto* (New York: Oxford University Press, 1992).

ROPER, KATHERINE, *German Encounters with Modernity: Novels of Imperial Berlin* (New York: Brill Academic, 1991).

ROSENBERG, BERNARD, and ERNEST GOLDSTEIN (eds.), *Creators and Disturbers: Reminiscences by Jewish Intellectuals of New York* (New York: Columbia University Press, 1982).

ROSMAN, MOSHE, *How Jewish Is Jewish History?* (Oxford: Littman Library of Jewish Civilization, 2007).

ROSSMORE, DERRICK, *Things I Can Tell* (London: E. Nash, 1912).

ROTH, CECIL, (ed.), *Anglo-Jewish Letters (1158–1917)* (London: Soncino Press, 1938).

——*Benjamin Disraeli, Earl of Beaconsfield* (New York: Philosophical Library, 1952).

——*The Great Synagogue, London, 1690–1940* (London: Goldston & Son, 1950).

——'The Haskalah in England', in H. J. Zimmels, J. Rabbinowitz, and I. Finestein (eds.), *Essays Presented to Chief Rabbi Israel Brodie on the Occasion of his Seventieth Birthday*, 2 vols. (London: Soncino Press, 1967), 365–76.

——*The Jewish Chronicle, 1841–1941: A Century of Newspaper History* (London: Jewish Chronicle, 1949).

ROTHSCHILD, MIRIAM, *Dear Lord Rothschild: Birds, Butterflies and History* (Philadelphia: Balaban Publishers, 1983).

ROZENBLIT, MARSHA L., *The Jews of Vienna, 1867–1914* (Albany: SUNY Press, 1983).

RUDERMAN, DAVID B., *Jewish Enlightenment in an English Key: Anglo-Jewry's Construction of Modern Jewish Thought* (Princeton: Princeton University Press, 2000).

RUPPIN, ARTHUR, *The Jews of To-day*, trans. Margery Bentwich (New York: Henry Holt, 1913).

RÜRUP, REINHARD, 'The European Revolutions of 1848 and Jewish Emancipation', in Werner E. Mosse, Arnold Paucker, and Reinhard Rürup (eds.), *Revolution and Evolution: 1848 in German-Jewish History* (Tübingen: J. C. B. Mohr, 1981), 1–53.

SALAMAN, CHARLES KENSINGTON, *Jews As They Are* (London: Simpkin, Marshall, 1882).

SALAMAN, REDCLIFFE NATHAN, *Whither Lucien Wolf's Anglo-Jewish Community?*, Lucien Wolf Memorial Lecture 1953 (London: Jewish Historical Society of England, 1954).

SALBSTEIN, M. C. N., *The Emancipation of the Jews in Britain: The Question of the Admission of the Jews to Parliament, 1828–1860* (Rutherford, NJ: Fairleigh Dickinson University Press, 1982).

SAMTER, NATHAN, *Judentaufen im neunzehnten Jahrhundert* (Berlin: M. Poppelauer, 1906).

SAMUEL, EDGAR, 'The First Fifty Years', in Vivian D. Lipman (ed.), *Three Centuries of Anglo-Jewish History* (London: Jewish Historical Society of England, 1961), 27–44.

——'The *Mahamad* as an Arbitration Court', *Transactions of the Jewish Historical Society of England*, 41 (2007), 9–30.

SARNA, JONATHAN D., *American Judaism: A History* (New Haven: Yale University Press, 2004).

——*JPS: The Americanization of Jewish Culture, 1888–1988* (Philadelphia: Jewish Publication Society, 1989).

SCHECHTER, SOLOMON, 'Zionism: A Statement', in id., *Seminary Addresses and Other Papers* (New York: Jewish Theological Seminary, 1959), 91–104.

SCHEINBERG, CYNTHIA, *Women's Poetry and Religion in Victorian England: Jewish Identity and Christian Culture* (Cambridge: Cambridge University Press, 2002).

SCHILLER-SZINESSY, SOLOMON MARCUS, *Harmony and Dis-harmony between Judaism and Christianity: Two Sermons Preached on the Sabbaths Shemot and Vaeira (December 25th 1858, and January 1st, 1859) at the Manchester Synagogue of British Jews* (Manchester [1859]).

SCHNITZLER, ARTHUR, *My Youth in Vienna*, trans. Catherine Hutter (New York: Holt, Rinehart & Winston, 1970).

——*The Road into the Open*, trans. Roger Byers (Berkeley: University of California Press, 1992).

SCHOLEM, GERSHOM, *From Berlin to Jerusalem*, trans. Harry Zohn (New York: Schocken, 1980).

——'On the Social Psychology of the Jews in Germany, 1900–1933', in David Bronsen (ed.), *Jews and Germans from 1860–1933: The Problematic Symbiosis* (Heidelberg: Winter, 1979), 9–32.

——'The Sabbatian Movement in Poland' (Heb.), in id., *Studies and Sources Regarding the History of Sabbatianism and its Metamorphoses* [Meḥkarim umekorot letoledot hashabta'ut vegilguleiha] (Jerusalem: Mosad Bialik, 1974), 68–140.

SCHOLEM, GERSHOM, 'With Gershom Scholem: An Interview', in Werner Dann-
hauser (ed.), *On Jews and Judaism in Crisis: Selected Essays* (New York: Schocken,
1976), 1–48.

SCHORSCH, ISMAR, 'The Ethos of Modern Jewish Scholarship', in id., *From Text to
Context: The Turn to History in Modern Jewish Scholarship* (Hanover, NH: University Press of New England, 1994), 158–76.

——*Jewish Reactions to German Anti-Semitism, 1870–1914* (New York: Columbia University Press, 1972).

——'The Myth of Sephardi Supremacy', *Leo Baeck Institute Year Book*, 34 (1989),
47–66.

—— *On the History of the Political Judgment of the Jew*, Leo Baeck Memorial Lecture 20
(New York: Leo Baeck Institute, 1976).

SCHREIBER, EMANUEL, *Die Selbstkritik der Juden* (Leipzig: W. Friedrich, 1980).

SCHÜLER-SPRINGORUM, STEFANIE, 'Assimilation and Community Reconsidered:
The Jewish Community in Königsberg, 1871–1914', *Jewish Social Studies*, NS 5/3
(1999), 104–31.

SCHWARZ, DANIEL R., *Disraeli's Fiction* (London: Macmillan, 1979).

SCRIVENER, MICHAEL, 'British Jewish Writing of the Romantic Era and the Prob-
lem of Modernity: The Example of David Levi', in Sheila A. Spector (ed.), *British
Romanticism and the Jews: History, Culture, Literature* (New York: Palgrave
Macmillan, 2002), 159–77.

——'The Philosopher and the Moneylender: The Relationship between William
Godwin and John King', in Robert Maniquis and Victoria Myers (eds.), *Godwin-
ian Moments* (Toronto: University of Toronto Press, forthcoming).

SEARLE, G. R., *Corruption in British Politics, 1895–1930* (Oxford: Clarendon Press,
1987).

SEED, JOHN, 'Unitarianism, Political Economy and the Antinomies of Liberal Culture in Manchester, 1830–1850', *Social History*, 7 (1982), 1–25.

SEGEL, HAROLD B. (ed.), *Stranger in Our Midst: Images of the Jew in Polish Literature*
(Ithaca, NY: Cornell University Press, 1996).

SELTZER, MICHAEL, 'Benjamin Disraeli's Knowledge of his Ancestry', *Disraeli Project Newsletter*, 1/2 (1976), 8–17.

SEMON, FELIX, *The Autobiography of Sir Felix Semon*, ed. Henry C. Semon and
Thomas McIntyre (London: Jarrolds, 1926).

SEPINWALL, ALYSSA GOLDSTEIN, 'Strategic Friendships: Jewish Intellectuals, the
Abbé Grégoire and the French Revolution', in Ross Brann and Adam Sutcliffe
(eds.), *Renewing the Past, Reconfiguring Jewish Culture: From Al-Andalus to the
Haskalah* (Philadelphia: University of Pennsylvania Press, 2004), 189–212.

SEWELL, WILLIAM, JR., 'AHA Forum on *A Crooked Line*', *American Historical Review*,
113 (2008), 393–405.

SHAEN, MARGARET J. (ed.), *Memorials of Two Sisters: Susanna and Catherine
Winkworth* (London: Longman, Green & Co., 1908).

SHAFTESLEY, JOHN M., 'Religious Controversies', in Salmond S. Levin (ed.), *A Century of Anglo-Jewish Life, 1870–1970: Lectures to Commemorate the Centenary of the United Synagogue* (London: United Synagogue, n.d.), 93–113.

SHAROT, STEPHEN, 'Reform and Liberal Judaism in London, 1840–1940', *Jewish Social Studies*, 41 (1979), 211–28.

SHATZKY, JACOB, 'Alexander Kraushar and his Road to Total Assimilation', *YIVO Annual*, 7 (1952), 146–74.

——'Warsaw Jews in the Polish Cultural Life of the Early 19th Century', *YIVO Annual*, 5 (1950), 41–54.

SIDGWICK, CECILY, *Home Life in Germany* (London: Methuen & Co., 1908).

——*Isaac Eller's Money* (London: Unwin, 1889).

——*Scenes of Jewish Life* (London: Edward Arnold, 1904).

SILBERNER, EDMUND, *Sozialisten zur Judenfrage* (Berlin: Colloquium, 1962).

SIMMEL, GEORG, *The Sociology of Georg Simmel*, trans. and ed. Kurt H. Wolff (Glencoe, Ill.: Free Press, 1950).

SIMON, M., 'Anti-Semitism in England', *Jewish Review*, 2 (1911), 294–307.

SIMON, OSWALD, *Correspondence between Mr. Oswald John Simon and the Dean of Litchfield, Rev. George Margoliouth, and Rev. A. E. Suffrin, on Parochial Missions to the Jews* (London: The Jewish World, 1887).

SIMON-NAHUM, PERRINE, *La Cité investie: La 'Science du judaïsme' français et la République* (Paris: Éditions du Cerf, 1991).

SIMPSON, COLIN, *The Partnership: The Secret Association of Bernard Berenson and Joseph Duveen* (London: Bodley Head, 1987).

SINGER, SIMEON, *Conversionist Activity and its Perils* (London: Jewish Chronicle, 1903).

——*The Literary Remains of the Rev. Simeon Singer*, 3 vols., ed. Israel Abrahams (London: George Routledge & Sons, 1908).

SINGER, STEVEN, 'Jewish Religious Observance in Early Victorian London, 1840–1860', *Jewish Journal of Sociology*, 28 (1986), 117–37.

——'Orthodox Judaism in Early Victorian England', Ph.D. diss. (Yeshiva University, 1981).

SMITH, GOLDWIN, 'The Jewish Question', *The Nineteenth Century*, 10 (1881), 494–513.

SMITH, PAUL, 'Disraeli's Politics', *Transactions of the Royal Historical Society*, 5th ser., 37 (1987), 65–85.

SMITH, SYDNEY, *The Letters of Sydney Smith*, 2 vols., ed. Nowell C. Smith (Oxford: Clarendon Press, 1953).

SOLOMONS, ISRAEL, *Notes and Queries*, 10th ser., 9 (1908), 428.

SORKIN, DAVID J., *Moses Mendelssohn and the Religious Enlightenment* (Berkeley: University of California Press, 1996).

SOUTHCOTT, JOANNA, *An Account of the Trials on Bills of Exchange wherein the Deceit of Mr. John King and his Confederates, under the Pretence of Lending Money, Is Exposed, and their Arts Brought to Light* (London, 1807).

SPENDER, STEPHEN, *World Within World* (London: Hamish Hamilton, 1951).

SPIRE, ANDRÉ, *Quelques Juifs*, 2nd edn. (Paris: Société du Mercure de France, 1913).

STANISLAWSKI, MICHAEL, 'Jewish Apostasy in Russia: A Tentative Apology', in Todd M. Endelman (ed.), *Jewish Apostasy in the Modern World* (New York : Holmes & Meier, 1987), 189–205.

——*Tsar Nicholas I and the Jews: The Transformation of Jewish Society in Russia, 1825–1855* (Philadelphia: Jewish Publication Society, 1983).

STANLEY, EDWARD HENRY, *Disraeli, Derby and the Conservative Party: Journals and Memoirs of Edward Henry, Lord Stanley, 1849–1869*, ed. John Vincent (Hassocks, Sussex: Harvester Press, 1978).

STEINMETZ, ANDREW, *The Gaming Table: Its Votaries and Victims, in All Times and Countries, Especially in England and in France*, 2 vols. (London: Tinsley Brothers, 1870).

STERLING, ELEONORE, 'Jewish Reaction to Jew-Hatred in the First Half of the 19th Century', *Leo Baeck Institute Year Book*, 3 (1958), 103–21.

STERN, FRITZ, *Gold and Iron: Bismarck, Bleichröder, and the German Empire* (New York: Alfred A. Knopf, 1977).

STERN, RUDOLPH A., 'Fritz Haber: Personal Recollections', *Leo Baeck Institute Year Book*, 8 (1963), 70–102.

STROUD, OSWALD E. (ed.), *The Story of the Stroud Family* (Bradford: privately published [c.1974]).

SZAJKOWSKI, ZOSA, 'Population Problems of Marranos and Sephardim in France from the 16th to the 20th Centuries', *Proceedings of the American Academy for Jewish Research*, 27 (1958), 1–23.

TAL, URIEL, *Jews and Christians in the Second Empire, 1870–1914* [Yahadut venatsrut bareikh hasheni' (1870–1914)] (Jerusalem: Magnes Press, 1969).

TAMA, DIOGENE (ed.), *Transactions of the Parisian Sanhedrim*, trans. F. D. Kirwan (London: C. Taylor, 1807); mimeograph (Cincinnati: Hebrew Union College, 1956).

TAYLOR, JOHN, *Records of My Life*, 2 vols. (London: E. Bull, 1832).

TETER, MAGDALENA, 'Jewish Conversions to Catholicism in the Polish–Lithuanian Commonwealth of the Seventeenth and Eighteenth Centuries', *Jewish History*, 17 (2003), 257–83.

THALE, MARY (ed.), *Selections from the Papers of the London Corresponding Society, 1792–1799* (Cambridge: Cambridge University Press, 1983).

THEILHABER, FELIX, *Der Untergang der deutschen Juden: Eine volkswirtschaftliche Studie*, 2nd edn. (Berlin: Jüdischer Verlag, 1921).

THOMPSON, EDWARD P., *The Making of the English Working Class* (London: Gollancz, 1963).

THON, JAKOB, *Die Juden in Oesterreich* (Berlin: L. Lamm, 1908).

TISHBY, ISAIAH, 'New Information on the Converso Community in London Based on the Letters of Sasportas from 1664–1665' (Heb.), in Aharon Mirsky et al. (eds.), *Exile after Exile: Essays in Jewish History Presented to Professor Haim Beinart on his Seventieth Birthday* [Galut aḥar golah: meḥkarim betoledot am yisra'el mugashim lifrofesor ḥayim beinart limlot lo shivim shanah] (Jerusalem: Ben Zvi Institute, 1988).

TOLAND, JOHN, *Reasons for Naturalizing the Jews in Great Britain and Ireland on the Same Foot with All Other Nations* (London, 1714).

TREITSCHKE, HEINRICH VON, 'Noch einige Bemerkungen zur Judenfrage', *Preussische Jahrbücher* (Jan. 1880), in Walter Boehlich (ed.), *Der Berliner Antisemitismusstreit* (Frankfurt am Main: Insel Verlag, 1965), 77–90.

TROPP, ASHER, *Jews in the Professions in Great Britain, 1891–1991* (London: The Maccabaeans, 1991).

TRUNK, ISAIAH, *Judenrat: The Jewish Councils in Eastern Europe under Nazi Occupation* (New York: Macmillan, 1973).

TSITRON, SAMUEL LEIB, *Behind the Curtain: Converts, Traitors, Deniers* [Me'aḥorei hapargod: mumarim, bogedim, mitkaḥashim], 2 vols. (Vilna: Zvi Matz, 1923–5).

VALMAN, NADIA, *The Jewess in Nineteenth-Century British Literary Culture* (Cambridge: Cambridge University Press, 2007).

VERNER, ANDREW M., 'What's in a Name? Of Dog-Killers, Jews and Rasputin', *Slavic Review*, 53 (1994), 1046–70.

VINCENT, JOHN, *Disraeli*, Past Masters (Oxford: Oxford University Press, 1990).

VITAL, DAVID, *A People Apart: The Jews in Europe, 1789–1939* (Oxford: Oxford University Press, 1999).

VOLKOV, SHULAMIT, *Germans, Jews, and Antisemites: Trials in Emancipation* (Cambridge: Cambridge University Press, 2006).

—— 'The Jews of Germany in the Nineteenth Century: Ambition, Success, Assimilation' (Heb.), in Yosef Kaplan and Menahem Stern (eds.), *Acculturation and Assimilation: Continuity and Change in Jewish and Non-Jewish Culture* [Hitbolelut utemiyah: hemshekhiyut utemurah betarbut ha'amim uvisra'el] (Jerusalem: Zalman Shazar Center for Jewish History, 1989), 173–88.

—— 'Unity and Assimilation: The Paradox of Jewish Identity in the Second Empire' (Heb.), in Moshe Zimmerman (ed.), *Crises of German National Consciousness in the 19th and 20th Centuries* [Mishberei hale'umiyut hagermanit bame'ah hatesha-esreh veha'esrim] (Jerusalem: Magnes Press, 1983), 169–85.

WALEY, SIGISMUND DAVID, *Edwin Montagu: A Memoir and an Account of his Visits to India* (London: Asia Publishing House, 1964).

WALPOLE, B. C., *The Life of the Late Right Honorable Charles James Fox* (New York: E. Duyckinck, 1811).

WARBURG, FREDRIC, *An Occupation for Gentlemen* (Boston: Houghton Mifflin, 1960).

WARNER, JESSICA, 'Violence Against and Among Jews in an Early Modern Town: Tolerance and its Limits in Portsmouth, 1718–1781', *Albion*, 35/3 (Fall 2003), 428–48.

WASSERMANN, HENRY, 'The Intimate Culture of German Jewry' (Heb.), in Moshe Zimmerman (ed.), *Crises of German National Consciousness in the 19th and 20th Centuries* [Mashberei hale'umiyut hagermanit bame'ah hatesha-esreh veha'esrim] (Jerusalem: Magnes Press, 1983), 187–98.

WASSERMANN, JAKOB, *My Life as German and Jew*, trans. S. N. Brainin (New York: Coward-McCann, 1933).

WEBER, MAX, ' "Objectivity" in Social Science and Social Policy', in id., *The Methodology of the Social Sciences*, ed. and trans. Edward A. Shils and Henry A. Finch (New York: The Free Press, 1949), 49–112.

——'Science as a Vocation', in id., *From Max Weber: Essays in Sociology*, ed. and trans. Hans H. Gerth and C. Wright Mills (New York: Oxford University Press, 1946), 129–56.

WEEKS, THEODORE R., 'The "International Jewish Conspiracy" Reaches Poland: Teodor Jeske-Choiński and his Works', *East European Quarterly*, 31 (1997), 231–41.

WEINERMAN, ELI, 'Racism, Racial Prejudice, and Jews in Late Imperial Russia', *Ethnic and Racial Studies*, 17 (1994), 442–95.

WEINRYB, BERNARD D., *The Jews of Poland: A Social and Economic History of the Jewish Community in Poland from 1100–1800* (Philadelphia: Jewish Publication Society, 1973).

WEINTRAUB, STANLEY, *Disraeli: A Biography* (New York: Truman Talley Books/Dutton, 1993).

WEIZMANN, CHAIM, *Trial and Error* (New York: Harper & Brothers, 1949).

WENGER, BETH S., *New York Jews and the Great Depression: Uncertain Promise* (New Haven: Yale University Press, 1996).

WERKMEISTER, LUCYLE, *A Newspaper History of England, 1792–1793* (Lincoln: University of Nebraska Press, 1967).

WERTHEIMER, JACK, *Unwelcome Strangers: East European Jews in Imperial Germany* (New York: Oxford University Press, 1987).

WHARTON, MICHAEL, *The Missing Will* (London: Hogarth Press, 1984).

WHITE, ARNOLD, *The Modern Jew* (London: W. Heinemann, 1899).

WHITFIELD, STEPHEN J., 'The Holocaust in the American Jewish Mind', in id., *Voices of Jacob, Hands of Esau: Jews in American Life and Thought* (Hamden, Conn: Archon Books, 1984), 30–41.

WIENER, MARTIN J., *English Culture and the Decline of the Industrial Spirit, 1850–1980* (Cambridge: Cambridge University Press, 1981).

WILLIAMS, BILL, *The Making of Manchester Jewry, 1740–1875* (Manchester: Manchester University Press, 1976).

WILLSTÄTTER, RICHARD, *From My Life: The Memoirs of Richard Willstätter*, ed. Arthur Stoll, trans. Lilli S. Hornig (New York: W. A. Benjamin, 1965).

WINSTANLEY, THOMAS, *A Sermon Preached at the Parish Church of St. George, Hanover Square, Sunday, October 28, 1753* (London, 1753).

WISTRICH, ROBERT S., *Revolutionary Jews from Marx to Trotsky* (New York: Harper & Row, 1976).

——*Socialism and the Jews: The Dilemmas of Assimilation in Germany and Austria-Hungary* (Rutherford, NJ: Fairleigh Dickinson University Press, 1982).

WOHL, ANTHONY, ' "Dizzi-Ben-Dizzi": Disraeli as Alien', *Journal of British Studies*, 34 (1995), 375–411.

WOLF, LUCIEN (ed.), *Jews in the Canary Islands, being a Calendar of Jewish Cases Extracted from the Records of the Canariote Inquisition in the Collection of the Marquess of Bute* (London: Jewish Historical Society of England, 1926).

WOLFE, HUMBERT, *Now a Stranger* (London: Cassell, 1933).

——*The Upward Anguish* (London: Cassell, 1938).

WOOLF, LEONARD, *Letters of Leonard Woolf*, ed. Frederic Spotts (London: Weidenfeld & Nicolson, 1989).

——*The Wise Virgins: A Story of Words, Opinions and a Few Emotions* (London: The Hogarth Press, 1979).

WYLIE, WILLIAM HOWIE, *Old and New Nottingham* (London: Longman, Brown, Green, and Longmans, 1853).

YERUSHALMI, YOSEF HAYIM, *Assimilation and Racial Anti-Semitism: The Iberian and the German Models*, Leo Baeck Institute Memorial Lecture 26 (New York: Leo Baeck Institute, 1982).

——*From Spanish Court to Italian Ghetto: Isaac Cardoso: A Study in Seventeenth-Century Marranism and Jewish Apologetics* (New York: Columbia University Press, 1971).

——*The Re-education of Marranos in the Seventeenth Century*, Rabbi Louis Feinberg Memorial Lecture in Judaic Studies 3 (Cincinnati: Judaic Studies Program, University of Cincinnati, 1980).

YOSHINO, KENJI, *Covering: The Hidden Assault on Our Civil Rights* (New York: Random House, 2006).

YOUNG, HARRY F., *Maximilian Harden: Censor Germaniae* (The Hague: Martinus Nijhoff, 1959).

YOVEL, YERMIYAHU, *Spinoza and Other Heretics*, 2 vols. (Princeton: Princeton University Press, 1989).

ZALESKI, ANTONI, *Towarzystwo warszawskie*, 2 vols. (Kraków: Drukarnia 'Czasu', 1886–7).

ZWEIG, STEFAN, *The World of Yesterday: An Autobiography* (London: Viking Press, 1943).

Index

Printed and bound by CPI Group (UK) Ltd, Croydon, CR0 4YY

09/06/2025

14685820-0003